Annual Editions: Psychology, 49/e

R. Eric Landrum

http://create.mheducation.com

ISBN-10: 1260488500 ISBN-13: 9781260488500

1 2 3 4 5 6 QVS/QVS 23 22 21 20 19

Contents

Detailed Table of Contents

Unit 1: The Science of Psychology

Unit 2: Biological Bases of Behavior

The Largest Health Disparity We Don't Talk About, Dhruv Khullar, *The New York Times*, 2018
Individuals suffering with a mental illness often do not receive the mental health services they need, but as it turns out, they often do not receive the physical health services they need as well. U.S. citizens with a mental disorder (such as depression or bipolar disorder) die 15-30 years younger than those without a mental disorder. For physicians, the two key factors that have been identified are probably therapeutic pessimism and diagnostic overshadowing.

Using Deviance Regulation Theory to Target Marijuana Use Intentions among College Students, Robert D. Dvorak et al., *Experimental and Clinical Psychopharmacology*, 2018
Deviance regulation theory (DRT) is based on the ideas that people who engage in uncommon behaviors tend to stand out and that information about these individuals is particularly important and valuable—this messaging is a signal to others how they would be perceived if they were to engage in the uncommon behavior. Using DRT and recognizing that marijuana use is on the rise with college-age samples, these researchers used a positively framed message about marijuana abstainers or a negatively framed message about marijuana users over three months and then measured students' intent to use.

Unit 3: Perceptual Processes

Some People Are More Likely to See Faces in Things, Moheb Constandi, *Braindecoder*, 2015
The ability to see images in places where those images are unlikely to exist (e.g., seeing the image of a famous historical figure in a slice of toast) is called pareidolia. This reporter writes about recent research where the ability to detect such images is related to both personality characteristics and current mood states.

A New Way to Trick the Brain and Beat Jet Lag, Randy Rieland, *Smithsonian*, 2016
There are certain tricks that researchers are uncovering about the relationship between brain function and interacting in our environment. In one study, researchers were able to reduce the amount of jet lag (sleepiness) by manipulating the light that passes through the eyelids. Other new research-based "tricks" involve not "watching" what you eat and not thinking too much about that new, desired habit.

Understanding Human Perception by Human-made Illusions, Claus-Christian Carbon, *Frontiers in Human Neuroscience*, 2014
Although visual illusions can be fun to view, researchers believe that by studying the limitations of human perception, the cognitive processes that drive perception can be better understood. The author believes that by garnering attention to the visual illusions, viewers can become more interested in understanding and studying the psychological phenomena that cause these illusions in the first place.

Evoking the Ineffable: The Phenomenology of Extreme Sports, Eric Brymer and Robert D. Schweitzer, *Psychology of Consciousness: Theory, Research, and Practice*, 2017
Extreme sports, characterized as a leisure activity in which a mistake or accident would likely cause death, are experiencing rapid growth while many traditional sports are suffering from declining participation. Based on interviews with 15 extreme sports participants in this research study, the authors extract three themes that shed insight into one's attraction to extreme sports: (a) extreme sports as invigorating experience, (b) inadequacy of words, and (c) participants' experience of transcendence.

Unit 4: Learning

You Have No Idea What Happened, Maria Konnikova, *The New Yorker*, 2015
Researchers now understand that memories for emotional events are truly different than memories for regular, everyday events. One's confidence in a recollection of events may be related to the emotionality of that event.

Unit 5: Cognitive Processes

Unit 6: Emotion and Motivation

Do Cholesterol Drugs Affect Aggression? Dennis Thompson, *HealthDay*, 2015
In previous studies, a person's level of cholesterol has been linked to aggression levels. Researchers have identified that drugs designed to lower cholesterol can have different effects on men and women in regard to their resulting aggression levels.

Unit 7: Development

A Brief History of Twin Studies, Ker Than, *Smithsonian*, 2016
This is a very nice research study that summarizes and highlights the benefits of twin studies on the relative contribution of nature and nurture, including studies about intelligence, eating disorders, sexual orientation, and when twins are not raised in the same household (reared apart).

How a Newborn Baby Sees You, Kjerstin Gjengedal, *University of Oslo*, 2015
Based on existing literature, technology, and mathematical calculations, researchers believe that they have identified what an infant 2–3 days old can see; they can perceive faces at 30 centimeters (almost 12 inches). The key to this new discovery was to focus on motion detection rather than the focus on a static (still) image, according to the researchers.

One in Five Teens May Be Bullied on Social Media, Randy Dotinga, *HealthDay*, 2015
Bullying, and particularly cyberbullying, continues to be hot topics with developmental researchers. After examining multiple studies, it is estimated that 23 percent of kids report being bullied via social media, although the amount of cyberbullying varied in studies from 5 percent to 74 percent.

How Do Smartphones Affect Childhood Psychology? Amy Williams, *Psych Central*, 2014
The use of smartphones is everywhere, and this includes usage by younger and younger children. Certain developmental achievements, such as language acquisition, rely on face-to-face interactions; researchers are concerned that with the increase in screen time by younger individuals, some developmental achievements may be impeded.

The Influence of Health-care Policies on Children's Health and Development, James M. Perrin, Thomas F. Boat, and Kelly J. Kelleher, *Society for Research in Child Development*, 2016
The data are clear—poverty affects a child's health; that is, children who are poorer suffer from more acute and chronic illnesses as well as having a higher mortality rate. These authors examine the role of health insurance for children in the United States and also describe how a community approach is desired in providing comprehensive health care to children.

Unit 8: Personality Processes

Good News about Worrying, Jan Hoffman, *The New York Times*, 2015
When receiving the results about a long-awaited outcome, most of the existing research examines the reaction to the news, such as coping strategies used when the news is bad news. However, researchers have also studied the waiting period for the big decision, and the outcomes of that study yielded surprising results.

How Are Horoscopes Still a Thing? Linda Rodriguez McRobbie, *Smithsonian*, 2016
Believers in astrology think that humans are currently affected by the movements of the sun, the moon, and the stars, and that our future is shaped by the relative positioning of the sun, moon, and stars on the day we are born. Given what we know about the causes of human behavior and the development of personality traits and characteristics, the author concludes that the reason that horoscopes remain popular today is simple: people like them.

A Potent Side Effect to the Flint Water Crisis: Mental Health Problems, Abby Goodnough and Scott Atkinson, *The New York Times*, 2016
Through the environmental crisis in Flint, Michigan regarding extremely high levels of lead in the water supply, these reporters present various stories about individuals experiencing mental health difficulties as they survive the situation.

A Mad World, Joseph Pierre, *Aeon Magazine*, 2014
Psychiatrists and psychologists share an interest in the effectiveness of psychotherapy, and practitioners from both disciplines rely on the DSM-V as a major diagnostic tool. The author explores the lens by which a psychiatrist views the world and views mental illness.

It's Not Just You—Politics Is Stressing Out America's Youth, Melissa DeJonckheere and Tammy Chang, *The Conversation*, 2018
When individuals aged 14 to 24 were surveyed before and after the 2016 U.S. presidential election, a majority of respondents reported physical distress (concentration difficulties, insomnia, over-eating) as well as emotional stressors (depression, anxiety, and fear). Youth distress has been on the rise in general, with rates of depression for adolescents increasing from 8.7 percent in 2005 to 11.3 percent in 2014.

Unit 11: Psychological Treatments

Fifty Psychological and Psychiatric Terms to Avoid: A List of Inaccurate, Misleading, Misused, Ambiguous, and Logically Confused Words and Phrases, Scott O. Lilienfeld et al., *Frontiers in Psychology*, 2015
These authors provide a highly valuable listing of psychological and psychiatric terms that should be avoided; moreover, the authors explain the problems with the term, provide an example of its misuse, and offer more palatable alternatives when they exist.

Study Finds Virtual Reality Can Help Treat Severe Paranoia, *Medical Research Council*, 2016
Based on a study in Britain, about 1–2 percent of individuals suffer from severe paranoia, which is evidenced by extreme distrust of others, believing that people are deliberately trying to harm the individual. Using virtual reality technology, patients with severe paranoia with specific instructions experienced reduced paranoia symptoms for the rest of the day, suggesting that there may be successful short-term coping techniques available.

Could Brain Scans Help Guide Treatment for OCD? Mary Elizabeth Dallas, *HealthDay*, 2015
About 2.5 percent of Americans are diagnosed with Obsessive Compulsive Disorder, and another 10 percent exhibit symptoms of Obsessive Compulsive Disorder; that is, they have a lesser form of the illness. Although cognitive behavioral therapy has been useful as a short-term treatment for individuals with OCD, brain scan technology is currently being used to explore treatments that may have longer-term effectiveness.

With the Help of Virtual Therapists, People with Eating Disorders Tackle Anxiety in Grocery Stores, Juli Fraga, *The Washington Post*, 2018
Anorexia is a mental health disorder affecting 1percent of Americans, and often people with anorexia are overwhelmed when surrounded by food, which makes grocery shopping difficult. Using procedures borrowed from telemedicine (FaceTime with headphones for privacy), therapists can now help individuals with anorexia with this adapted version of exposure therapy called grocery store therapy.

Preface

The *Annual Editions: Psychology* series has been around for over two generations, year after year, edition after edition. I was certainly not the originator of this lovely idea, but I am the current curator, a responsibility I take seriously. The idea seems simple, yet is not so simple—it's like your favorite cookie or confection that you buy during the holidays—you think you could make it yourself at home, replicate the recipe, and it would taste just as good. Perhaps even one holiday you tried to make those special cookies with your family, rather than buying them as family tradition dictates—well, how did that turn out? And how much money did you special trying to recreate that "simple" recipe?

The folks at McGraw-Hill have settled on a recipe that works—find an academic in the discipline who cares about the introductory course, have that person curate readable yet research-based articles that will link to nearly every introductory psychology textbook/course structure in existence, have an expert team secure the permissions for those articles, generate learning objectives, critical thinking questions, and follow-up websites for interested readers for every article in the volume—and package that all in one place—in your hands right now as you read the longest run-on sentence I've written in a long time [99 words!]. Your instructor, your Department of Psychology could do this too, but sometimes, homemade is not better. We believe we've created a superior and readable resource that can help you better understand psychology, whether you're enrolled in an introductory psychology course or just looking to read more about a fascinating topic—our own human behavior—and what can be more fascinating than that?

Like any academic or professional discipline, psychology is filled with jargon and nuance—characteristics that are challenging for those new to any topic to absorb. For this reason, McGraw-Hill publishes *Annual Editions,* an anthology of current, clearly written, and highly understandable articles about psychology. The editorial staff at McGraw-Hill has designed *Annual Editions: Psychology* to meet the needs of lay people and students who are curious about psychological science and its applications.

Annual Editions: Psychology provides a large selection of readable, informative articles primarily from popular magazines and newspapers, but we also include empirical journal articles where relevant. Many of the popular press articles are written by journalists, but some are authored by psychologists. The articles for this volume are representative of current research and thinking in psychology, and many of these pieces are cutting-edge with 2018 publication dates.

This is a series that has been successful for quite some time. How do some articles get added to *Annual Editions: Psychology* whereas others are dropped? Were the articles that were dropped from the previous edition not very good? No, that's not the case at all! As new research emerges, a book like *Annual Editions: Psychology* allows both faculty members and students to stay current. So for some articles, it was time to update the work to more recent sources. McGraw-Hill also values instructor feedback highly, so sometimes an article on an important topic just didn't work out well when students are trying to read and comprehend the content. Results from instructor surveys and input from the Academic Advisor Board (keep reading) were also instrumental in helping determine what should absolutely stay, and what areas might be updated; seriously, some reviewer recommendations based on the last edition have been incorporated into this edition.

What would be the best way to get the most out of this book? Read it (and take your time too). Seriously, the book won't do you any good without reading it. As you read about the biological bases of behavior in your introductory psychology course, also read the similar content available to you in *Annual Editions: Psychology.* Concepts you may find difficult to understand from your textbook or from your instructor may become clearer to you once you read about the same topics when discussed by a knowledgeable journalist or the actual researcher. Read and deeply engage with the articles provided in *Annual Editions: Psychology* and you'll be on your way to a better understanding of the science of human behavior—psychology, and the most fascinating topic of all—ourselves.

Editor of This Volume

R. Eric Landrum is a professor of psychology at Boise State University, receiving his PhD in cognitive psychology from Southern Illinois University-Carbondale. His research interests center on the educational conditions that best facilitate student success in all forms. Eric is a member of the American Psychological Association, a fellow in APA's Division Two (Society for the Teaching of Psychology [STP]); he is also a member of the Association for Psychological Science and an APS Fellow. He served as STP secretary (2009–2011) and president (2014), is past-president of the Rocky Mountain Psychological Association, and currently serves as president of Psi Chi, the international honor society in psychology.

Academic Advisory Board

Members of the Academic Advisory Board are instrumental in the final selection of articles for each edition of Annual Editions. Their review of articles for content, level, and appropriateness provides critical direction to the editors and staff. We think that you will find their careful consideration well reflected in this volume.

Eric Miller
Kent State University

Stephanie Moore
Northeast Mississippi Community College

Lorenz Neuwirth
College of Staten Island

Vicki Ritts
St. Louis Community College, Meramec

Terry M. Salem
Lake Land College

Holly Schofield
Central Carolina Community College

Mark R. Schweizer
Camden County College

Laurence Segall
Housatonic Community College

Carolyn Simoneaux
Urshan College

Jason S. Spiegelman
Community College of Baltimore County

Margaret Stanton
Valencia College

Stephen P. Stelzner
College of Saint Benedict and St. John's University

Colleen Stevenson
Muskingum University

Todd Steward, Sr.
Pittsville High School

Loren Toussaint
Luther College

Bettina Viereck
University of Hartford

Heidi Villanueva
Virginia Union University

John E. Walsh
University of Colorado

Unit 1

UNIT

Prepared by: R. Eric Landrum, *Boise State University*

The Science of Psychology

Contemporary psychology is defined as the science of human behavior. Compared to other sciences (like chemistry or physics), psychology is a younger discipline. Some aspects of modern psychology are particularly biological, such as neuroscience, perception, psychobiology, and behavioral genetics. In fact, many of our recent advances in cognitive and social psychology emerge from neuroscience.

Modern psychology encompasses the full spectrum of human behavior, thought, and emotion. There is no aspect of human life that does not fall under psychology's purview. In fact, if you can think of a behavior, then there is surely a branch of psychology that focuses on the study of that behavior. From homelife to the workplace to the athletic field to the church, synagogue, and mosque, psychologists seek to understand our behaviors and our thoughts. Some psychologists work to understand these behaviors simply for the sake of advancing new knowledge. Other psychologists take this new knowledge and apply it to improving the quality of everyday life. Still other psychologists focus exclusively on the most challenging problems facing the world today, such as war, hunger, poverty, sexual and other forms of abuse, drug and alcohol addiction, environmental change and global warming, and so on.

Psychologists work in varied settings. Many psychologists are academics, teaching, and conducting psychological research on college and university campuses. Others work in applied settings such as hospitals, mental health clinics, industry, local, state, and federal government facilities, and schools. Other psychologists work primarily in private practice in which they see clients for personal therapy and counseling sessions. Despite this diversity of settings, psychologists share a keen interest in understanding and explaining human thought and behavior. Psychologists receive rigorous training in their respective subfields of psychology. Undergraduates who are interested in becoming professional psychologists attend graduate school to receive specialized training. Some of these students earn their master's degree in psychology, whereas others go on to complete their doctorate (PhD or PsyD). For some subfields of psychology, such as clinical psychology, individuals must obtain a license to practice psychology. In this case, in addition to completing the graduate degree, the individual must also complete an internship in which he or she receives advanced and closely supervised training in the specialty.

Psychology is an incredibly diverse discipline that offers valuable insights into work, play, suffering, and love. It addresses many fascinating issues, dilemmas, and questions. Not only are individual psychologists successful in advancing careers, but psychologists on the whole continue to be successful in advancing our knowledge about animal and human behavior. This unit offers you a glimpse at some of the pressing challenges that face psychologists in their work today and offers some insight into what you can expect from your study of psychology.

Article

Prepared by: R. Eric Landrum, *Boise State University*

Investigating Variation in Replicability: A "Many Labs" Replication Project

RICHARD A. KLEIN, ET AL.

Learning Outcomes

After reading this article, you will be able to:

- Understand the importance of a replication study.
- Define what a WEIRD sample is and why it matters.

Replication is a central tenet of science; its purpose is to confirm the accuracy of empirical findings, clarify the conditions under which an effect can be observed, and estimate the true effect size (Brandt et al., 2013; Open Science Collaboration, 2012, 2014). Successful replication of an experiment requires the recreation of the essential conditions of the initial experiment. This is often easier said than done. There may be an enormous number of variables influencing experimental results, and yet only a few tested. In the behavioral sciences, many effects have been observed in one cultural context, but not observed in others. Likewise, individuals within the same society, or even the same individual at different times (Bodenhausen, 1990), may differ in ways that moderate any particular result.

Direct replication is infrequent, resulting in a published literature that sustains spurious findings (Ioannidis, 2005) and a lack of identification of the eliciting conditions for an effect. While there are good epistemological reasons for assuming that observed phenomena generalize across individuals and contexts in the absence of contrary evidence, the failure to directly replicate findings is problematic for theoretical and practical reasons. Failure to identify moderators and boundary conditions of an effect may result in overly broad generalizations of true effects across situations (Cesario, 2014) or across individuals (Henrich, Heine, & Norenzayan, 2010). Similarly, overgeneralization may lead observations made under laboratory observations to be inappropriately extended to ecological contexts that differ in important ways (Henry, MacLeod, Phillips, & Crawford, 2004). Practically, attempts to closely replicate research findings can reveal important differences in what is considered a direct replication (Schmidt, 2009), thus leading to refinements of the initial theory (e.g., Aronson, 1992; Greenwald, Pratkanis, Leippe, & Baumgardner, 1986). Close replication can also lead to the clarification of tacit methodological knowledge that is necessary to elicit the effect of interest (Collins, 1974).

Overview of the Present Research

Little attempt has been made to assess the variation in replicability of findings across samples and research contexts. This project examines the variation in replicability of 13 classic and contemporary psychological effects across 36 samples and settings. Some of the selected effects are known to be highly replicable; for others, replicability is unknown. Some may depend on social context or participant sample, others may not. We bundled the selected studies together into a brief, easy-to-administer experiment that was delivered to each participating sample through a single infrastructure (http://projectimplicit.net/).

There are many factors that can influence the replicability of an effect such as sample, setting, statistical power, and procedural variations. The present design standardizes procedural characteristics and ensures appropriate statistical power in order to examine the effects of sample and setting on replicability. At one extreme, sample and situational characteristics might have little effect on the tested effects – variation in effect magnitudes may not exceed expected random error. At the other extreme, effects might be highly contextualized – for example, replicating only with sample and situational characteristics that are highly consistent with the original circumstances. The primary contribution of this investigation is to establish a paradigm for testing replicability across samples and settings and provide a rich data set that allows the determinants of replicability to be explored. A secondary purpose is to demonstrate support for replicability for the 13 chosen effects. Ideally, the results will stimulate theoretical developments about the conditions under which replication will be robust to the inevitable variation in circumstances of data collection.

Method

Researcher Recruitment and Data Collection Sites

Project leads posted a call for collaborators to the online forum of the Open Science Collaboration on February 21, 2013 and to the SPSP Discussion List on July 13, 2013. Other colleagues were contacted personally. For inclusion, each replication team had to: (1) follow local ethical procedures, (2) administer the protocol as specified, (3) collect data from at least 80 participants,[1] (4) post a video simulation of the setting and administration procedure, and (5) document key features of recruiting, sample, and any changes to the standard protocol. In total, there were 36 samples and settings that collected data from a total of 6,344 participants (27 data collections in a laboratory and 9 conducted online; 25 from the US, 11 from other countries; see Table 1 for a brief description of sites and for a full descriptions of sites, site characteristics, and participant characteristics by site).

Selection of Replication Studies

Twelve studies producing 13 effects were chosen based on the following criteria:

1. *Suitability for online presentation.* Our primary concern was to give each study a "fair" replication that was true to the original design. By administering the study through a web browser, we were able to ensure procedural consistency across sites.
2. *Length of study.* We selected studies that could be administered quickly so that we could examine many of them in a single study session.
3. *Simple design.* With the exception of one correlational study, we selected studies that featured a simple, two-condition design.
4. *Diversity of effects.* We sought to diversify the sample of effects by topic, time period of original investigation, and differing levels of certainty and existing impact. Justification for study inclusion is described in the registered proposal (http://osf.io/project/aBEsQ/).

Table 1 Data Collection Sites

Site identifier	Location	*N*	Online (O) or laboratory (L)	US or international (I)
Abington	Penn State Abington, Abington, PA	84	L	US
Brasilia	University of Brasilia, Brasilia, Brazil	120	L	I
Charles	Charles University, Prague, Czech Republic	84	L	I
Conncoll	Connecticut College, New London, CT	95	L	US
CSUN	California State University, Northridge, LA, CA	96	O	US
Help	HELP University, Malaysia	102	L	I
Ithaca	Ithaca College, Ithaca, NY	90	L	US
JMU	James Madison University, Harrisonburg, VA	174	O	US
KU	Koç University, Istanbul, Turkey	113	O	I
Laurier	Wilfrid Laurier University, Waterloo, Ontario, Canada	112	L	I
LSE	London School of Economics and Political Science, London, UK	277	L	I
Luc	Loyola University Chicago, Chicago, IL	146	L	US
McDaniel	McDaniel College, Westminster, MD	98	O	US
MSVU	Mount Saint Vincent University, Halifax, Nova Scotia, Canada	85	L	I

MTURK	Amazon Mechanical Turk (US workers only)	1,000	O	US
OSU	Ohio State University, Columbus, OH	107	L	US
Oxy	Occidental College, LA, CA	123	L	US
PI	Project Implicit Volunteers (US citizens/ residents only)	1,329	O	US
PSU	Penn State University, University Park, PA	95	L	US
QCCUNY	Queens College, City University of New York, NY	103	L	US
QCCUNY2	Queens College, City University of New York, NY	86	L	US
SDSU	SDSU, San Diego, CA	162	L	US
SWPS	University of Social Sciences and Humanities Campus Sopot, Sopot, Poland	79	L	I
SWPSON	Volunteers visiting www.badania.net	169	O	I
TAMU	Texas A&M University, College Station, TX	187	L	US
TAMUC	Texas A&M University-Commerce, Commerce, TX	87	L	US
TAMUON	Texas A&M University, College Station, TX (Online participants)	225	O	US
Tilburg	Tilburg University, Tilburg, Netherlands	80	L	I
UFL	University of Florida, Gainesville, FL	127	L	US
UNIPD	University of Padua, Padua, Italy	144	O	I
UVA	University of Virginia, Charlottesville, VA	81	L	US
VCU	VCU, Richmond, VA	108	L	US
Wisc	University of Wisconsin-Madison, Madison, WI	96	L	US
WKU	Western Kentucky University, Bowling Green, KY	103	L	US
WL	Washington & Lee University, Lexington, VA	90	L	US
WPI	Worcester Polytechnic Institute, Worcester, MA	87	L	US

The Replication Studies

All replication studies were translated into the dominant language of the country of data collection ($N = 7$ languages total; 3/6 translations from English were back-translated). Next, we provide a brief description of each experiment, original finding, and known differences between original and replication studies. Most original studies were conducted with paper and pencil, all replications were conducted via computer. Exact wording for each study, including a link to the study, can be found in the supplementary materials. The relevant findings from the original studies can be found in the original proposal.

1. *Sunk costs (Oppenheimer, Meyvis, & Davidenko, 2009).* Sunk costs are those that have already been incurred and cannot be recovered (Knox & Inkster, 1968). Oppenheimer et al. (2009; adapted from Thaler, 1985) asked participants to imagine that they have tickets to see their favorite football team play an important game, but that it is freezing cold on the day of the game. Participants rated their likelihood of attending the game on a 9-point scale (1 = *definitely stay at home*, 9 = *definitely go to the game*). Participants were marginally more likely to go to the game if they had paid for the ticket than if the ticket had been free.
2. *Gain versus loss framing (Tversky & Kahneman, 1981).* The original research showed that changing the focus from losses to gains decreases participants' willingness to take risks – that is, gamble to get a better outcome rather than take a guaranteed result. Participants imagined that the US was preparing for the outbreak of an unusual Asian disease, which is expected to kill 600 people. Participants were then asked to select a course of action to combat the disease from logically identical sets of alternatives framed in terms of gains as follows: Program A will save 200 people (400 people will die), or Program B which has a 1/3 probability that 600 people

will be saved (nobody will die) and 2/3 probability that no people will be saved (600 people will die). In the "gain" framing condition, participants are more likely to adopt Program A, while this effect reverses in the loss framing condition. The replication replaced the phrase "the United States" with the country of data collection, and the word "Asian" was omitted from "an unusual Asian disease."

3. *Anchoring (Jacowitz & Kahneman, 1995).* Jacowitz and Kahneman (1995) presented a number of scenarios in which participants estimated size or distance after first receiving a number that was clearly too large or too small. In the original study, participants answered 3 questions about each of 15 topics for which they estimated a quantity. First, they indicated if the quantity was greater or less than an anchor value. Second, they estimated the quantity. Third, they indicated their confidence in their estimate. The original number served as an anchor, biasing estimates to be closer to it. For the purposes of the replication we provided anchoring information before asking just for the estimated quantity for four of the topics from the original study – distance from San Francisco to New York City, population of Chicago, height of Mt. Everest, and babies born per day in the US for countries that use the metric system, we converted anchors to metric units and rounded them.
4. *Retrospective gambler's fallacy (Oppenheimer & Monin, 2009).* Oppenheimer and Monin (2009) investigated whether the rarity of an independent, chance observation influenced beliefs about what occurred before that event. Participants imagined that they saw a man rolling dice in a casino. In one condition, participants imagined witnessing three dice being rolled and all came up 6s. In a second condition two came up 6s and one came up 3. In a third condition, two dice were rolled and both came up 6s. All participants then estimated, in an open-ended format, how many times the man had rolled the dice before they entered the room to watch him. Participants estimated that the man rolled dice more times when they had seen him roll three 6s than when they had seen him roll two 6s or two 6s and a 3. For the replication, the condition in which the man rolls two 6s was removed leaving two conditions.
5. *Low-versus-high category scales (Schwarz, Hippler, Deutsch, & Strack, 1985).* Schwarz and colleagues (1985) demonstrated that people infer from response options what are low and high frequencies of a behavior, and self-assess accordingly. In the original demonstration, participants were asked how much TV they watch daily on a low-frequency scale ranging from "up to half an hour" to "more than two and a half hours," or a high-frequency scale ranging from "up to two and a half hours" to "more than four and a half hours." In the low-frequency condition, fewer participants reported watching TV for more than two and a half hours than in the high-frequency condition.
6. *Norm of reciprocity (Hyman & Sheatsley, 1950).* When confronted with a decision about allowing or denying the same behavior to an ingroup and outgroup, people may feel an obligation to reciprocity, or consistency in their evaluation of the behaviors (Hyman & Sheatsley, 1950). In the original study, American participants answered two questions: whether communist countries should allow American reporters in and allow them to report the news back to American papers and whether America should allow communist reporters into the United States and allow them to report back to their papers. Participants reported more support for allowing communist reporters into America when that question was asked after the question about allowing American reporters into the communist countries. In the replication, we changed the question slightly to ensure the "other country" was a suitable, modern target (North Korea). For international replication, the target country was determined by the researcher heading that replication to ensure suitability (see supplementary materials).
7. *Allowed/Forbidden (Rugg, 1941).* Question phrasing can influence responses. Rugg (1941) found that respondents were less likely to endorse forbidding speeches against democracy than they were to not endorse allowing speeches against democracy. Respondents in the United States were asked, in one condition, if the US should allow speeches against democracy or, in another condition, whether the US should forbid speeches against democracy. Sixty-two percent of participants indicated "No" when asked if speeches against democracy should be allowed, but only 46% indicated "Yes" when asked if these speeches should be forbidden. In the replication, the words "The United States" were replaced with the name of the country the study was administered in.
8. *Quote Attribution (Lorge & Curtiss, 1936).* The source of information has a great impact on how that information is perceived and evaluated. Lorge and Curtiss (1936) examined how an identical quote would be perceived if it was attributed to a liked or disliked individual. Participants were asked to rate their agreement with a list of quotations. The quotation of

interest was, "I hold it that a little rebellion, now and then, is a good thing, and as necessary in the political world as storms are in the physical world." In one condition the quote was attributed to Thomas Jefferson, a liked individual, and in the other it was attributed to Vladimir Lenin, a disliked individual. More agreement was observed when the quote was attributed to Jefferson than Lenin (reported in Moskowitz, 2004). In the replication, we used a quote attributed to either George Washington (liked individual) or Osama Bin Laden (disliked individual).

9. *Flag Priming (Carter, Ferguson, & Hassin, 2011; Study 2).* The American flag is a powerful symbol in American culture. Carter et al. (2011) examined how subtle exposure to the flag may increase conservatism among US participants. Participants were presented with four photos and asked to estimate the time of day at which they were taken. In the flag-prime condition, the American flag appeared in two of these photos. In the control condition, the same photos were presented without flags. Following the manipulation, participants completed an 8-item questionnaire assessing views toward various political issues (e.g., abortion, gun control, affirmative action). Participants in the flag-primed condition indicated significantly more conservative positions than those in the control condition. The priming stimuli used to replicate this finding were obtained from the authors and identical to those used in the original study. Because it was impractical to edit the images with unique national flags, the American flag was always used as a prime. As a consequence, the replications in the United States were the only ones considered as direct replications. For international replications, the survey questions were adapted slightly to ensure they were appropriate for the political climate of the country, as judged by the researcher heading that particular replication (see supplementary materials). Further, the original authors suggested possible moderators that they have considered since publication of the original study. We included three items at the very end of the replication study to test these moderators: (1) How much do you identify with being American? (1 = *not at all*; 11 = *very much*), (2) To what extent do you think the typical American is a Republican or Democrat? (1 = Democrat; 7 = Republican), (3) To what extent do you think the typical American is conservative or liberal? (1 = *Liberal*; 7 = *Conservative*).

10. *Currency priming (Caruso, Vohs, Baxter, & Waytz, 2013).* Money is a powerful symbol. Caruso et al. (2013) provide evidence that merely exposing participants to money increases their endorsement of the current social system. Participants were first presented with demographic questions, with the background of the page manipulated between subjects. In one condition the background showed a faint picture of US$100 bills; in the other condition the background was a blurred, unidentifiable version of the same picture. Next, participants completed an 8-question "system justification scale" (Kay & Jost, 2003). Participants in the money-prime condition scored higher on the system justification scale than those in the control condition. The authors provided the original materials allowing us to construct a near identical replication for US participants. However, the stimuli were modified for international replications in two ways: First, the US dollar was usually replaced with the relevant country's currency (see supplementary materials); Second, the system justification questions were adapted to reflect the name of the relevant country.

11. *Imagined contact (Husnu & Crisp, 2010; Study 1).* Recent evidence suggests that merely imagining contact with members of ethnic outgroups is sufficient to reduce prejudice toward those groups (Turner, Crisp, & Lambert, 2007). In Husnu and Crisp (2010), British non-Muslim participants were assigned to either imagine interacting with a British Muslim stranger or to imagine that they were walking outdoors (control condition). Participants imagined the scene for one minute, and then described their thoughts for an additional minute before indicating their interest and willingness to interact with British Muslims on a four-item scale. Participants in the "imagined contact" group had significantly higher contact intentions than participants in the control group. In the replication, the word "British" was removed from all references to "British Muslims." Additionally, for the predominately Muslim sample from Turkey the items were adapted so Christians were the outgroup target.

12. *Sex differences in implicit math attitudes (Nosek, Banaji, & Greenwald, 2002).* As a possible account for the sex gap in participation in science and math, Nosek and colleagues (2002) found that women had more negative implicit attitudes toward math compared to arts than men did in two studies of Yale undergraduates. Participants completed four Implicit Association Tests (IATs) in random order, one of which measured associations of math and arts with positivity and negativity. The replication simplified the design for length to be just a single IAT.

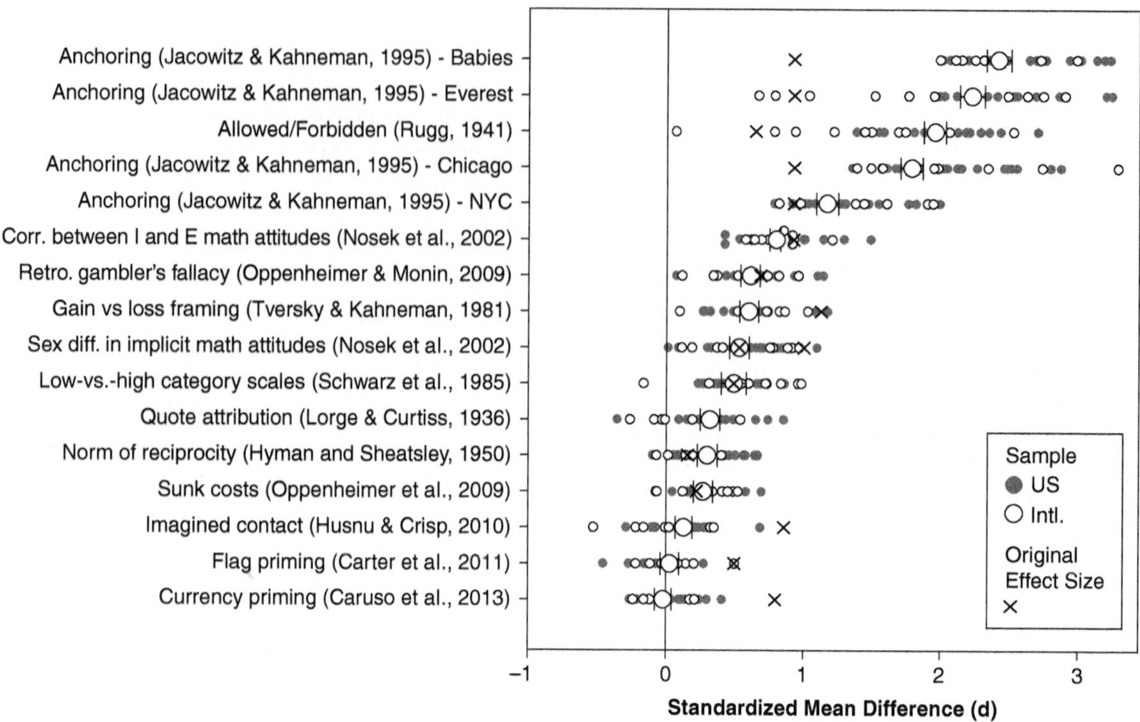

Figure 1 Replication results organized by effect. "X" indicates the effect size obtained in the original study. Large circles represent the aggregate effect size obtained across all participants. Error bars represent 99% noncentral confidence intervals around the effects. Small circles represent the effect sizes obtained within each site (black and white circles for US and international replications, respectively).

13. *Implicit math attitudes relations with self-reported attitudes (Nosek et al., 2002).* In the same study as Effect 12, self-reported math attitudes were measured with a composite of feeling thermometers and semantic differential ratings, and the composite was positively related with the implicit measure. The replication used a subset of the explicit items (see supplementary materials).

Procedure

The experiments were implemented on the Project Implicit infrastructure and all data were automatically recorded in a central database with a code identifying the sample source. After a paragraph of introduction, the studies were presented in a randomized order, except that the math IAT and associated explicit measures were always the final study. After the studies, participants completed an instructional manipulation check (IMC; Oppenheimer et al., 2009), a short demographic questionnaire, and then the moderator measures for flag priming. See Table S1[2] for IMC and summary demographic information by site. The IMC was not analyzed further for this report. Each replication team had a private link for their participants, and they coordinated their own data collection. Experimenters in laboratory studies were not aware of participant condition for each task, and did not interact with participants during data collection unless participants had questions. Investigators who led replications at specific sites completed a questionnaire about the experimental setting (responses summarized in Table S1), and details and videos of each setting along with the actual materials, links to run the study, supplemental tables, datasets, and original proposal are available at https://osf.io/ydpbf/.

Confirmatory Analysis Plan

Prior to data collection, we specified a confirmatory analysis plan. All confirmatory analyses are reported either in text or in supplementary materials. A few of the tasks produced highly erratic distributions (particularly anchoring) requiring revisions to those analysis plans. A summary of differences between the original plans and actual analysis is reported in the supplementary materials.

Results

Summary Results

Figure 1 presents an aggregate summary of replications of the 13 effects, presenting each of the four anchoring effects separately. Table 2 presents the original effect size, median effect size, weighted and unweighted effect size and 99% confidence intervals, and proportion of samples that rejected the null hypothesis in the expected and unexpected direction. In the aggregate, 10 of the 13 studies replicated the original results with varying distance from the original effect size. One study, imagined contact, showed a significant effect in the expected direction in just 4 of the 36 samples (and once in the wrong direction), but the confidence intervals for the aggregate effect size suggest that it is slightly different than zero. Two studies – flag priming and currency priming – did not replicate the original effects. Each of these had just one p-value < .05 and it was in the wrong direction for flag priming. The aggregate effect size was near zero whether using the median, weighted mean, or unweighted mean. All confidence intervals included zero. Figure 1 presents all 36 samples for flag priming, but only US data collections were counted for the confirmatory analysis (see Table 2). International samples also did not show a flag priming effect (weighted mean d = .03, 99% CI [–.04, .10]). To rule out the possibility that the priming effects were contaminated by the contents of other experimental materials, we reexamined only those participants who completed these tasks first. Again, there was no effect (Flag Priming: $t(431) = 0.33$, $p = .75$, 95% CI [–.171, .240], Cohen's d = .03; Currency Priming: $t(605) = -0.56$, $p = .57$, 95% CI [–.201, .112], Cohen's d = .05).[3]

When an effect size for the original study could be calculated, it is presented as an "X" in Figure 1. For three effects (contact, flag priming, and currency priming), the original effect is larger than for any sample in the present study, with the observed median or mean effect at or below the lower bound of the 95% confidence interval for the original effect.[4] Though the sex difference in implicit math attitudes effect was within the 95% confidence interval of the original result, the replication estimate combined with another large-scale replication (Nosek & Smyth, 2011) suggests that the original effect was an overestimate.

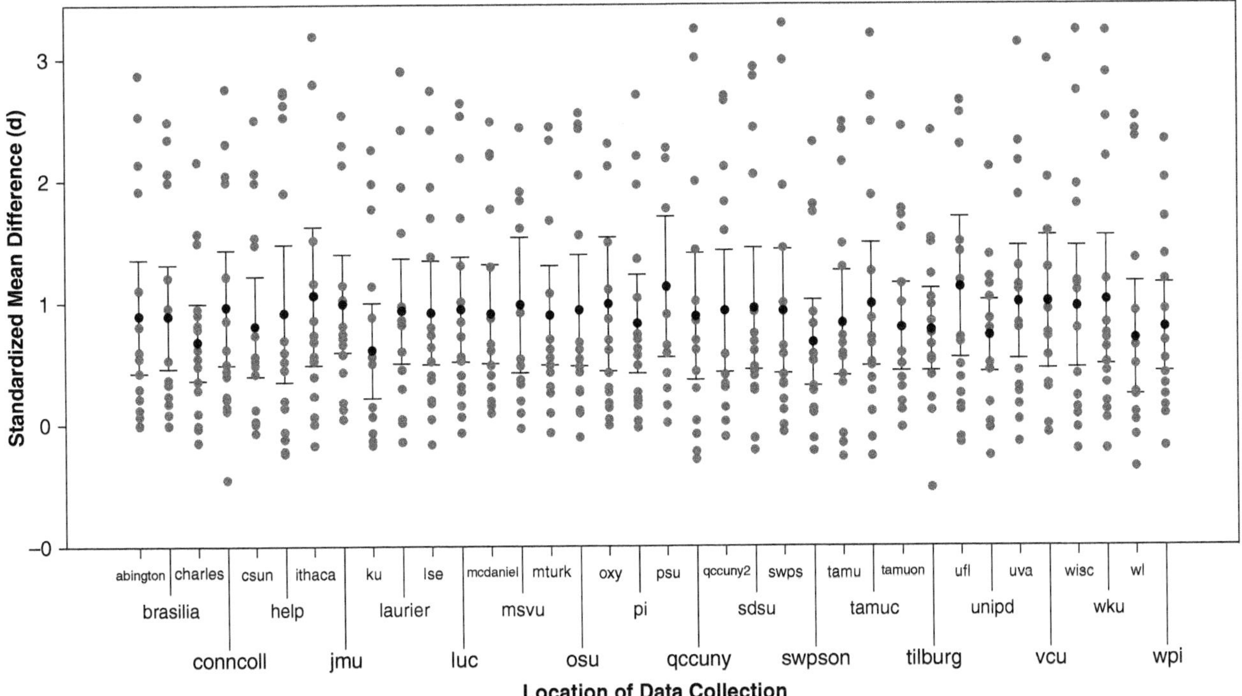

Figure 2 Replication results organized by site. Gray circles represent the effect size obtained for each effect within a site. Black circles represent the mean effect size obtained within a site. Error bars represent 95% confidence interval around the mean.

Table 2 Summary Confirmatory Results for Original and Replicated Effects

	Original study			**Unweighted**		**Weighted**		**Null hypothesis significance tests by sample ($N = 36$)**			**Null hypothesis significance tests of aggregate**			
Effect	ES	95% CI lower, upper	Median replication ES	Replication ES	99% CI lower, upper	Replication ES	99% CI lower, upper	Proportion $p < .05$, opposite direction	Proportion $p < .05$, same direction	Proportion *ns*	Key statistics	*df*	*N*	*p*
Anchoring – babies bom	0.93	.51, 1.33	2.43	2.60	2.41, 2.79	2.42	2.33, 2.51	0.00	1.00	0.00	$t = 90.49$	5,607	5,609	<.001
Anchoring – Mt. Everest	0.93	.51, 1.33	2.00	2.45	2.12, 2.77	2.23	2.14, 2.32	0.00	1.00	0.00	$t = 83.66$	5,625	5,627	<.001
Allowed/forbidden	0.65	.57, .73	1.88	1.87	1.58, 2.16	1.96	1.88, 2.04	0.00	0.97	0.03	$\chi^2 = 3{,}088.7$	1	6,292	<.001
Anchoring – Chicago	0.93	.51, 1.33	1.88	2.05	1.84, 2.25	1.79	1.71. 1.87	0.00	1.00	0.00	$t = 65.00$	5,282	5,284	<.001
Anchoring – distance to NYC	0.93	.51, 1.33	1.18	1.27	1.13, 1.40	1.17	1.09, 1.25	0.00	1.00	0.00	$t = 42.86$	5,360	5,362	<001
Relations between I and E math attitudes	0.93	.77, 1.08	0.84	0.79	0.63, 0.96	0.79	0.75, 0.83	0.00	0.94	0.06	$r = .38$		5,623	<.001
Retrospective gambler fallacy	0.69	.16, 1.21	0.61	0.59	0.49, 0.70	0.61	0.54, 0.68	0.00	0.83	0.17	$t = 24.01$	5,940	5,942	<001
Gain vs. loss framing	1.13	.89, 1.37	0.58	0.62	0.52, 0.71	0.60	0.53, 0.67	0.00	0.86	0.14	$\chi^2 = 516.4$	1	6,271	<.001
Sex differences in	1.01	.54, 1.48	0.59	0.56	0.45, 0.68	0.53	0.46, 0.60	0.00	0.71	0.29	$r = 19.28$	5,840	5,842	<.001

implicit math attitudes	0.50	.15, .84	0.50	0.51	0.42, 0.61	0.49	0.40, 0.58	0.00	0.67	0.33	$\chi^2 = 342.4$	1	5,899	<.001
Low vs. high category scales														
Quote attribution	na		0.30	0.31	0.19, 0.42	0.32	0.25, 0.39	0.00	0.47	0.53	$t = 12.79$	6,323	6,325	<.001
Norm of reciprocity	0.16	.06, .27	0.27	0.27	0.18, 0.36	0.30	0.23,0.37	0.00	0.36	0.64	$\chi^2 = 135.3$	1	6,276	<.001
Sunk costs	0.23	–.04, .50	0.32	0.31	0.22, 0.39	0.27	0.20, 0.34	0.00	0.50	0.50	$t = 10.83$	6,328	6,330	<.001
Imagined contact	0.86	.14, 1.57	0.12	0.10	0.00, 0.19	0.13	0.07, 0.19	0.03	0.11	0.86	$t = 5.05$	6,334	6,336	<.001
Flag priming	0.50	.01, .99	0.02	0.01	–0.07, 0.08	0.03	–0.04, 0.10	0.04	0.00	0.96	$t = 0.88$	4,894	4,896	0.38
Currency priming	0.80	.05, 1.54	0.00	0.01	–0.06, 0.09	–0.02	–0.08, 0.04	0.00	0.03	0.97	$t = -0.79$	6,331	6,333	0.83

Notes. All effect sizes (ES) presented in Cohen's *d* units. Weighted statistics are computed on the whole aggregated dataset ($N > 6{,}000$); Unweighted statistics are computed on the disaggregated dataset ($N = 36$). 95% CI's for original effect sizes used cell sample sizes when available and assumed equal distribution across conditions when not available. The original anchoring article did not provide sufficient information to calculate effect sizes for individual scenarios, therefore an overall effect size is reported. The Anchoring original effect size is a mean point-biserial correlation computed across 15 different questions in a test–retest design, whereas the present replication adopted a between-subjects design with random assignments. One sample was removed from sex difference and relations between implicit and explicit math attitudes because of a systemic error in that laboratory's recording of reaction times. Flag priming includes only US samples. Confidence intervals around the unweighted mean are based on the central normal distribution. Confidence intervals around the weighted effect size are based on noncentral distributions.

Variation Across Samples and Settings

Figure 1 demonstrates substantial variation for some of the observed effects. That variation could be a function of the true effect size, random error, sample differences, or setting differences. Comparing the intra-class correlation of samples across effects (ICC = .005; $F(35, 385) = 1.06$, $p = .38$, 95% CI [–.027, .065]) with the intra-class correlation of effects across samples (ICC = .75; $F(12,420) = 110.62$, $p < .001$, 95% CI [.60, .89]) suggests that very little in the variability of effect sizes can be attributed to the samples, and substantial variability is attributable to the effect under investigation. To illustrate, Figure 2 shows the same data as Figure 1 organized by sample rather than by effect. There is almost no variation in the average effect size across samples.

However, it is possible that particular samples would elicit larger magnitudes for some effects and smaller magnitudes for others. That might be missed by the aggregate analyses. Table 3 presents tests of whether the heterogeneity of effect sizes for each effect exceeds what is expected by measurement error. Cochran's Q and I^2 statistics revealed that heterogeneity of effect sizes was largely observed among the very large effects – anchoring, allowed-forbidden, and relations between implicit and explicit attitudes. Only one other effect – quote attribution – showed substantial heterogeneity. This appears to be partly attributable to this effect occurring more strongly in US samples and to a lesser degree in international samples.

To test for moderation by key characteristics of the setting, we conducted a Condition × Country (US or other) × Location

Table 3 Tests of Effect Size Heterogeneity

	Heterogeneity statistics				Moderation tests					
Effect	***Q***	***DF***	***p***	***I^2***	**US or international**	***p***	**η_p^2**	**Laboratory or online**	***p***	**η_p^2**
Anchoring – babies born	59.71	35	0.01	0.402	0.16	0.69	0.00	16.14	<0.01	0.00
Anchoring – Mt. Everest	152.34	35	<.0001	0.754	94.33	<0.01	0.02	119.56	<0.01	0.02
Allowed/forbidden	180.40	35	<.0001	0.756	70.37	<0.01	0.01	0.55	0.46	0.00
Anchoring – Chicago	312.75	35	<0001	0.913	0.62	0.43	0.00	32.95	<0.01	0.01
Anchoring – distance to NYC	88.16	35	<.0001	0.643	9.35	<0.01	0.00	15.74	<0.01	0.00
Relations between I and E math attitudes	54.84	34	<.0001	0.401	0.41*	0.52	<.001*	2.80*	0.09	<001*
Retrospective gambler fallacy	50.83	35	0.04	0.229	0.40	0.53	0.00	0.34	0.56	0.00
Gain vs. loss framing	37.01	35	0.37	0.0001	0.09	0.76	0.00	1.11	0.29	0.00
Sex differences in implicit math attitudes	47.60	34	0.06	0.201	0.82	0.37	0.00	1.07	0.30	0.00
Low vs. high category scales	36.02	35	0.42	0.192	0.16	0.69	0.00	0.02	0.88	0.00
Quote attribution	67.69	35	<.001	0.521	8.81	<0.01	0.001	0.50	0.48	0.00
Norm of reciprocity	38.89	35	0.30	0.172	5.76	0.02	0.00	0.64	0.43	0.00
Sunk costs	35.55	35	0.44	0.092	0.58	0.45	0.00	0.25	0.62	0.00
Imagined contact	45.87	35	0.10	0.206	0.53	0.47	0.00	4.88	0.03	0.00
Flag priming	30.33	35	0.69	0	0.53	0.47	0.00	1.85	0.17	0.00
Currency priming	28.41	35	0.78	0	1.00	0.32	0.00	0.11	0.74	0.00

Notes. Tasks ordered from largest to smallest observed effect size (see Table 2). Heterogeneity tests conducted with R-package metafor. REML was used for estimation for all tests. One sample was removed from sex difference and relations between implicit and explicit math attitudes because of a systemic error in that laboratory's recording of reaction times.

*Moderator statistics are *F* value of the interaction of condition and the moderator from an ANOVA with condition, country, and location as independent variables with the exception of relations between impl. and expl. math attitudes for is reported the *F* value associated with the change in R squared after the product term between the independent variable and the moderator is added in a hierarchical linear regression model. Details of all analyses are available in the supplement.

(lab or online) ANOVA for each effect. Table 3 presents the essential Condition × Country and Condition × Location effects. Full model results are available in supplementary materials. A total of 10 of the 32 moderation tests were significant, and seven of those were among the largest effects – anchoring and allowed forbidden. Even including those, none of the moderation effect sizes exceeded a η_p^2 of .022. The heterogeneity in anchoring effects may be attributable to differences in knowledge of the height of Mt Everest, distance to NYC, or population of Chicago between the samples. Overall, whether the sample was collected in the US or elsewhere, or whether data collection occurred online or in the laboratory, had little systematic effect on the observed results.

Additional possible moderators of the flag priming effect were suggested by the original authors. On the US participants only ($N \sim 4{,}670$), with five hierarchical regression models, we tested whether the items moderated the effect of the manipulation. They did not (*ps* = .48, .80, .62, .07, .05, all $\Delta R^2 < .001$). Details are available in the online supplement.

Discussion

A large-scale replication with 36 samples successfully replicated eleven of 13 classic and contemporary effects in psychological science, some of which are well-known to be robust, and others that have been replicated infrequently or not at all. The original studies produced underestimates of some effects (e.g., anchoring-and-adjustment and allowed versus forbidden message framing), and overestimates of other effects (e.g., imagined contact producing willingness to interact with outgroups in the future). Two effects – flag priming influencing conservatism and currency priming influencing system justification – did not replicate.

A primary goal of this investigation was to examine the heterogeneity of effect sizes by the wide variety of samples and settings, and to provide an example of a paradigm for testing such variation. Some studies were conducted online, others in the laboratory. Some studies were conducted in the United States, others elsewhere. And, a wide variety of educational institutions took part. Surprisingly, these factors did not produce highly heterogeneous effect sizes. Intraclass correlations suggested that most of the variation in effects was due to the effect under investigation and almost none to the particular sample used. Focused tests of moderating influences elicited sporadic and small effects of the setting, while tests of heterogeneity suggested that most of the variation in effects is attributable to measurement error. Further, heterogeneity was mostly restricted to the largest effects in the sample – counter to an intuition that small effects would be the most likely to be variable across sample and setting. Further, the lack of heterogeneity is particularly interesting considering that there is substantial interest and commentary about the contingency of effects on our two moderators, lab versus online (Gosling, Vazire, Srivastava, & John, 2004; Paolacci, Chandler, & Ipeirotis, 2010), and cultural variation across nations (Henrich et al., 2010).

All told, the main conclusion from this small sample of studies is that, to predict effect size, it is much more important to know what effect is being studied than to know the sample or setting in which it is being studied. The key virtue of the present investigation is that the study procedure was highly standardized across data collection settings. This minimized the likelihood that factors other than sample and setting contributed to systematic variation in effects. At the same time, this conclusion is surely constrained by the small, nonrandom sample of studies represented here. Additionally, the replication sites included in this project cannot capture all possible cultural variation, and most societies sampled were relatively Western, Educated, Industrialized, Rich, and Democratic (WEIRD; Henrich et al., 2010). Nonetheless, the present investigation suggests that we should not necessarily assume that there are differences between samples; indeed, even when moderation was observed in this sample, the effects were still quite robust in each setting.

The present investigation provides a summary analysis of a very large, rich dataset. This dataset will be useful for additional exploratory analysis about replicability in general, and these effects in particular. The data are available for download at the Open Science Framework (https://osf.io/ydpbf/).

Conclusion

This investigation offered novel insights into variation in the replicability of psychological effects, and specific information about the replicability of 13 effects. This methodology – crowdsourcing dozens of laboratories running an identical procedure – can be adapted for a variety of investigations. It allows for increased confidence in the existence of an effect and for the investigation of an effect's dependence on the particular circumstances of data collection (Open Science Collaboration, 2014). Further, a consortium of laboratories could provide mutual support for each other by conducting similar large-scale investigations on original research questions, not just replications. Thus, collective effort could accelerate the identification and verification of extant and novel psychological effects.

Notes

1. One sample fell short of this requirement ($N = 79$) but was still included in the analysis. All sites were encouraged to collect as many participants as possible beyond the required 80, but the decision to end data collection was determined independently by each site. Researchers had no access to the data prior to completing data collection.

2. Table names that begin with the prefix "S" (e.g., Table S1) refer to tables that can be found in the supplementary materials. Tables with no prefix are in this paper.
3. None of the effects was moderated by which position in the study procedure it was administered.
4. The original anchoring report did not distinguish between topics so the aggregate effect size is reported.

References

Aronson, E. (1992). The return of the repressed: Dissonance theory makes a comeback. *Psychological Inquiry, 3*, 303–311.

Bodenhausen, G. V. (1990). Stereotypes as judgmental heuristics: Evidence of circadian variations in discrimination. *Psychological Science, 1*, 319–322.

Brandt, M. J., IJzerman, H., Dijksterhuis, A., Farach, F. J., Geller, J., Giner-Sorolla, R., . . . van 't Veer, A. (2013). The replication recipe: What makes for a convincing replication? *Journal of Experimental Social Psychology, 50*, 217–224.

Carter, T. J., Ferguson, M. J., & Hassin, R. R. (2011). A single exposure to the American flag shifts support toward Republicanism up to 8 months later. *Psychological Science, 22*, 1011–1018.

Caruso, E. M., Vohs, K. D., Baxter, B., & Waytz, A. (2013). Mere exposure to money increases endorsement of free-market systems and social inequality. *Journal of Experimental Psychology: General, 142*, 301–306.

Cesario, J. (2014). Priming, replication, and the hardest science. *Perspectives on Psychological Science, 9*, 40–48.

Collins, H. M. (1974). The TEA set: Tacit knowledge and scientific networks. *Science Studies, 4*, 165–185.

Crisp, R. J., Miles, E., & Husnu, S. (2014). Support for the replicability of imagined contact effects. Commentaries and rejoinder on Klein et al. (2014). *Social Psychology*. Advance online publication. doi: 10.1027/1864-9335/1000202

Ferguson, M. J., Carter, T. J., & Hassin, R. R. (2014). Commentary on the attempt to replicate the effect of the American flag on increased republican attitudes. Commentaries and rejoinder on Klein et al. (2014). *Social Psychology*. Advance online publication. doi: 10.1027/1864-9335/1000202

Gosling, S. D., Vazire, S., Srivastava, S., & John, O. P. (2004). Should we trust web-based studies? A comparative analysis of six preconceptions about Internet questionnaires. *American Psychologist, 59*, 93.

Greenwald, A. G., Pratkanis, A. R., Leippe, M. R., & Baumgardner, M. H. (1986). Under what conditions does theory obstruct research progress? *Psychological Review, 93*, 216–229.

Henrich, J., Heine, S. J., & Norenzayan, A. (2010). Most people are not WEIRD. *Nature, 466*, 29.

Henry, J. D., MacLeod, M. S., Phillips, L. H., & Crawford, J. R. (2004). A meta-analytic review of prospective memory and aging. *Psychology and Aging, 19*, 27.

Husnu, S., & Crisp, R. J. (2010). Elaboration enhances the imagined contact effect. *Journal of Experimental Social Psychology, 46*, 943–950.

Hyman, H. H., & Sheatsley, P. B. (1950). The current status of American public opinion. In J. C. Payne (Ed.), *The teaching of contemporary affairs: 21st yearbook of the National Council of Social Studies* (pp. 11–34). New York, NY: National Council of Social Studies.

Ioannidis, J. P. (2005). Why most published research findings are false. *PLoS Medicine, 2*, e124.

Jacowitz, K. E., & Kahneman, D. (1995). Measures of anchoring in estimation tasks. *Personality and Social Psychology Bulletin, 21*, 1161–1166.

Kahneman, D. (2014). A new etiquette for replication. Commentaries and rejoinder on Klein et al. (2014). *Social Psychology*. Advance online publication. doi: 10.1027/1864-9335/1000202

Kay, A. C., & Jost, J. T. (2003). Complementary justice: Effects of "poor but happy" and "poor but honest" stereotype exemplars on system justification and implicit activation of the justice motive. *Journal of Personality and Social Psychology*, 85, 823–837.

Klein, R. A., Ratliff, K. A., Vianello, M., Adams, R. B. Jr., Bahník, Š., Bernstein, M. J., . . . Nosek, B. A. (2014). Theory building through replication: Response to commentaries on the "Many Labs" replication project. Commentaries and rejoinder on Klein et al. (2014). *Social Psychology*. Advance online publication. doi: 10.1027/1864-9335/1000202

Knox, R. E., & Inkster, J. A. (1968). Postdecision dissonance at post time. *Journal of Personality and Social Psychology, 8*, 319.

Lorge, I., & Curtiss, C. C. (1936). Prestige, suggestion, and attitudes. *The Journal of Social Psychology, 7*, 386–402.

Monin, B., & Oppenheimer, D. M. (2014). The limits of direct replications and the virtues of stimulus sampling. Commentaries and rejoinder on Klein et al. (2014). *Social Psychology*. Advance online publication. doi: 10.1027/1864-9335/1000202

Moskowitz, G. B. (2004). *Social cognition: Understanding self and others.* New York: Guilford Press.

Nosek, B. A., Banaji, M. R., & Greenwald, A. G. (2002). Math = male, Me = female, therefore math ≠ Me. *Journal of Personality and Social Psychology, 83*, 44–59.

Nosek, B. A., & Smyth, F. L. (2011). Implicit social cognitions predict sex differences in math engagement and achievement. *American Educational Research Journal, 48*, 1125–1156.

Open Science Collaboration. (2012). An open, large-scale, collaborative effort to estimate the reproducibility of psychological science. *Perspectives on Psychological Science, 7*, 657–660.

Open Science Collaboration. (2014). The reproducibility project: A model of large-scale collaboration for empirical research on reproducibility. In V. Stodden, F. Leisch, & R. Peng (Eds.), *Implementing reproducible computational research (A volume in the R series)* (pp. 299–323). New York, NY: Taylor & Francis.

Oppenheimer, D. M., Meyvis, T., & Davidenko, N. (2009). Instructional manipulation checks: Detecting satisficing to increase statistical power. *Journal of Experimental Social Psychology, 45*, 867–872.

Oppenheimer, D. M., & Monin, B. (2009). The retrospective gambler's fallacy: Unlikely events, constructing the past, and multiple universes. *Judgment and Decision Making, 4*, 326–334.

Paolacci, G., Chandler, J., & Ipeirotis, P. (2010). Running experiments on Amazon Mechanical Turk. *Judgment and Decision Making, 5*, 411–419.

Rugg, D. (1941). Experiments in wording questions: II. *Public Opinion Quarterly, 5*, 91–92.

Schmidt, S. (2009). Shall we really do it again? The powerful concept of replication is neglected in the social sciences. *Review of General Psychology, 13*, 90–100.

Schwarz, N., Hippler, H. J., Deutsch, B., & Strack, F. (1985). Response scales: Effects of category range on reported behavior and comparative judgments. *Public Opinion Quarterly, 49*, 388–395.

Schwarz, N., & Strack, F. (2014). Does merely going through the same moves make for a "direct" replication? Concepts, contexts, and operationalizations. Commentaries and rejoinder on Klein et al. (2014). *Social Psychology*. Advance online publication. doi: 10.1027/1864-9335/1000202

Thaler, R. (1985). Mental accounting and consumer choice. *Marketing Science, 4*, 199–214.

Turner, R. N., Crisp, R. J., & Lambert, E. (2007). Imagining intergroup contact can improve intergroup attitudes. *Group Processes and Intergroup Relations, 10*, 427–441.

Tversky, A., & Kahneman, D. (1981). The framing of decisions and the psychology of choice. *Science, 211*, 453–458.

Critical Thinking

1. What are the practical implications when a study does not replicate? So what? Provide three reasons why it is important to demonstrate replicability in psychological research.
2. One of the topics frequently mentioned in the article is effect size. What is effect size, and how does it differ from statistical significance?

Internet References

Estimating the reproducibility of psychological science
http://science.sciencemag.org/content/349/6251/aac4716

Psychology, replication & beyond
https://bmcpsychology.biomedcentral.com/articles/10.1186/s40359-016-0135-2

The replication crisis in psychology
http://nobaproject.com/modules/the-replication-crisis-in-psychology

What is replication? Why many psychology studies fail to replicate
https://www.verywell.com/what-is-replication-2795802

Article

Prepared by: R. Eric Landrum, *Boise State University*

That's So Random: Why We Persist in Seeing Streaks

CARL ZIMMER

Learning Outcomes

After reading this article, you will be able to:

- Better understand the nature of random events.
- Understand the instinctual nature of looking for patterns and trends in our world.

From time to time, athletes get on a streak. Suddenly, the basketball goes through the net every time, or a batter gets a hit in every game. This blissful condition is often known as the hot hand, and players have come to believe it is real—so much so that they have made it a part of their strategy for winning games.

"On offense, if someone else has a hot hand, I constantly lay the ball on him," wrote the N.B.A. legend Walt Frazier in his 1974 memoir, *Rockin' Steady: A Guide to Basketball & Cool.*

In the 1980s, Thomas Gilovich, a psychologist at Cornell University, and his colleagues did a study of the hot hand. They confirmed that the vast majority of basketball players believed in it. The audiences at basketball games were also convinced. But then Dr. Gilovich and his colleagues analyzed the hot hand statistically, and it fell apart.

The hot hand was, they concluded, an illusion caused "by a general misconception of chance."

Today, there still isn't much evidence for a hot hand in basketball or beyond. But our belief in it is unquestionably real. Roulette players will bet on more numbers after they win than after they lose, psychologists have found. A store that issues a winning lottery ticket will tend to sell more lottery tickets afterward, economists have observed. Investors often assume that a rising stock's price will keep rising.

Time and again, we don't want to believe that streaks can be the result of pure chance—probably because the bias appears to be deeply ingrained in our minds, researchers say. Indeed, a new study in *The Journal of Experimental Psychology: Animal Learning and Cognition* suggests that the hot hand phenomenon is so ancient that monkeys display it, too.

"What it suggests is that there's something going back at least 25 million years," said Benjamin Y. Hayden, a neuroscientist at the University of Rochester who wrote the study with his graduate student, Tommy C. Blanchard, and a psychologist at Clarkson University, Andreas Wilke.

The new study builds on earlier tests that Dr. Wilke and his colleagues carried out on people. In one such study, the scientists had volunteers play a computer game that showed a picture of either a pear or a bunch of cherries. The volunteers had to guess which fruit would appear next.

The order was random, and yet the volunteers tended to guess that the next fruit would be the same as the current one. In other words, they expected the fruit to arrive in streaks.

In another trial, Dr. Wilke and his colleagues let volunteers choose among different versions of the game so that they could increase their winnings. One version of the game was more likely to switch the fruit each time. As a result, the game had fewer streaks.

It should have been an easy game to win. All Dr. Wilke's volunteers needed to do was guess that the next fruit would be different each time. And yet the volunteers tended to avoid the alternating game in favor of the random game, "where they see a pattern that doesn't exist," said Dr. Wilke.

Dr. Wilke and his colleagues argue that this mental quirk is a side effect of how our brains have evolved.

"Our idea is that the driving force of the hot hand phenomenon was our history of foraging," said Dr. Wilke.

Our ancestors were constantly searching for food, either gathering plants or hunting animals. As they searched, they had to continually decide where to look next. The wrong choice could mean starvation.

Dr. Wilke argues that this threat led our ancestors to evolve some rules of thumb based on the fact that animals and plants aren't scattered randomly across a landscape. Instead, they can be found in clumps.

This meant that if our ancestors picked up a fruit from the ground, they were likely to find more by looking nearby, rather than going somewhere else. As a result, they became very sensitive to these streaks. They were an indication that good fortune would keep coming.

On the other hand, if our ancestors kept looking in a place for food and found nothing, they could predict that another look wouldn't yield anything to eat.

In the modern world, Dr. Wilke argues, we can't get rid of this instinct to think that streaks will continue, even when we're dealing with random patterns.

To vet this hypothesis, Dr. Wilke has collaborated with H. Clark Barrett of the University of California, Los Angeles, to give his hot hand tests to a group of people who live deep in the Amazon rain forest and depend in part on hunting and foraging for their food. They had the same bias found in American volunteers, suggesting that the hot hand phenomenon went beyond Western societies obsessed with basketball and slot machines.

Dr. Wilke's latest experiment sought to test whether the hot hand bias was even more universal.

"The strongest test to see if it's evolutionary is to find it in another species," said Dr. Hayden, who studies how monkeys make decisions.

So, he and Dr. Wilke developed a game for monkeys to play. In each round, the monkeys saw either a purple rectangle on the left side of a computer screen or a blue rectangle on the right. In order to get a reward, the monkeys had to guess which rectangle would appear next, directing their gaze to the left or right side of the screen.

The monkeys played thousands of rounds, developing a strategy to get the biggest reward they could. And their performance revealed that they have a hot hand bias in their decision-making, researchers said.

When streaks were common, the scientists found, the monkeys learned to get a high score. In other versions of the game, with fewer streaks, they did worse. They couldn't help guessing that a new rectangle would be the same as the previous one.

Dr. Barrett, who was not involved in the new study, cautioned that the results need to be replicated. Nevertheless, he agreed that it raised the possibility that foraging gave rise to the hot hand phenomenon millions of years ago.

"This may be a deep evolutionary history indeed, stretching back to before we were human," Dr. Barrett said.

Similarly, Laurie Santos, a psychologist at Yale, said, "They're on to something." But she questioned whether the new study actually showed that monkeys experienced the same feeling as a basketball player on a streak.

Just because the monkeys expected the rectangles to come in streaks didn't mean that they believed their own actions had anything to do with it. Some psychologists distinguish between these two effects, calling them "hot hands" and "hot outcomes."

Dr. Santos was confident that Dr. Hayden and his colleagues could devise another experiment to test the two alternatives. "That's harder, but Ben does all kinds of crazy things," said Dr. Santos. "I'm sure he could find a way to do it."

Dr. Wilke said that hot hands and hot outcomes both could have evolved from the same underlying rules of thumb for searching for food. By understanding their origins, we may be able to better understand the particular ways they influence our thinking today.

In the July issue of *Evolution and Human Behavior*, Dr. Wilke and his colleagues report that habitual gamblers have a stronger hot hand bias than non-gamblers. It might eventually be possible to predict who will be at risk of problem gambling by measuring hot hand bias in advance.

"That's a first step into some sort of application of this research," said Dr. Wilke.

Critical Thinking

1. If people believe so much in the hot hand yet the scientific evidence does not support that belief, what problems might that cause when individuals believe in something that isn't real?
2. To what extent does gambling, such as playing the lottery, capitalize on people's beliefs about hot hands and non-random events?

Internet References

Hot hands in basketball

http://psych.cornell.edu/sites/default/files/Gilo.Vallone.Tversky.pdf

Monkeys also believe in winning streaks

http://www.rochester.edu/newscenter/monkeys-also-believe-in-winning-streaks-study-shows

Article

Prepared by: R. Eric Landrum, *Boise State University*

Trigger Warnings in Psychology: Psychology Teachers' Perspectives and Practices

Guy A. Boysen and Loreto R. Prieto

Learning Outcomes

After reading this article, you will be able to:

- Understand what a trigger warning is in the context of a psychology course.
- Identify what the expectations are regarding students and trigger warnings in psychology course (Table 2).
- Report on the structure of a research-based journal article in psychology (introduction, method, results, and discussion).

Recent reports in the news media indicate that college students without documented mental disorders are requesting that faculty issue trigger warnings before covering certain topics that they find personally distressing (Lukianoff & Haidt, 2015; Wilson, 2015). The Americans with Disabilities Act (1990) strongly encourages teachers to provide accommodations that foster equal educational access for students, and warnings about course topics could be one such accommodation for students whose distress is related to trauma-based mental disorders. Academic accommodations are a well-established practice in the educational system, and college teachers tend to view them positively (Leyser et al., 2011; Sniatecki, Perry, & Snell, 2015). In contrast, there has been a significant controversy among college teachers about issuing warnings for topics that are unrelated to documented disabilities but that students still find personally sensitive (American Association of University Professors, 2014). Despite the ongoing controversy, almost no empirical data exist on college teachers' use of warnings in relation to topics that are directly related to clinically defined trauma (e.g., sexual assault) or those that are merely sensitive in nature (e.g., race); thus, the purpose of the current study was to assess how psychology teachers at four-year colleges and universities view and use trigger warnings.

The Genesis of Trigger Warnings

The concept of trigger warnings stems from the clinical symptomology associated with post-traumatic stress disorder (PTSD). A hallmark symptom of the disorder is psychological reexperiencing of a traumatic event (American Psychiatric Association [APA], 2013). Patients with PTSD can have flashbacks in which they feel as if a trauma is reoccurring, and they can experience extreme emotional reactions when they encounter specific environmental stimuli that trigger memories of their traumatic experience. In the lay public, a general recognition that exposure to topics related to trauma might be distressing has led to the practice of prefacing discussion of such topics with a warning (Medina, 2014; Vingiano, 2014). Based upon this use of warnings among the lay public, college students began to request that teachers provide trigger warnings before covering sensitive topics in classes (Essig, 2014; Lukianoff & Haidt, 2015; Shaw-Thornburg, 2014; Stokes, 2014). Although the debate on trigger warnings has primarily concerned undergraduate education, the issue is also relevant to psychology education in high school and graduate school settings where the issue is even more complex because high school teachers work with minors and because graduate faculty serve as gatekeepers for the profession.

Although trigger warnings have been the subject of much debate, no consensus has emerged in the scholarly literature about their definition or appropriate use. A broad definition used in some scholarly discussions is that trigger warnings refer to faculty issuing any type of warning about any topic that might possibly lead students to feel distress (Veraldi & Veraldi, 2015; Wyatt, 2016). According to this broad definition, examples of trigger warnings could include warning students in a human sexuality course that pictures of infected genitalia might produce disgust or warning students in a diversity course that discussing race-based issues might cause discomfort. As these examples illustrate, the problem with the broad definition is that it ignores the origins of trigger warnings as a tool for averting negative reactions due to the symptoms of PTSD (Boysen, 2017). For people with PTSD, the purpose of a trigger warning is not to avoid a stimulus itself, but to avoid clinically significant levels of distress that occur automatically from exposure to the stimulus (Ehlers, Hackmann, & Michael, 2004; Grillon et al., 2009; Kleim et al., 2013; Simmons et al., 2013).

A more precise definition is needed to separate warnings issued for trauma-related topics from warnings about topics that may be personally sensitive but are not directly related to students' mental health status. In this vein, Boysen (2017, p. 164) defined trigger warnings as "teachers offering prior notification of an educational topic so that students may prepare for or avoid distress that is automatically evoked by that topic due to clinical mental health problems." This definition purposefully excludes topics that are merely sensitive (e.g., racism, sex) or that may generally elicit emotional reactions (e.g., nudity, images of bodily injury). As such, this definition narrows the scope of trigger warnings from any topic that might be distressing, to topics for which students might receive accommodations according to the Americans with Disabilities Act (1990). There are undoubtedly sound pedagogical reasons to offer warnings before teaching about many psychology topics. Thus, teachers would benefit from information about teachers' typical practices when offering warnings about topics that are potential triggers of trauma-related distress versus topics that are merely sensitive.

The Trigger Warning Debate

The debate over trigger warnings in college classrooms represents a conflict between the belief that students should not be forced to encounter distressing content in their courses versus the belief that teachers should be free to select and present relevant content within their discipline. Advocates emphasize use of trigger warning as a protection for students' mental health, not as a method for avoiding sensitive issues. They argue that trigger warnings are analogous to accommodations for psychiatric conditions such as a distraction-free testing environment for students with attention-deficit/hyperactivity disorder (Wyatt, 2016). Advocates also assert that the use of trigger warnings can send a message of inclusion and respect for people with trauma-based mental disorders (Carter, 2015). Finally, supporters note that the use of trigger warnings by faculty requires no alteration to course content and only a slight modification to normal classroom activities (Godderis & Root, 2016; Manne, 2015; Wyatt, 2016). One limitation of focusing on trigger warnings as an accommodation for disability is that it does not address students who have suffered a trauma but have not developed a mental disorder or who have not received documentation for their mental disorder; such students may be left unprotected by disability-focused trigger warnings.

Critics of trigger warnings argue that confronting sensitive topics is a central part of higher education and that standardized implementation of trigger warnings does not follow the established procedures for disability accommodations at universities (American Association of University Professors, 2014). Critics acknowledge that, according to the Americans with Disabilities Act (1990), teachers should provide accommodations that allow students with documented diagnoses of mental disorders to have equal access to academic opportunities. However, they assert that no such legal protection exists when it comes to addressing individual students' personal preferences for comfort in the classroom. If an accommodation, such as a warning about content, were to occur for a sensitive topic, it would need to be based on a documented diagnosis of a mental disorder and sanctioned by an official campus office.

Critics also view trigger warnings as too problematic for widespread adoption in the college classroom. Triggers of distress are extremely varied and unique to individuals, and this leaves teachers unable to provide warnings for every possible traumatic association or sensitivity that students may have (American Association of University Professors, 2014; Wyatt, 2016). In addition, trigger warnings are designed to facilitate the avoidance of trauma-related stimuli, and avoidance is a symptom of PTSD, not a treatment or appropriate coping method. As such, the use of trigger warnings would seem to contradict the type of controlled, safe exposure to reminders of trauma that is fundamental to treating PTSD (Wyatt, 2016). Some critics have even suggested that trigger warnings in the classroom are scientifically meaningless because they extend the original concept of triggered distress in PTSD well beyond its intended meaning in the clinical literature (Veraldi & Veraldi, 2015).

Empirical Research on Trigger Warnings

Despite the ongoing debate in higher education, there is little empirical research to guide teachers' uses of trigger warnings in the classroom. A vast clinical literature on post-traumatic stress provides mixed support for the assumptions underlying the use of classroom trigger warnings (Boysen, 2017), but the generalizability of that research to a classroom setting needs further investigation. Only one published study on classroom trigger warnings has emerged, and it focused on their use among abnormal psychology instructors (Boysen, Wells, & Dawson, 2016). Results from that investigation showed that 49 percent of these instructors had never issued a trigger warning, 31 percent had issued such warnings, and 20 percent were unfamiliar with the term. Instructors' attitudes about trigger warnings were ambivalent; 44 percent had a negative opinion toward the use of such warnings, 25 percent a positive opinion, and 31 percent were neutral. When prompted to report if they provided warnings for certain abnormal psychology topics, almost half of the instructors regularly or always provided warnings before covering trauma-related topics such as suicide or descriptions of specific traumatic experiences, but less than ⅓ of instructors regularly or always provided warnings about topics that might merely be personally sensitive to some students such as gender identity and sexual dysfunction. The study's results provided course-specific evidence that psychology instructors have mixed attitudes about trigger warnings and that the use of trigger warnings differs for trauma-related topics and topics that are merely sensitive.

The Current Study

The purpose of the current study was to extend previous research on trigger warning use by teachers of abnormal psychology to teachers of psychology courses in general. A sample of psychology teachers from specialties across the discipline completed a survey assessing their attitudes about trigger warnings, use of trigger warnings for specific topics, and perceptions of student distress in reaction to specific topics. Although there is a strong argument to be made for defining trigger warnings as relating only to clinical distress (Boysen, 2017), the current study included warnings related to a wide variety of potentially sensitive topics. The inclusion of PTSD-related trauma topics, as well as potentially sensitive non-PTSD-related trauma topics, was necessary to formulate a complete picture of teachers' attitudes and practices and to allow for comparison of the two types of topics. This approach allowed for the examination of four research questions:

1. What are psychology teachers' general attitudes about trigger warnings?
2. What are psychology teachers' typical trigger warning practices?
3. Do psychology teachers observe students as being distressed by potentially sensitive topics?
4. Do teachers report differences between topics associated with events defined as traumas in the diagnosis of PTSD (e.g., sexual assault, suicide, child abuse) and topics that may be sensitive to students (e.g., race, sexual orientation, social class issues) but are not PTSD-related traumas?

The answers to these questions will help establish basic knowledge about trigger warnings in psychology.

Method

Participants

Participants (N = 284) consisted of psychology teachers who were primarily female (55 percent) and European American (84 percent), and who had an average age of 49 years (SD = 12). Participants represented a wide variety of specialty areas including clinical (26 percent), cognitive/neuroscience (17 percent), social (16 percent), counseling (9 percent), developmental (9 percent), experimental (6 percent), school/educational (5 percent), industrial/organizational (3 percent), and personality (2 percent), with 9 percent of the sample reporting their specialty as "other." Participants described their institutions as undergraduate liberal arts colleges/universities (30 percent), doctoral universities (29 percent), master's universities (21 percent), baccalaureate colleges (19 percent), and other (1 percent). Private (52 percent) and public (48 percent) institutions were approximately equally represented. Most participants taught face-to-face courses (94 percent) in tenure-track positions (71 percent), and the sample had an average of 20 (SD = 12) years of teaching experience. Participants estimated that 81 percent (SD = 26) of their teaching responsibility was at the undergraduate level and their average class contained 31 (SD = 21) students. The recruitment method consisted of sending e-mail requests for participation to full-time psychology faculty selected from a random sample of Carnegie classified four-year institutions (26 percent response rate).

Materials and Procedure

The study received human subjects' committee approval, and all procedures were consistent with APA guidelines. The procedure consisted of participants receiving an e-mail request for participation and then completing an online survey. Invitations explained the purpose of the study was to identify "how teachers deal with sensitive topics in the classroom (e.g., trigger warnings)."

Attitudes about Trigger Warnings. The survey included several items assessing teachers' attitudes about trigger warnings. Two items asked participants to rate their opinion about the use of trigger warnings in college classrooms, as well as specifically in

Table 1 Teachers' Ratings of Warning Necessity and Frequency

	Warning Necessity						Warning frequency				
Topic	*M* (*SD*)	**Not at all (%)**	**Slightly (%)**	**Somewhat (%)**	**Very (%)**	**Abso-lutely (%)**	*M* (*SD*)	**Never (%)**	**Rarely (%)**	**Occ. (%)**	**Always (%)**
Sexual assault	2.86 (1.33)	23	16	26	24	12	2.72 (1.23)	27	13	22	38
Child abuse	2.62 (1.33)	28	21	23	18	10	2.47 (1.24)	35	11	26	28
Violent/cata-strophic trauma	2.56 (1.31)	29	21	23	18	9	2.28 (1.24)	42	13	21	24
Suicide	2.48 (1.34)	34	19	20	19	8	2.16 (1.23)	46	13	18	22
Self-harm	2.23 (1.28)	41	21	17	15	1	1.96 (1.13)	52	14	21	14
Sexual orienta-tion/gender identity	2.06 (1.28)	46	18	22	11	3	1.99 (1.12)	50	16	21	14
Eating disorders	2.06 (1.18)	47	19	19	13	3	1.87 (1.10)	56	13	19	12
Psychiatric symptoms	2.04 (1.17)	51	14	20	14	3	2.16 (1.23)	51	14	21	14
Racial issues	2.04 (1.17)	46	20	20	12	3	2.07 (1.18)	49	13	21	17
Sexism	1.98 (1.14)	46	18	22	11	3	1.96 (1.10)	51	14	23	12
Human sexuality	1.96 (1.15)	51	17	18	13	1	1.89 (1.11)	55	15	17	13
Mental illness stigma	1.88 (1.19)	56	17	12	11	3	1.77 (1.10)	62	12	14	13
Substance abuse	1.86 (1.12)	56	15	18	10	2	1.63 (0.94)	63	17	14	6
Religious issues	1.83 (1.07)	54	21	17	7	2	1.76 (1.02)	58	17	17	9
Physical disability	1.81 (1.06)	56	19	16	9	1	1.65 (0.95)	63	14	17	6
Social class/SES	1.71 (1.01)	60	17	16	6	1	1.63 (0.96)	65	13	15	6

Note: Occ. = occasionally; SES = socioeconomic status.

psychology classrooms, using a Likert-type scale ranging from 1 (*extremely negative*) to 5 (*extremely favorable*). Participants also rated how helpful they thought trigger warnings were to the psychological health of students using a Likert-type scale ranging from 1 (*extremely harmful*) to 5 (*extremely helpful*). Following methods established in previous research, these initial items were not accompanied by an *a priori* definition of trigger warnings, which allowed for an assessment of participants' preexisting attitudes about trigger warnings and assessment of the percentage of participants who were unfamiliar with the concept (Boysen et al., 2016). Participants also rated how necessary they believed it is for psychology teachers to offer trigger warnings for the 16 topics listed in Table 1 using a Likert-type scale ranging from 1 (*not at all necessary*) to 5 (*absolutely necessary*). A separate section of the survey included 11 items assessing more specific attitudes about trigger warnings and their role in psychology education (Table 2). Participants rated these items using a Likert-type scale ranging from 1 (*strongly disagree*) to 5 (*strongly agree*).

Common Practices in the Use of Trigger Warnings. One item asked participants to report in how many different psychology courses they had provided warnings about topics "that some students might find sensitive, personally disturbing, controversial, or could elicit troublesome emotions." Participants also selected all of the methods they used to provide warnings using the following options: (a) in their course syllabus, (b) via a class announcement in the first class session, (c) via a class announcement when a distressing topic first arose in class, (d) via a class announcement when students expressed or showed visible discomfort in class, and (e) via a class announcement when students privately reported discomfort to the instructor. To assess the frequency of trigger warning use by topic, participants indicated how often they warned students about the 16 topics listed in Table 1 using a 4-point scale (*never, rarely, occasionally, always*); they could also indicate that the topic did not arise in their courses.

Table 2 Agreement with Statements about Warnings

Statement	Teachers, *M* (*SD*)
Psychology students should understand that education in psychology can and will expose them to potentially controversial or disturbing content in their courses or classroom discussions.	4.71 (0.64)
Psychology students are taught and exposed to potentially controversial or disturbing content in their courses or classroom discussions because such content is relevant to their training and future careers.	4.67 (0.65)
Psychology instructors who purposefully avoid covering potentially controversial or disturbing content in their courses or classroom discussions compromise and limit the full learning potential of their psychology students.	4.50 (0.91)
Psychology students should be at a point in their maturity and understanding of the world to realize that controversial or disturbing content in their courses or classroom discussions are necessary aspects of their learning.	4.46 (0.80)
Even when psychology instructors warn their students that potentially controversial or disturbing content will be a part of the course or classroom discussions, some students will still experience distress and this is acceptable.	4.27 (0.78)
Psychology instructors generally use good professional judgment when deciding to expose psychology students to potentially controversial or disturbing content in their courses or classroom discussions.	4.19 (0.78)
Psychology instructors should always warn their students when potentially controversial or disturbing content will be a part of the course or classroom discussions.	2.56 (1.33)
Psychology students who are bothered by controversial or disturbing content in their courses or classroom discussions should use that experience to guide them away from psychology courses, minors, and majors.	2.41 (1.16)
Psychology students who are bothered by controversial or disturbing content in their courses or classroom discussions should be, without penalty, provided with alternate nondisturbing content to learn instead.	2.04 (1.17)
Psychology instructors have a professional responsibility to make sure their students are not disturbed in any way by potentially controversial or disturbing content in courses or classroom discussions.	1.81 (1.11)
Psychology instructors should avoid covering any controversial or disturbing content that has the chance of adversely affecting students in their courses or classroom discussions.	1.11 (0.35)

Note: The rating scale ranged from 1 (*strongly disagree*) to 5 (*strongly agree*).

Observed Student Reactions to Topics. Three sections of the survey assessed participants' perceptions of students' reactions to potentially sensitive topics. A *yes/no* item asked if participants had covered a topic that "led to students being visibly disturbed (as shown by their vocal, facial, or behavioral reactions)" and also asked participants to select each of the 16 topics that had elicited visible student distress. Similarly, a yes/no question asked participants if their psychology students had ever asked them to provide "a warning about a specific sensitive topic before covering it in class" and then asked them to select each of the 16 topics that had brought such requests. Finally, a yes/no item asked if students had ever asked "for an accommodation or exception to course policy." Participants could then list the accommodations requested.

Results

Attitudes toward Trigger Warnings

Eighty-six percent of participants initially reported being familiar with the concept of trigger warnings. Among those familiar with the concept, 43 percent held a favorable opinion about their use in psychology classrooms, 30 percent a negative opinion, and 28 percent were neutral; on average, opinions were neutral (M = 3.14, SD = 1.09). Opinions about the general use of trigger warnings in college classrooms showed a similar pattern (41 percent favorable, 34 percent negative, 25 percent neutral; M = 3.05, SD = 1.09). In terms of perceptions of trigger warnings' effect on the psychological health of students, 48 percent of participants believed they were helpful, 17 percent believed they were harmful, and 35 percent were neutral (M = 3.35, SD = 0.91).

Means, standard deviations, and frequencies for participants' ratings of the necessity of trigger warnings for specific topics can be seen in Table 1. Participants' mean ratings of the necessity of trigger warnings across the 16 topics indicated that they viewed them as *slightly necessary* overall; *not at all necessary* was the most frequent response for all topics except sexual assault. Individual topics with means that rose above *slightly necessary* included sexual assault, child abuse, and violent trauma; participants' perceived warnings for these topics as *somewhat necessary*. However, a larger percentage of participants rated warnings as *not at all* to *slightly necessary* than rated them as *very* to *absolutely necessary*.

Participants rated their level of agreement with 11 statements about sensitive topics in psychology education (see Table 2). Participants agreed that the discipline of psychology deals some sensitive topics that are essential to the curriculum. However, participants also believed that students must take responsibility for learning about sensitive topics if they are psychology majors. Participants disagreed with the notion that teachers are responsible for ensuring that students avoid any topics that might distress them.

Common Practices

Forty-seven percent of participants indicated they did not provide trigger warnings in their classes, 39 percent reported they did, and 14 percent indicated that they were not familiar with the concept. Participants familiar with the concept reported that they had warned students about sensitive topics in approximately four different courses (M = 3.61, SD = 3.92). Table 1 includes the frequencies of warnings related to the 16 specific topics, excluding participants who did not cover the topics in their courses. Examination of these frequencies illustrates that most teachers reported *never* providing warnings for 11 of the 16 topics. However, 10 percent or more of faculty reported *always* providing warnings about 11 of topics. In terms of overall mean ratings, participants reported that they *rarely* provided warnings for 15 of the 16 topics.

The most commonly selected response, as to when teachers issued warnings, was when sensitive issues arose during class (52 percent). The next most common responses were during the first day of class (36 percent), as a written statement in the syllabus (24 percent), when students privately dents showed or expressed discomfort in class (11 percent).

Observed Student Reactions

The majority of participants (68 percent) indicated that they had at some time covered a sensitive topic in class that led students to show visible signs of distress; the frequency of visible student distress by topic can be seen in Table 3. Teachers could also write in topics that elicited student distress that were not listed on the survey. Of the 49 write-in responses, five topics were cited by more than one participant: child-birth or sexually transmitted infections (8 percent), death (3 percent), animal experiments/cruelty (2 percent), bullying (1 percent), and specific phobias (1 percent).

Eighteen percent of participants reported having had a student request a trigger warning for potentially sensitive topics covered in class. Topics that led to these student requests and the frequency of student requests can be seen in Table 3. Teachers could also write in topics, and of the 10 write-in responses, the only topic mentioned by more than one participant was death (7 percent). In terms of students having asked participants for accommodations or other policy exceptions related to the coverage of a sensitive topic, 22 percent of participants had received such a request. Of the 51 open-ended responses describing these student requests, the most frequent was to miss the portion of class related to the topic (60 percent). Other student requests mentioned by more than one participant included students requesting an alternative assignment (18 percent), requesting extra time to do an assignment (4 percent), and requesting to be totally excused from doing an assignment (4 percent).

Table 3 Topics of Teacher-observed Student Disturbance and Teacher-reported Warning Requests

Topic	Disturbance observed (%)	Warnings Requested (%)
Sexual assault	42	54
Racial issues	33	11
Child abuse	31	27
Violent/catastrophic trauma	26	16
Sexual orientation/ gender identity	21	25
Suicide	18	18
Sexism	18	9
Psychiatric symptoms	17	18
Religious issues	17	9
Human sexuality	15	
Self-harm	12	
Eating disorders	10	
Mental illness stigma	9	
Social class/SES	8	
Substance abuse	8	14
Physical disability	2	11

Note: Participants could select more than one topic. SES = socioeconomic status.

Student Distress and Requests for Trigger Warnings by Topic

The diagnosis of PTSD requires that a person has experienced an "exposure to actual or threatened death, serious injury, or sexual violence," or learning of such trauma unexpectedly befalling a close friend or family member (APA, 2013, p. 271). Only 4 of the 16 topics presented on our survey can be directly associated with the traumatic experiences required for the diagnosis of PTSD: childhood abuse, sexual assault, suicide, and violent/catastrophic trauma. The other 12 topics are potentially sensitive and could theoretically serve as personal reminders of traumatic experiences, but they are not traumas in and of themselves according to the diagnostic criteria for PTSD. Therefore, the next analyses compared participants' responses related to the four PTSD-related trauma topics and the remaining 12 topics not related to PTSD traumas.

Regarding attitudes about issuing trigger warnings, a paired-samples t test indicated that teachers rated the necessity of warnings for PTSD-related trauma topics (M = 2.62, SD = 1.24) significantly higher than the necessity of warnings for non-PTSD topics (M = 1.96, SD = 1.03), $t(227) = 12.97$, $p < .001$, $d = 0.56$. With respect to the frequency of issued trigger warnings, participants indicated that they warned about PTSD-related trauma topics (M = 2.42, SD = 1.11) significantly more frequently than non-PTSD topics (M = 1.87, SD = 0.93), $t(141) = 9.82$, $p < .001$, $d = 0.53$.

The next analysis examined the frequency of observed student disturbance related to PTSD-related trauma topics versus non-PTSD topics, and the frequency of requested accommodations related to these topics. The analyses only included participants who indicated that they had observed student disturbance ($n = 44$) or who had received a request for a warning ($n = 44$). χ^2 analyses examined the proportion of participants indicating that they had (or had not) observed student disturbance when covering PTSD-related trauma topics versus non-PTSD topics. There was a significant difference in the frequency of observed disturbances between the topics, $\chi^2(1) = 89.22$, $p < .001$, $d = 0.38$. The proportion of student disturbances observed for PTSD-related trauma topics (31 percent) was higher than expected by chance, and the proportion of disturbances observed for non-PTSD topics (14 percent) was lower than expected by chance. Next, χ^2 analyses examined the proportion of participants indicating that a student had (or had not) requested a warning for PTSD-related trauma topics versus non-PTSD topics. This test was also significant, $\chi^2(1) = 9.68$, $p < .002$, $d = 0.25$, with the proportion of student requests for warnings concerning PTSD-related trauma topics (25 percent) being higher than expected by chance, and the proportion warning requests for non-PTSD topics (14 percent) being lower than expected by chance.

Discussion

The purpose of the current research was to examine the use of trigger warnings among a broad base of psychology teachers. Four research questions guided the study. Research Question 1 asked, What are psychology teachers' attitudes about trigger warnings? The majority of teachers were split between favorable and unfavorable attitudes, with the average reflecting no strong trend in either direction, and on the whole, teachers viewed trigger warnings as only slightly necessary for almost all sensitive topics. Research Question 2 asked, what are psychology teachers' typical trigger warning practices? Many teachers in our sample indicated that they had issued trigger warnings to their students at some point, yet for most topics, they did so only rarely. Research Question 3 asked, do psychology teachers observe students as being distressed by potentially sensitive topics? A large majority of teachers noticed students showing visible signs of distress in reaction to course topics; nonetheless, comparatively few teachers reported receiving student requests for trigger warnings. Research Question 4 asked if there were differences between topics related to PTSD-based trauma and topics not associated with PTSD traumas. Teachers viewed warnings for PTSD-related topics as more necessary and offered them more frequently.

Several comparisons are possible between the results of the current study and earlier research on abnormal psychology instructors (Boysen et al., 2016). A slightly larger percentage of teachers from the current sample offered trigger warnings than in the previous study (39 percent vs. 31 percent). Finding a higher percentage among teachers of psychology courses in general is unexpected when considering the content of abnormal psychology, which often requires teachers to cover multiple potentially sensitive topics, including topics meeting the criteria for PTSD-related traumas. This finding could indicate that abnormal psychology teachers and students are aware that highly sensitive, and even disturbing, topics will be covered, making specific warnings less necessary. In both studies, trends emerged suggesting a difference in warning frequency between PTSD-related and non-PTSD-related topics; this suggests that teachers are most likely to accept the necessity of warnings for topics associated with PTSD.

In comparison to abnormal psychology instructors (Boysen et al., 2016), a larger percentage of teachers in the current sample viewed trigger warnings favorably (43 percent vs. 25 percent) and believed that they are helpful to students' mental health (48 percent vs. 34 percent). Several factors may explain these differences. The routine immersion of instructors of abnormal psychology in trauma-related content may lead them to be more accustomed to, and less concerned by, the impact of that content on students. The essential nature of trauma-related topics to the abnormal psychology course may also lead teachers to view the topics as something students must confront and accept if they are enrolled in the course. It is also possible that abnormal psychology instructors' more negative view of trigger warnings' impact on health represents their expert knowledge that the avoidance behavior encouraged by trigger warnings maintains and exacerbates symptoms of disorders such as PTSD (Ehring, Ehlers, & Glucksman, 2008; Polusny et al., 2011).

A chief finding of the current study was that psychology teachers do not, on average, offer trigger warnings to students when covering most potentially sensitive topics. Across 14 of the 16 topics that participants considered, the majority of teachers indicated that they rarely or never provide warnings. These results strongly suggest that trigger warnings are not a typical practice for sensitive topics in psychology. Two potential exceptions are the topics of sexual assault and child abuse. They were the only topics for which the majority of teachers reported that they offer warnings at least occasionally. The frequency of warnings about sexual assault converges with teachers' reports that this topic was the most frequent cause of visible student disturbance and prompted the highest number of student requests for trigger warnings.

Teachers believed that warnings for PTSD-trauma-related topics (sexual assault, child abuse, self-harm, suicide, and catastrophe/violence) are more necessary than warnings for other potentially sensitive topics, and they also reported a higher frequency of offering warnings for these topics. The effect sizes were mostly medium to large for the differences in teachers' perceptions of topics related to experiences that meet criteria for PTSD in the *DSM-5* (APA, 2013) versus those that could not meet the PTSD trauma criteria. This may suggest a practically meaningful difference in perceptions of how the topics should be treated in the classroom. For topics directly associated with traumatic experiences that meet criteria for PTSD, true trigger warnings about automatically activated distress may be necessary. That is, teachers may choose to explicitly state that particular topics could trigger reexperiencing symptoms among students with PTSD-related traumatic experiences. Teachers may also encourage self-advocacy by informing students at the start of courses to contact the campus office of disability resources or student affairs if they require topic-based accommodations such as trigger warnings. In contrast, "topic warnings" about sensitive issues need not be framed in relation to the concepts of disability, disorder, or accommodation; rather, teachers may simply choose to warn students that a topic can be difficult or uncomfortable for some students. Although both types of warnings are consistent with the standard pedagogical practice of preparing students to learn, they are not equivalent in their message, nor in their relation to disabilities that must be accommodated.

Although the current results are relevant to establishing typical classroom practices and instructor attitudes about trigger warnings, they do not speak to the effectiveness of issuing warnings to students. No direct evidence concerning the effect of trigger warnings on students' ability to learn or deal with personally distressing topics is available. In order to determine the utility of trigger warnings in the psychology classroom, future researchers must examine the effect of randomly assigning students to receive or not receive trigger warnings on emotions, learning, and other classroom behaviors. In addition, the effectiveness of trigger warnings should be examined separately for students with and without relevant mental health and trauma histories. As is often the case in education, perceptions of what works in the classroom may not match up with reality, and what benefits one student may be irrelevant or even detrimental to other students.

Additional research is also needed to confirm and extend the results of the current study. Specifically, our sample only included faculty at four-year institutions; therefore, further research is needed on trigger warnings as they relate to secondary schools, community colleges, graduate education, and online instruction. Research on the influence of classroom variables on the use and effect of trigger warnings is also needed. For example, trigger warnings may have different utilities in smaller, discussion-based classes where there is ample opportunity for ongoing student–teacher communication about distress. In contrast, online courses, especially those with larger enrollments, may necessitate more explicit warnings due to the primary use of electronic communication and reduced oversight of students. Another factor to explore is the role of academic major. Psychology majors, relative to nonmajors, may have less need for warnings due to their increased familiarity with the typical topics covered in psychology courses. Conversely, students who pursue psychology as field of study in order to better understand personal mental health problems may have an increased need for warnings related to those mental health problems.

Several limitations of the current study should be noted. A major limitation was the use of a self-selected sample. Psychology teachers who were willing to complete the survey may not be representative of the population and may have held a greater interest in, or stronger opinions about, the use of trigger warnings. Another limitation relates to teachers' ability to accurately assess and describe student behaviors. Even if teachers can accurately notice visible distress in their students, they may be unable to truly gauge the full amount of student discomfort caused by a classroom topic. Some students may preemptively remove themselves from the classroom due to an expectation of becoming distressed, some students may mask their immediate distress, and some students may have distress that emerges outside of class. Therefore, observations by teachers are likely to be an underestimate of student distress. In addition, we did not assess whether teachers offered trigger warnings as a result of documented student disabilities, informal student requests, or personal judgments of necessity. Therefore, it is not clear if teachers issued warnings as a formal mechanism to accommodate specific students' disabilities or as an informal method intended to generally reduce students' discomfort.

In summary, the heated debate surrounding trigger warnings will not be fruitful in the absence of scientific data. An opportunity exists for the field of psychology to provide information about the typical attitudes, classroom practices, and educational outcomes associated with trigger warnings. The current research takes one step toward providing this information by demonstrating that teachers of psychology do not issue trigger warnings as standard practice. In addition, although they are open to providing trigger warnings in some instances, teachers also believe that students' sensitivity to topics should not compromise the goals of psychology education.

References

American Association of University Professors. (2014). *On trigger warnings*. Retrieved from www.aaup.org/report/trigger-warnings

American Psychiatric Association. (2013). *Diagnostic and statistical manual of mental disorders* (5th ed.). Washington, DC: Author.

Americans with Disabilities Act of 1990, Pub. L. No. 101–336, 104 Stat. 328 (1990).

Boysen, G. (2017). Evidence-based answers to questions about trigger warnings for clinically-based distress: A review for teachers. *Scholarship of Teaching and Learning in Psychology, 3*, 163–177. Retrieved from http://dx.doi.org/10.1037/stl0000084

Boysen, G. A., Wells, A. M., & Dawson, K. J. (2016). Instructors' use of trigger warnings and behavior warnings in abnormal psychology. *Teaching of Psychology, 43*, 334 –339. Retrieved from http://dx.doi.org/10.1177/0098628316662766

Carter, A. M. (2015). Teaching with trauma: Disability pedagogy, feminism, and the trigger warnings debate. *Disability Studies Quarterly, 35*, 1–9. Retrieved from http://dx.doi.org/10.18061/dsq.v35i2.4652

Ehlers, A., Hackmann, A., & Michael, T. (2004). Intrusive re-experiencing in post-traumatic stress disorder: Phenomenology, theory, and therapy. *Memory, 12*, 403– 415. Retrieved from http://dx.doi.org/10.1080/09658210444000025

Ehring, T., Ehlers, A., & Glucksman, E. (2008). Do cognitive models help in predicting the severity of posttraumatic stress disorder, phobia, and depression after motor vehicle accidents? A prospective longitudinal study. *Journal of Consulting and Clinical Psychology, 76*, 219 –230. Retrieved from .org/10.1037/0022-006X.76.2.219

Essig, L. (2014, March 10). Trigger warnings trigger me. *The Chronicle of Higher Education*. Retrieved from www.chronicle.com/blogs/conversation/2014/03/10/trigger-warnings-trigger-me/

Godderis, R., & Root, J. L. (2016). Trigger warnings: Compassion is not censorship. *Radical Pedagogy, 13*, 130 –138.

Grillon, C., Pine, D. S., Lissek, S., Rabin, S., Bonne, O., & Vythilingam, M. (2009). Increased anxiety during anticipation of unpredictable aversive stimuli in posttraumatic stress disorder but not in generalized anxiety disorder. *Biological Psychiatry, 66*, 47–53. Retrieved from http://dx.doi.org/10.1016/j.biopsych.2008.12.028

Kleim, B., Graham, B., Bryant, R. A., & Ehlers, A. (2013). Capturing intrusive re-experiencing in trauma survivors' daily lives using ecological momentary assessment. *Journal of Abnormal Psychology, 122*, 998–1009. Retrieved from http://dx.doi.org/10.1037/a0034957

Leyser, Y., Greenberger, L., Sharoni, L., & Vogel, G. (2011). Students with disability in teacher education: Changes in faculty attitudes toward accommodations over ten years. *International Journal of Sexual Education, 26*, 161–174.

Lukianoff, G., & Haidt, J. (2015, September). The coddling of the American mind. *The Atlantic*. Retrieved from www.theatlantic.com/magazine/archive/2015/09/the-coddling-of-the-american-mind/399356/?utm_source=hpfb

Manne, K. (2015, September 9). Why I use trigger warnings. *The New York Times*. Retrieved from https://www.nytimes.com/2015/09/20/opinion/sunday/why-i-use-trigger-warnings.html

Medina, J. (2014, May 17). Warning: The literary cannon makes students squirm. *The New York Times*. Retrieved from www.nytimes.com/2014/05/18/us/warning-the-literary-canon-could-make-students-squirm.html

Polusny, M. A., Ries, B. J., Meis, L. A., DeGarmo, D., McCormick-Deaton, C. M., Thuras, P., & Erbes, C. R. (2011). Effects of parents' experiential avoidance and PTSD on adolescent disaster-related posttraumatic stress symptomatology. *Journal of Family Psychology, 25*, 220–229. Retrieved from http://dx.doi.org/10.1037/a0022945

Shaw-Thornburg, A. (2014, June 16). This is a trigger warning. *The Chronicle of Higher Education*. Retrieved from www.chronicle.com/article/This-Is-a-Trigger-Warning/147031

Simmons, A. N., Flagan, T. M., Wittmann, M., Strigo, I. A., Matthews, S. C., Donovan, H., . . . Paulus, M. P. (2013). The effects of temporal unpredictability in anticipation of negative events in combat veterans with PTSD. *Journal of Affective Disorders, 146*, 426–432. Retrieved from http://dx.doi.org/10.1016/j.jad.2012.08.006

Sniatecki, J. L., Perry, H. B., & Snell, L. H. (2015). Faculty attitudes and knowledge regarding college students with disabilities. *Journal of Postsecondary Education and Disability, 28*, 259–275.

Stokes, M. (2014, May 29). In defense of trigger warnings. *The Chronicle of Higher Education*. Retrieved from www.chronicle.com/blogs/conversation/2014/05/29/in-defense-of-trigger-warnings/

Veraldi, L., & Veraldi, D. M. (2015). Stressors, triggers, and trauma: Considering the *DSM-5* in the debate over campus trigger warnings. *American Journal of Forensic Psychology, 33*, 5–17.

Vingiano, A. (2014, May 5). How the "trigger warning" took over the Internet. *BuzzFeedNews*. Retrieved from www.buzzfeed.com/alisonvingiano/how-the-trigger-warning-took-over-the-internet?utm_term=.dyOQKXp34#.xv9arPm2Z

Wilson, R. (2015, September 14). Students' requests for trigger warnings grow more varied. *The Chronicle of Higher Education*. Retrieved from http://chronicle.com/article/Students-Requests-for/233043

Wyatt, W. (2016). The ethics of trigger warnings. *Teaching Ethics, 16*, 17–35. Retrieved from http://dx.doi.org/10.5840/tej201632427

Critical Thinking

1. Think about your own college experiences to date. Previous instructors may not have called it specifically a "trigger warning," but can you think of any instances where you were given a "heads up" that the topics discussed in a particular class could be upsetting? Did the instructor give you some options on what to do if this were to happen during class?
2. Do you think the topics that might trigger intense feelings for you in the college classroom are the same for everyone else? Explore this a bit with some self-reflection. Why or why not?
3. Are there some topics that are just so sensitive or so off-limits that they should not ever be discussed in a college classroom? If so, why do you think that is?

Internet References

Harvard Study: Trigger Warnings Might Coddle the Mind

https://www.psychologytoday.com/us/blog/happiness-and-the-pursuit-leadership/201808/harvard-study-trigger-warnings-might-coddle-the

It's Official—Trigger Warnings Might Actually Be Harmful

https://medium.com/@CraigHarper19/its-official-trigger-warnings-might-actually-be-harmful-3e8acaae098b

The Trapdoor of Trigger Words

http://www.slate.com/articles/double_x/cover_story/2016/09/what_science_can_tell_us_about_trigger_warnings.html

Why I Use Trigger Warnings

https://www.nytimes.com/2015/09/20/opinion/sunday/why-i-use-trigger-warnings.html

Article

Prepared by: R. Eric Landrum, *Boise State University*

A Manifesto for Reproducible Science

Marcus R. Munafò, et al.

Learning Outcomes

After reading this article, you will be able to:

- Understand how reproducibility is a concern in science.
- Articulate what it means in research to utilize a registered report.
- Explain why data sharing is important.

What proportion of published research is likely to be false? Low sample size, small effect sizes, data dredging (also known as *P*-hacking), conflicts of interest, large numbers of scientists working competitively in silos without combining their efforts, and so on may conspire to dramatically increase the probability that a published finding is incorrect.[1] The field of metascience—the scientific study of science itself—is flourishing and has generated substantial empirical evidence for the existence and prevalence of threats to efficiency in knowledge accumulation (Refs. 2–7; Figure 1).

Data from many fields suggest reproducibility is lower than is desirable;[8–14] one analysis estimates that 85 percent of biomedical research efforts are wasted,[14] while 90 percent of respondents to a recent survey in *Nature* agreed that there is a "reproducibility crisis".[15] Whether "crisis" is the appropriate term to describe the current state or trajectory of science is debatable, but accumulated evidence indicates that there is substantial room for improvement with regard to research practices to maximize the efficiency of the research community's use of the public's financial investment in research.

Here, we propose a series of measures that we believe will improve research efficiency and robustness of scientific findings by directly targeting specific threats to reproducible science. We argue for the adoption, evaluation, and ongoing improvement of these measures to optimize the pace and efficiency of knowledge accumulation. The measures are organized into the following categories:[16] methods, reporting and dissemination, reproducibility, evaluation, and incentives. They are not intended to be exhaustive, but provide a broad, practical, and evidence-based set of actions that can be implemented by researchers, institutions, journals, and funders. The measures and their current implementation are summarized in Table 1.

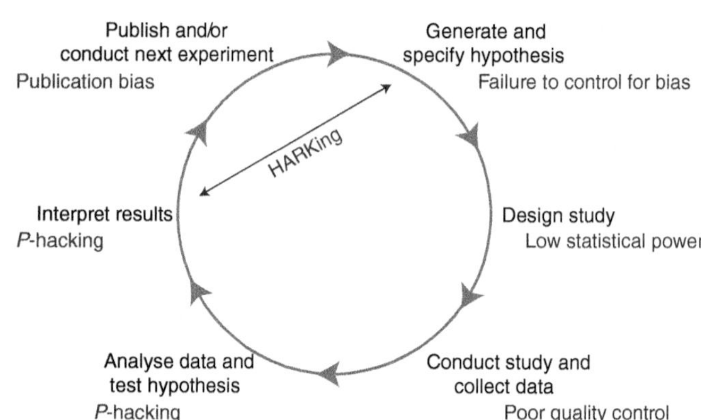

Figure 1 Threats to reproducible science. An idealized version of the hypothetico-deductive model of the scientific method is shown. Various potential threats to this model exist, including lack of replication,5 hypothesizing after the results are known (HARKing),7 poor study design, low statistical power,2 analytical flexibility,51 P-hacking,4 publication bias,3 and lack of data sharing.6 Together these will serve to undermine the robustness of published research and may also impact on the ability of science to self-correct.

The Problem

A hallmark of scientific creativity is the ability to see novel and unexpected patterns in data. John Snow's identification of links between cholera and water supply,[17] Paul Broca's work on language lateralization,[18] and Jocelyn Bell Burnell's discovery of pulsars[19] are examples of breakthroughs achieved by

Table 1 A Manifesto for Reproducible Science

Theme	Proposal	Examples of Initiatives/Potential Solutions (Extent of Current Adoption)	Stakeholder(s)
Methods	Protecting against cognitive biases	All of the initiatives listed below (* to ****) Blinding (**)	J, F
	Improving methodological training	Rigorous training in statistics and research methods for future researchers (*) Rigorous continuing education in statistics and methods for researchers (*)	I, F
	Independent methodological support	Involvement of methodologists in research (**) Independent oversight (*)	F
	Collaboration and team science	Multisite studies/distributed data collection (*) Team-science consortia (*)	I, F
Reporting and dissemination	Promoting study preregistration	Registered reports (*) Open Science Framework (*)	J, F
	Improving the quality of reporting	Use of reporting checklists (**) Protocol checklists (*)	J
	Protecting against conflicts of interest	Disclosure of conflicts of interest (***) Exclusion/containment of financial and nonfinancial conflicts of interest (*)	J
Reproducibility	Encouraging transparency and open science	Open data, materials, software, and so on (* to **) Preregistration (**** for clinical trials, * for other studies)	J, F, R
Evaluation	Diversifying peer review	Preprints (* in biomedical/behavioral sciences, **** in physical sciences) Pre- and post-publication peer review, for example, Publons, PubMed Commons (*)	J
Incentives	Rewarding open and reproducible practices	Badges (*) Registered reports (*) Transparency and Openness Promotion guidelines (*) Funding replication studies (*) Open-science practices in hiring and promotion (*)	J, I, F

Estimated extent of current adoption: *, <5 percent; **, 5 percent to 30 percent; ***, 30 percent to 60 percent; ****, >60 percent. Abbreviations for key stakeholders: J, journals/publishers; F, funders; I, institutions; R, regulators.

interpreting observations in a new way. However, a major challenge for scientists is to be open to new and important insights while simultaneously avoiding being misled by our tendency to see structure in randomness. The combination of apophenia (the tendency to see patterns in random data), confirmation bias (the tendency to focus on evidence that is in line with our expectations or favored explanation), and hindsight bias (the tendency to see an event as having been predictable only after it has occurred) can easily lead us to false conclusions.[20] Thomas Levenson documents the example of astronomers who became convinced they had seen the fictitious planet Vulcan because their contemporary theories predicted its existence.[21] Experimenter effects are an example of this kind of bias.[22]

Overinterpretation of noise is facilitated by the extent to which data analysis is rapid, flexible, and automated.[23] In a high-dimensional data set, there may be hundreds or thousands of reasonable alternative approaches to analyzing the same data.[24,25] For example, in a systematic review of functional magnetic resonance imaging (fMRI) studies, Carp showed that there were almost as many unique analytical pipelines as there were studies.[26] If several thousand potential analytical pipelines can be applied to high-dimensional data, the generation of false-positive findings is highly likely. For example, applying almost 7,000 analytical pipelines to a single fMRI data set resulted in over 90 percent of brain voxels showing significant activation in at least one analysis.[27]

During data analysis, it can be difficult for researchers to recognize *P*-hacking[28] or data dredging because confirmation and hindsight biases can encourage the acceptance of outcomes that fit expectations or desires as appropriate, and the rejection of outcomes that do not as the result of suboptimal designs or analyses. Hypotheses may emerge that fit the data and are then reported without indication or recognition of their *post hoc* origin.[7] This, unfortunately, is not scientific discovery, but self-deception.[29] Uncontrolled, it can dramatically increase the false discovery rate. We need measures to counter the natural tendency of enthusiastic scientists who are motivated by discovery to see patterns in noise.

Methods

In this section, we describe measures that can be implemented when performing research (including, e.g., study design, methods, statistics, and collaboration).

Protecting against Cognitive Biases

There is a substantial literature on the difficulty of avoiding cognitive biases. An effective solution to mitigate self-deception and unwanted biases is blinding. In some research contexts, participants and data collectors can be blinded to the experimental condition that participants are assigned to, and to the research hypotheses, while the data analyst can be blinded to key parts of the data. For example, during data preparation and cleaning, the identity of experimental conditions or the variable labels can be masked so that the output is not interpretable in terms of the research hypothesis. In some physical sciences, this approach has been extended to include deliberate perturbations in or masking of data to allow data preparation (e.g., identification of outliers) to proceed without the analyst being able to see the corresponding results.[30] Preregistration of the study design, primary outcome(s), and analysis plan (see "Promoting Study Preregistration" section below) is a highly effective form of blinding because the data do not exist and the outcomes are not yet known.

Improving Methodological Training

Research design and statistical analysis are mutually dependent. Common misperceptions, such as the interpretation of *P* values,[31] limitations of null-hypothesis significance testing,[32] the meaning and importance of statistical power,[2] the accuracy of reported effect sizes,[33] and the likelihood that a sample size that generated a statistically significant finding will also be adequate to replicate a true finding,[34] could all be addressed through improved statistical training. Similarly, basic design principles are important, such as blinding to reduce experimenter bias, randomization or counterbalancing to control for confounding, and the use of within-subjects designs, where possible, to maximize power. However, integrative training in research practices that can protect oneself against cognitive biases and the effects of distorted incentives is arguably more important. Moreover, statistical and methodological best practices are under constant revision and improvement, so that senior as well as junior researchers need continuing methodological education, not least because much training of early-career researchers is informal and flows from their supervisor or mentor. A failure to adopt advances in methodology—such as the very slow progress in increasing statistical power[35,36]—may be partly a function of failing to inculcate a continuing professional education and development ethic.

Without formal requirements for continuing education, the most effective solutions may be to develop educational resources that are accessible, easy to digest, and immediately and effectively applicable to research (i.e., brief, web-based modules for specific topics, and combinations of modules that are customized for particular research applications). A modular approach simplifies the process of iterative updating of those materials. Demonstration software and hands-on examples may also make the lessons and implications particularly tangible to researchers at any career stage: the Experimental Design Assistant (https://edas.nc3rs.org.uk) supports research design for whole animal experiments, while *P*-hacker (http://shinyapps.org/apps/p-hacker/) shows just how easy it is to generate apparently statistically significant findings by exploiting analytic flexibility.

Implementing Independent Methodological Support

The need for independent methodological support is well-established in some areas—many clinical trials, for example, have multidisciplinary trial steering committees to provide advice and oversee the design and conduct of the trial. The need for these committees grew out of the well-understood financial conflicts of interest that exist in many clinical trials. The sponsor of a trial may be the company manufacturing the product, and any intentional or unintentional influence can distort the study design, analysis, and interpretation of results for the ultimate financial benefit of the manufacturer at the cost of the accuracy of the science and the health benefit to the consumers.[37,38] Nonfinancial conflicts of interest also exist, such as the beliefs and preconceptions of individual scientists and the stakes that researchers have in obtaining publishable results in order to progress their career.[39,40] Including independent researchers (particularly, methodologists with no personal investment in a research topic) in the design, monitoring, analysis, or interpretation of research outcomes may mitigate some of those influences, and can be done either at the level of the individual research project or through a process facilitated by a funding agency (see Box 1).

Box 1 Independent Oversight: The Case of CHDI Foundation

CHDI Foundation—a privately funded nonprofit drug development organization targeting Huntington's disease—convened a working group in 2013 to identify practical and viable steps that could be taken to help ensure the rigor of their research.[76] One concrete product of this meeting was the establishment of the Independent Statistical Standing Committee (ISSC; http://chdi-foundation.org/independent-statistical-standing-committee/) designed to provide independent, unbiased, and objective evaluation and expert advice regarding all aspects of experimental design and statistics. CHDI has made this resource available to the wider Huntington's disease research community on a priority basis. The ISSC is comprised of individuals with specific expertise in research design and statistics. Critically, committee members are not themselves engaged in Huntington's disease research, and have no investment in study results, or other conflicts of interest. The committee provides a number of services, including (but not limited to) provision of expert assistance in developing protocols and statistical analysis plans, and evaluation of prepared study protocols. Their oversight and input, particularly at the study design stage, may mitigate low statistical power, inadequate study design, and flexibility in data analysis and reporting.[6,71] As recently highlighted, "asking questions at the design stage can save headaches at the analysis stage: careful data collection can greatly simplify analysis and make it more rigorous."[77]

Encouraging Collaboration and Team Science

Studies of statistical power persistently find it to be below (sometimes well below) 50 percent, across both time and the different disciplines studied.[2,35,36] Low statistical power increases the likelihood of obtaining both false-positive and false-negative results,[2] meaning that it offers no advantage if the purpose is to accumulate knowledge. Despite this, low-powered research persists because of dysfunctional incentives, poor understanding of the consequences of low power, and lack of resources to improve power. Team science is a solution to the latter problem—instead of relying on the limited resources of single investigators, distributed collaboration across many study sites facilitates high-powered designs and greater potential for testing generalizability across the settings and populations sampled. This also brings greater scope for multiple theoretical and disciplinary perspectives, and a diverse range of research cultures and experiences, to be incorporated into a research project.

Multicenter and collaborative efforts have a long and successful tradition in fields, such as randomized controlled trials, in some areas of clinical medicine, and in genetic association analyses, and have improved the robustness of the resulting research literatures. Multisite collaborative projects have also been advocated for other types of research, such as animal studies,[41–43] in an effort to maximize their power, enhance standardization, and optimize transparency and protection from biases. The Many Labs projects illustrate this potential in the social and behavioral sciences, with dozens of laboratories implementing the same research protocol to obtain highly precise estimates of effect sizes, and evaluate variability across samples and settings.[44,45] It is also possible, and desirable, to incorporate a team science ethos into student training (see Box 2).

Box 2 Distributed Student Projects

Student assessment requirements, and limited access to populations of interest, may hinder extensive collaboration within a single institution, but it could be achieved across multiple institutions in the form of a distributed student project. Under this model, academics and students from several institutions would form a consortium, collaboratively develop a research question, protocol, and analysis plan, and publicly preregister it prior to data collection. The protocol would be implemented by each student at each participating center, and the resulting data pooled for analysis. Consortium meetings before and after data collection could be used to integrate training in research design, while offering opportunities for creative input from the students. Conclusions based on results would be mutually agreed in preparation for wider dissemination, using inclusive authorship conventions such as those adopted by genetic consortia. Students would learn rigorous research methods through active participation in research that is sufficiently well designed and conducted to be genuinely meaningful. Critically, collaborative team science would be instilled at an early stage of training.

The Collaborative Replications and Education Project (https://osf.io/wfc6u/) is an example of this concept in psychology, albeit in a more centralized form. A coordinating team identifies recently published research that could be replicated in the context of a semester-long undergraduate course on research methods. A Central Commons provides the materials and guidance to incorporate the replications into projects or classes, and the data collected across sites are aggregated into manuscripts for publication. The Pipeline[78] and Many Labs[44,45] projects also offer opportunities to contribute to large-scale replication efforts with coordinated data collection across many locations simultaneously.

Reporting and Dissemination

In this section, we describe measures that can be implemented when communicating research (including, i.e., reporting standards, study preregistration, and disclosing conflicts of interest).

Promoting Study Preregistration

Preregistration of study protocols for randomized controlled trials in clinical medicine has become standard practice.[46] In its simplest form, it may simply comprise the registration of the basic study design, but it can also include a detailed prespecification of the study procedures, outcomes, and statistical analysis plan. It was introduced to address two problems: publication bias and analytical flexibility (in particular, outcome switching in the case of clinical medicine). Publication bias,[47] also known as the file drawer problem,[48] refers to the fact that many more studies are conducted than published. Studies that obtain positive and novel results are more likely to be published than studies that obtain negative results or report replications of prior results.[47,49,50] The consequence is that the published literature indicates stronger evidence for findings than exists in reality. Outcome switching refers to the possibility of changing the outcomes of interest in the study depending on the observed results. A researcher may include 10 variables that could be considered outcomes of the research, and—once the results are known—intentionally or unintentionally select the subset of outcomes that show statistically significant results as the outcomes of interest. The consequence is an increase in the likelihood that reported results are spurious by leveraging chance, while negative evidence gets ignored. This is one of several related research practices that can inflate spurious findings when analysis decisions are made with knowledge of the observed data, such as selection of models, exclusion rules, and covariates. Such data-contingent analysis decisions constitute what has become known as *P*-hacking,[51] and preregistration can protect against all of these.

The strongest form of preregistration involves both registering the study (with a commitment to make the results public) and closely prespecifying the study design, primary outcome, and analysis plan in advance of conducting the study or knowing the outcomes of the research. In principle, this addresses publication bias by making all research discoverable, whether or not it is ultimately published, allowing all of the evidence about a finding to be obtained and evaluated. It also addresses outcome switching, and *P*-hacking more generally, by requiring the researcher to articulate analytical decisions prior to observing the data, so that these decisions remain data-independent. Critically, it also makes clear the distinction between data-independent confirmatory research that is important for testing hypotheses, and data-contingent exploratory research that is important for generating hypotheses.

While preregistration is now common in some areas of clinical medicine (due to requirements by journals and regulatory bodies, such as the Food and Drug Administration in the United States and the European Medicines Agency in the European Union), it is rare in the social and behavioral sciences. However, support for study preregistration is increasing; websites such as the Open Science Framework (http://osf.io/) and AsPredicted (http://AsPredicted.org/) offer services to preregister studies, the Preregistration Challenge offers education and incentives to conduct preregistered research (http://cos.io/prereg), and journals are adopting the Registered Reports (RR) publishing format[52,53] to encourage preregistration and add results-blind peer review (see Box 3).

Box 3 Registered Reports

The RR initiative seeks to eliminate various forms of bias in hypothesis-driven research,[52,53] and in particular, the evaluation of a study based on the results. Unlike conventional journal articles, RRs split the peer review process into two stages, before and after results are known. At the first stage, reviewers and editors assess a detailed protocol that includes the study rationale, procedure, and a detailed analysis plan. Following favorable reviews (and probably revision to meet strict methodological standards), the journal offers in-principle acceptance: publication of study outcomes is guaranteed provided the authors adhere to the approved protocol, the study meets prespecified quality checks, and conclusions are appropriately evidence-bound. Once the study is completed, the authors resubmit a complete manuscript that includes the results and discussion. The article is published at the end of this two-stage process. By accepting articles before results are known, RRs prevent publication bias. By reviewing the hypotheses and analysis plans in advance, RRs should also help neutralize *P*-hacking and HARKing by authors and critiquing after the results are known by reviewers with their own investments in the research outcomes, although empirical evidence will be required to confirm that this is the case.

Perhaps the most commonly voiced objection to RRs is that the format somehow limits exploration or creativity by requiring authors to adhere to a prespecified methodology. However, RRs place no restrictions on creative analysis practices or serendipity. Authors are free to report the outcomes of any unregistered exploratory analyses, provided such tests are clearly labeled as *post hoc*. Thus, the sole requirement is that exploratory outcomes are identified transparently as exploratory (for a list of frequently asked questions, see https://cos.io/rr/#faq). Of course, RRs are not intended for research that is solely exploratory.

As of November 2016, RRs have been adopted by over 40 journals, including *Nature Human Behaviour*, covering a wide range of life, social, and physical sciences (for a curated list, see https://cos.io/rr/#journals). The concept also opens the door to alternative forms of research funding that place a premium on transparency and reproducibility. For example, authors could submit a detailed proposal before they have funding for their research. Following simultaneous review by both the funder and the journal, the strongest proposals would be offered financial support by the funder and in-principle acceptance for publication by the journal (https://cos.io/rr/#funders).

Improving the Quality of Reporting

Preregistration will improve discoverability of research, but discoverability does not guarantee usability. Poor usability reflects difficulty in evaluating what was done, in reusing the methodology to assess reproducibility, and in incorporating the evidence into systematic reviews and meta-analyses. Improving the quality and transparency in the reporting of research is necessary to address this. The Transparency and Openness Promotion (TOP) guidelines offer standards as a basis for journals and funders to incentivize or require greater transparency in planning and reporting of research.[54] TOP provides principles for how transparency and usability can be increased, while other guidelines provide concrete steps for how to maximize the quality of reporting in particular areas. For example, the Consolidated Standards of Reporting Trials (CONSORT) statement provides guidance for clear, complete, and accurate reporting of randomized controlled trials.[55–57] Over 300 reporting guidelines now exist for observational studies, prognostic studies, predictive models, diagnostic tests, systematic reviews and meta-analyses in humans, a large variety of studies using different laboratory methods, and animal studies. The Equator Network (http://www.equator-network.org/) aggregates these guidelines to improve discoverability.[58] There are also guidelines for improving the reporting of research planning, for example, the Preferred Reporting Items for Systematic Reviews and Meta-analyses (PRISMA) statement for reporting of systematic reviews and meta-analyses,[59] and PRISMA-P for protocols of systematic reviews.[60] The Preregistration Challenge workflow and the preregistration recipe for social-behavioral research[61] also illustrate guidelines for reporting research plans.

The success of reporting guidelines depends on their adoption and effective use. The social and behavioral sciences are behind the biomedical sciences in their adoption of reporting guidelines for research, although with rapid adoption of the TOP guidelines and related developments by journals and funders that gap may be closing. However, improved reporting may be insufficient on its own to maximize research quality. Reporting guidelines are easily perceived by researchers as bureaucratic exercises rather than means of improving research and reporting. Even with preregistration of clinical trials, one study observed that just 13 percent of trials published outcomes completely consistent with the preregistered commitments. Most publications of the trials did not report preregistered outcomes and added new outcomes that were not part of the registered design (see www.COMPare-trials.org). Franco and colleagues observed similar findings in psychology[62]; using protocol preregistrations and public data from the Time-sharing Experiments for the Social Sciences project (http://www.tessexperiments.org/), they found that 40 percent of published reports failed to mention one or more of the experimental conditions of the experiments, and approximately 70 percent of published reports failed to mention one or more of the outcome measures included in the study. Moreover, outcome measures that were not included were much more likely to be negative results and associated with smaller effect sizes than outcome measures that were included.

The positive outcome of reporting guidelines is that they make it possible to detect and study these behaviors and their impact. Otherwise, these behaviors are simply unknowable in any systematic way. The negative outcome is the empirical evidence that reporting guidelines may be necessary, but will not alone be sufficient, to address reporting biases. The impact of guidelines and how best to optimize their use and impact will be best assessed by randomized trials (see Box 4).

Box 4 Evidence for the Effectiveness of Reporting Guidelines

In medicine, there is strong evidence for the effectiveness of CONSORT guidelines—journals that do not endorse the CONSORT statement show poorer reporting quality compared with endorsing journals.[79] For the Animal Research: Reporting of *In Vivo* Experiments (ARRIVE) guidelines,[80] studies comparing the reporting of ARRIVE items in specific fields of research before and after the guidelines were published report mixed results.[81–83] A randomized controlled trial is in progress to assess the impact of mandating a completed ARRIVE checklist with manuscript submissions on the quality of reporting in published articles (https://ecrf1.clinicaltrials.ed.ac.uk/iicarus). The success of these efforts will require journals and funders to adopt guidelines and support the community's iterative evaluation and improvement cycle.

Reproducibility

In this section, we describe measures that can be implemented to support verification of research (including, i.e., sharing data and methods).

Promoting Transparency and Open Science

Science is a social enterprise: independent and collaborative groups work to accumulate knowledge as a public good. The credibility of scientific claims is rooted in the evidence supporting them, which includes the methodology applied, the data acquired, and the process of methodology implementation, data analysis, and outcome interpretation. Claims become credible by the community reviewing, critiquing, extending, and reproducing the supporting evidence. However, without transparency, claims only achieve credibility based on trust in the confidence or authority of the originator. Transparency is superior to trust.

Open science refers to the process of making the content and process of producing evidence and claims transparent and accessible to others. Transparency is a scientific ideal, and adding "open" should therefore be redundant. In reality, science often lacks openness: many published articles are not available to people without a personal or institutional subscription, and most data, materials, and code supporting research outcomes are not made accessible, for example, in a public repository (Refs. 63 and 64; Box 5).

Box 5 Data Sharing

Sharing data in public repositories offers field-wide advantages in terms of accountability, data longevity, efficiency, and quality (for example, reanalyses may detect crucial mistakes or even data fabrication).[84] Unfortunately, many scientific disciplines, including most of those devoted to the study of human behavior, do not have a culture that values open data.[6] In the past, data sharing has rarely been enforced or facilitated. Recent initiatives, however, aim to change the normative culture. Hopefully, these initiatives will change the culture on data sharing. Once accepted as the norm, we doubt that data sharing will ever go out of fashion.

Transparency and Openness Promotion (TOP)

In 2015, Nosek and colleagues[54] proposed author guidelines to help journals and funders adopt transparency and reproducibility policies. As of November 2016, there were 757 journal and 64 organization signatories to the TOP guidelines. For example, the journal *Science* decided to "publish papers only if the data used in the analysis are available to any researcher for purposes of reproducing or extending the analysis"[65] and the conglomerate of Springer Nature journals adopted similar data sharing policies.

Badges to Acknowledge Open-science Practices

The Center for Open Science has suggested that journals assign a badge to articles with open data (as well as to other open practices such as preregistration and open materials). The main purpose of the badges is to signal that the journal values these practices. The journal *Psychological Science* has adopted these badges, and there is evidence that the open data badge has had a positive effect, increasing data sharing by more than tenfold (Figure 2).

The Peer Reviewers' Openness Initiative

Researchers who sign this initiative (https://opennessinitiative.org) pledge that as reviewers they will not offer comprehensive review for any manuscript that does not make data publicly available without a clear reason.[85]

Requirements from Funding Agencies

In recent years, prominent funding agencies, such as Research Councils UK in the United Kingdom and the National Institutes of Health (NIH) and National Science Foundation (NSF) in the United States, have increased pressure on researchers to share data. For instance, the 2015 NIH Public Access Plan (https://grants.nih.gov/grants/NIH-Public-Access-Plan.pdf) states: "NIH intends to make public access to digital scientific data the standard for all NIH-funded research." Since 2010, NSF requires submission of a data-management plan that stipulates how data will be stored and shared.

Very little of the research process (i.e., study protocols, analysis workflows, and peer review) is accessible because, historically, there have been few opportunities to make it accessible even if one wanted to do so. This has motivated calls for open access, open data, and open workflows (including analysis pipelines), but there are substantial barriers to meeting these ideals, including vested financial interests (particularly in scholarly publishing) and few incentives for researchers to pursue open practices. For example, current incentive structures promote the publication of "clean" narratives, which may require the incomplete reporting of study procedures or results. Nevertheless, change is occurring. The TOP guidelines[54,65] promote open practices, while an increasing number of journals and funders require open practices (for example, open data), with some offering their researchers free, immediate open-access publication with transparent post-publication peer review (for example, the Wellcome Trust, with the launch of Wellcome Open Research). Policies to promote open science can include reporting guidelines or specific disclosure statements (see Box 6). At the same time, commercial and nonprofit organizations are building new infrastructure such as the Open Science Framework to make transparency easy and desirable for researchers.

Box 6 Disclosure

Full disclosure refers to the process of describing in full the study design and data collected that underlie the results reported, rather than a curated version of the design, and/or a subset of the data collected. The need for disclosure is clear: in order to adequately evaluate results, we need to know how they were obtained. For example, the informational value of a dependent variable exhibiting an effect of interest is different if only one variable was collected or if 15 were. The probability of a single variable achieving $P < 0.05$ just by chance is 5 percent, but the probability of 1 of 15 variables achieving $P < 0.05$ is 54 perecent.[1] It is obvious that cherry-picking 1 from 15 variables invalidates the results unless it is clear that this has happened. If readers know, then they can adjust their interpretation accordingly. From this simple fact, it follows that if authors do not tell us whether they collected 1 or 15 variables readers cannot evaluate their research.[51]

The simplest form of disclosure is for authors to assure readers via an explicit statement in their article that they are disclosing the data fully. This can be seen as a simple item of reporting guidance where extra emphasis is placed on some aspects that are considered most essential to disclose. For example, including the following 21-word statement: "We report how we determined our sample size, all data exclusions (if any), all manipulations, and all measures in the study."[86] Alternatively, a more complex, but also more enforceable and accountable process is for journals to require explicit and specific disclosure statements. The journal *Psychological Science* (PSCI), for example, now requires authors to "Confirm that (a) the total number of excluded observations and (b) the reasons for making these exclusions have been reported in the Method section(s)."[87]

Evaluation

In this section, we describe measures that can be implemented when evaluating research (including, for example, peer review).

Diversifying Peer Review

For most of the history of scientific publishing, two functions have been confounded—evaluation and dissemination. Journals have provided dissemination via sorting and delivering content to the research community, and gatekeeping via peer review to determine what is worth disseminating. However, with the advent of the Internet, individual researchers are no longer dependent on publishers to bind, print, and mail their research to subscribers. Dissemination is now easy and can be controlled by researchers themselves. For example, preprint services (arXiv for some physical sciences, bioRxiv and PeerJ for the life sciences, engrXiv for engineering, PsyArXiv for psychology, and SocArXiv and the Social Science Research Network for the social sciences) facilitate easy sharing, sorting, and discovery of research prior to publication. This dramatically accelerates the dissemination of information to the research community.

With increasing ease of dissemination, the role of publishers as a gatekeeper is declining. Nevertheless, the other role of publishing—evaluation—remains a vital part of the research enterprise. Conventionally, a journal editor will select a limited number of reviewers to assess the suitability of a submission for a particular journal. However, more diverse evaluation processes are now emerging, allowing the collective wisdom of the scientific community to be harnessed.[66] For example, some preprint services support public comments on manuscripts, a form of prepublication review that can be used to improve the manuscript. Other services, such as PubMed Commons and PubPeer, offer public platforms to comment on published works facilitating post-publication peer review. At the same time, some journals are trialing "results-free" review, where editorial decisions to accept are based solely on review of the rationale and study methods alone (that is, results-blind).[67]

Both pre- and post-publication peer review mechanisms dramatically accelerate and expand the evaluation process.[68] By sharing preprints, researchers can obtain rapid feedback on their work from a diverse community, rather than waiting several months for a few reviews in the conventional, closed peer review process. Using post-publication services, reviewers can make positive and critical commentary on articles instantly, rather than relying on the laborious, uncertain, and lengthy process of authoring a commentary and submitting it to the publishing journal for possible publication, eventually.

As public forms of pre- and post-publication review, these new services introduce the potential for new forms of credit and reputation enhancement.[69] In the conventional model, peer review is done privately, anonymously, and purely as a service. With public commenting systems, a reviewer that chooses to be identifiable may gain (or lose) reputation based on the quality of review. There are a number of possible and perceived risks of non-anonymous reviewing that reviewers must consider and research must evaluate, but there is evidence that open peer review improves the quality of reviews received.[70] The opportunity for accelerated scholarly communication may both improve the pace of discovery and diversify the means of being an active contributor to scientific discourse.

Incentives

Publication is the currency of academic science and increases the likelihood of employment, funding, promotion, and tenure. However, not all research is equally publishable. Positive, novel, and clean results are more likely to be published than negative results, replications, and results with loose ends; as a consequence, researchers are incentivized to produce the former, even at the cost of accuracy.[40] These incentives ultimately increase the likelihood of false positives in the published literature.[71] Shifting the incentives therefore offers an opportunity to increase the credibility and reproducibility of published results. For example, with simulations, Higginson and Munafò developed an optimality model that predicted the most rational research strategy, in terms of the proportion of research effort spent on seeking novel results rather than on confirmatory studies, and the amount of research effort per exploratory study.[72] This showed that, for parameter values derived from the scientific literature, researchers acting to maximize their "fitness" should spend most of their effort seeking novel results and conduct small studies that have a statistical power of only 10–40 percent. Critically, their model suggests that altering incentive structures, by considering more of a researcher's output and giving less weight to strikingly novel findings when making appointment and promotion decisions, would encourage a change in researcher behavior that would ultimately improve the scientific value of research.

Funders, publishers, societies, institutions, editors, reviewers, and authors all contribute to the cultural norms that create and sustain dysfunctional incentives. Changing the incentives is therefore a problem that requires a coordinated effort by all stakeholders to alter reward structures. There will always be

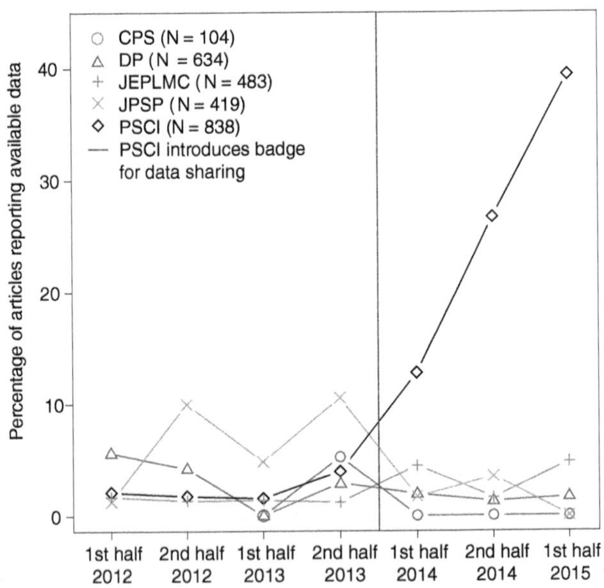

Figure 2 The impact of introducing badges for data sharing. In January 2014, the journal Psychological Science (PSCI) introduced badges for articles with open data. Immediately afterward, the proportion of articles with open data increased steeply, and by October 2015, 38 percent of articles in PSCI had open data. For comparison journals (Clinical Psychological Science (CPS), Developmental Psychology (DP), Journal of Experimental Psychology: Learning, Memory and Cognition (JEPLMC), and Journal of Personality and Social Psychology (JPSP)), the proportion of articles with open data remained uniformly low. Figure adapted from Ref. 75, PLoS.

incentives for innovative outcomes—those who discover new things will be rewarded more than those who do not. However, there can also be incentives for efficiency and effectiveness—those who conduct rigorous, transparent, and reproducible research could be rewarded more than those who do not. There are promising examples of effective interventions for nudging incentives. For example, journals are adopting badges to acknowledge open practices (Figure 2), RR as a results-blind publishing model (see Box 3), and TOP guidelines to promote openness and transparency. Funders are also adopting transparency requirements, and piloting funding mechanisms to promote reproducibility such as the Netherlands Organisation for Scientific Research and the US NSF's Directorate of Social, Behavioral, and Economic Sciences, both of which have announced funding opportunities for replication studies. Institutions are wrestling with policy and infrastructure adjustments to promote data sharing, and there are hints of open-science practices becoming part of hiring and performance evaluation (i.e., http://www.nicebread.de/open-science-hiring-practices/). Collectively, and at scale, such efforts can shift incentives such that what is good for the scientist is also good for science—rigorous, transparent, and reproducible research practices producing credible results.

Conclusion

The challenges to reproducible science are systemic and cultural, but that does not mean they cannot be met. The measures we have described constitute practical and achievable steps toward improving rigor and reproducibility. All of them have shown some effectiveness and are well suited to wider adoption, evaluation, and improvement. Equally, these proposals are not an exhaustive list; there are many other nascent and maturing ideas for making research practices more efficient and reliable.[73] Offering a solution to a problem does not guarantee its effectiveness, and making changes to cultural norms and incentives can spur additional behavioral changes that are difficult to anticipate. Some solutions may be ineffective or even harmful to the efficiency and reliability of science, even if conceptually they appear sensible.

The field of metascience (or metaresearch) is growing rapidly, with over 2,000 relevant publications accruing annually.[16] Much of that literature constitutes the evaluation of existing practices and the identification of alternative approaches. What was previously taken for granted may be questioned, such as widely used statistical methods; for example, the most popular methods and software for spatial extent analysis in fMRI imaging were recently shown to produce unacceptably high false-positive rates.[74] Proposed solutions may also give rise to other challenges; for example, while replication is a hallmark for reinforcing trust in scientific results, there is uncertainty about which studies deserve to be replicated and what would be the most efficient replication strategies. Moreover, a recent simulation suggests that replication alone may not suffice to rid us of false results.[71]

These cautions are not a rationale for inaction. Reproducible research practices are at the heart of sound research and integral to the scientific method. How best to achieve rigorous and efficient knowledge accumulation is a scientific question; the most effective solutions will be identified by a combination of brilliant hypothesizing and blind luck, by iterative examination of the effectiveness of each change, and by a winnowing of many possibilities to the broadly enacted few. True understanding of how best to structure and incentivize science will emerge slowly and will never be finished. That is how science works. The key to fostering a robust metascience that evaluates and improves practices is that the stakeholders of science must not embrace the status quo, but instead pursue self-examination continuously for improvement and self-correction of the scientific process itself.

As Richard Feynman said, "The first principle is that you must not fool yourself—and you are the easiest person to fool."

References

1. Ioannidis, J. P. A. Why most published research findings are false. *PLoS Med.* **2**, e124 (2005).
2. Button, K. S. *et al.* Power failure: why small sample size undermines the reliability of neuroscience. *Nat. Rev. Neurosci.* **14**, 365–376 (2013).
3. Fanelli, D. "Positive" results increase down the Hierarchy of the Sciences. *PloS ONE* **5**, e10068 (2010).
4. John, L. K., Loewenstein, G. & Prelec, D. Measuring the prevalence of questionable research practices with incentives for truth telling. *Psychol. Sci.* **23**, 524–532 (2012).
5. Makel, M. C., Plucker, J. A. & Hegarty, B. Replications in psychology research: how often do they really occur? *Perspect. Psychol. Sci.* **7**, 537–542 (2012).
6. Wicherts, J. M., Borsboom, D., Kats, J. & Molenaar, D. The poor availability of psychological research data for reanalysis. *Am. Psychol.* **61**, 726–728 (2006).
7. Kerr, N. L. HARKing: hypothesizing after the results are known. *Pers. Soc. Psychol. Rev.* **2**, 196–217 (1998).
8. Al-Shahi Salman, R. *et al.* Increasing value and reducing waste in biomedical research regulation and management. *Lancet* **383**, 176–185 (2014).
9. Begley, C. G. & Ioannidis, J. P. Reproducibility in science: improving the standard for basic and preclinical research. *Circ. Res.* **116**, 116–126 (2015).
10. Chalmers, I. *et al.* How to increase value and reduce waste when research priorities are set. *Lancet* **383**, 156–165 (2014).
11. Chan, A. W. *et al.* Increasing value and reducing waste: addressing inaccessible research. *Lancet* **383**, 257–266 (2014).
12. Glasziou, P. *et al.* Reducing waste from incomplete or unusable reports of biomedical research. *Lancet* **383**, 267–276 (2014).

13. Ioannidis, J. P. *et al.* Increasing value and reducing waste in research design, conduct, and analysis. *Lancet* **383**, 166–175 (2014).
14. Macleod, M. R. *et al.* Biomedical research: increasing value, reducing waste. *Lancet* **383**, 101–104 (2014).
15. Baker, M. 1,500 scientists lift the lid on reproducibility. *Nature* **533**, 452–454 (2016).
16. Ioannidis, J. P., Fanelli, D., Dunne, D. D. & Goodman, S. N. Meta-research: evaluation and improvement of research methods and practices. *PLoS Biol.* **13**, e1002264 (2015).
17. Paneth, N. Assessing the contributions of John Snow to epidemiology: 150 years after removal of the broad street pump handle. *Epidemiology* **15**, 514–516 (2004).
18. Berker, E. A., Berker, A. H. & Smith, A. Translation of Broca's 1865 report. Localization of speech in the third left frontal convolution. *Arch. Neurol.* **43**, 1065–1072 (1986).
19. Wade, N. Discovery of pulsars: a graduate student's story. *Science* **189**, 358–364 (1975).
20. Nickerson, R. S. Confirmation bias: a ubiquitous phenomenon in many guises. *Rev. Gen. Psychol.* **2**, 175–220 (1998).
21. Levenson, T. *The Hunt for Vulcan...and How Albert Einstein Destroyed a Planet, Discovered Relativity, and Deciphered the University* (Random House, 2015).
22. Rosenthal, R. *Experimenter Effects in Behavioral Research* (Appleton-Century-Crofts, 1966).
23. de Groot, A. D. The meaning of "significance" for different types of research [translated and annotated by Eric-Jan Wagenmakers, Denny Borsboom, Josine Verhagen, Rogier Kievit, Marjan Bakker, Angelique Cramer, Dora Matzke, Don Mellenbergh, and Han L. J. van der Maas]. *Acta Psychol.* **148**, 188–194 (2014).
24. Heininga, V. E., Oldehinkel, A. J., Veenstra, R. & Nederhof, E. I just ran a thousand analyses: benefits of multiple testing in understanding equivocal evidence on gene-environment interactions. *PloS ONE* **10**, e0125383 (2015).
25. Patel, C. J., Burford, B. & Ioannidis, J. P. Assessment of vibration of effects due to model specification can demonstrate the instability of observational associations. *J. Clin. Epidemiol.* **68**, 1046–1058 (2015).
26. Carp, J. The secret lives of experiments: methods reporting in the fMRI literature. *Neuroimage* **63**, 289–300 (2012).
27. Carp, J. On the plurality of (methodological) worlds: estimating the analytic flexibility of FMRI experiments. *Front. Neurosci.* **6**, 149 (2012).
28. Simonsohn, U., Nelson, L. D. & Simmons, J. P. *P*-curve: a key to the file-drawer. *J. Exp. Psychol. Gen.* **143**, 534–547 (2014).
29. Nuzzo, R. Fooling ourselves. *Nature* **526**, 182–185 (2015).
30. MacCoun, R. & Perlmutter, S. Blind analysis: hide results to seek the truth. *Nature* **526**, 187–189 (2015).
31. Greenland, S. *et al.* Statistical tests, *P* values, confidence intervals, and power: a guide to misinterpretations. *Eur. J. Epidemiol.* **31**, 337–350 (2016).
32. Sterne, J. A. & Davey Smith, G. Sifting the evidence—What's wrong with significance tests? *BMJ* **322**, 226–231 (2001).
33. Brand, A., Bradley, M. T., Best, L. A. & Stoica, G. Accuracy of effect size estimates from published psychological research. *Percept. Motor Skill.* **106**, 645–649 (2008).
34. Vankov, I., Bowers, J. & Munafò, M. R. On the persistence of low power in psychological science. *Q. J. Exp. Psychol.* **67**, 1037–1040 (2014).
35. Sedlmeier, P. & Gigerenzer, G. Do studies of statistical power have an effect on the power of studies? *Psychol. Bull.* **105**, 309–316 (1989).
36. Cohen, J. The statistical power of abnormal-social psychological research: a review. *J. Abnorm. Soc. Psychol.* **65**, 145–153 (1962).
37. Etter, J. F., Burri, M. & Stapleton, J. The impact of pharmaceutical company funding on results of randomized trials of nicotine replacement therapy for smoking cessation: a meta-analysis. *Addiction* **102**, 815–822 (2007).
38. Etter, J. F. & Stapleton, J. Citations to trials of nicotine replacement therapy were biased toward positive results and high-impact-factor journals. *J. Clin. Epidemiol.* **62**, 831–837 (2009).
39. Panagiotou, O. A. & Ioannidis, J. P. Primary study authors of significant studies are more likely to believe that a strong association exists in a heterogeneous meta-analysis compared with methodologists. *J. Clin. Epidemiol.* **65**, 740–747 (2012).
40. Nosek, B. A., Spies, J. R. & Motyl, M. Scientific utopia: II. Restructuring incentives and practices to promote truth over publishability. *Perspect. Psychol. Sci.* **7**, 615–631 (2012).
41. Bath, P. M. W., Macleod, M. R. & Green, A. R. Emulating multicentre clinical stroke trials: a new paradigm for studying novel interventions in experimental models of stroke. *Int. J. Stroke* **4**, 471–479 (2009).
42. Dirnagl, U. *et al.* A concerted appeal for international cooperation in preclinical stroke research. *Stroke* **44**, 1754–1760 (2013).
43. Milidonis, X., Marshall, I., Macleod, M. R. & Sena, E. S. Magnetic resonance imaging in experimental stroke and comparison with histology systematic review and meta-analysis. *Stroke* **46**, 843–851 (2015).
44. Klein, R. A. *et al.* Investigating variation in replicability: a "many labs" replication project. *Soc. Psychol.* **45**, 142–152 (2014).
45. Ebersole, C. R. *et al.* Many Labs 3: evaluating participant pool quality across the academic semester via replication. *J. Exp. Soc. Psychol.* **67**, 68–82 (2016).
46. Lenzer, J., Hoffman, J. R., Furberg, C. D. & Ioannidis, J. P. A. Ensuring the integrity of clinical practice guidelines: a tool for protecting patients. *BMJ* **347**, f5535 (2013).
47. Sterling, T. D. Publication decisions and their possible effects on inferences drawn from tests of significance—or vice versa. *J. Am. Stat. Assoc.* **54**, 30–34 (1959).
48. Rosenthal, R. File drawer problem and tolerance for null results. *Psychol. Bull.* **86**, 638–641 (1979).
49. Sterling, T. D. Consequence of prejudice against the null hypothesis. *Psychol. Bull.* **82**, 1–20 (1975).
50. Franco, A., Malhotra, N. & Simonovits, G. Publication bias in the social sciences: unlocking the file drawer. *Science* **345**, 1502–1505 (2014).
51. Simmons, J. P., Nelson, L. D. & Simonsohn, U. False-positive psychology: undisclosed flexibility in data collection and analysis allows presenting anything as significant. *Psychol. Sci.* **22**, 1359–1366 (2011).

52. Chambers, C. D. Registered Reports: a new publishing initiative at Cortex. *Cortex* **49**, 609–610 (2013).
53. Nosek, B. A. & Lakens, D. Registered Reports: a method to increase the credibility of published results. *Soc. Psychol.* **45**, 137–141 (2014).
54. Nosek, B. A. *et al.* Promoting an open research culture. *Science* **348**, 1422–1425 (2015).
55. Begg, C. *et al.* Improving the quality of reporting of randomized controlled trials: the CONSORT statement. *JAMA* **276**, 637–639 (1996).
56. Moher, D., Dulberg, C. S. & Wells, G. A. Statistical power, sample size, and their reporting in randomized controlled trials. *JAMA* **272**, 122–124 (1994).
57. Schulz, K. F., Altman, D. G., Moher, D. & Group, C. CONSORT 2010 statement: updated guidelines for reporting parallel group randomised trials. *BMJ* **340**, c332 (2010).
58. Grant, S. *et al.* Developing a reporting guideline for social and psychological intervention trials. *Res. Social Work Prac.* **23**, 595–602 (2013).
59. Liberati, A. *et al.* The PRISMA statement for reporting systematic reviews and meta-analyses of studies that evaluate health care interventions: explanation and elaboration. *PLoS Med.* **6**, e1000100 (2009).
60. Shamseer, L. *et al.* Preferred reporting items for systematic review and meta-analysis protocols (PRISMA-P) 2015: elaboration and explanation. *BMJ* **349**, g7647 (2015); erratum **354**, i4086 (2016).
61. van 't Veer, A. & Giner-Sorolla, R. Pre-registration in social psychology: a discussion and suggested template. *J. Exp. Soc. Psychol.* **67**, 2–12 (2016).
62. Franco, A., Malhotra, N. & Simonovits, G. Underreporting in psychology experiments: evidence from a study registry. *Soc. Psychol. Per. Sci.* **7**, 8–12 (2016).
63. Alsheikh-Ali, A. A., Qureshi, W., Al-Mallah, M. H. & Ioannidis, J. P. Public availability of published research data in high-impact journals. *PloS ONE* **6**, e24357 (2011).
64. Iqbal, S. A., Wallach, J. D., Khoury, M. J., Schully, S. D. & Ioannidis, J. P. Reproducible research practices and transparency across the biomedical literature. *PLoS Biol.* **14**, e1002333 (2016).
65. McNutt, M. Taking up TOP. *Science* **352**, 1147 (2016).
66. Park, I. U., Peacey, M. W. & Munafò, M. R. Modelling the effects of subjective and objective decision making in scientific peer review. *Nature* **506**, 93–96 (2014).
67. Button, K. S., Bal, L., Clark, A. G. & Shipley, T. Preventing the ends from justifying the means: withholding results to address publication bias in peer-review. *BMC Psychol.* **4**, 59 (2016).
68. Berg, J. M. *et al.* Preprints for the life sciences. *Science* **352**, 899–901 (2016).
69. Nosek, B. A. & Bar-Anan, T. Scientific utopia: I. Opening scientific communication. *Psychol. Inq.* **23**, 217–243 (2012).
70. Walsh, E., Rooney, M., Appleby, L. & Wilkinson, G. Open peer review: a randomised trial. *Brit. J. Psychiat.* **176**, 47–51 (2000).
71. Smaldino, P. E. & McElreath, R. The natural selection of bad science. *R. Soc. Open Sci.* **3**, 160384 (2016).
72. Higginson, A. D. & Munafò, M. Current incentives for scientists lead to underpowered studies with erroneous conclusions. *PLoS Biol.* **14**, e2000995 (2016).
73. Ioannidis, J. P. How to make more published research true. *PLoS Med.* **11**, e1001747 (2014).
74. Eklund, A., Nichols, T. E. & Knutsson, H. Cluster failure: why fMRI inferences for spatial extent have inflated false-positive rates. *Proc. Natl Acad. Sci. USA* **113**, 7900–7905 (2016).
75. Kidwell, M. C. *et al.* Badges to acknowledge open practices: a simple, low-cost, effective method for increasing transparency. *PLoS Biol.* **14**, e1002456 (2016).
76. Munafò, M. *et al.* Scientific rigor and the art of motorcycle maintenance. *Nat. Biotechnol.* **32**, 871–873 (2014).
77. Kass, R. E. *et al.* Ten simple rules for effective statistical practice. *PLoS Comput. Biol.* **12**, e1004961 (2016).
78. Schweinsberg, M. *et al.* The pipeline project: pre-publication independent replications of a single laboratory's research pipeline. *J. Exp. Psychol. Gen.* **66**, 55–67 (2016).
79. Stevens, A. *et al.* Relation of completeness of reporting of health research to journals' endorsement of reporting guidelines: systematic review. *BMJ* **348**, g3804 (2014).
80. Kilkenny, C. *et al.* Survey of the quality of experimental design, statistical analysis and reporting of research using animals. *PloS ONE* **4**, e7824 (2009).
81. Baker, D., Lidster, K., Sottomayor, A. & Amor, S. Two years later: journals are not yet enforcing the ARRIVE guidelines on reporting standards for pre-clinical animal studies. *PLoS Biol.* **12**, e1001756 (2014).
82. Gulin, J. E., Rocco, D. M. & Garcia-Bournissen, F. Quality of reporting and adherence to ARRIVE guidelines in animal studies for Chagas disease preclinical drug research: a systematic review. *PLoS Negl. Trop. Dis.* **9**, e0004194 (2015).
83. Liu, Y. *et al.* Adherence to ARRIVE guidelines in Chinese journal reports on neoplasms in animals. *PloS ONE* **11**, e0154657 (2016).
84. Gotzsche, P. C. & Ioannidis, J. P. Content area experts as authors: helpful or harmful for systematic reviews and meta-analyses? *BMJ* **345**, e7031 (2012).
85. Morey, R. D. *et al.* The Peer Reviewers' Openness Initiative: incentivizing open research practices through peer review. *R. Soc. Open Sci.* **3**, 150547 (2016).
86. Simmons, J. P., Nelson, L. D. & Simonsohn, U. A 21 word solution. Preprint at http://dx.doi.org/10.2139/ssrn.2160588 (2012).
87. Eich, E. Business not as usual. *Psychol. Sci.* **25**, 3–6 (2014).

Critical Thinking

1. A researcher conducts a research study and publishes it in a journal. Explain in your own words why it is fundamentally important that someone else, using basically the same techniques, be able to obtain basically the same results.
2. Sometimes errors in science are due to sloppiness, and at other times, errors are due to fraud. Thinking about the methodological proposals in this article, how might they address both of these sources of error?

Internet References

A Quick Guide to the Replication Crisis in Psychology

https://www.psychologytoday.com/us/blog/the-nature-nurture-nietzsche-blog/201509/quick-guide-the-replication-crisis-in-psychology

Psychology's Replication Crisis Can't Be Wished Away

https://www.theatlantic.com/science/archive/2016/03/psychologys-replication-crisis-cant-be-wished-away/472272/

The Replication Crisis in Psychology

https://nobaproject.com/modules/the-replication-crisis-in-psychology

Why Students Are the Answer to Psychology's Replication Crisis

http://theconversation.com/why-students-are-the-answer-to-psychologys-replication-crisis-90286

Unit 2

UNIT

Prepared by: R. Eric Landrum, *Boise State University*

Biological Bases of Behavior

As a child, Angel vowed that she did not want to turn out like either of her parents. Angel's mother was passive and silent about her father's drinking. When her father was drunk, her mom always called his boss to report that he was "sick" and then acted as if there was nothing wrong at home. Angel's childhood was a nightmare. Her father's behavior was erratic and unpredictable. If he drank a little, he seemed to be happy. If he drank a lot (which was usually the case), he often became belligerent.

Despite vowing not to become like her father, as an adult Angel found herself as an inpatient in the alcohol rehabilitation unit of a large hospital. Angel's employer could no longer tolerate her on-the-job mistakes or her unexplained absences from work. Angel's supervisor referred her to the clinic for help. As Angel pondered her fate, she wondered whether her genes preordained her to follow in her father's drunken footsteps or whether the stress of her childhood had brought her to this point in her life. After all, being the adult child of an alcoholic is difficult.

Psychologists are concerned with discovering the causes (when possible) of human behavior. Once the cause is known, treatments for problematic behaviors can be developed. In fact, certain behaviors might even be prevented when the cause is identified early enough. But for Angel, prevention was too late. One of the paths to understanding human behavior is the task of understanding its biological underpinnings. Genes and chromosomes, the body's chemistry (as found in hormones, neurotransmitters, and enzymes), and the central and peripheral nervous systems are all implicated in human behavior.

Physiological psychologists, biopsychologists, and neuroscientists examine the role of biology in behavior. These experts often utilize one of a handful of techniques to understand the biology-behavior connection. Animal studies involving manipulation, stimulation, or destruction of certain parts of the brain offer one method of study, but these studies remain controversial with many. There is an alternative technique that involves the study of individuals born with unusual or malfunctioning brains or those whose brains are damaged by accidents or disease, and some case studies of these individuals are famous in psychology for the insights yielded. By studying an individual's behavior in comparison to both natural and adoptive parents, or by studying identical twins reared together or apart, we also can begin to understand the role of genetics and environment on human behavior.

Article

Prepared by: R. Eric Landrum, *Boise State University*

Sleep Deprivation and False Confessions

STEVEN J. FRENDA, ET AL.

Learning Outcomes

After reading this article, you will be able to:

- Define what a false confession is, and be able to explain how some of the methods by which they occur.
- Describe the general effects of sleep deprivation.

In the United States, an alarming number of people are convicted of crimes they did not commit (1). Although it has proven exceedingly difficult to measure the scope of this problem, a recent investigation suggested that at least 4% of people who have been sentenced to death in the United States were actually innocent (2). Studies of known wrongful convictions reveal that false confessions are a substantial contributor to this problem, implicated in 15–25% of cases (1, 3). A false confession occurs when an innocent person makes a false admission of guilt and subsequently produces a postadmission narrative, which includes details about how or why the crime was committed (4). Confessions are extremely powerful forms of evidence. An admission of guilt alone, even without a postadmission narrative, will have serious consequences for an innocent suspect who is the target of a criminal investigation, as will confessions that are later recanted (5). Surprisingly, even when jurors understand that a confession has been coerced, it nonetheless inflates their perception of the defendant's guilt and influences their construal of other, unrelated evidence (5, 6).

False confessions can clearly have dire consequences and it might seem that they would only arise after some form of physical coercion. However, interrogators more often capitalize on psychologically coercive interrogation strategies, which are known to increase the risk of false confession in innocent suspects (3, 4, 7–10). As such, the use of these strategies contribute to an inordinately stressful and mentally taxing experience for an innocent suspect (11), who must rely on a number of complex cognitions and decision-making skills to protect their interests and avoid self-incrimination during a potentially lengthy interrogation.

A robust literature reveals that sleep deprivation impairs many of the cognitive skills that may be crucial in resisting this type of coercive environment. In addition to disrupting mood and impairing a whole host of cognitive operations (12, 13), there is evidence suggesting that sleep deprivation reduces inhibitory control, leading people to make riskier decisions (14–16), and interferes with their ability to anticipate and measure the consequences of their actions (17). Finally, recent research has linked sleep deprivation with false and distorted memories of past events (18), suggesting that sleep-deprived people may be especially vulnerable to suggestive influences.

These findings are cause for serious concern; studies have shown that as many as 17% of interrogations occur during typical sleep hours (between midnight and 8:00 AM) (19). Studies of known false confessions have found that a majority occurred following interrogations that lasted more than 12 h, with many lasting for longer than 24 consecutive hours (20). Moreover, as the Senate Select Committee on Intelligence recently revealed, the Central Intelligence Agency routinely used sleep deprivation for up to 1 wk to assist in their hardline interrogations of detainees, some of whom were later revealed to be wrongfully held (21). It is increasingly evident that the interrogation of unrested, possibly sleep-deprived, suspects is not out of the ordinary and may even be commonplace.

In the present research, we capitalized on available laboratory techniques for examining false confession processes (22) and compared the tendency of rested and sleep-deprived participants to falsely admit to wrongdoing that never occurred. Specifically, participants completed computer-based tasks, writing exercises, and questionnaires during three separate laboratory sessions (see Figures. S1–S3). Throughout their time in the laboratory, participants were repeatedly warned to never press the Escape key on their computer keyboards because doing so, they were told, would result in the loss of important study data. Importantly, the location of the Escape key on a standard PC keyboard made it highly unlikely that participants would have pressed this key accidentally during the course of the experiment.

Significance

False confessions occur surprisingly frequently in the context of interrogations and criminal investigations. Indeed, false confessions are thought to account for approximately 15–25% of wrongful convictions in the United States. Here we demonstrate that sleep deprivation increases the likelihood that a person will falsely confess to wrongdoing that never occurred. Furthermore, our data suggest that it may be possible to identify certain individuals who are especially likely to falsely confess while sleep deprived. The present research is a crucial step toward understanding the role of sleep deprivation in the problem of false confession and, in turn, raises complex questions about the use of sleep deprivation in the interrogation of innocent and guilty suspects.

Author contributions: S.J.F., S.R.B., E.F.L., and K.M.F. designed research; S.J.F. and K.M.F. performed research; S.J.F. and K.M.F. analyzed data; and S.J.F., S.R.B., E.F.L., and K.M.F. wrote the paper.

Reviewers: M.W.L.C., Duke NUS Graduate Medical School; and S.K., John Jay College of Criminal Justice.

The authors declare no conflict of interest.

This article contains supporting information online at www.pnas.org/lookup/suppl/doi:10.1073/pnas.1521518113/-/DCSupplemental.

Following session 2, participants either slept for 8 h in laboratory bedrooms or remained awake throughout the night, carefully monitored by research staff (see Table S1). The morning following either their night of sleep or sleep deprivation, all participants were shown a personalized statement describing their time in the laboratory, purportedly written by a member of the research staff. Critically, the statement falsely alleged that the participant pressed the Escape key during their first visit to the laboratory, thereby compromising the study data. Participants were asked to read the statement and type their name beneath it to confirm its accuracy. If participants refused to sign their name to the statement, they were immediately shown the statement a second time and again encouraged to type their name (Fig. S3).

Our results indicate that after the initial request, 8 of the 44 rested participants (18%) signed the statement, as did 22 (50%) of the 44 sleep-deprived participants. As shown in Table 1, 9 of the additional rested participants (for a total of 39%) signed after the second request, as did 8 additional sleep-deprived participants (for a total of 68%). The odds of signing the statement were significantly greater for sleep-deprived participants than for the rested participants after the initial request, odds ratio (OR) (95% C.I.) = 4.5 (1.7, 11.8), and after both requests, OR = 3.4 (1.4, 8.2). It should be noted that despite the robust effect of sleep deprivation on false confession, participants' false admissions did not include a detailed postadmission narrative, which is commonly obtained in a criminal confession.

During the initial session (1 wk before the overnight session), we assessed participants' tendency to adopt an impulsive problem-solving strategy by using the Cognitive Reflection Task (CRT; ref. 23; see Fig. S2). As predicted, the effect of sleep deprivation on the likelihood of false confession was markedly increased among participants who showed higher impulsive responding, as shown in Fig. 1. In a logistic regression analysis, with false admission (yes or no) entered as the dependent variable, the main effect of CRT score approached significance, OR = 1.5 (1.0, 2.3), and there was a significant interaction between study condition (sleep-deprived or rested) and intuitive response rates, OR = 3.0 (1.1, 8.0), suggesting that individuals with an impulsive cognitive style were more vulnerable to the effects of sleep deprivation on false confessions.

Table 1 Percentages (and Raw Numbers) of Rested and Sleep-deprived (TSD) Participants who Signed the Statement Containing a False Admission of Wrongdoing after the First Request (Left Side) and Both Requests (Right Side)

False admission (first request)?	Rested	TSD	False admission (both requests)?	Rested	TSD
Yes	18% (8)	50% (22)	Yes	38.6% (17)	68.2% (30)
Refused	82% (36)	50% (22)	Refused	61.4% (27)	31.8% (14)
Total	100% (44)	100% (44)	Total	100% (44)	100% (44)

Sleep-deprived participants reported increased sleepiness, and decreased positive and negative affect compared with rested participants (see Fig. S4 for further analyses). Of note, participants who signed the statement containing the false allegation showed no difference in positive affect, $t(86) = 1.47$, $P = 0.14$, or negative affect, $t(86) = 0.75$, $P = 0.45$, relative to participants who did not sign the statement. This finding suggests that changes in affect as a result of sleep-deprivation did not account for elevated rates of false confession. However, high ratings of sleepiness (i.e., 6 or a 7 on the 7-point scale) strongly predicted the likelihood of false confession, as shown in Fig. 2. An implication of this finding is that a suspect's self-reported sleepiness may be a powerful indicator of risk. Regardless of experimental condition, the odds of confessing were 4.5 times higher for participants who reported high levels of sleepiness, relative to participants who reported low-to-medium levels of sleepiness.

We considered the possibility that sleep-deprived participants were less able (or willing) to read and comprehend the statement containing the false allegation. As detailed in *Materials and Methods* below, we gave all participants a comprehension check in the morning. Two participants (one rested, one sleep-deprived) failed to demonstrate that they were reading and comprehending our materials, and excluding these subjects from our analyses had no effect on any results reported here. Relatedly, it is worth noting that in the context of a criminal investigation, an innocent suspect who signs a confession statement (even if they did not read or comprehend it) may face serious consequences as a result.

These findings are a crucial step in better understanding the role of sleep deprivation in false confessions as they unfold in the context of a police interrogation. We propose that sleep deprivation sets the stage for a false confession by impairing complex decision-making abilities—specifically, the ability to anticipate risks and consequences, inhibit behavioral impulses, and resist suggestive influences.

Despite the strength of our findings, the present study has a few limitations. Although we found evidence suggesting that sleep deprivation may increase the risk of false confessions, our study sheds no light on the impact of sleep deprivation on true confessions. Sleep deprivation may increase confession rates of both innocent and guilty suspects. If sleep deprivation increases both true and false confessions, then law enforcement and military personnel may want to carefully weigh the costs and benefits of sleep deprivation in an interrogation, particularly when collecting intelligence that could prevent the loss of innocent lives. Future research would do well to examine the role of sleep deprivation on both true and false confessions.

Additionally, the consequences of signing the statement were ambiguous and unknown to the participants. We recognize that this scenario may differ in important ways from the situation a suspect may face in an interrogation room. Although obtaining more ecologically valid interrogation conditions are bound to present significant challenges for laboratory researchers because of ethical constraints, further research might profitably investigate whether the severity of the purported wrongdoing and its perceived consequences moderate the effects of sleep deprivation. Finally, the extent to which cultural and/or demographic factors (e.g., age, education) moderate the effect of sleep deprivation on confessions remains an open question.

Nonetheless, to the extent that the same psychological processes are implicated both by laboratory studies and real-life interrogations, our findings have important implications for policies and procedures related to interrogations, particularly those involving innocent suspects. Depriving a suspect of sleep—whether intentionally as part of an interrogation strategy or incidentally as the result of a lengthy interrogation—may compromise the reliability of evidence obtained from an innocent suspect in an interrogation and put innocent suspects at increased risk. To this end, our findings provide an additional justification for the importance of videotaping all interrogations, thus providing judges, attorneys, experts, and jurors with additional opportunities to evaluate the probative value of any confession that is obtained.

Furthermore, we recommend that interrogators assess suspects' sleep habits for the days preceding the interrogation and measure suspects' sleepiness by using validated self-report scales (24, 25) before entering the interrogation room and over the course of the interrogation. It is worth noting that in our sample, participants who indicated a high degree of sleepiness on the single-item Stanford Sleepiness Scale were significantly more likely to sign off on the false allegation compared with participants who reported less severe sleepiness, irrespective of condition. This scale takes only seconds to administer, yet here

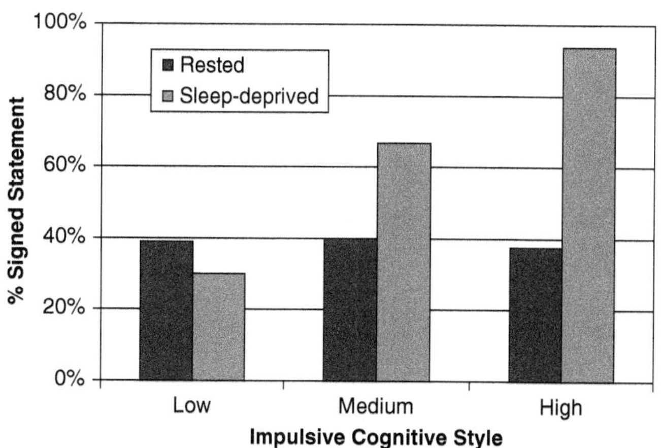

Figure 1 Percentage of participants that signed the statement following both requests as a function of scores on the CRT.

it proved to be a reliable indicator of heightened risk for innocent suspects.

A false admission of wrongdoing can have disastrous consequences in a legal system already fraught with miscarriages of justice. We are hopeful that researchers will continue to uncover the sleep-related factors that influence processes related to false confession.

Materials and Methods

Participants were 88 undergraduates from Michigan State University who enrolled in the study in exchange for course credit. Their mean age was 19.3 (SD = 1.3; range = 18–23) and just under half were female (49%). Participants reported their race/ethnicity as Native American (2.3%), Asian (4.6%), Black (5.7%), Latino (1.1%), Middle Eastern (2.3%), and White (84.1%).

Several additional participants began the study but did not complete it and were excluded from all subsequent procedures and analyses. These participants either: napped on the day of the experiment (n = 1), consumed alcohol on the night of the experiment (n = 1), became ill during the deprivation night (n = 1), or chose to leave in the middle of the deprivation night because they had completed their credit requirement (n = 1). One additional participant chose to leave when the condition was revealed; this individual was assigned to the sleep condition but wanted to be in the deprivation condition to study for an examination the following day. All participants gave informed consent for experimental procedures before completing any experimental tasks. Furthermore, the experiment and informed consent procedures were approved by the Institutional Review Board at Michigan State University.

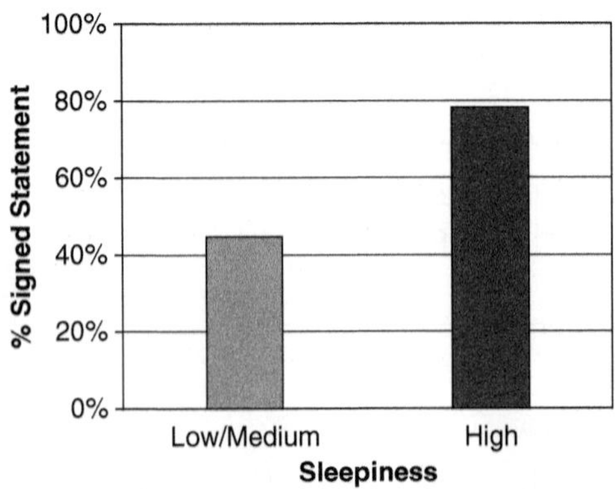

Figure 2 Percentage of participants (collapsed across conditions) that signed the statement as a function of self-reported sleepiness by using the Stanford Sleepiness Scale. Participants who selected a 6 or 7 on the 7-point Stanford Sleepiness scale (25) were categorized as high in sleepiness, whereas participants who selected a rating of less than 6 were categorized as low/medium sleepiness. OR (95% C.I.) = 4.5 (1.5, 13.5).

As shown in Fig. S1, the 88 participants who completed the study attended three laboratory sessions. In session 1, participants provided demographic information and received the first of several warnings not to press the Escape key during the study procedures. Specifically, they were shown a screen with the word "WARNING" at the top, followed by an instruction that read as follows: "Please remember: it's very important that while you work on the computer today that you do NOT press the 'escape key,' located at the top left corner of the keyboard, for any reason—this could cause the computer to lose valuable data. If you have any questions about today's study procedures or questionnaires, please be sure to raise your hand and a member of our research staff will quietly escort you out of the room so as not to disturb the other participants." Participants were asked to click a button to indicate that they understood the warning. To dissuade participants who may have been tempted to press the forbidden Escape key, a member of the research staff watched as participants completed the computer tasks.

Measures relevant to the present research questions were the Pittsburg Sleep Quality Index, a measure of general sleep quality (26) and the CRT (23) (Table S2 and Fig. S2). The CRT measures a person's "cognitive impulsiveness," or their tendency to hastily arrive at intuitive—yet incorrect—answers to a series of logic puzzles. For instance, one question reads, "A bat and a ball cost $1.10 in total. The bat costs $1.00 more than the ball. How much does the ball cost?" The correct answer to this question is $0.05, but the more intuitive (yet incorrect) response is $0.10. People who give intuitive answers to the puzzles are thought to prefer an impulsive thinking and problem-solving style. We measured cognitive impulsiveness by totaling the number of intuitive responses that each participant gave (out of three). We designated participants as "high" in cognitive impulsiveness if they gave intuitive responses to all of the puzzles on the CRT, "medium" if they gave intuitive responses to two puzzles, and "low" if they gave intuitive responses to either zero or one puzzle.

Session 2 took place on an evening ~7 d later. Participants returned to the laboratory at 10:00 PM and were first shown the Escape key warning, which was identical to the warning they received in session 1. Then, participants completed baseline measures of positive and negative affect [Positive and Negative Affect Schedule (PANAS); ref. 27] and sleepiness (Stanford Sleepiness Scale; ref. 25), and a series of filler computer tasks not relevant to the present study.

Half of the participants then slept for 8 h in laboratory bedrooms (n = 44, 21 female) and half remained awake throughout the night in the laboratory while being monitored by research staff (n = 44, 22 female) (Table S1). Participants were quasi-randomly assigned to condition. We used quasi-random assignment to ensure that the time interval between sessions 1 and 2 was equal across conditions. Specifically, participants' first session was roughly 1 wk before their overnight [mean (M) = 7.26 d, SD = 1.0]. Importantly, the interval between session 1 and session 2 was similar for the sleep (M = 7.2, SD = 1.1, range = 6–10) and the deprivation (M = 7.3, SD = 0.9) groups $t(86) = 0.58$, $P = 0.55$. When they arrived to the first session, before completing any computer tasks, participants selected their overnight session. This procedure was designed so that if a participant could not attend any of the available evenings, we could reschedule their first session to maintain an average of 7 d between session 1 and the overnight. Although the experimenter knew which nights would be deprivation nights and which would be sleep nights, the participants remained blind to condition until after the computer tasks on the evening of their overnight session. Put simply, the participants were blind to condition until the last possible moment (e.g., ~11:00 PM, which is when we had to start setting sleep participants up for polysomnography).

Session 3 took place the next morning, after the night of sleep or sleep deprivation. Each participant began the morning procedure by reading, once again, the Escape key warning, completing measures of affect and sleepiness, and filler tasks and questionnaires. Next, participants completed a comprehension check. In this task, we asked them to indicate whether they completed certain activities in the laboratory. Hidden among a list of events that actually occurred (e.g., "You filled out computer questionnaires") were foil events that could not possibly have occurred (e.g., "You drank a beer in the lab"). Only two participants (one rested, one sleep-deprived) failed to successfully complete the task, and when these participants were excluded from our analyses, all results and patterns of significance remained identical.

The critical outcome of interest was the participants' response to the false allegation. Before leaving the laboratory, each participant was shown a personalized statement, purportedly written by a member of the research staff. The statement described the participant's activities in the laboratory over the course of the week, and falsely alleged that the participant pressed the Escape key during their first visit to the laboratory (the prior week when no participants had been sleep deprived), thereby compromising the study data. Participants were asked to read the statement, check a box confirming its accuracy, and type their name beneath the statement. If participants refused to confirm the accuracy of the statement, they were shown the statement a second time and again encouraged to sign it (Fig. S3). Participants who refused to sign the statement were asked which parts of the statement they believed were inaccurate and given an opportunity to freely respond. After signing their name (or refusing both requests, whichever came first), they were fully debriefed.

ACKNOWLEDGMENTS

We thank Nicholas Nicoletti and Joseph O'Connor for their invaluable assistance in coordinating and running this study and two reviewers for insightful comments on an earlier draft of this manuscript.

1. Gross SR, Shaffer M (2012) Exonerations in the United States 1989 through 2012 (Natl. Registry Exonerations Report). Available at www.law.umich.edu/special/exoneration/Documents/exonerations_us_1989_2012_full_report.pdf. Accessed October 30, 2015.
2. Gross SR, O'Brien B, Hu C, Kennedy EH (2014) Rate of false conviction of criminal defendants who are sentenced to death. *Proc Natl Acad Sci USA* 111(20):7230–7235.
3. Garrett BL (2011) *Convicting the Innocent: Where Criminal Prosecutions Go Wrong* (Harvard Univ Press, Cambridge, MA).
4. Leo RA (2009) False confessions: Causes, consequences, and implications. *J Am Acad Psychiatry Law* 37(3):332–343.
5. Kassin SM, Sukel H (1997) Coerced confessions and the jury: An experimental test of the "Harmless Error" rule. *Law Hum Behav* 21(1):27–46.
6. Hasel LE, Kassin SM (2009) On the presumption of evidentiary independence: Can confessions corrupt eyewitness identifications? *Psychol Sci* 20(1):122–126.
7. Kassin SM (2008) Confession evidence: Commonsense myths and misconceptions. *Crim Justice Behav* 35(10):1309–1322.
8. Kassin SM, Gudjonsson GH (2004) The psychology of confession evidence: A review of the literature and issues. *Psychol Sci Public Interest* 5(2):33–67.
9. Kassin SM, McNall K (1991) Police interrogations and confessions: Communicating promises and threats by pragmatic implications. *Law Hum Behav* 15(3):233–251.
10. Narchet FM, Meissner CA, Russano MB (2011) Modeling the influence of investigator bias on the elicitation of true and false confessions. *Law Hum Behav* 35(6):452–465.
11. Kassin SM, et al. (2010) Police-induced confessions: Risk factors and recommendations. *Law Hum Behav* 34(1):3–38.
12. Ratcliff R, Van Dongen HPA (2009) Sleep deprivation affects multiple distinct cognitive processes. *Psychon Bull Rev* 16(4):742–751.
13. Pilcher JJ, Huffcutt AI (1996) Effects of sleep deprivation on performance: A meta-analysis. *Sleep* 19(4):318–326.
14. Killgore WD, Balkin TJ, Wesensten NJ (2006) Impaired decision making following 49 h of sleep deprivation. *J Sleep Res* 15(1):7–13.
15. Chuah YML, Venkatraman V, Dinges DF, Chee MWL (2006) The neural basis of interindividual variability in inhibitory efficiency after sleep deprivation. *J Neurosci* 26(27):7156–7162.
16. Drummond SP, Paulus MP, Tapert SF (2006) Effects of two nights sleep deprivation and two nights recovery sleep on response inhibition. *J Sleep Res* 15(3):261–265.

17. Harrison Y, Horne JA (2000) The impact of sleep deprivation on decision making: A review. *J Exp Psychol Appl* 6(3):236–249.
18. Frenda SJ, Patihis L, Loftus EF, Lewis HC, Fenn KM (2014) Sleep deprivation and false memories. *Psychol Sci* 25(9):1674–1681.
19. Kassin SM, et al. (2007) Police interviewing and interrogation: A self-report survey of police practices and beliefs. *Law Hum Behav* 31(4):381–400.
20. Drizin S, Leo R (2004) The problem of false confessions in the post-DNA world. *North Carol Law Rev* 82:891–1007.
21. U.S. Senate Select Committee on Intelligence (2014) *Committee Study of the Central Intelligence Agency's Detention and Interrogation Program.* Available at: www.intelligence.senate.gov/press/committee-releases-study-cias-detention-and-interrogation-program. Accessed October 30, 2015.
22. Kassin SM, Kiechel K (1996) The social psychology of false confessions: Compliance, internalization, and confabulation. *Psychol Sci* 7(3):125–128.
23. Frederick S (2005) Cognitive reflection and decision making. *J Econ Perspect* 19(4): 25–42.
24. Johns MW (1991) A new method for measuring daytime sleepiness: The Epworth sleepiness scale. *Sleep* 14(6):540–545.
25. Hoddes E, Zarcone V, Smythe H, Phillips R, Dement WC (1973) Quantification of sleepiness: A new approach. *Psychophysiology* 10(4):431–436.
26. Buysse DJ, Reynolds CF, Monk TH, Berman SR, Kupfer DJ (1989) The Pittsburgh Sleep Quality Index: A new instrument for psychiatric practice and research. *Psychiatry Res* 28(2):193–213.
27. Watson D, Clark LA, Tellegen A (1988) Development and validation of brief measures of positive and negative affect: The PANAS scales. *J Pers Soc Psychol* 54(6):1063–1070.

Critical Thinking

1. Figuring out how many individuals are falsely imprisoned is akin to estimating the number of individuals not counted during a census. How do researchers determine false imprisonments?
2. The researchers described some of the effects of sleep deprivation. Thinking about your own situation, how might the effects of sleep deprivation be affecting you?

Internet References

False confessions or admissions—The Innocence Project
https://www.innocenceproject.org/causes/false-confessions-admissions/

False confessions: Causes, consequences, and implications
http://jaapl.org/content/37/3/332

Why do innocent people confess?
http://www.nytimes.com/2012/02/26/opinion/sunday/why-do-innocent-people-confess.html

Article

Prepared by: R. Eric Landrum, *Boise State University*

Could a Dose of Sunshine Make You Smarter?

Moderate ultraviolet light exposure boosts the brainpower of mice thanks to increased production of the neurotransmitter glutamate.

RUTH WILLIAMS

Learning Outcomes

After reading this article, you will be able to:

- Identify the brain chemical that UV light activates in rats.
- Begin to understand the relationship between neuronal functioning and UV light exposure.

The sun's ultraviolet (UV) radiation is a major cause of skin cancer, but it offers some health benefits too, such as boosting production of essential vitamin D and improving mood. Today (May 17), a report in Cell adds enhanced learning and memory to UV's unexpected benefits.

Researchers have discovered that, in mice, exposure to UV light activates a molecular pathway that increases production of the brain chemical glutamate, heightening the animals' ability to learn and remember.

"The subject is of strong interest, because it provides additional support for the recently proposed theory of UV light's regulation of the brain and central neuroendocrine system," dermatologist Andrzej Slominski of The University of Alabama who was not involved in the research writes in an e-mail to *The Scientist.*

"It's an interesting and timely paper investigating the skin–brain connection," notes skin scientist Martin Steinhoff of University College Dublin's Center for Biomedical Engineering who also did not participate in the research. "The authors make an interesting observation linking moderate UV exposure to . . . [production of] the molecule urocanic acid. They hypothesize that this molecule enters the brain, activates glutaminergic neurons through glutamate release, and that memory and learning are increased."

While the work is "fascinating, very meticulous, and extremely detailed," says dermatologist David Fisher of Massachusetts General Hospital and Harvard Medical School, "it does not imply that UV is actually good for you. . . . Across the board, for humanity, UV really is dangerous."

Wei Xiong of the University of Science and Technology of China who led the research did not set out to investigate the effects of UV light on the brain or the skin–brain connection. He stumbled upon his initial finding "almost accidentally," he explains in an email to *The Scientist.* Xiong and his colleagues were using a mass spectrometry technique they had recently developed for analyzing the molecular contents of single neurons, when their results revealed the unexpected presence of urocanic acid—a little-known molecule produced in the skin in response to UV light.

"It was a surprise because we checked through all the literature and found no reports of the existence of this small molecule in the central nervous system," writes Xiong.

With little information to go on, Xiong and his colleagues decided to see whether UV light could also boost levels of urocanic acid in the brain. They exposed shaved mice to a low dose of UVB—responsible for sunburn in humans—for two hours, then performed mass spectrometry on the animals' individual brain cells. Sure enough, levels of urocanic acid increased in neurons of the animals exposed to the light, but not in those of control animals.

Urocanic acid can absorb UV rays and, as a result, may be able to protect skin against the sun's harmful effects. But in the liver and other peripheral tissues, the acid is also known to be an intermediate molecule generated in the metabolic pathway that converts histidine to glutamate. Given glutamate's role in the brain as an excitatory neurotransmitter, Xiong and his colleagues were interested to test whether the observed UV-dependent increase in urocanic acid in neurons might be coupled with increased glutamate production. It was.

Next, the team showed that UV light enhanced electrical transmission between glutaminergic neurons in brain slices taken from animals exposed to UV, but not in those from control animals. This UV-induced effect was prevented when the researchers inhibited activity of the enzyme urocanase, which converts urocanic acid to glutamate, indicating that the acid was indeed the mediator of the UV-induced boost in glutaminergic activity.

Lastly, the team showed that mice exposed to UV performed better in motor learning and recognition memory tasks than their unexposed counterparts. And, as before, treating the animals with a urocanase inhibitor prevented the UV-induced improvements in learning and memory. Administering urocanic acid directly to animals not exposed to UV light also spurred similar learning and memory improvements to those achieved with UV exposure.

Whether the results obtained in mice, which are nocturnal and rarely see the sun, will hold true in humans is yet to be determined. But, Fisher says, if the results do hold, the finding that urocanic acid alone can enhance learning and memory might suggest "a way to utilize this information to benefit people without exposing them to the damaging effects of UV."

H. Zhu et al., "Moderate UV exposure enhances learning and memory by promoting a novel glutamate biosynthetic pathway in the brain," Cell, doi: 10.1016/j.cell.2018.04.014, 2018.

Critical Thinking

1. It's often the case that exposure to some phenomenon in nature is not exclusively good or exclusively bad, but can have trade-offs. According to this article, what is the new information now available about the trade-offs regarding exposure to sunlight/UV radiation?
2. Scientists are very careful about making causal claims. As best as you can from the article, what is the sequence of events that connects these links: exposure to UV radiation, glutamate, urocanic acid, glutaminergic neurons, urocanase, and recognition memory.

Internet References

Sunlight Boosted Memory in Mice—Could It Do the Same for Humans?
https://www.newsweek.com/sunlight-could-make-you-smarter-975879

Sunshine for Your Mind
http://stke.sciencemag.org/content/11/537/eaau6107

UV Light May Make Brain Work Better, Researchers Find
http://english.cas.cn/newsroom/news/201805/t20180531_193655.shtml

Article

Prepared by: R. Eric Landrum, *Boise State University*

The Largest Health Disparity We Don't Talk About

DHRUV KHULLAR

Learning Outcomes

After reading this article, you will be able to:

- Recognize the degree to which a person's lifespan is shortened when they have a mental illness.
- Understand the concept of therapeutic pessimism and the role this belief plays in the reduction of treatment for individuals with a mental disorder.
- Appreciate the role of diagnostic overshadowing and how it adds to the complexing of treating the physical health symptoms of individuals with mental health challenges.

I didn't think our relationship would last, but neither did I think it would end so soon.

My patient had struggled with bipolar disorder his entire life, and his illness dominated our years together. He had, in a fit of hopelessness, tried to take his life with a fistful of pills. He had, in an episode of mania, driven his car into a tree. But the reason I now held his death certificate—his sister and mother in tears by his bed—was more pedestrian: a ruptured plaque in his coronary artery. A heart attack.

Americans with depression, bipolar disorder, or other serious mental illnesses die 15 to 30 years younger than those without mental illness—a disparity larger than for race, ethnicity, geography, or socioeconomic status. It's a gap, unlike many others, that has been growing, but it receives considerably less academic study or public attention. The extraordinary life expectancy gains of the past half-century have left these patients behind, with the result that Americans with serious mental illness live shorter lives than those in many of the world's poorest countries.

National conversations about better mental health care tend to follow a mass shooting or the suicide of a celebrity. These discussions obscure a more rampant killer of millions of Americans with mental illness: chronic disease.

We may assume that people with mental health problems die of "unnatural causes" like suicide, overdoses, and accidents, but they're much more likely to die of the same things as everyone else: cancer, heart disease, stroke, diabetes, and respiratory problems. Those with serious mental illness are more likely to struggle with homelessness, poverty, and social isolation. They have higher rates of obesity, physical inactivity, and tobacco use. Nearly half don't receive treatment, and for those who do, there's often a long delay.

When these patients do make it into our clinics and hospitals, it's clear that we could do better. A troubled mind can distract doctors from an ailing heart or a budding cancer.

For doctors, two related biases are probably at play. The first is therapeutic pessimism. Clinicians, including mental health professionals, often hold gloomy views about whether patients with serious mental illness can get better. This can lead to a resigned passivity, meaning that certain tests and treatments aren't offered or pursued.

As Lisa Rosenbaum, a cardiologist at Brigham and Women's Hospital in Boston, writes: "Many of us have internalized the directive to seek a test or procedure only if 'there's something you can do about it.' For mentally ill patients with medical illness, however, this principle often justifies doing nothing."

The second is a concept called diagnostic overshadowing, by which patients' physical symptoms are attributed to their mental illness. When doctors know a patient has depression, for example, they're less likely to think her headache or abdominal pain portends a serious illness.

In a recent article in *The New England Journal of Medicine*, Dr. Brendan Reilly, a physician at Dartmouth, describes his late brother's devastating story. Over the course of months, he wrote, countless physicians, hospitals, and rehab facilities missed the spinal cord damage that left him quadriplegic—instead variously ascribing his inability to move to his mental illness, his medications, or his will.

"Once they find out you have a mental illness," Dr. Reilly quoted his brother as saying, "it's like the lights go out."

This isn't an isolated event. Patients with mental illness are much less likely to undergo cardiac catheterization when they show heart attack symptoms. They're also less likely to get standard diabetes care like blood tests or eye exams, or to be screened and treated for cancer.

This is, at times, understandable, particularly when it comes to managing complex chronic diseases. For both clinicians and loved ones of patients with serious mental illness, contending with an episode of psychosis or severe depression can be so overwhelming that controlling cholesterol or managing blood pressure seems like mowing the lawn while the house is on fire.

It may help to organize and pay for mental health care more like physical health care. We've been redesigning care for patients with diabetes, heart failure, or knee problems, but have made few dedicated efforts for those with mental illness. A recent review, for instance, found that there are currently no good trials on how to increase cancer screening for people with mental illness.

The few tailored programs that do exist have shown promise in meeting the distinct needs of these patients and overcoming the health system's biases. One study recruited nearly 300 overweight patients from community-based psychiatric programs and randomly assigned them either to "usual care"—general nutrition and exercise information—or a behavioral weight loss program. The weight loss program was devised for patients with serious mental illness, who often struggle with memory, attention, and learning issues.

The patients were taught material in small chunks with frequent repetition, role-played the selection of healthy foods, and got help organizing their homes to enable a healthier lifestyle. At the end of the study, patients in the control group weighed essentially what they did at the beginning. But those in the specialized program lost on average 7.5 pounds; nearly 40 percent had lost 5 percent of their total body weight.

Across the country, heart failure patients leaving the hospital are routinely seen in specialized clinics within a week of discharge. Not so for psychiatric patients, who often wait months before seeing a mental health professional.

To narrow that gap, UT Health San Antonio created a transitional clinic for patients with mental illness discharged from hospitals and emergency departments throughout the city. The goal is to get these patients evaluated within days. They meet with psychiatrists, social workers, and therapists. They receive training in how to buy groceries and use public transportation. They're visited at home by case workers who help organize not only their psychiatric drugs but also their cholesterol and blood pressure medications.

"With the right kind of care, people with serious mental illness can integrate back into society," said Dr. Dawn Velligan, professor at UT Health San Antonio and a director at the clinic. "They can have regular jobs, relatively normal lives. We just need to intervene before things get unmanageable."

Early results are promising: historically, about 7 percent of psychiatric patients return to the hospital within a month, but only 1 percent of those seen in the transitional clinic do. Despite the program's success, inconsistent funding has limited the number of patients the clinic can reach—a reflection of how society continues to undervalue mental health.

"When there's a commitment to these patients, there's a lot we can do," Dr. Velligan said. "But right now, they're not a priority. People have to want to care for them. We have to care."

After decades of fragmenting medicine into specialties and subspecialties, it's perhaps not surprising that a siloed system often fails those in need of whole-person care. I still sometimes wonder if I had let my patient's mental illness overshadow his physical needs. Did I overlook some subtle cue?

I may never know the answer, but next time, I hope I'm not asking the question.

Critical Thinking

1. In the United States, we struggle to provide health care to all individuals. Now consider the added struggle to provide mental health care to those individuals who need it. In additional to what the article has mentioned, what are some of the other obstacles to providing routine physical health care to individuals with mental health challenges?
2. The notion of therapeutic pessimism is that if the doctor does not believe that the person with the mental illness will not get better, the doctor may not be overly motivated to offer help, order tests, and so on. Think about how this concept applies to other aspects of life. If a teacher does not believe a child can learn, or if a parent does not believe a child has value, what happens? If you do not believe in yourself, if you do not believe that you can be successful in what you do (i.e., achieve self-efficacy), what happens? Explain.

Internet References

A Patient's Experience with Diagnostic Overshadowing

https://www.kevinmd.com/blog/2014/11/patients-experience-diagnostic-overshadowing.html

Depression and Diagnostic Overshadowing

https://www.psychologytoday.com/us/blog/two-takes-depression/201510/depression-and-diagnostic-overshadowing

Diagnostic Overshadowing Dangers

https://psnet.ahrq.gov/webmm/case/412/diagnostic-overshadowing-dangers

Dhruv Khullar is a physician at NewYork-Presbyterian Hospital, a researcher at the Weill Cornell Department of Healthcare Policy and Research, and a director of policy dissemination at the Physicians Foundation Center for Physician Practice and Leadership.

Article

Prepared by: R. Eric Landrum, *Boise State University*

Using Deviance Regulation Theory to Target Marijuana Use Intentions among College Students

ROBERT D. DVORAK, ET AL.

Learning Outcomes

After reading this article, you will be able to:

- Articulate the concept of descriptive norms and how it relates to base rates.
- Explain the two parts of deviance regulation theory: uncommon behaviors tend to be memorable because they stand out, and the information attached to the individuals exhibiting the uncommon behaviors is critical—thus, you can be bringing attention to the positive uncommon behavior or encourage others to not stand out when the uncommon behavior is viewed negatively.

There has been increasing acceptance and use of recreational marijuana over the last several years (Hasin et al., 2015; Miech et al., 2015). In a large, nationally representative sample, Hasin and colleagues found that past year marijuana use prevalence doubled from 4.1 percent in 2001–2002 to 9.5 percent in 2012–2013 (Hasin et al., 2015). In the most recent Monitoring the Future survey, annual marijuana use among college students had grown from 30.2 percent in 2006 to 39.3 percent in 2016. In addition, there has been an increase in daily marijuana use from 5.3 percent to 7.8 percent among all 19–22-year-olds during this same time frame (Schulenberg et al., 2017). This may be linked to increasing support for marijuana legalization (Kerr et al., 2017; Miech et al., 2015). In addition to higher use rates, recreational use may result in risks associated with physical and mental health such as increased anxiety, decreased cardiovascular health, and possible substance dependence (Dvorak & Day, 2014; Keith et al., 2015). Given the various health risks associated with recreational marijuana use and the apparent rise in marijuana acceptability, it is of the utmost importance that prevention efforts be identified. Previous research has shown web-delivered norm-based approaches can be successful and have the potential to reduce marijuana use (Elliott & Carey, 2012; Palfai et al., 2014; Walters, Lee, & Walker, 2012). The current study examines a web-delivered norm-based approach, grounded in DRT, as a means to reduce marijuana use intentions.

Norm-Based Interventions

Descriptive norms are the beliefs that individuals hold regarding the base rate of a given behavior in the population. As an example, asking a student what percent of individuals at their school use marijuana will elicit the student's normative belief (i.e., descriptive norm) about the frequency of marijuana use at their school. Previous research has shown that descriptive normative beliefs about substance use are reasonable predictors of actual use (Neighbors, Geisner, & Lee, 2008; Pearson, Liese, Dvorak, & the Marijuana Outcomes Study Team, 2017). Furthermore, individuals tend to believe substance use is higher in the population than it actually is (Prentice & Miller, 1993). Capitalizing on this, feedback highlighting the discrepancy between individual's beliefs about the norm and the actual norm (i.e., norm-based interventions) have been found to be effective at reducing substance use behaviors broadly (Lewis & Neighbors, 2006; Patrick, Lee, & Neighbors, 2014). Indeed, this approach is so effective that it has become a staple of virtually every web-based alcohol use intervention. Web-based interventions have shown to economically reach a larger number of people (Lee et al., 2010; Strecher, Shiffman, & West, 2006) without sacrificing the integrity of participant responses (Gosling et al., 2004). Furthermore, there is evidence that web-based interventions do not impede the effectiveness of the intervention (Bewick et al., 2008). Thus, web-based interventions are useful both in that they seem to be effective while simultaneously reaching more individuals at a lower cost.

However, the few studies that have specifically tested norm-based web-delivered interventions for marijuana use have seen limited success (Elliott & Carey, 2012; Lee et al., 2010; Palfai et al., 2014). For example, Elliott and Carey (2012) found reductions in marijuana use descriptive norms and lower rates of peer disapproval of abstinence among those receiving the intervention. However, there were no effects on use/initiation. Similarly, Palfai et al. (2014) found a decrease in perceived norms of peer marijuana use as well as a small reduction in marijuana-related consequences, but no change in actual marijuana use. Despite the limited success of these initial ventures, they do show promise for the use of norm-based web-delivered interventions for recreational marijuana use. Recently, researchers have begun testing an alternative norm-based approach that does not use normative feedback (Dvorak et al., 2017; Dvorak, Pearson, Neighbors, Martens, & Williams, 2015; Dvorak et al., 2016). This new approach utilizes DRT. DRT approaches capitalize on perceived norms but do not provide corrective feedback on norm discrepancies. Instead, this approach utilizes the norm as a mechanism for delivering a targeted message about the behavior (Blanton & Christie, 2003).

DRT

DRT is a model of behavioral intention and action, based on the interaction of social norms and message framing (Blanton & Christie, 2003; Blanton, Stuart, & Van den Eijnden, 2001). The primary tenets of DRT are twofold. First, uncommon behaviors (i.e., low base-rate behaviors) are salient, as they are opposite to public perception. That is, individuals who engage in uncommon behavior are in the minority and tend to *stand out*. An example might be a person who picks their nose during meetings. DRT predicts they would stand out as they are engaging in behavior that is uncommon. Second, information about characteristics of individuals who engage in uncommon behaviors is particularly important, as it places a spotlight on this highly visible group or individual. Thus, messages or beliefs indicating that people who pick their noses are "gross" and/or "disrespectful" conveys special meaning, as it tells the individual that this is how they would be seen if they were to engage in this uncommon behavior. Essentially, DRT operates on desires to stand out in a positive way by bringing attention to positive uncommon behavior or to *not stand out* in a negative way when the uncommon behavior is viewed more negatively (Blanton & Christie, 2003). Thus, in the above example, if an individual believes that picking your nose is uncommon, then negative information about individuals who engage in this behavior is important and should result in less nose picking. In contrast, if a person believes that everyone picks their nose, then positive information about the minority of individuals who do not engage in this behavior is important and should result in less nose picking. The effect of the message is dependent on the perceived base rate of a given behavior.

Interestingly, the perception of base rates need not be accurate for DRT to exert effects. This is important as research indicates that normative perceptions of substance use vary considerably across people and typically have an overestimation bias (Berkowitz, 2004). Further, this bias is one factor driving substance use(Prentice & Miller, 1993). Indeed, normative feedback interventions utilize this overestimation bias as the mechanism of change (Lewis & Neighbors, 2006). However, DRT does not seek to change the perceived norm. Instead a DRT approach seeks to identify which message would be most effective, given a person's normative beliefs (Blanton et al., 2001). Thus, if a person believes that the base rate of a behavior is high, then a message highlighting the opposite behavior is recommended. As an example, if an individual believes that substance use is common, then a message highlighting the positive characteristics of nonusers would be recommended as nonusers would be the minority. In contrast, if a person believes that substance use is uncommon (i.e., low base rates), then a message highlighting the negative characteristics of users would be recommended as users would be the minority from this person's perspective.

In a series of recent studies, Dvorak and colleagues (Dvorak et al., 2015, 2016, 2017) examined the use of DRT to change intentions to engage in protective behavior strategies when drinking. In each of these studies, the researchers randomly assigned a participant to receive a positive message about students that use protective behaviors when drinking or a negative message about people that do not use protective behaviors when drinking. Though the findings vary a little across studies, the take-home message was that this approach resulted in increased intentions to use these strategies, lower rates of alcohol use, and, in some cases, fewer alcohol-related consequences. In addition, they found that the use of DRT actually strengthens the association between intentions and behavior (Dvorak et al., 2016). This latter finding is particularly important as most of the initial tests of this approach have examined changes in behavioral intentions (Blanton & Burkley, 2008; Blanton & Christie, 2003; Blanton et al., 2001).

Several models of behavior change place intentions as a proximal predictor of behavior (Ajzen, 1991; Ajzen, Albarracín, & Hornik, 2007; Ajzen & Madden, 1986; Gollwitzer, 1999; Gollwitzer & Sheeran, 2006; Pomery et al., 2009; Sheeran et al., 2002). Thus, modifying intentions remains an important initial step in the early stages of developing behavior change approaches. Recent research has found that a DRT-based approach can effectively change substance use behavioral intentions (Dvorak et al., 2015, 2016). Furthermore, DRT-based approaches not only modify intentions but also decrease the intention–action gap (Dvorak et al., 2016). Given the success in previous alcohol research utilizing a DRT framework (Dvorak et al., 2015, 2016, 2017), it reasons that DRT-based approaches, targeting marijuana, may be successful in reducing use intentions.

Overview

The current study examines the effects of a web-based DRT approach on marijuana use intentions. It was hypothesized that a positive message about individuals who do not use marijuana would result in lower marijuana use intentions among those who believed marijuana use was common among university peers (i.e., high perceived marijuana use norms). In contrast, a negative message about marijuana users was expected to produce lower rates of marijuana use intentions among those who believed marijuana use was relatively uncommon (i.e., low perceived marijuana use norms). Finally, we controlled for the extent to which a person believes the message and the extent to which they agree with the message as way to reduce differences in message strength across frames.

Method

Participants.

Participants (n = 694; 66.81 percent female) were college students attending a Midwest university. Participants were recruited via a mass university listserv email. The email went out to all on campus undergraduate students (approximately 13,000). Participants were required to register online to participate. The sample ranged in age from 18 to 37 (M = 19.30, SD = 2.05). The sample was 92 percent white, 6 percent Asian, 3 percent African American, 1 percent Native American, and 8 percent were other or did not wish to respond. The response rate was approximately 5 percent; however, the reported demographics were quite consistent with those at the university. Two individuals reported an age less than 18 and were excluded from the analysis.

Procedure

Study Design. Participants were recruited via mass university email for a study on "Marijuana Use Perceptions." The recruitment email indicated marijuana use was not a prerequisite for participation. Participants were offered the chance to win one of four $50 gift cards for participating. Participants logged on to a secure server where they completed informed consent. Afterward, participants were redirected to the study website. At the study website, participants provided demographic information, reported on recent marijuana use, and indicated pre-manipulation perceived marijuana use norms. They were then randomly assigned to receive a negative frame about individuals who *do* use marijuana or a positive frame about individuals who *do not* use marijuana. After the presentation of the frame, participants rated their intentions to use marijuana over the next three months. At the conclusion of the study, all participants were emailed for debriefing. This email included the actual base rates of marijuana use on campus, described the selection of positively and negatively framed items, and provided a more detailed overview of study goals. The data on base rates of use was obtained from the President's Council on Alcohol and Other Drugs at North Dakota State University (NDSU). These data was collected using the CORE Drug and Alcohol Survey data collected annually in conjunction with the Core Institute. The university institutional review board approved this study, and all participants were treated in accordance with American Psychological Association ethical guidelines.

Intervention. The intervention followed procedures from previous DRT studies. The framing items were developed from a focus group (n = 12; *males* = 5, *females* = 7) of students at NDSU. During this focus group, participants discussed common negative perceptions of marijuana users as well as common positive perceptions of nonmarijuana users. The top 10 perceptions were selected and then framed either positively (e.g., nonusers are more dependable and responsible) or negatively (e.g., users are undependable and irresponsible). Across all of the messages, all but one message occurred in the focus group in both a positive and negative manner, though often phrased slightly different (i.e., a positive message stated ". . . nonusers seem to have more self-control." While a negative message was ". . . users are just impulsive."). However, there was no matching negative message for "nonusers are more intelligent." Thus, we created an opposing negative message. In addition, members of the focus group highlighted that "marijuana use" gave the perception of prescription medication, while "pot use" was the term typically associated with recreational use at NDSU. Thus, in the intervention, the term "pot" was used, rather than, the more common, "marijuana" or "cannabis." To prevent potential contamination, none of the individuals from the focus group were allowed to participate in the larger DRT study. This approach to developing the messages for DRT has been effectively used in previous research (Dvorak et al., 2015, 2017). A list of all 20 statements can be obtained from the first author.

Frame Manipulation. For the manipulation, participants were randomly assigned to receive a positive frame about individuals who do not use marijuana or a negative frame about individuals who do use marijuana. Within each frame, participants were told:

> We've recently started examining the perceptions of pot users by other students. In general, we have found 10 basic perceptions about NDSU students who [Positive Frame: DO NOT use pot; Negative Frame: DO use pot]. Did you know, NDSU students who [Positive Frame: DO NOT USE pot; Negative Frame: DO USE pot] are seen by other students as . . .

This prompt was followed by the 10 positively or negatively framed statements.

Measures

Marijuana Use. Marijuana use over the last 3 months was assessed by a single item that asked, "How often have you used pot in the last 3 months?" Responses were coded on a 5-point Likert-type scale (0 = *not at all*, 1 = *1–3 times*, 2 = *4–6 times*, 3 = *7–9 times*, 4 = *10+ times*). This variable was used as a covariate in the analyses to control for recent marijuana use. Individuals also indicated if they had ever used marijuana in their lifetime (0 = *no*, 1 = *yes*).

Perceived Marijuana Use Norms. Prior to the intervention, participants were asked, "We're curious about your perception of pot use among NDSU students. Based on your experience, what percent of students at NDSU, do you think, have used pot?" Participants could select a value between 0 percent and 100 percent. Consistent with DRT, this value was examined as a moderator of the message frame.

Frame Belief. After the presentation of the message frame, but before individuals rated their use intentions, participants were asked, "How strongly do you believe this research?" which they responded to on a Likert-type scale of 0 (*not at all*) to 10 (*extremely*). This was added as a covariate in the analysis.

Message Agreement. After the presentation of the message frame, but before individuals rated their use intentions, participants were asked, "How much do you personally agree with the above statements?" which they responded to on a Likert-type scale of 0 (*not at all*) to 10 (*extremely*). This was added as a covariate in the analysis.

Marijuana Use Intentions. Immediately after the frame presentation, participants responded to the following three items meant to assess future intentions to use marijuana: "I intend to use pot over the next three months." and "Given the opportunity, I would likely use or try pot over the next three months." Both rated on a Likert-type sliding scale where individuals could move a cursor along the 11-point axis (1 = *no!!!*, 3 = *probably not*, 6 = *maybe*,9 = *probably*, 11 = *yes!!!*). The third item asked "How strong is your desire to use pot over the next three months?" rated on a Likert-type sliding scale where individuals could move a cursor along the 11-point axis (1 = *not at all*, 3 = *unlikely*, 6 = *somewhat*, 9 = *quite a bit*, 11 = *extremely*). Internal consistency for these items was good (a = .95).

Data Preparation and Analysis Plan

Data was examined for skew and multivariate outliers. Two individuals reported an age less than 18 and thus were removed from analysis. The outcome variable had substantial positive skew (skew = 1.73), and the residuals were not normally distributed using an ordinary least squares model. To account for this, we examined a number of generalized linear model outcome distributions. Given that the outcome was positively skewed, continuous (ranging from 1 to 11), and had a standard deviation approximately equivalent to the mean (M = 2.50, SD = 2.52), we selected a generalized linear model with a gamma distribution and log-link function for the final model (Ng & Cribbie, 2016). Simple slopes were calculated for each message frame for significant interactions (Aiken & West, 1991). Below we report both raw coefficients as well as relative risk ratios (RRRs) as a measure of parameter effects.

Results

Descriptive Statistics

A lifetime history of marijuana use was endorsed by 47.98 percent of the sample. In the past three months, 26.80 percent reported some marijuana use (none = 73.20 percent, 1–3 times = 10.81 percent, 4–6 times = 6.20 percent, 7–9 times = 3.31 percent, 10+ times = 6.48 percent). Across frames, there were no differences in marijuana use in the past three months ($t(692) = 0.01, p = .995$), age ($t(692) = 0.28, p = 0.778$), gender distribution, $\chi^2(1) = 0.04$, $p = 0.851$, marijuana use descriptive norms ($t(692) = 0.73$, $p = .467$), or frame belief ($t(692) = -1.22$, $p = 0.222$). Interestingly, individuals in the positive frame endorsed stronger agreement with the message frame ($t(692) = -4.11$, $p < 0.001$, Cohen's $d = -0.31$). Men reported significantly more marijuana use over the last three months, $t(343) = 4.98$, $p <$ 001, Cohen's $d = 0.39$. Men were also more likely to have a lifetime history of marijuana use (men: 56 percent, women: 44 percent), $X^2(1) = 8.57$, $p = 0.003$.

Gender differences in marijuana use norms were not significant, $t(692) = 0.86$, $p = 0.395$. There was a positive association between marijuana use norms and both lifetime marijuana use, $r = 0.153$, $p < 0.001$ and past 3 months marijuana use, $r = 0.079$, $p = 0.037$. Overall, the marijuana use rates were consistent with those observed in college students across the country (Pearson et al., 2017).

Primary Analysis

Marijuana use intentions were regressed onto lifetime marijuana use, past three months marijuana use, message frame, marijuana norms, frame belief, message agreement, Message Frame X Marijuana Norms, Message Frame X Lifetime Marijuana Use, Lifetime Marijuana Use X Marijuana Norms, and Message Frame X Marijuana Norms X Lifetime Marijuana Use. In the initial model, the three-way interaction of Message Frame X Marijuana Norms X Lifetime Marijuana Use was not significant ($B = 0.008$, RRR = 1.00, $p = 0.180$). As use history did not moderate the DRT effect, the interactions with use history were removed and the model was reestimated. The final model, depicted in Table 1, accounted for 49.46 percent of the variance in use intentions.

There were positive associations between use intentions over the next three months and past three months marijuana use, year in school, and lifetime history of marijuana use. Frame belief and message agreement were inversely associated with marijuana use intentions. Consistent with DRT, there was a significant interaction of Message Frame X Marijuana Norms ($B = -.006$, RRR = 0.994, $p = 0.023$). The Message Frame X Marijuana Norms interaction was probed using simple slopes analysis (Figure 1). Consistent with hypothesis, among those who received a negative frame, marijuana use norms were positively associated with marijuana use intentions ($B = 0.009$, RRR = 1.01, $p < 0.001$). Among those who received a positive frame, marijuana use norms were not associated with the likelihood of marijuana use intentions ($B = 0.002$, RRR = 1.00, $p = 0.177$).

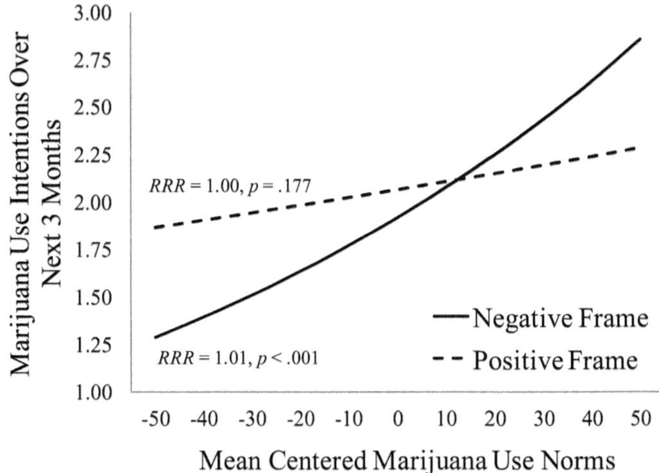

Figure 1 Association between marijuana use norms and marijuana use intentions as a function of message frame.

Table 1 Generalized Linear Model Predicting Marijuana Use Intentions

Predictors	Coefficient	RRR	*SE*	*p*	95% CI
Gender	0.017	1.018	0.047	0.697	[0.930, 1.114]
Age	–0.025	0.976	0.013	0.061	[0.951, 1.001]
Year in school	0.063	1.065	0.027	0.013	[1.013, 1.119]
Message agreement	–0.032	0.968	0.013	0.015	[0.943, 0.994]
Message believability	–0.041	0.960	0.014	0.005	[0.934, 0.988]
Past three-month MJ use	0.304	1.356	0.032	0.000	[1.293, 1.421]
Lifetime MJ use	0.438	1.550	0.099	0.000	[1.368, 1.756]
Message frame	0.074	1.077	0.049	0.105	[0.985, 1.178]
MJ use norms	0.006	1.005	0.001	0.000	[1.003, 1.008]
Frame X use Norms	–0.006	0.994	0.003	0.023	[0.989, 0.999]
Model intercept	0.687	1.987	0.045	0.000	[1.901, 2.077]

Note: All variables are mean centered. RRR = relative risk ratio; *SE* = robust standard errors; 95 Percent CI = 95 percent confidence intervals of the RRR; MJ = marijuana.

Discussion

The current study examined the utility of a web-based DRT approach on marijuana use intentions in a sample of college students. The results were partially consistent with hypotheses. A negative frame about individuals that do use marijuana was associated with lower use intentions among those with low marijuana perceived norms. In contrast, a positive frame about individuals who do not use marijuana was associated with lower use intentions among those with high marijuana use perceived norms. These findings are discussed in greater detail below.

One of the most complicated, even controversial, issues of the current study is the use of a negative frame regarding individuals that do use marijuana. Among those with the lowest levels of perceived marijuana use norms, the negative frame was associated with the lowest use intentions. However, use intentions were highest among those who received a negative frame and held the highest levels of marijuana use perceptions. Thus, caution should be urged with the use of this frame. It seems plausible that the negative frame could elicit reactance/resistance, especially as marijuana use becomes increasingly common. There is a cautionary tale found within the literature on message framing and marijuana use. Skenderian, Siegel, Crano, Alvaro, and Lac (2008) found that changes in future intentions to use marijuana were most robust if adolescents transitioned from abstainers to marijuana users. This was attributed to violations of negative expectancies, perhaps as a function of negative media exposure, following a first exposure to marijuana. Thus, negative messages describing marijuana users may be contraindicated if individuals have had no exposure to marijuana use/users. This remains an important area for future research prior to the implementation of prevention programs using this approach. This may be good news given the rise in popularity in marijuana and the legalizations across the country. According to DRT, the most salient group is the minority group. As marijuana use becomes increasingly normative, the use of a negative frame should become increasingly irrelevant.

As noted above, one might expect an increase in normative perceptions of use as legalization continues to gain steam across the country. Previous research has linked marijuana use norms to actual marijuana use (Pearson et al., 2017). Indeed, in the current data, marijuana use norms were positively correlated with a history of marijuana use. Thus, those with the highest use norm perceptions are also at the highest risk for recreational use. However, in the positive frame, there was no relationship between use norms and use intentions. This seems to suggest that the link between marijuana use norms and marijuana use intentions can be uncoupled by presenting positive information about nonusers. It is unclear if this would result in changes in actual use. Indeed, previous research has shown that changing use norms does not necessarily translate into changes in actual marijuana use (Elliott & Carey, 2012; Palfai et al., 2014). It is possible that changing intentions would be just as futile, though this remains a question for future research.

Clinical Implications

Recent research has indicated increasing use of marijuana among college-aged students (Schulenberg et al., 2017; Terry-McElrath et al., 2017). In addition, we have seen rises in marijuana use disorders among this age group (Hasin & Grant, 2015; Hasin et al., 2015). This has led to a call for researchers to develop interventions to target this population (Miech et al., 2015). The current findings suggest that intentions to use marijuana may be modified using an Internet-based intervention that requires little clinical training and labor to implement. It is unclear whether actual marijuana use would be modified alongside intentions. These findings also suggest that highlighting the positive aspects of nonusers may be the safest course of action when an individual's perception of use norms is unknown. On the same note, highlighting the negative aspects of users could lead to increased intentions to use if the individual perceives marijuana use to be normative. Thus, the use of negative message is contraindicated for this group.

Limitations and Future Directions

These findings should be interpreted in the context of the limitations of the study. First, the sample was comprised predominantly of Caucasian undergraduate students at a Midwest university. In addition, the response rate was quite low, which might be expected for a study that offers no compensation while also asking about illicit drug use. However, the demographic sample closely matched that of the university at large. Despite this, generalizability should be done with caution, and these methods/results surely warrant replication attempts in more diverse samples. In addition, we assessed intentions, but did not examine the effects on actual use behavior. Examining these effects in a prospective or longitudinal design is warranted. We are hopeful that this approach would lead to decreases in use behavior, as recent research indicates that DRT operates in two distinct ways: (a) modifying behavioral intentions *and* (b) strengthening the association between intentions and behavior (Dvorak et al., 2016). Another potential limitation is that we asked about the believability of the message frames. It seems possible that simply asking this could foster distrust; the alternative also seems plausible that asking how much a person believes the frame solidifies belief in the message. This remains a question for future research. Along these same lines, participants endorsed higher agreement with the messages in the positive frame than the negative frame. Certainly, there are better approaches to developing and delivering messages that ensure individuals endorse consistent agreement across message frames. This will be an important next step. Finally, we did not include a control condition. Thus, we are unable to make statements about causality. This remains an important next step.

Conclusions

The present study examined the effects of a DRT-based approach on marijuana use intentions. Overall, these results were consistent with DRT predictions. They suggest that a negative frame may be best among those with the lowest perceived norms while a positive frame may be effective at decoupling the relationship between marijuana use norms and use intentions by reducing use intentions among those with the highest perceived use norms. This latter finding may be especially relevant as marijuana use, and subsequently perceived use norms, become increasingly more common.

References

Aiken, L. S., & West, S. G. (1991). *Multiple regression: Testing and interpreting interactions.* Newbury Park, CA: Sage.

Ajzen, I. (1991). The theory of planned behavior. *Organizational Behavior and Human Decision Processes, 50,* 179–211. doi:10.1016/0749-5978(91)90020-T

Ajzen, I., Albarracín, D., & Hornik, R. (2007). *Prediction and change of health behavior: Applying the reasoned action approach.* Mahwah, NJ: Erlbaum.

Ajzen, I., & Madden, T. J. (1986). Prediction of goal-directed behavior: Attitudes, intentions, and perceived behavioral control. *Journal of Experimental Social Psychology, 22,* 453–474. http://dx.doi.org/10.1016/0022-1031(86)90045-4

Berkowitz, A. D. (2004). *The social norms approach: Theory, research and annotated bibliography.* Newton, MA: Higher Education Center for Alcohol and Other Drug Abuse and Violence Prevention.

Bewick, B. M., Trusler, K., Mulhern, B., Barkham, M., & Hill, A. J. (2008). The feasibility and effectiveness of a web-based personalised feedback and social norms alcohol intervention in UK university students: A randomised control trial. *Addictive Behaviors, 33,* 1192–1198. http://dx.doi.org/10.1016/j.addbeh.2008.05.002

Blanton, H., & Burkley, M. (2008). Deviance regulation theory: Applications to adolescent social influence. In M. J. Prinstein & K. A. Dodge (Eds.), *Understanding peer influence in children and adolescents* (pp. 94–121). New York, NY: Guilford Press.

Blanton, H., & Christie, C. (2003). Deviance regulation: A theory of action and identity. *Review of General Psychology, 7,* 115–149. http://dx.doi.org/10.1037/1089-2680.7.2.115

Blanton, H., Stuart, A. E., & Van den Eijnden, R. J. J. M. (2001). An introduction to deviance-regulation theory: The effect of behavioral norms on message framing. *Personality and Social Psychology Bulletin, 27,* 848–858. http://dx.doi.org/10.1177/0146167201277007

Dvorak, R. D., & Day, A. M. (2014). Marijuana and self-regulation: Examining likelihood and intensity of use and problems. *Addictive Behaviors, 39,* 709–712. http://dx.doi.org/10.1016/j.addbeh.2013.11.001

Dvorak, R. D., Kramer, M. P., Stevenson, B. L., Sargent, E. M., & Kilwein, T. M. (2017). An application of deviance regulation theory to reduce alcohol-related problems among college women during spring break. *Psychology of Addictive Behaviors, 31,* 295–306. http://dx.doi.org/10.1037/adb0000258

Dvorak, R. D., Pearson, M. R., Neighbors, C., & Martens, M. P. (2015). Fitting in and standing out: Increasing the use of alcohol protective behavioral strategies with a deviance regulation intervention. *Journal of Consulting and Clinical Psychology, 83,* 482–493. http://dx.doi.org/10.1037/a0038902

Dvorak, R. D., Pearson, M. R., Neighbors, C., Martens, M. P., Stevenson, B. L., & Kuvaas, N. J. (2016). A road paved with safe intentions: Increasing intentions to use alcohol protective behavioral strategies via deviance regulation theory. *Health Psychology, 35,* 604–613. http://dx.doi.org/10.1037/hea0000327

Elliott, J. C., & Carey, K. B. (2012). Correcting exaggerated marijuana use norms among college abstainers: A preliminary test of a preventive intervention. *Journal of Studies on Alcohol and Drugs, 73,* 976–980. http://dx.doi.org/10.15288/jsad.2012.73.976

Gollwitzer, P. M. (1999). Implementation intentions: Strong effects of simple plans. *American Psychologist, 54,* 493–503. http://dx.doi.org/10.1037/0003-066X.54.7.493

Gollwitzer, P. M., & Sheeran, P. (2006). Implementation intentions and goal achievement: A meta-analysis of effects and processes. *Advances in Experimental Social Psychology, 38,* 69–119. http://dx.doi.org/10.1016/ S0065-2601(06)38002-1

Gosling, S. D., Vazire, S., Srivastava, S., & John, O. P. (2004). Should we trust web-based studies? A comparative analysis of six preconceptions about internet questionnaires. *American Psychologist, 59,* 93–104. http:// dx.doi.org/10.1037/0003-066X.59.2.93

Hasin, D. S., & Grant, B. F. (2015). The National Epidemiologic Survey on Alcohol and Related Conditions (NESARC) Waves 1 and 2: Review and summary of findings. *Social Psychiatry and Psychiatric Epidemiology, 50,* 1609–1640. http://dx.doi.org/10.1007/s00127-015-1088-0

Hasin, D. S., Saha, T. D., Kerridge, B. T., Goldstein, R. B., Chou, S. P., Zhang, H., . . . Grant, B. F. (2015). Prevalence of marijuana use disorders in the United States between 2001–2002 and 2012–2013. *Journal of the American Medical Association Psychiatry, 72,* 1235–1242. http://dx.doi.org/10.1001/jamapsychiatry.2015.1858

Keith, D. R., Hart, C. L., McNeil, M. P., Silver, R., & Goodwin, R. D. (2015). Frequent marijuana use, binge drinking and mental health problems among undergraduates. *The American Journal on Addictions, 24,* 499–506. http://dx.doi.org/10.1111/ajad.12201

Kerr, D. C. R., Bae, H., Phibbs, S., & Kern, A. C. (2017). Changes in undergraduates' marijuana, heavy alcohol and cigarette use following legalization of recreational marijuana use in Oregon. *Addiction, 112,* 1992–2001. http://dx.doi.org/10.1111/add.13906

Lee, C. M., Neighbors, C., Kilmer, J. R., & Larimer, M. E. (2010). A brief, web-based personalized feedback selective intervention for college student marijuana use: A randomized clinical trial. *Psychology of Addictive Behaviors, 24,* 265–273. http://dx.doi.org/10.1037/a0018859

Lewis, M. A., & Neighbors, C. (2006). Social norms approaches using descriptive drinking norms education: A review of the research on personalized normative feedback. *Journal of American College Health, 54,* 213–218. http://dx.doi.org/10.3200/JACH.54.4.213-218

Miech, R. A., Johnston, L., O'Malley, P. M., Bachman, J. G., Schulenberg, J., & Patrick, M. E. (2015). Trends in use of marijuana and attitudes toward marijuana among youth before and after decriminalization: The case of California 2007–2013. *International Journal of Drug Policy, 26,* 336–344. http://dx.doi.org/10.1016/j.drugpo.2015.01.009

Neighbors, C., Geisner, I. M., & Lee, C. M. (2008). Perceived marijuana norms and social expectancies among entering college student marijuana users. *Psychology of Addictive Behaviors, 22,* 433–438. http://dx.doi.org/10.1037/0893-164X.22.3.433

Ng, V. K. Y., & Cribbie, R. A. (2016). Using the gamma generalized linear model for modeling continuous, skewed and heteroscedastic outcomes in psychology. *Current Psychology: A Journal for Diverse Perspectives on Diverse Psychological Issues, 36,* 225–235. http://dx.doi.org/10.1007/s12144-015-9404-0

Palfai, T. P., Saitz, R., Winter, M., Brown, T. A., Kypri, K., Goodness, T. M., . . . Lu, J. (2014). Web-based screening and brief intervention for student marijuana use in a university health center: Pilot study to examine the implementation of eCHECKUP TO GO in different contexts. *Addictive Behaviors, 39,* 1346–1352. http://dx.doi.org/10.1016/j.addbeh.2014.04.025

Patrick, M. E., Lee, C. M., & Neighbors, C. (2014). Web-based intervention to change perceived norms of college student alcohol use and sexual behavior on spring break. *Addictive Behaviors, 39,* 600–606. http://dx.doi.org/10.1016/j.addbeh.2013.11.014

Pearson, M. R., Liese, B. S., & Dvorak, R. D., & the Marijuana Outcomes Study Team. (2017). College student marijuana involvement: Perceptions, use, and consequences across 11 college campuses. *Addictive Behaviors, 66,* 83–89. http://dx.doi.org/10.1016/j.addbeh.2016.10.019

Pomery, E. A., Gibbons, F. X., Reis-Bergan, M., & Gerrard, M. (2009). From willingness to intention: Experience moderates the shift from reactive to reasoned behavior. *Personality and Social Psychology Bulletin, 35,* 894–908. http://dx.doi.org/10.1177/0146167209335166

Prentice, D. A., & Miller, D. T. (1993). Pluralistic ignorance and alcohol use on campus: Some consequences of misperceiving the social norm. *Journal of Personality and Social Psychology, 64,* 243–256. http://dx.doi.org/10.1037/0022-3514.64.2.243

Schulenberg, J. E., Johnston, L. D., O'Malley, P. M., Bachman, J. G., Miech, R. A., & Patrick, M. E. (2017). *Monitoring the future national survey results on drug use, 1975–2016: Volume II, College students and adults ages 19–55.* Ann Arbor, MI: Institute for Social Research, University of Michigan.

Sheeran, P., Trafimow, D., Finlay, K. A., & Norman, P. (2002). Evidence that the type of person affects the strength of the perceived behavioural control-intention relationship. *British Journal of Social Psychology, 41,* 253–270. http://dx.doi.org/10.1348/014466602760060129

Skenderian, J. J., Siegel, J. T., Crano, W. D., Alvaro, E. E., & Lac, A. (2008). Expectancy change and adolescents' intentions to use marijuana. *Psychology of Addictive Behaviors, 22,* 563–569. http://dx.doi.org/10.1037/a0013020

Strecher, V. J., Shiffman, S., & West, R. (2006). Moderators and mediators of a web-based computer-tailored smoking cessation program among nicotine patch users. *Nicotine & Tobacco Research, 8,* S95–S101.

Terry-McElrath, Y. M., O'Malley, P. M., Johnston, L. D., Bray, B. C., Patrick, M. E., & Schulenberg, J. E. (2017). Longitudinal patterns of marijuana use across ages 18–50 in a US national sample: A descriptive examination of predictors and health correlates of repeated measures latent class membership. *Drug and Alcohol Dependence, 171,* 70–83. http://dx.doi.org/10.1016/j.drugalcdep.2016.11.021

Walters, S. T., Lee, C. M., & Walker, D. D. (2012). Brief interventions for marijuana use. In H. R. White, D. L. Rabiner, H. R. White, & D. L. Rabiner (Eds.), *College drinking and drug use* (pp. 184–202). New York, NY: Guilford Press.

Critical Thinking

1. This is an interesting theory because behavior change is based on the beliefs of the person. If you believe that substance use is common, what type of message would be suggested according to DRT? Explain.
2. Continuing from the item above, if you believed that substance use is uncommon, what type of message would be suggested in order to change behavior according to DRT? Explain?
3. Actual research was conducted to test the framing message concerning marijuana use. In your own words, what happened?

Internet References

Deviance Regulation Theory

https://wikivisually.com/wiki/Deviance_regulation_theory

Early Applications of Deviance Regulation Theory to Norms Based Health Communication

https://chipcontent.chip.uconn.edu//chipweb/lectures/20091015_Hart_Blanton/Presentation/HBlanton.pdf

Unit 3

UNIT

Prepared by: R. Eric Landrum, *Boise State University*

Perceptual Processes

Marina and her roommate Claire have been friends since their first year of college. Because they share so much in common, they decided to become roommates in their sophomore year. They both want to travel abroad one day. They both enjoy the same restaurants and share the same preference for red wine. Both have significant others from the same hometown, both are education majors, and both want to work with young children someday. Today they are at the local art museum. As they walk around the galleries, Marina is astonished at Claire's taste in art. Whatever Claire likes, Marina finds hideous. The paintings and sculptures that Marina admires are the very ones to which her roommate turns up her nose. "How can our tastes in art be so different when we share so much in common?" Marina wonders. What Marina and Claire experience is a difference in perception—the interpretation of the sensory stimulation entering the brain. Perception and sensation are closely connected topics in psychology, as well as the topic of this unit. As you will learn in your study of psychology, the study of sensation and perception dates back to psychology's earliest beginnings, and even prior to psychology's formal start. Understanding how the physical energy of sound waves is translated into the language we hear and how waves of light are translated into the images we see are processes occurring in the nervous system and have long fascinated psychologists. Although the laboratory study of sensation and perception is well over 100 years old, psychologists are still seeking to further their understanding of these phenomena.

For many years, it was popular for psychologists to consider sensation and perception as two distinct processes. Sensation was defined in passive terms as the simple event of some stimulus energy (e.g., a sound wave) impinging on a specific sensory organ (e.g., the ear) that then reflexively transmitted the appropriate information to the central nervous system and brain. Perception, on the other hand, was defined as the interpretive process that the higher centers of the brain supposedly accomplish based on sensory information and available memories of similar events. Interesting aberrations can occur however, such as when individuals who suffer from the amputation of a limb still report pain from that missing limb (called phantom pain). Sometimes these aberrations can be delightful, as in visual illusions.

The dichotomy of sensation and perception is no longer widely accepted by today's psychologists. The revolution came in the mid-1960s, when a psychologist published a then-radical treatise in which he reasoned that perceptual processes included all sensory events that he believed were directed by an actively searching central nervous system. This viewpoint provided that certain perceptual patterns, such as recognition of a piece of artwork, may be species-specific. Thus, all humans, independent of learning history, should share some of the same perceptual repertoires. Optical illusions are intriguing because the sensations collected by the visual system, once the brain attempts to translate sensations into perceptions, cause humans to deduce that what was "seen" cannot be true. This is probably one of the reasons that magic tricks are so entertaining to so many people, and sometimes we are blind to events that occur right before our eyes. This unit on perceptual processes is designed to expand your understanding of these incredibly interesting processes. As you will find, understanding perception is a complex process that is made even more difficult by the fact that perception is fluid, continual, and often takes place below everyday levels of consciousness.

Article

Prepared by: R. Eric Landrum, *Boise State University*

Some People Are More Likely to See Faces in Things

MOHEB CONSTANDI

Learning Outcomes

After reading this article, you will be able to:

- Know the name of the phenomenon where people believe they can see faces in things.
- List the personality traits which are significantly correlated with the ability to see faces in things.

Anyone can see the face of Jesus on a slice of toast, a rocky face on Mars, or a man in the moon. But although seeing nonexistent faces is generally quite common, some people may be more likely than others to experience the phenomenon: personality, sex, and emotional state may influence our tendency to perceive faces and other meaningful patterns when they don't actually exist, according to new research presented earlier this month at the 19th annual meeting of the Association for the Scientific Study of Consciousness in Paris.

This phenomenon, called pareidolia, occurs as a result of how the brain works. One area of the brain, called the right fusiform face area, is specialized to process true faces, and the same area also activates when people see a face pattern inside noise. This universal experience has led to countless photographs, a $28,000 sale of an old grilled cheese sandwich, and was famously exploited by the Swiss psychologist Hermann Rorschach to develop his inkblot test, which is still used today to gauge the mental state of psychiatric patients or examine personality traits of anyone in general.

In the new study, Norimichi Kitagawa of the NNT Communication Science Laboratory in Tokyo and his colleagues designed an experiment to test whether one's personality traits and emotional state can affect the tendency to experience pareidolia, and the characteristics of the pareidolic images that people experience might predict their personality and emotional state.

The researchers recruited 166 healthy undergraduate students and asked them to complete the Ten Item Personality Inventory and the Positive and Negative Affect Scale, questionnaires designed to assess the "big five" personality traits and emotional mood, respectively. They showed all the participants the same pattern of random dots, asking them to report whatever shapes they saw within it, and also to trace the shapes they saw onto the pattern with a pen.

They found that some of the participants had a greater tendency than others to perceive meaningful shapes in the random pattern of dots—including not only faces, but also animals and plants—and that this tendency was correlated with particular traits and moods.

Overall, those with a higher neuroticism score were more likely to experience pareidolia, as were those who reported being in a less negative mood. But that the physical characteristics of the pareidolic images they perceived was not related to the participants' personality traits or emotional states. The researchers also found that women were more likely than men to experience pareidolia.

Exactly why certain traits might make one more susceptible to pareidolia is still unclear, but Kitagawa and his colleagues propose that an evolutionary purpose may have been behind women's higher tendency for pareidolia. Females are often physically weaker than males, and this, the researchers say, may have made them more sensitive to meaningful stimuli within noise, better enabling them to detect predators in a forest.

Neurotic people tend to be less emotionally stable than others, and this, too, may make them tend to see meaningful patterns that aren't actually there. Likewise, certain moods may increase the tendency to see such patterns. "We think positive moods enhance creativity," says Kitagawa, "so people with higher positive mood scores may find more possible interpretations of the dots"

Critical Thinking

1. What are the psychological characteristics that turned out to be positive predictors of the ability to see faces in things?
2. An explanation was provided as to why gender differences exist on the ability to see faces in things? What do you think of this argument, and why?

Internet References

Pareidolia: Seeing faces in unusual places
https://www.livescience.com/25448-pareidolia.html

Pareidolia: Why we see faces in hills, the Moon and toasties
http://www.bbc.com/news/magazine-22686500

What do YOU see in these photos? If it's faces, you suffer from pareidolia...it's not a sign of madness but a well-wired brain
http://www.dailymail.co.uk/femail/article-3280816/What-photos-s-faces-suffer-facial-pareidolia.html

Article

Prepared by: R. Eric Landrum, *Boise State University*

A New Way to Trick the Brain and Beat Jet Lag

RANDY RIELAND

Learning Outcomes

After reading this article, you will be able to:

- Describe the impact of light on a person's sleep cycle.
- List different ways that our brains can be tricked.

The human brain is a remarkable, stunningly complex organ. And yet, scientists are discovering something about it that the likes of Harry Houdini and other great magicians have known for a long time—the brain can be surprisingly easy to trick.

That's because in order to be so efficient, it has evolved to create shortcuts in response to outside stimuli, such as light or sound. But those shortcuts and the consistency with which the brain follows them can also make it vulnerable to deception.

Take, for example, recent research by Stanford scientists exploring a new way to fight jet lag. For a while, researchers have known that exposure to light before taking a trip can help your body adjust to the changes in your sleep cycles that come with traveling across time zones. The most common preventive treatment involves sitting in front of bright lights for hours at a time during the day.

But the Stanford team, led by Jamie Zeitzer, an assistant professor of psychiatry and behavioral sciences, tried a different approach. First, it looked at light exposure while someone was actually sleeping, and it found that the body's circadian rhythms, which control sleep cycles, are more sensitive to light at night—even when a person's eyes are closed.

Then, the researchers wondered if the kind of light passing through the eyelids makes a difference. They recruited 39 volunteers and had them get on a regular sleep cycle for two weeks—going to bed and waking up at the same times every day. Then they brought them into a sleep lab.

They divided the participants into two groups. Once they had fallen asleep, the people in one group were given the conventional treatment—exposure to continuous light for an hour. But the others were treated with a different kind of light—quick flashes 10 seconds apart, like a strobe.

What they found the next night is that the people exposed to the flashing light felt sleepy about two hours later than they had the first evening. For those given the continuous light treatment, sleepiness was delayed by only 36 minutes.

Biological hacking

Zeitzer, who refers to this therapy as "biological hacking," says the light exposure works better at night because it fools the brain, as you fall asleep, into thinking the day is longer than it actually is. And that resets the body clock.

But why would a flashing light do this more effectively than a constant one?

According to Zeitzer, it has to do with the cells at the back of the eye, which send messages to the part of the brain that sets circadian rhythms. Those cells, he says, use the times of darkness between flashes to recover or recalibrate, and that apparently helps them be more responsive to the light when it reoccurs.

So far, he noted, most of those tested haven't had a problem sleeping through the flashing lights. In the real world, Zeitzer sees the therapy working like this: Say, you're flying across the U.S. from the West Coast to the East Coast. If you usually wake up at 8 a.m., you'd set a device to start the light flashes at 5 a.m. By the time you land, he says, your body clock should already be adjusting to East Coast time.

More tricks

Here are three other recent studies in which researchers have found how the brain can be deceived.

Don't watch what you eat: If you can't see what you're eating, you're less likely to eat as much. That's the conclusion of scientists at the University of Konstanz in Germany after asking 90 students to eat three different flavors of ice cream.

Forty were told to evaluate the taste and texture of the ice cream, and then estimate how much they had eaten and whether they would buy that ice cream. Pretty straightforward. But the other 50 were thrown a bit of a curve. They were asked to do the same taste test blindfolded.

The results, published in the journal Food Quality and Preference, suggested that those who couldn't see what they were eating estimated they had eaten almost twice as much as they actually did. They also ate less than the people without the blindfolds. Plus, they were less likely to say they would buy the ice cream.

Based on their findings, the researchers said that those who want to lose weight should try to eat with their eyes closed more often.

Beware of overthinking: A study at the University of Southern California found that if you want to develop a new habit, you should avoid thinking too much about it.

The researchers asked a group of people to watch a video that shows how to make sushi. And they determined that when people were able to watch the video over and over without any other specific instructions, they learned the sushi-making process better than those who were told to try to remember what came next.

The reason, according to researcher Jennifer Labrecque, is that habits are encoded in the brain by what's known as the procedural memory system, which doesn't involve much deliberative thinking. That's what involved when you get back on a bike. But when you plan and concentrate on learning, you engage the declarative memory system, which remembers facts and personal experiences.

When you try to use both systems at once, they can interfere with your learning, she said. You're better off not thinking too hard when you're trying to learn something new.

Is someone there?: Do you ever have that feeling where you can sense the presence of another person in the room with you when no one else is around? Well, scientists at the Swiss Federal Institute of Technology say it's likely a case of your brain perceiving something that's not there.

That's based, in part, on research done with a group of people who were blindfolded, given ear plugs and had their fingers connected to a device. The subjects were told to move the device, and when they did, a robotic arm poked them in the back. Because the poke was synchronized with their movements, the subjects' brains recognized it as something they had done to themselves.

But when the researchers caused a slight delay between when the people moved the device and when they were poked, the study participants had a different reaction. They swore that not only was someone else touching them, but that they could actually feel another person's presence. A few, in fact, found the experience so unsettling that they chose not to finish the experiment.

That strange sensation, according to the scientists, was caused by an altered perception within their brains, one that made them feel their own bodies had been replaced by someone else's presence.

Now that's creepy.

Critical Thinking

1. Can you think of another example of "biological hacking" in addition to the light exposure therapy for enhancing sleep? Explain.
2. Based on the article, what is the relationship between vision and eating? What would be the evidence-based dieting suggestion?

Internet References

Jet lag
http://thebrain.mcgill.ca/flash/i/i_11/i_11_s/i_11_s_hor/i_11_s_hor.html

Jet lagged and forgetful? It's no coincidence
http://news.berkeley.edu/2010/11/24/jetlag/

Physicists have figured out why jet lag is worse when you fly East
https://www.sciencealert.com/physicists-think-they-know-why-jet-lag-is-so-much-worse-when-you-fly-east

Article Prepared by: R. Eric Landrum, *Boise State University*

Understanding Human Perception by Human-made Illusions

Claus-Christian Carbon

Learning Outcomes

After reading this article, you will be able to:

- Describe the idea of top-down processes.
- Understand the importance of illusions in understanding the function of the human brain.

About the Veridicality of Perception

The Relationship Between Reality and Object

Sensory perception is often the most striking proof of something factual—when we perceive something, we interpret it and take it as "objective", "real." Most obviously, you can experience this with eyewitness testimonies: If an eyewitness has "seen it with the naked eye," judges, jury members and attendees take the reports of these *percepts* not only as strong evidence, but usually as fact—despite the active and biasing processes on basis of perception and memory. Indeed, it seems that there is no better, no more "proof" of something being factual knowledge than having perceived it. The assumed link between perception and physical reality is particularly strong for the visual sense—in fact, we scrutinize it only when sight conditions have been unfortunate, when people have bad vision or when we know that the eyewitness was under stress or was lacking in cognitive faculties. When people need even more proof of reality than via the naked eye, they intuitively try to touch the to-be-analyzed entity (if at all possible) in order to investigate it haptically. Feeling something by touch seems to be the ultimate perceptual experience in order for humans to speak of physical proof (Carbon and Jakesch, 2013).

We can analyze the quality of our perceptual experiences by standard methodological criteria. By doing so we can regularly find out that our perception is indeed mostly very reliable and also objective (Gregory and Gombrich, 1973)—but only if we employ standard definitions of "objective" as being consensual among different beholders. Still, even by meeting these methodological criteria, we cannot give something in evidence about physical reality. It seems that knowledge about the physical properties of objects cannot be gained by perception, so perception is neither "veridical" nor "valid" in the strict sense of the words—the properties of the "thing in itself" remain indeterminate in any empirical sense (Kant, 1787/1998). We "reliably" and "objectively" might perceive the sun going up in the morning and down in the evening; the physical relations are definitely different, as we have known at least since Nicolaus Copernicus's proposed heliocentricism—it might also be common sense that the Earth is a spheroid for most people, still the majority of people have neither perceived the Earth as spherical nor represented it like that; one reason for this is that in everyday life contexts the illusion of a plane works perfectly well to guide us in the planning and execution of our actions (Carbon, 2010b).

Limitations of the Possibility of Objective Perception

The limitations of perception are even more far reaching: our perception is not only limited when we do not have access to the thing in itself, it is very practically limited to the quality of processing and the general specifications of our perceptual system. For instance, our acoustic sense can only register and process a very narrow band of frequencies ranging from about 16

Hz–20 kHz as a young adult—this band gets narrower and narrower with increasing age. Typically, infrasonic and ultrasonic bands are just not perceivable despite being essential for other species such as elephants and bats, respectively. The perception of the environment and, consequently, the perception and representation of the world as such, is different for these species—what would be the favorite music of an elephant, which preference would a bat indicate if "honestly asked"? What does infrasonic acoustics sound and feel like? Note: infrasonic frequencies can also be perceived by humans; not acoustically in a strict sense but via vibrations—still, the resulting experiences are very different (cf. Nagel, 1974). To make such information accessible we need transformation techniques; for instance, a Geiger-Müller tube for making ionizing radiation perceivable as we have not developed any sensory system for detecting and feeling this band of extremely high frequency electromagnetic radiation.

But even if we have access to given information from the environmental world, it would be an illusion to think of "objective perception" of it—differences in perception across different individuals seem to be obvious: this is one reason for different persons having different tastes, but it is even more extreme: even within a lifetime of one person, the perceptual qualities and quantities which we can process change. Elderly people, for instance, often have yellowish corneas yielding biased color perception reducing the ability to detect and differentiate bluish color spectra. So even objectivity of perceptions in the sense of consensual experience is hardly achievable, even within one species, even within one individual—just think of fashion phenomena (Carbon, 2011a), of changes in taste (Martindale, 1990) or the so-called cycle of preferences (Carbon, 2010a)! Clearly, so-called objective perception is impossible, it is an illusion.

Illusory Construction of the World

The problem with the idea of veridical perception of the world is further intensified when taking additional perceptual phenomena, which demonstrate highly constructive qualities of our perceptual system, into account. A very prominent example of this kind is the perceptual effect which arises when any visual information which we want to process falls on the area of the retina where the so-called blind spot is located.

Interestingly, visual information that is mapped on the blind spot is not just dropped—this would be the easiest solution for the visual apparatus. It is also not rigidly interpolated, for instance, by just doubling neighbor information, but intelligently complemented by analysing the meaning and Gestalt of the context. If we, for example, are exposed to a couple of lines, the perceptual system would complement the physically non-existing information of the blind spot by a best guess heuristic how the lines are interconnected in each case, mostly yielding a very close approximation to "reality" as it uses most probable solutions. Finally, we experience clear visual information, seemingly in the same quality as the one which mirrors physical perception—in the end, the "physical perception" and the "constructed perception", are of the same quality, also because the "physical perception" is neither a depiction of physical reality, but is also constructed by top-down processes based on best guess heuristic as a kind of hypothesis testing or problem solving (Gregory, 1970).

Beside this prominent example which has become common knowledge up to now, a series of further phenomena exist where we can speak of full perceptual constructions of the world outside without any direct link to the physical realities. A very intriguing example of this kind will be described in more detail in the following: When we make fast eye movements (so-called saccades) our perceptual system is suppressed, with the result that we are functionally blind during such saccades. Actually, we do not perceive these blind moments of life although they are highly frequent and relatively long as such—actually, Rayner et al. estimated that typical fixations last about 200–250 ms and saccades last about 20–40 ms (Rayner et al., 2001), so about 10% of our time when we are awake is susceptible to such suppression effects. In accordance with other filling-in phenomena, missing data is filled up with the most plausible information: Such a process needs hypotheses about what is going on in the current situation and how the situation will evolve (Gregory, 1970, 1990). If the hypotheses are misleading because the underlying mental model of the situation and its further genesis is incorrect, we face an essential problem: what we then perceive (or fail to perceive) is incompatible with the current situation, and so will mislead our upcoming action. In most extreme cases, this could lead to fatal decisions: for instance: if the model does not construct a specific interfering object in our movement axis, we might miss information essential to changing our current trajectory resulting in a collision course. In such a constellation, we would be totally startled by the crash, as we would not have perceived the target object at all—this is not about missing an object but about entirely overlooking it due to a non-existing trace of perception.

Despite the knowledge about these characteristics of the visual system, we might doubt such processes as the mechanisms are working to so great an extent in most everyday life situations that it provides the perfect illusion of continuous, correct and super-detailed visual input. We can, however, illustrate this mechanism very easily by just observing our eye movements in a mirror: when executing fast eye movements, we cannot observe them by directly inspecting our face in the mirror—we can only perceive our fixations and the slow movements of the eyes. If we, however, film the same scene with a video camera, the whole procedure looks totally different: Now we clearly also see the fast movements; so we can directly experience the specific operation of the visual system in this respect by comparing the same scene captured by two differently working visual systems: our own, very cognitively operating, visual system and the rigidly filming video system which just catches the scene frame by frame without further processing, interpreting and tuning it.[1] We call this moment of temporary functional blindness phenomenon "saccade blindness" or "saccade suppression", which again illustrates the illusionary aspects of human perception "saccadic suppression", Bridgeman et al., 1975; "tactile suppression", Ziat et al., 2010). We can utilize this phenomena for testing interesting hypotheses on the mental representation of the visual environment: if we change details of a visual display during such functional blind phases of saccadic movements, people usually do not become aware of such changes, even if very important details, e.g., the expression of the mouth, are changed (Bohrn et al., 2010).

Illusions By Top-Down Processes

Gregory proposed that perception shows the quality of hypothesis testing and that illusions make us clear how these hypotheses are formulated and on which data they are based (Gregory, 1970). One of the key assumptions for hypothesis testing is that perception is a constructive process depending on top-down processing. Such top-down processes can be guided through knowledge gained over the years, but perception can also be guided by preformed capabilities of binding and interpreting specific forms as certain Gestalts. The strong reliance of perception on top-down processing is the essential key for assuring reliable perceptual abilities in a world full of ambiguity and incompleteness. If we read a text from an old facsimile where some of the letters have vanished or bleached out over the years, where coffee stains have covered partial information and where decay processes have turned the originally white paper into a yellowish crumbly substance, we might be very successful in reading the fragments of the text, because our perceptual system interpolates and (re-)constructs. If we know or understand the general meaning of the target text, we will even read over some passages that do not exist at all: we fill the gaps through our knowledge—we change the meaning towards what we expect.

A famous example which is often cited and shown in this realm is the so-called man-rat-illusion where an ambiguous sketch drawing is presented whose content is not clearly decipherable, but switches from showing a man to showing a rat—another popular example of this kind is the bistable picture where the interpretation flips from an old woman to a young woman an v.v.—most people interpret this example as a fascinating illusion demonstrating humans' capability of switching from one meaning to another, but the example also demonstrates an even more intriguing process: what we will perceive at first glance is mainly guided through the specific activation of our semantic network. If we have been exposed to a picture of a man before, or if we think of a man or have heard the word "man", the chance is strongly increased that our perceptual system interprets the ambiguous pattern towards a depiction of a man—if the prior experiences were more associated with a rat, a mouse or another animal of such a kind, we will, in contrast, tend to interpret the ambiguous pattern more as a rat.

So, we can literally say that we perceive what we know—if we have no prior knowledge of certain things we can even overlook important details in a pattern because we have no strong association with something meaningful. The intimate processing between sensory inputs and our semantic networks enables us to recognize familiar objects within a few milliseconds, even if they show the complexity of human faces (Locher et al., 1993; Willis and Todorov, 2006; Carbon, 2011b).

Top-down processes are powerful in schematizing and easing-up perceptual processes in the sense of compressing the "big data" of the sensory inputs towards tiny data packages with pre-categorized labels on such schematized "icons" (Carbon, 2008). Top-down processes, however, are also susceptible to characteristic fallacies or illusions due to their guided, model-based nature: When we have only a brief time slot for a snapshot of a complex scene, the scene is (if we have associations with the general meaning of the inspected scene at all) so simplified that specific details get lost in favor of the processing and interpretation of the general meaning of the whole scene.

Biederman (1981) impressively demonstrated this by exposing participants to a sketch drawing of a typical street scene where typical objects are placed in a prototypical setting, with the exception that a visible hydrant in the foreground was not positioned on the pavement *besides* a car but unusually directly *on* the car. When people were exposed to such a scene for only 150 ms, followed by a scrambled backward mask, they "re-arranged" the setting by top-down processes based on their knowledge of hydrants and their typical positions on pavements. In this specific case, people have indeed been deceived, because they report a scene which was in accordance with their

[1] There is an interesting update in technology for demonstrating this effect putting forward by one of the reviewers. If you use the 2nd camera of your smartphone (the one for shooting "selfies") or your notebook camera and you look at your depicted eyes very closely, then the delay of building up the film sequence is seemingly a bit longer than the saccadic suppression yielding the interesting effect of perceiving your own eye movements directly. Note: I have tried it out and it worked, by the way best when using older models which might take longer for building up the images. You will perceive your eye movements particular clearly when executing relatively large saccades, e.g., from the left periphery to the right and back.

knowledge but not with the assessment of the presented scene—but for everyday actions this seems unproblematic. Although you might indeed lose the link to the fine-detailed structure of a specific entity when strongly relying on top-down processes, such an endeavor works quite brilliantly in most cases as it is a best guess estimation or approximation—it works particularly well when we are running out of resources, e.g., when we are in a specific mode of being pressed for time and/or you are engaged in a series of other cognitive processes. Actually, such a mode is the standard mode in everyday life. However, even if we had the time and no other processes needed to be executed, we would not be able to adequately process the big data of the sensory input.

The whole idea of this top-down processing with schematized perception stems from F. C. Bartlett's pioneering series of experiments in a variety of domains (Bartlett, 1932). Bartlett already showed that we do not read the full information from a visual display or a narrative, but that we rely on schemata reflecting the essence of things, stories, and situations being strongly shaped by prior knowledge and its specific activation (see for a critical reflection of Bartlett's method; Carbon and Albrecht, 2012).

Perception as a Grand Illusion

Reconstructing Human Psychological Reality

There is clearly an enormous gap between the big data provided by the external world and our strictly limited capacity to process them. The gap widens even further when taking into account that we not only have to process the data but ultimately have to make clear sense of the core of the given situation. The goal is to make one (and only one) decision based on the unambiguous interpretation of this situation in order to execute an appropriate action. This very teleological way of processing needs inhibitory capabilities for competing interpretations to strictly favor one single interpretation which enables fast action without quarrelling about alternatives. In order to realize such a clear interpretation of a situation, we need a mental model of the external world which is very clear and without ambiguities and indeterminacies. Ideally, such a model is a kind of caricature of physical reality: If there is an object to be quickly detected, the figure-ground contrast, e.g., should be intensified. If we need to identify the borders of an object under unfavorable viewing conditions, it is helpful to enhance the transitions from one border to another, for instance. If we want to easily diagnose the ripeness of a fruit desired for eating, it is most helpful when color saturation is amplified for familiar kinds of fruits. Our perceptual system has exactly such capabilities of intensifying, enhancing and amplifying—the result is the generation of schematic, prototypical, sketch-like perceptions and representations. Any metaphor for perception as a kind of tool which makes photos is fully misleading because perception is much more than blueprinting: it is a cognitive process aiming at reconstructing any scene at its core.

All these "intelligent perceptual processes" can most easily be demonstrated by perceptual illusions: For instance, when we . . . observe a continuous shift from light to dark gray and from left to right, although there is no physical change in the gray value—in fact only one gray value is used for creating this region. The illusion is induced by the distribution of the peripheral gray values which indeed show a continuous shift of gray levels, although in a reverse direction. The phenomenon of simultaneous contrast helps us to make the contrast clearer; helping us to identify figure-ground relations more easily, more quickly and more securely.

A similar principle of intensifying given physical relations by the perceptual system is now known as the Chevreul-Mach bands, independently introduced by chemist Michel Eugène Chevreul (see Chevreul, 1839) and by physicist and philosopher Ernst Waldfried Josef Wenzel Mach (Mach, 1865). Via the process of lateral inhibition, luminance changes from one bar to another are exaggerated, specifically at the edges of the bars. This helps to differentiate between the different areas and to trigger edge-detection of the bars.

Constructing Human Psychological Reality

This reconstructive capability is impressive and helps us to get rid of ambiguous or indeterminate percepts. However, the power of perception is even more intriguing when we look at a related phenomenon. When we analyze perceptual illusions where entities or relations are not only enhanced in their recognizability but even entirely constructed without a physical correspondence, then we can quite rightly speak of the "active construction" of human psychological reality. A very prominent example is the Kanizsa triangle where we clearly perceive illusory contours and related Gestalts—actually, none of them exists at all in a physical sense. The illusion is so strong that we have the feeling of being able to grasp even the whole configuration.

To detect and recognize such Gestalts is very important for us. Fortunately, we are not only equipped with a cognitive mechanism helping us to perceive such Gestalts, but we also feel rewarded when having recognized them as Gestalts despite indeterminate patterns (Muth et al., 2013): in the moment of the insight for a Gestalt the now determinate pattern gains liking (the so-called "Aesthetic-Aha-effect," Muth and Carbon, 2013). The detection and recognition process adds affective value to the pattern which leads to the activation of even more cognitive energy to deal with it as it now means something to us.

Conclusions

Perceptual illusions can be seen, interpreted and used in two very different aspects: on the one hand, and this is the common property assigned to illusions, they are used to entertain people. They are a part of our everyday culture, they can kill time. On the other hand, they are often the starting point for creating insights. And insights, especially if they are based on personal experiences through elaborative processes actively, are perfect pre-conditions to increase understanding and to improve and optimize mental models (Carbon, 2010b). We can even combine both aspects to create an attractive learning context: by drawing people's attention via arousing and playful illusions, we generate attraction towards the phenomena underlying the illusions. If people get really interested, they will also invest sufficient time and cognitive energy to be able to solve an illusion or to get an idea of how the illusion works. If they arrive at a higher state of insight, they will benefit from understanding what kind of perceptual mechanism is underlying the phenomenon.

We can of course interpret perceptual illusions as malfunctions indicating the typical limits of our perceptual or cognitive system—this is probably the standard perspective on the whole area of illusions. In this view, our systems are fallible, slow, malfunctioning, and imperfect. We can, however, also interpret illusory perceptions as a sign of our incredible, highly complex and efficient capabilities of transforming sensory inputs into understanding and interpreting the current situation in a very fast way in order to generate adequate and goal-leading actions in good time (see Gregory, 2009)—this view is not yet the standard one to be found in beginners' text books and typical descriptions or non-scientific papers on illusions. By taking into account how perfectly we act in most everyday situations, we can experience the high "intelligence" of the perceptual system quite easily and intuitively. We might not own the most perfect system when we aim to reproduce the very details of a scene, but we can assess the core meaning of a complex scene.

Typical perceptual processes work so brilliantly that we can mostly act appropriately, and, very important for a biological system, we can act in response to the sensory inputs very fast—this has to be challenged by any technical, man-made system, and will always be the most important benchmark for artificial perceptual systems. Following the research and engineering program of *bionics* (Xie, 2012),where systems and processes of nature are transferred to technical products, we might be well-advised to orient our developments in the field of perception to the characteristic processing of biological perceptual systems, and their typical behavior when perceptual illusions are encountered.

Acknowledgments

This paper was strongly inspired by Richard L. Gregory's talks, texts and theories which I particularly enjoyed during the first years of my research career. The outcome of these "perceptions" changed my "perception on reality" and so on "reality" as such. I would also like to thank two anonymous reviewers who put much effort in assisting me to improve a previous version of this paper. Last but not least I want to express my gratitude to Baingio Pinna, University of Sassari, who edited the whole Research Topic together with Adam Reeves, Northeastern University, USA.

References

Bartlett, F. C. (1932). *Remembering: A Study in Experimental and Social Psychology.* Cambridge: Cambridge University Press.

Biederman, I. (1981). "On the semantics of a glance at a scene," in *Perceptual Organization*, eds M. Kubovy and J. R. Pomerantz (Hillsdale, New Jersey: Lawrence Erlbaum), 213–263.

Bohrn, I., Carbon, C. C., and Hutzler, F. (2010). Mona Lisa's smile—perception or deception? *Psychol. Sci.* 21, 378–380. doi: 10.1177/0956797610362192

Bridgeman, G., Hendry, D., and Stark, L. (1975). Failure to detect displacement of visual world during saccadic eye movements. *Vision Res.* 15, 719–722. doi: 10. 1016/0042-6989(75)90290-4

Carbon, C. C. (2008). Famous faces as icons. The illusion of being an expert in the recognition of famous faces. *Perception* 37, 801–806. doi: 10.1068/p5789

Carbon, C. C. (2010a). The cycle of preference: long-term dynamics of aesthetic appreciation. *Acta Psychol. (Amst)* 134, 233–244. doi: 10.1016/j.actpsy.2010.02.004

Carbon, C. C. (2010b). The earth is flat when personally significant experiences with the sphericity of the earth are absent. *Cognition* 116, 130–135. doi: 10. 1016/j.cognition.2010.03.009

Carbon, C. C. (2011a). Cognitive mechanisms for explaining dynamics of aesthetic appreciation. *Iperception* 2, 708–719. doi: 10.1068/i0463aap

Carbon, C. C. (2011b). The first 100 milliseconds of a face: on the microgenesis of early face processing. *Percept. Mot. Skills* 113, 859–874. doi: 10.2466/07.17.22. pms.113.6.859-874

Carbon, C. C., and Albrecht, S. (2012). Bartlett's schema theory: the unreplicated "portrait d'homme" series from 1932. *Q. J. Exp. Psychol. (Hove)* 65, 2258–2270. doi: 10.1080/17470218.2012.696121

Carbon, C. C., and Jakesch, M. (2013). A model for haptic aesthetic processing and its implications for design. *Proc. IEEE* 101, 2123–2133. doi: 10.1109/jproc.2012. 2219831

Chevreul, M.-E. (1839). *De La loi du Contraste Simultané des Couleurs et de L'assortiment des Objets Colorés: Considéré D'après cette loi Dans ses rapports avec La peinture, les Tapisseries des Gobelins, les Tapisseries de Beauvais pour meubles, les Tapis, la Mosaique, les Vitraux colorés, L'impression des étoffes, L'imprimerie, L'enluminure, La decoration des édifices, L'habillement et L'horticulture.* Paris, France: Pitois-Levrault.

Gregory, R. L. (1970). *The Intelligent Eye.* London: Weidenfeld and Nicolson.

Gregory, R. L. (1990). *Eye and Brain: The Psychology of Seeing.* 4th Edn. Princeton, N.J.: Princeton University Press.

Gregory, R. L. (2009). *Seeing Through Illusions.* Oxford: Oxford University Press.

Gregory, R. L., and Gombrich, E. H. (1973). *Illusion in Nature and Art.* London/UK: Gerald Duckworth and Company Ltd.

Kanizsa, G. (1955). Margini quasi-percettivi in campi con stimolazione omogenea. *Riv. Psicol.* 49, 7–30.

Kant, I. (1787/1998). *Kritik der Reinen Vernunft [Critique of Pure Reason].* Ham

burg: Meiner. Lingelbach, B. (2014). The barn. *Perception.* doi: 10.1068/p7743

Locher, P., Unger, R., Sociedade, P., and Wahl, J. (1993). At 1st glance: accessibility of the physical attractiveness stereotype. *Sex Roles* 28, 729–743. doi: 10. 1007/bf00289990

Mach, E. (1865). Über die wirkung der räumlichen vertheilung des lichtreizes auf die Netzhaut. *Sitzungsberichte der Mathematisch-Naturwissenschaftlichen Classe der Kaiserlichen Akademie der Wissenschaften* 52, 303–322.

Martindale, C. (1990). *The Clockwork Muse: The Predictability of Artistic Change.* New York: Basic Books.

Muth, C., and Carbon, C. C. (2013). The aesthetic aha: on the pleasure of having insights into Gestalt. *Acta Psychol. (Amst)* 144, 25–30. doi: 10.1016/j.actpsy.2013.05.001

Muth, C., Pepperell, R., and Carbon, C. C. (2013). Give me Gestalt! preference for cubist artworks revealing high detectability of objects. *Leonardo* 46, 488–489. doi: 10.1162/leon_a_00649

Nagel, T. (1974). What is it like to be a bat? *Philos. Rev.* 83, 435–450.

Rayner, K., Foorman, B. R., Perfetti, C. A., Pesetsky, D., and Seidenberg, M. S. (2001). How psychological science informs the teaching of reading. *Psychol. Sci.* 2, 31–74. doi: 10.1111/1529-1006.00004

Willis, J., and Todorov, A. (2006). First impressions: making up your mind after a 100-ms exposure to a face. *Psychol. Sci.* 17, 592–598. doi: 10.1111/j.1467-9280. 2006.01750.x

Xie, H. (2012). A study on natural bionics in product design. *Manuf. Eng. Automation* 591–593, 209–213. doi: 10.4028/www. scientific.net/amr.591.593.209

Ziat, M., Hayward, V., Chapman, C. E., Ernst, M. O., and Lenay, C. (2010). Tactile suppression of displacement. *Exp. Brain Res.* 206, 299–310. doi: 10.1007/s00221010-2407-z

Conflict of Interest Statement: The author declares that the research was conducted in the absence of any commercial or financial relationships that could be construed as a potential conflict of interest.

Received: 01 June 2014; accepted: 11 July 2014; published online: 31 July 2014.

Citation: Carbon C-C (2014) Understanding human perception by human-made illusions. Front. Hum. Neurosci. 8:566. doi: 10.3389/fnhum.2014.00566 This article was submitted to the journal Frontiers in Human Neuroscience.

Critical Thinking

1. What is the main task of human perception? Explain fully.
2. Do we read and process everything in the visual field, or do we extract key details and draw conclusions? Explain.

Internet References

Optical illusions: When your brain can't believe your eyes

http://abcnews.go.com/Health/EyeHealth/optical-illusions-eye-brain-agree/story?id=8455573

Perception and perceptual illusions

https://www.psychologytoday.com/blog/theory-knowledge/201305/perception-and-perceptual-illusions

Sensory illusions

http://www.brainfacts.org/sensing-thinking-behaving/awareness-and-attention/articles/2011/sensory-illusions/

Article

Prepared by: R. Eric Landrum, *Boise State University*

Evoking the Ineffable: The Phenomenology of Extreme Sports

Eric Brymer and Robert D. Schweitzer

Learning Outcomes

After reading this article, you will be able to:

- Articulate which type of psychological conditions and behavioral patterns are more likely for buildings antennae span earth (BASE) jumpers.
- Debate whether the motivation for extreme sports participation is for the risk-focused adrenaline or for feelings of everyday enhancement such as peace, calm, and stillness.
- Define the word ineffable.

Extreme sports refer to independent leisure activities in which a mismanaged mistake or accident would most likely result in death (Brymer, 2005). Typical activities include surfing big waves over 60-feet (20+ meter) tall; jumping from solid structures, such as bridges, cliffs, and buildings, with only a parachute (Buildings Antennae Span and Earth [BASE] jumping); climbing difficult routes on mountains and cliffs without the aid of ropes or other protection; skiing sheer cliffs; and kayaking over waterfalls 100-feet high (30+ m). Few statistics are available that focus specifically on participation rates in extreme sports. However, research in the broader action and extreme sport field suggests that while many traditional sports, such as golf and basketball, have witnessed declining participation over the past three decades, participation rates in extreme sports have grown exponentially (Howe, 1998; Pain & Pain, 2005). For example, in 1996, snowboarding was the fastest growing sport in the United States, with over 3.7 million participants (Howe, 1998). By 2002, approximately 86 million individuals were taking up some sort of action or extreme sport (Ostrowski, 2002). In 2003, approximately 30 percent of all sporting goods sold in the United States, equating to $14 billion, were extreme sports related (Liberman, 2004).

Although extreme sports are still widely assumed to be a Western pastime, there has been considerable uptake of such sports in other parts of the world. For example, in 2016, approximately 130 million people engaged in outdoor activities in China (Asia Outdoors, 2017). The Chinese mountaineering association estimated that about 50 percent of these individuals participated in more intense adventure experiences. In June 2016, the Iran Surfing Federation became the 100th member of the international surf association. In Iran, women are the surfing pioneers. These trends of increased participation in action and extreme sports are continuing (Brymer & Houge Mackenzie, 2016).

The idea that adventure sports are only for the young is also changing, as participation rates across the generations are growing. Baby boomers are enthusiastic participants of adventure sports, more generally. A survey conducted in the United Kingdom in 2015 suggested that more pensioners expressed an interest in participating in adventure and extreme sports compared with individuals between the ages of 18 and 25 years (Inghams, 2015). Extreme sports provide significant opportunities for women to participate on equal ground with men. For example, in June 2016, a British woman completed the explorer's grand slam in seven months and 19 days, breaking the previous record. The feat involved climbing the highest peaks on each continent as well as reaching the North and South Poles. She joined a handful of people who have completed the challenge in less than a year. At the time of writing, fewer than 50 people have completed all nine challenges.

Attempts to understand extreme sport participation have drawn on a range of theoretical conceptualizations. Nevertheless to date, these approaches have failed to consider what we term the ineffable or transcendental nature of the experience. Theoretical models that purport to explain motivation to participate in extreme sports include sensation seeking (Rossi & Cereatti, 1993; Slanger & Rudestam, 1997; Zarevski, Marusic, Zolotic, Bunjevac, & Vukosav, 1998; Zuckerman, 2007), psychoanalytic interpretation of unconscious motivation (Hunt, 1995, 1996; Elmes & Barry, 1999), and personality orientation with reference to a typology referred to as Type T or thrill-seeking personality (Self, Henry, Findley, & Reilly, 2007).

These models assume that participation is motivated by a need to take risks or pursue the "adrenaline buzz" (Allman, Mittlestaedt, Martin, & Goldenberg, 2009; Brymer, 2005; Delle Fave, Bassi, & Massimini, 2003; Hunt, 1995; Lambton, 2000; Olivier, 2006; Pizam, Reichel, & Uriely, 2002; Rinehart, 2000; Rossi & Cereatti, 1993; Self et al., 2007; Simon, 2002). From these perspectives, extreme sport participation is most often judged to be deviant in some way and socially unacceptable (Elmes & Barry, 1999; Hunt, 1996; Pain & Pain, 2005; Monasterio, 2007; Self et al., 2007). For example, Elmes and Barry (1999, p. 163) argued that extreme sports—in this case, high-altitude climbing—foster "the emergence of pathologically narcissistic, competitive, and regressive dynamics." Self et al. (2007) argued that extreme sports are deviant activities in which participants lack the capacity to regulate emotions and behaviors in a socially acceptable manner. Extreme sports have also been associated with drug abuse and criminal behavior. Michel, Cazenave, Delpouve, Purper-Ouakil, and LeScanff (2009) administered a battery of tests to 11 BASE jumpers and found that the BASE jumpers in the group tested consumed more illicit drugs than a control group. The authors reported that the BASE jumpers showed significantly more clinical pathological personality features from Cluster B of the *Diagnostic and Statistical Manual of Mental Disorders, Fourth Edition, Text Revision* classification compared with control participants. Finally, Ranieri (2009) has speculated that extreme sports athletes evidence personality deficits and a pathological addiction to extreme risk seeking that contributes to their involvement in these activities.

We argue that there are a number of significant problems with the risk-focused perspective we reviewed, including the fact that this perspective is simply not consonant with the experience of extreme sports participants. We challenge a number of assumptions of this perspective and popular beliefs regarding extreme sports, beginning with the mistaken assumption that all participants are young, male, and under 30 years of age. This widespread belief negates the experiences of many female athletes and participants in extreme sports over 30. Second, the extant literature challenges the risk-seeking stereotype of extreme sports enthusiasts (Brymer & Schweitzer, 2013a; Celsi, Rose, & Leigh, 1993; Soreide, Ellingsen, & Knutson, 2007; Storry, 2003). For example, researchers have found that extreme climbers were high in extraversion and emotional stability but low in neuroticism (Freixanet, 1991). Researchers have also reported that extreme BASE jumping athletes and extreme mountaineers were more curious and less fearful than the general population (Monasterio, Alamri, & Mei-Dan, 2014; Monasterio, Mulder, Frampton, & Mei-Dan, 2012). Monasterio and Brymer (in press) showed that mountaineers' scores did not differ significantly from the normative population on characteristics, such as cooperativeness, persistence, and social dependency, and that the large variation in the standard deviations across all measures was neither indicative of a discretely defined mountaineering personality profile nor a risk-taking profile.

The assumptions that have underpinned prevalent stereotypes regarding extreme sports participants have reflected not only popular misconceptions of such sports but also a lack of research on the lived experience of extreme sports participants. An exclusive theory-driven focus on risk has ensured that other salient aspects of the experience of extreme sports mostly have been ignored (Brymer, Downey, & Gray, 2009; Brymer & Oades, 2009; Brymer & Schweitzer, 2013a, 2013b, 2015; Willig, 2008). For example, Brymer et al. (2009) found that extreme sports participants develop a deep and profound relationship with the natural world, which they often described as a partnership or dance that is expressed as feeling part of nature. Participants were clear that risk taking was not a motive for participation (Brymer, 2010). Furthermore, risk-focused accounts are necessarily deficit oriented and fail to capture the potentially profound and transformational nature of the experience (Brymer, 2005; Brymer & Oades, 2009; Brymer & Schweitzer, 2013a, 2013b; Celsi et al., 1993; Wiersma, 2014; Willig, 2008).

Participation in Extreme Sports as Positive Experience

The notion that experiences associated with extreme sports can be profound and positive is gaining more widespread traction, as investigators have begun to explore the subjective experiences of extreme athletes. For example, as alluded to previously, participant descriptions of a deep connection to nature and feelings of being at one with nature also seem to enhance feelings of well-being in everyday life (Brymer & Gray, 2009, 2010; Brymer et al., 2009). Veteran skydivers report regular extraordinary experiences such as peace, calm, stillness, and altered perceptions of time and space while engaging in skydiving (Lipscombe, 1999). Extreme sport athletes also describe deep and meaningful experiences epitomized by feelings of freedom as a state of mind (Brymer & Schweitzer, 2013a, 2013b). In summary, far from the traditional risk-focused assumptions, extreme sports participation may well facilitate more positive psychological experiences and express human values such as humility, harmony, creativity, spirituality, and a vital sense of self that enriches everyday life (Brymer & Oades, 2009; Brymer & Schweitzer, 2013a, 2013b; Willig, 2008).

The current study focuses on the lived experience of extreme sport, with the goal of explicating themes that are consistent with participants' experience. To undertake such a study, we refer to nonordinary states of mind, which we refer to, in this case, as "ineffable" and "transformative." The findings thus have the potential to contribute to our understanding of the full range of human experiences and, ultimately, what it means to be human.

The Ineffable in Phenomenology

Phenomenology considers consciousness as intentional, that is, consciousness is always directed at something. We use the term *ineffable* from the Latin *ineffabilis* to refer to "that which is beyond words" to describe a particular experience or form of consciousness. In our description of ineffable aspects of extreme sport, we draw on Dienske's (2000, p. 3) phenomenological description of the ineffable, as an entity in its own right existing as an enriching experience not just as the absence of "linguistic utterance".

From a phenomenological perspective, an experience can be ineffable due to (a) a limited vocabulary, as exemplified by a young child's attempt to find the words to describe an emotion or feeling; (b) certain oppressions or taboos, such as those reportedly encountered in some religious or cultural contexts where particular experiences are incompatible with the dominant perspective; (c) a response to complexity or nuance of feeling, such as the attempt to describe experiences such as love; and (d) the experience of atmosphere (sensorial qualities available in everyday space) that surrounds our everyday life, such as the mist in the autumn morning.

However, beyond the more everyday ineffable experiences highlighted above, the ineffable is also, not uncommonly, associated with nonordinary or extraordinary human experiences (White, 1988, 1993). Such experiences are characterized by tacit rich and bodily experiences, such as the experience of unity with nature (Brymer et al., 2009). Ineffable experiences exemplified by bodily or tacit rich experiences are by definition not easy to describe; instead, words can only partially evoke the experience; to truly appreciate or fully comprehend the experience, one must arguably live the experience.

Ineffable experiences have been observed in events such as near-death experiences (Fox, 2003; Grof, 1985) and bodily activities such as sport (Murphy & White, 1978; Watson & Parker, 2015) and are often characterized by an "extension of consciousness within ordinary space–time reality" (Grof, 1993, p. 12) or "beyond space–time reality" (Grof, 1993, p. 12). In these instances, the experience is invariably described as being beyond words, embodied, invigorating, and transcendent. Time often takes on new meaning and is said to "slow down," the perceiver and perceived are described as merging, senses are enhanced, and space seems altered to include new ways of perceiving the body–space continuum (Valle, 1998; Valle & Mohs, 1998). In these cases, ineffability, as a phenomenological construct, reflects the extraordinary nature of the experience itself. At its core, the ineffable is real, important, and enriching.

Hermeneutic Phenomenology and Methodology

This article draws on findings from a larger hermeneutic phenomenological study of the extreme sport experience in an effort to better understand the relationship between the ineffable and extreme sports. In the tradition of phenomenology, the initial hermeneutic phenomenological study aimed to gain a deeper understanding of the extreme sport experience from the point of view of extreme sport participants (van Manen, 1997; Wertz, 2015). Findings in this study are particularly poignant because the larger phenomenological study did not set out to specifically explore the experience of the ineffable as an entity in its own right.

Phenomenological research seeks to illuminate the essence of an experience, as it is experienced in the lifeworld of people having the experience (Wertz, 2015). Hermeneutic phenomenology, as differentiated from other variants of this philosophical school, acknowledges that the process of gaining insights into lived experience is interpretive rather than purely descriptive (Willis, 2001). This hermeneutic process is undertaken as a means to offer insights into the experience examined, as opposed to explaining or classifying the experience.

Hermeneutic phenomenological researchers contend that although language and explicit accounts are a crucial tool in understanding experience, much of immediate experience is prereflective and thus not determined entirely or captured adequately by language (Ajjawi & Higgs, 2007). Nevertheless, the aim of hermeneutic phenomenology is to penetrate deeper, beyond the reflective interpretation of an event, to reveal the essence of an experience. As Willis (2001, p. 7) points out: "When speech, language and thought patterns generated from experiences in the world are used, they always involve an interpretive process"; however, the aim here is to try to disclose the most naive and basic interpretation that is already present but as yet is unelaborated in the lifeworld experience, a phenomenological hermeneutic.

From this position, as hermeneutic phenomenological researchers, we interpreted the accounts of extreme sports participants, who might have struggled to disclose their own experience, in an attempt to recuperate the elusive primacy of intense, even transformative extreme sport experiences. The analysis proceeded across different individuals' accounts, because what may be a trace of the inexpressible in a single interview may recur across several different accounts as participants seek to articulate a shared aspect of the phenomenon, which is not easy to render into explicit form.

The hermeneutic approach is particularly appropriate when attempting to assemble a phenomenological account of people's lived experiences, especially when this experience is studied for the first time, when a particular topic requires a fresh perspective, or when the experience is difficult to access (Cohen, Kahn, & Steeves, 2000). Rather than projecting the analysts' own biases or preconceived understandings of what is occurring, the hermeneutic phenomenological approach carefully obtains and analyzes first-hand accounts of an experience from those who have engaged with the experience. In practice, this process requires that the researcher be open to what the informant reports during the data gathering and analysis process, which requires that the researcher suspend or "bracket" previous knowledge or subjective understandings about the experience. Even though, as a researcher, we may not have personal experience with the experience investigated, phenomenological analysis often produces a rich textual description of the phenomenon that resonates with our own experiences or experiences we could conceivably have in the future (Smith, 1997; van Manen, 1990; Wertz, 2015). The current study focuses on one aspect of human experience, participation in extreme sports, and, more specifically, the experiences best captured by the term ineffable.

Method

Participants

Following ethics approval from the university of the first author, 15 extreme sport participants (10 men and 5 women aged 30–70 years) were recruited across three continents: Europe, Australia, and North America. Extreme sport participants were required to meet the inclusion criterion that they participated in "extreme sports" and they were willing to explore, through reflection, the extreme sport experience. Participants' affiliation with extreme sports included BASE jumping ($n = 4$), big-wave surfing ($n = 2$), extreme skiing ($n = 2$), waterfall kayaking ($n = 2$), extreme mountaineering ($n = 3$), and solo rope-free climbing ($n = 2$). Initially, participants were recruited through social media and the first author's network, followed by snowball sampling.

Interviews

The phenomenological approach requires that the researcher enters the project with an open mind; preexisting understandings are "bracketed" or set aside to the extent possible (Giorgi, 1997). Interviews were conducted face-to-face ($n = 13$) or by phone ($n = 2$), by the first author, at a prearranged time and place that suited the participant. Twelve of the face-to-face interviews were conducted at the participants' homes, and one participant was interviewed in a quiet, distraction-free room at the university of the first author. Although the face-to-face interviews facilitated the development of rapport, the phone interviews made it easier to make notes and draw attention to words and phrases that required deeper explication.

The interview process was guided by the question, "What is your experience of your activity?" Follow-up prompts were used to more deeply explore aspects of participants' experience. Examples of prompts were "Tell me more about . . .," "How was that for you?," and "Please elaborate." In other words, the open-ended format sought especially to encourage participants to elaborate on topics that they themselves raised in the course of answering very basic, open-ended initial questions. The open-ended, response-driven interview process is especially suitable for hermeneutical phenomenology, because the themes are explored in terms introduced by the informants themselves, not by the interviewer. Pseudonyms have been used to protect confidentiality.

Data Explication

The first stage of process of explication was undertaken by the first author and involved listening to each tape immediately following the interview (Amlani, 1998; Ettling, 1998). The second step involved repeatedly listening to and reading individual interviews and transcripts. Each individual tape/transcript was listened to, read, and thematically analyzed ideographically. All transcripts were revisited as themes became more explicit. Both formal and nonformal understandings of potential themes were continually questioned, challenged, and assessed for relevance. A series of questions checked the explication process: "What is the meaning implicit in the text as presented?" "Am I interpreting this text from a position of interference from theory or personal bias?" "What am I missing?" Interesting phrases and relevant nonverbal considerations were noted. These notes were reconsidered from a nomothetic stance in terms of potential underlying thematic phrases or meaning units (DeMares, 1998; Moustakas, 1994).

Thematic ideas that emerged were clustered into groups and further defined, giving rise to second-order themes. These second-order themes were refined and developed by both authors and considered against the original transcripts to ensure accuracy of explication. For example, we made sure that the analysis did not group concepts that participants used to make fine but important distinctions. This process of moving between the parts and the whole was repeated recursively to the point of saturation. To ensure research rigor, second-order themes were shared with participants for comments and checking to ensure that our explication reflected their experience. All participants agreed with the themes as identified and with the explication of the data as reflecting their lived experience.

Results

The following sections are organized by three themes that are presented in a hierarchical order; that is, each theme builds on the prior theme. Each theme is explicated, and direct quotes provide evidence for the emergent nature of the thematic process. The three themes are extreme sports as invigorating experience, inadequacy of words, and participants' experience as transcendence (see supplemental Table 1), themes all related to the experience of what we here term the *ineffable*.

Extreme Sports as Invigorating Experience

A significant characteristic of the extreme sport experience reflected the profound vigor associated with the activity. The term *vigor*, from the original, *invigorate*, is considered particularly apt, as it is derived from the Latin *invigorat*—which is "to give vigor to, strengthen, animate" (Donald, 1965, p. 272)—from *in*-toward and *vigorare*, which includes both "active strength" and "vital strength in animals and plants" (Donald, 1965, p. 530). An extreme skier interviewed for this study put it this way:

> It's just three hours of AAAAAARRRRR (yells out) and when I get back to the car, like that's my memory of going skiing, it's just this crazy wild ride for three hours in the day. (Nikki, extreme skier)

On further reflection, Nikki depicted the feeling as "being cool" and as if every cell was twitching and alive. An extreme surfer spent a considerable length of time considering the experience and attempting to describe how the experience made him feel invigorated:

> It's like you're just wound up and YEAH and going NO WAY you know "how did I make that" just CRRRRR! Oh mate it's just amazing what it does to you . . . like seeing something that was totally um like you'd never seen before and you cannot believe it you know like GRRRRRRR what do you do? (Aaron, big-wave surfer)

Participants typically described the experience as enhancing the way that they felt to an extent that they experienced the feeling as tapping into an aspect of themselves that was far beyond the mundane and was difficult, if not impossible, to describe. It was also typical for participants to accept that while the experience was invigorating, words were an ineffective tool. Tim, an extreme kayaker observed,

> I often dream that I'm able to take somebody else's being and put it inside my body just to let them look out through my eyes because it's such an amazing situation to be in. There's no way they could possibly understand the feelings, to feel what I'm feeling and to see what I'm seeing because you never get to see those things. It feels like being in another world.

The journey into the "other world" is better than the everyday world. The experience of sitting at the top of the waterfall is described as quiet and "totally cut off in this really artificial world" (Tim), where he readies himself to enter the other world. Priya, a BASE jumper, described the experience as an ultimate metaphor for life in which a participant is committed to experiencing life rather than "quivering on the edge." James, a mountaineer, described the experience as a life altering powerful energy, which we refer to as vigor. The invigorating experiences described signify that extreme sports enable a state of being beyond the confines of everyday life, and one that often defies adequate description.

Inadequacy of Words

Without exception, those interviewed were clear that words were inadequate tools for exploring the central elements of the extreme sport experience. A typical response was that not only could words not fully explore or describe the experience, but finding an appropriate simile was also difficult. For example, Priya, a BASE jumper, deemed that words were inadequate, as the sensations felt had no comparisons:

> There are no words, I think English is a very limited language and there are no words because it is a complete sensation. It's a sensation that's taking in all your senses and then some that you didn't know you had.

Later on in the interview, Priya returned to her description and attempted to clarify and explicate her feelings further:

> It's more of a self-discovery activity, it's more of a spiritual esoteric . . . umm . . . it's another form of expression that's so outside any normal type of activity yet you can get results from it that are so outside anything you'd expect from any normal activity.

Jenny, a mountaineer, attempted to describe the essence of the experience by likening it to sexual orgasm; however, on reflection, even this was deemed an inadequate representation. Other interview participants offered a similar response. For example, Dave, a big-wave surfer, described the extreme sport experience as more significant than the sexual orgasm. Aaron, a big-wave surfer, explored the notion of fulfillment and enjoyment only to accept that nothing else compared:

> It's just better than sex, better than any shit like that it's just very hard to describe, like I say only the guys that have done it would be able to put it into words . . . if they can.

Certain elements of the experience emerge as being beyond description, or at the very least beyond words comprising the English language. While some participants felt that perhaps it was just they who did not have the ability to verbalize the experience, the above quotes epitomized their collective experience. Metaphor emerged as the only means of expression, and thus the only vehicle for interpretation. For example, Suresh, a BASE jumper, searched for parallels to point to the essence of the experience. Suresh was adamant that the extreme sport experience could not be compared with any other single experience and that it was complex, involving a variety of characteristics. He drew on a number of metaphors including sexual orgasm and taking control of a spinning and out of control car. Nevertheless, even this mixture of metaphors was considered an inadequate representation of the essence of the extreme sport experience.

Participants' Experience of Transcendence

The extreme sport experience was described as being beyond the normal on psychological, physical, and descriptive levels. Sam, an extreme mountaineer, maintained that the experience was akin to losing himself through the action of participation. Fred, an extreme climber, described an experience whereby the essential movements required were beyond description and explanation. In particular, a climb was recalled, whereby

> to get over the bulge in the ice and I had a real weird feeling at that point . . . I felt as if I was going up onto a higher plane and I can't tell you today how I did that move but I felt something go like there was no way I was going to go back.

Sam, an extreme mountaineer, reflected on the experience as being "the call of the wild," which one can either ignore or answer. Jenny, an extreme mountaineer, spoke of connecting to a primal, animal-like state as if connecting to all animals. Priya, a BASE jumper, spoke about the power of the energy involved in the experience, an energy that comes from the environment. Jenny, an extreme mountaineer, also reported feeling a powerful energy coming from the environment as well as an instinctual element as if reacting to the environment. Sam, an extreme mountaineer, was quite clear that the only reason he participated was to satisfy a base and indescribable instinct hidden deep within.

The extreme sport experience should not be confused with the immediate aftereffects of the experience. That is, while benefits might transfer to everyday life, the essential element of the experience seems to be during the activity, most often related to the feelings of freedom and fear mentioned in previous accounts of extreme sports (Brymer & Schweitzer, 2013a, 2013b). Fred, an extreme climber, observed that "You do it because you are obviously hitting some sort of plane that you can't normally hit." Priya described experiencing time "slowing down" and an increased ability to notice detail in the environment, even while traveling at 125 miles (200 kilometers) per hour:

> On every BASE jump you experience something interesting in that your awareness of one second expands enormously. What we would normally perceive in one second is very little compared to what you perceive in one second on a BASE jump. Your mind, so you can deal with everything that you have to, slows things down so when you're doing it, it feels like it's in slow motion.

She later continued,

> When you watch it back on footage you look and go WOW, that's over in a blip (clicks fingers), but when you're doing it you know you can see the tiny little creases in the rock and different colors in the sky and you're totally aware of where your body is in space and how its moving and . . . it's very surreal.

Here, Priya describes the difference between living the experience and watching the experience, noting that perceptions of time are different in each case. What is over in a "blip" when watching herself on video was perceived as much longer when living the experience. The extreme sport experience seems to be a medium for alternative perceptions of space, time, and a clarity or augmented state of sensual awareness, which tends to enhance participants' ability to act. Time, as "normally" perceived, drops away and time is experienced as being lost or slowing. Senses grasp or take in more detail than otherwise available. Focus is opened in new or transcendent ways. Jim, a BASE jumper, differentiated this experience from other experiences that he described as "tunnel vision":

> The more experienced you become, you know your mind is clearer. I've had situations where I've had tunnel vision and it cuts your brain off as well where you can't control it, you know you've got [sensory] overload. I nearly died actually in California on one of my early jumps where I got tunnel vision.

Frank, a BASE jumper, expressed a similar perception: "I like to see the rock come by but I'm also fully aware of everything else that is going around me. It's the opposite of tunnel vision." Suresh, also a BASE jumper, put it this way:

> It's incredibly, incredibly intense and mostly because if something goes wrong in a BASE jump, you have to do something about it extremely quickly. You're at this level of alertness that you're not in a normal life. You've only got seconds to sort it out or you die.

Suresh explains how the experience facilitates an intense alertness directly linked to the need to be ready for the possibility of something going wrong. BASE jumpers often travel at speeds approaching 155 miles (250 km) per hour for perhaps only a few hundred yards (meters). If something does go wrong, if the parachute opens and twists, then there is very little time to resolve any problems. This existential readiness appears to facilitate experiences beyond those available in modern everyday life where death is rarely even considered.

Discussion

The extreme sport experience can be conceptualized as an altered state of consciousness that encompasses novel perceptions of time and enhanced human senses to process sensory experiences meaningfully (Grof, 1993). We have explicated three themes associated with extreme sports: invigorating experience, the inadequacy of words to fully capture the experience, and the experience of transcendence. Participants report that they are totally absorbed in the experience and are able to sense and experience themselves and their environment in unfamiliar ways during every moment of the experience. For example, the sense of time transcends measured time. At some point during a particular extreme sport event, beginning with the commitment to jump, climb, or paddle over the waterfall, participants metaphorically leave this world for another. During the ensuing moments, senses are enhanced and physical potentials are realized, which is often described as being like a particular animal. Participants typically describe transcending everyday human capabilities while also connecting with a self-described inner power, characterized as relaxing and peaceful. Participants experience "being powerful" in a way that feels like being "alive," as if primal elements of their being are in direct contact with a universal life force. Participants invariably describe feeling conscious or more fully aware of "nonmaterial" potentials not experienced during other parts of their lives. Experiences such as these have previously been associated with and even grouped together with mystical type or spiritual experiences (Watson & Parker, 2015). For example, mystical-type experiences resemble the experiences recounted by extreme athletes in that the former are often characterized by ineffability; a sense of loss of self and transcending the environment, the mundane senses, and the boundaries of time and space; peace and joy; and a noetic quality (see Lynn & Evans, in press).

Nevertheless, mystical experiences in a purely religious context are, by definition, more likely to encompass a sense of sacredness and the acceptance of a higher "Being" external to the self. Accordingly, although the extreme sport experience might be similar in terms of sharing certain characteristics with a religiously oriented mystical experience, the fundamental interpretation and focus regarding the two experiences differ. Further, ineffability in the context of extreme sports is often evoked through experiences that reflect what Dienske (2000) terms *bodily* or *tacit-rich knowledge* and *nonordinary experiences* rather than a lack of vocabulary or cultural limitations, which is evident in the explication of the three themes (i.e., invigorating activity, inadequacy of words, transcendence).

Each of the three themes are well captured in Dienske's definition of the ineffable. The notion of transcendence is particularly salient in capturing the idea that some experiences are potentially not able to be expressed in ordinary discourse. That is, the experience of transformation or transcendence can only exist in opposition to what phenomenologists may term a *mundane mode of being in the world*. This idea is consistent with Dienske's notion of tacit knowledge and meaning being derived from our senses. A good example of the use of such metaphor is well expressed by a participant whose only way of expressing her experience of immediacy and vitality was "it's just three hours of AAAAAARRRRR (yells out)."

Several limitations and areas for further research are important to acknowledge. Sample size is often an issue in phenomenological research. It would be useful for researchers to acquire larger samples and consider the experience of a wider group of participants to enhance the generalizability of the findings (e.g., relatively old vs. young; different ethnic groups; beginners vs. more experienced participants). Indeed, the participants in the current study might have been nonrepresentative of extreme sports athletes in that they were willing to participate in a study that involved considerable self-reflection. Our sample was necessarily constrained by language and the activities that formed the basis of the participants' experience. It would also be worthwhile to replicate the three themes identified and examine the intercorrelations among the three themes and to explore the aftereffects of extreme sports and follow participants over time, beginning with their first involvement with the sport. Future studies could address potential interview demand characteristics, and researchers would do well to develop standardized interviews with established interrater reliabilities and self-report measures with established psychometric properties to address common and unique aspects of extreme athletes' experiences across different sports.

A more general criticism of phenomenological studies is that they do not capitalize on or flow from on previous research. Although the current findings challenge previous deficit-based accounts, it would be worthy for future researchers to build on the emerging literature in the phenomenology of extreme sports and to consider how current findings can be integrated and accommodated into data-driven conceptual models that specify and predict subjective experiences during and after extreme sports and serve as heuristics for comprehensive studies. We envision a role for mixed-method controlled studies that compare participants who engage in extreme sports with individuals who participate in a range of alternative activities, such as intense exercise and yoga practices, that purport to induce mystical or ineffable experiences. Such studies could include well-standardized measures, such as the Mystical Experience Questionnaire (Barrett, Johnson, & Griffiths, 2015).

The methodology adopted in the current study as well as the topic provides us with an exemplar to study lived experience. In this instance, such experience is conceptualized as potentially representing endeavors at the extreme end of human agency, that is, making choices to engage in activity, which may, in certain circumstances, lead to death. However, such experiences have been shown to be affirmative of life and the potential for transformation. It is arguable that as humans engage increasingly with a digital reality, the yearning for a more direct relationship with nature will result in greater engaging in extreme activities such as those outlined in the current study (Brymer & Schweitzer, 2015). Future research may well benefit by combining sociology, leisure studies, and psychology to gain a more comprehensive understanding of human motivation and to utilize our understanding of extreme sport-related experiences to better understand the nature and range of experiences of modern living. Extreme sports have the potential to induce nonordinary states of consciousness that are at once powerful and meaningful. These experiences enrich the lives of participants and provide a further glimpse into what it means to be human.

Summary

We explored an aspect of the lifeworld of extreme sports participants from a phenomenological perspective. We focused on describing the ineffable element of the extreme sport experience. However, any attempt to describe the indescribable immediately reduces the intensity and power of such an experience to defined, bound verbalizations and conceptualizations. Attempts to clarify certain experiences potentially results in the experience being lost or, perhaps worse still, being obliterated in the process. A contemporary phenomenologist, van Manen (2002, p. 239) contended, "In the act of naming we cannot help but kill the things that we name." Still, beyond the world of words is a rich landscape of experiences that needs to be better grasped and explicated, as it forms an important element of the human experience—often ineffable yet enriching and meaningful—that resides outside the boundaries of the mundane.

References

Ajjawi, R., & Higgs, J. (2007). Using hermeneutic phenomenology to investigate how experienced practitioners learn to communicate clinical reasoning. *Qualitative Report, 12,* 612–638.

Allman, T. L., Mittlestaedt, R. D., Martin, B., & Goldenberg, B. (2009). Exploring the motivations of BASE jumpers: Extreme sport enthusiasts. *Journal of Sport & Tourism, 14,* 229–247. Retrieved from http://dx.doi.org/10.1080/14775080903453740

Amlani, A. (1998). Internal events and archetypes. In W. Braud & R. Anderson (Eds.), *Transpersonal research methods for the social sciences: Honoring human experience* (pp. 179–183). Thousand Oaks, CA: Sage.

Asia Outdoors. (2017). The 9th Asia Outdoor in Nanjing: The Chinese outdoor industry looks optimistic in the future. Retrieved from http://www.asian-outdoor.com/en/audience.php?about=&id=617

Barrett, F. S., Johnson, M. W., & Griffiths, R. R. (2015). Validation of the revised Mystical Experience Questionnaire in experimental sessions with psilocybin. *Journal of Psychopharmacology, 29,* 1182–1190. Retrieved from http://dx.doi.org/10.1177/0269881115609019

Brymer, E. (2005). *Extreme dude: The phenomenology of the extreme sport experience* (Unpublished doctoral thesis). University of Wollongong, Wollongong, New South Wales, Australia.

Brymer, E. (2010). Risk and extreme sports: A phenomenological perspective. *Annals of Leisure Research, 13*(1–2), 218–239. Retrieved from http://dx.doi.org/10.1080/11745398.2010.9686845

Brymer, E., Downey, G., & Gray, T. (2009). Extreme sports as a precursor to environmental sustainability. *Journal of Sport & Tourism, 14*(2–3), 193–204. Retrieved from http://dx.doi.org/10.1080/14775080902965223

Brymer, E., & Gray, T. (2009). Dancing with nature: Rhythm and harmony in extreme sport participation. *Journal of Adventure Education and Outdoor Learning, 9,* 135–149. Retrieved from http://dx.doi.org/10.1080/14729670903116912

Brymer, E., & Gray, T. (2010). Developing an intimate "relationship" with nature through extreme sports participation. *Leisure/Loisir, 34,* 361–374. Retrieved from http://dx.doi.org/10.1080/14927713.2010.542888

Brymer, E., & Houge Mackenzie, S. (2016). Psychology and the extreme sport experience. In F. Felletti (Ed.), *Extreme sports medicine* (pp. 3–13). New York, NY: Springer. Retrieved from http://dx.doi.org/10.1007/978-3-319-28265-7_1

Brymer, E., & Oades, L. (2009). Extreme sports: A positive transformation in courage and humility. *Journal of Humanistic Psychology, 49,* 114–126. Retrieved from http://dx.doi.org/10.1177/0022167808326199

Brymer, E., & Schweitzer, R. (2013a). Extreme sports are good for your health: A phenomenological understanding of fear and anxiety in extreme sport. *Journal of Health Psychology, 18,* 477–487. Retrieved from http://dx.doi.org/10.1177/1359105312446770

Brymer, E., & Schweitzer, R. (2013b). The search for freedom in extreme sports: A phenomenological exploration. *Psychology of Sport and Exercise, 14,* 865–873. Retrieved from http://dx.doi.org/10.1016/j.psychsport.2013.07.004

Brymer, E., & Schweitzer, R. (2015). Phenomenology and extreme sports in natural landscapes. In S. Gammon & S. Elkington (Eds.), *Landscapes of leisure: Space, place and identities* (pp. 135–146). Oxford, England: Palgrave Macmillan. Retrieved from http://dx.doi.org/10.1057/9781137428530_10

Celsi, R. L., Rose, R. L., & Leigh, T. W. (1993). An exploration of high-risk leisure consumption through skydiving. *Journal of Consumer Research, 20,* 1–23.

Cohen, M. Z., Kahn, D. L., & Steeves, R. H. (2000). *Hermeneutic phenomenological research: A practical guide for nurse researchers.* Thousand Oaks, CA: Sage.

Delle Fave, A., Bassi, M., & Massimini, F. (2003). Quality of experience and risk perception in high-altitude climbing. *Journal of Applied Sport Psychology, 15,* 82–98. Retrieved from http://dx.doi.org/10.1080/10413200305402

DeMares, R. (1998). Peak experiences with cetaceans: A phenomenological study (Doctoral thesis). The Union Institute Graduate College, Cincinnati, OH.

Dienske, I. (2000). Beyond words: On the experience of the ineffable. *Phenomenology + Pedagogy, 3,* 3–19.

Donald, J. (Ed.). (1965). *Chambers etymological dictionary of the English language.* Edingburgh, England: W & R Chambers Ltd., University of Edinburgh.

Elmes, M., & Barry, D. (1999). Deliverance, denial, and the Death Zone: A study of narcissism and regression in the May 1996 Everest climbing disaster. *The Journal of Applied Behavioral Science, 35,* 163–187. Retrieved from http://dx.doi.org/10.1177/0021886399352003

Ettling, D. (1998). Levels of listening. In W. Braud & R. Anderson (Eds.), *Transpersonal research methods for the social sciences: Honoring human experience* (pp. 176–179). Thousand Oaks, CA: Sage.

Fox, M. (2003). *Religion, spirituality and the near death experience.* London, UK: Routledge.

Freixanet, M. G. (1991). Personality profile of subjects engaged in high physical risk sports. *Personality and Individual Differences, 12,* 1087–1093.

Giorgi, A. (1997). The theory, practice, and evaluation of the phenomenological method as a qualitative research procedure. *Journal of Phenomenological Psychology, 28,* 235–260. Retrieved from http://dx.doi.org/10.1163/156916297X00103

Grof, S. (1985). *Beyond the brain: Birth, death and transcendence in psychotherapy.* Albany, NY: SUNY Press.

Grof, S. (1993). *The holotropic mind: The three levels of human consciousness and how they shape our lives.* New York, NY: Harper Collins.

Howe, S. (1998). *Sick: A cultural history of snowboarding.* New York, NY: St. Martin's Press.

Hunt, J. C. (1995). Divers' accounts of normal risk. *Symbolic Interaction, 18,* 439–462. Retrieved from http://dx.doi.org/10.1525/si.1995.18.4.439

Hunt, J. C. (1996). Diving the wreck: Risk and injury in sport scuba diving. *Psychoanalytic Quarterly, LXV,* 591–622. Retrieved from http://www.psychomedia.it/pm/grpind/sport/sub2.htm

Inghams. (2015). Inghams asks: Why aren't we trying something new? Retrieved from http://blog.inghams.co.uk/ski/inghams-asks-arent-trying-something-new/

Lambton, D. (2000). Extreme sports flex their muscles. *Allsport, September* (SB49), 19–22.

Liberman, N. (2004). New heights or a crash landing? *Street & Smith's Sports Business Journal, 12,* 18–25.

Lipscombe, N. (1999). The relevance of the peak experience to continued skydiving participation: A qualitative approach to assessing motivations. *Leisure Studies, 18,* 267–288. Retrieved from http://dx.doi.org/10.1080/026143699374853

Lynn, S. J., & Evans, J. (in press). Hypnotic suggestion produces mystical-type experiences in the laboratory: A demonstration proof. *Psychology of Consciousness.*

Michel, G., Cazenave, N., Delpouve, C., Purper-Ouakil, D., & LeScanff, C. (2009). Personality profiles and emotional function in extreme sports: An exploratory study among BASE-jumpers. *Annales Médico-Psychologiques, 167,* 72–77. Retrieved from http://dx.doi.org/10.1016/j.amp.2008.11.008

Monasterio, E. (2007, November 19). The risks of adventure sports/people. *The Alpinist* [Web log post]. Retrieved from http://www.alpinist.com/doc/web07f/rb-erik-monasterio-mountaineering-medicine

Monasterio, E., Alamri, Y. A., & Mei-Dan, O. (2014). Personality characteristics in a population of mountain climbers. *Wilderness & Environmental Medicine, 25,* 214–219. Retrieved from http://dx.doi.org/10.1016/j.wem.2013.12.028

Monasterio, E., & Brymer, E. (in press). The Mountaineering experience. In A. Carr, G. Musa, & J. Higham. (Eds.), *Mountain climbing tourism*: London, UK: Routledge.

Monasterio, E., Mulder, R., Frampton, C., & MeiDan, O. (2012). Personality characteristics of BASE jumpers. *Journal of Applied Sport Psychology, 24,* 391–400.

Moustakas, C. E. (1994). *Phenomenological research methods.* Thousand Oaks, CA: Sage.

Murphy, M., & White, R. A. (1978). *The psychic side of sports.* Menlo Park, CA: Addison Wesley Publishing. Retrieved from http://dx.doi.org/10.4135/9781412995658

Olivier, S. (2006). Moral dilemmas of participation in dangerous leisure activities. *Leisure Studies, 25,* 95–109. Retrieved from http://dx.doi.org/10.1080/02614360500284692

Ostrowski, J. (2002). Corporate America makes pitchmen of pariahs. *Street & Smith's Sports Business Journal, 19,* 26.

Pain, M. T. G., & Pain, M. A. (2005). Essay: Risk taking in sport. *Lancet, 366,* S33–S34. Retrieved from http://dx.doi.org/10.1016/S0140-6736(05)67838-5

Pizam, A., Reichel, A., & Uriely, N. (2002). Sensation seeking and tourist behavior. *Journal of Hospitality & Leisure Marketing, 9*(3–4), 17–33.

Ranieri, F. (2009) La quête de risques extrêmes [Extreme risk seeking]. *Psychotropes, 1,* 115–135.

Rinehart, R. (2000). Emerging arriving sports: Alternatives to formal sports. In J. Coakley & E. Dunning (Eds.), *Handbook of sports studies* (pp. 501–520). London, UK: Sage.

Rossi, B., & Cereatti, L. (1993). The sensation seeking in mountain athletes as assessed by Zuckerman's Sensation Seeking Scale. *International Journal of Sport Psychology, 24,* 417–431.

Self, D., Henry, E., Findley, C., & Reilly, E. (2007). Thrill seeking: The type T personality and extreme sports. *International Journal of Sport Management and Marketing, 2,* 175–190. Retrieved from http://dx.doi.org/10.1504/IJSMM.2007.011397

Simon, J. (2002). Taking risks: Extreme sports and the embrace of risk in advanced liberal societies. In T. Baker & J. Simon (Eds.), *Embracing risk: The changing culture of insurance and responsibility* (pp. 177–208). Chicago, IL: University of Chicago Press.

Slanger, E., & Rudestam, K. E. (1997). Motivation and disinhibition in high risk sports: Sensation seeking and self-efficacy. *Journal of Research in Personality, 31,* 355–374. Retrieved from http://dx.doi.org/10.1006/jrpe.1997.2193

Smith, D. (1997). Phenomenology: Methodology and method. In J. Higgs (Ed.), *Qualitative research: Discourse on methodologies* (pp. 75–80). Sydney, NSW: Hampden Press.

Soreide, K., Ellingsen, C., & Knutson, V. (2007). How dangerous is BASE jumping? An analysis of adverse events in 20,850 jumps from the Kjerag Massif, Norway. *Journal of Trauma-Injury Infection & Critical Care, 62,* 1113–1117.

Storry, T. (2003). Ours to reason why. *Journal of Adventure Education and Outdoor Learning, 3,* 133–143. Retrieved from http://dx.doi.org/10.1080/14729670385200321

Valle, R. (1998). Transpersonal awareness: Implications for phenomenological research. In R. Valle (Ed.), *Phenomenological inquiry: Existential and transpersonal dimensions* (pp. 273–279). New York, NY: Plenum Press. Retrieved from http://dx.doi.org/10.1007/978-1-4899-0125-5_12

Valle, R., & Mohs, M. (1998). Transpersonal awareness in phenomenological inquiry: Philosophy, reflections and recent research. In W. Braud & R. Anderson (Eds.), *Transpersonal research methods for the social sciences: Honouring human experience* (pp. 95–113). Thousand Oaks, CA: Sage.

van Manen, M. (1990). *Researching lived experience: Human science for an action sensitive pedagogy.* New York, NY: State University of New York Press.

van Manen, M. (1997). *Researching lived experience: Human science for an action sensitive pedagogy* (2nd ed.). London, Ontario, Canada: The Althouse Press.

van Manen, M. (2002). Writing in the dark. In M. van Manen (Ed.), *Writing in the dark: Phenomenological studies in interpretive inquiry* (pp. 237–253). London, Ontario, Canada: The Althouse Press.

Watson, N. J., & Parker, A. (2015). The mystical and sublime in extreme sports: Experiences of psychological well-being or Christian revelation? *Studies in World Christianity, 21,* 260–281. Retrieved from http://dx.doi.org/10.3366/swc.2015.0127

Wertz, F. J. (2015). Phenomenology: Methods, historical development, and applications in psychology. In J. Martin, J. Sugarman, & K. L. Slaney (Eds.), *The Wiley handbook of theoretical and philosophical psychology: Methods, approaches, and new directions for social sciences* (pp. 85–101). Chichester, UK: John Wiley and Sons, Ltd. Retrieved from http://dx.doi.org/10.1002/97811 18748213.ch6

White, R. A. (1988). List of potential exceptional human experiences. In R. A. White (Ed.), *Exceptional human experiences: Special issue, background papers II. The EHE Network, 1995–1998. Progress and Possibilities* (pp. 41–43). New Bern, NC: The Exceptional Human Experience Network.

White, R. A. (1993). *Exceptional human experiences as a vehicle of grace: Parapsychology, faith, and the outlier mentality.* Paper presented at the Annual Conference of the Academy of Religion and Psychical Research Proceedings.

Wiersma, L. D. (2014). A phenomenological investigation of the psychology of big-wave surfing at Maverick's. *The Sport Psychologist, 28,* 151–163. Retrieved from http://dx.doi.org/10.1123/tsp.2013-0001

Willig, C. (2008). A phenomenological investigation of the experience of taking part in 'Extreme Sports'. *Journal of Health Psychology, 13,* 690–702. Retrieved from http://dx.doi.org/10.1177/1359105307082459

Willis, P. (2001). The "Things Themselves" in phenomenology. *The Indo-Pacific Journal of Phenomenology, 1,* 1–16. Retrieved from http://dx.doi.org/10.1080/20797222.2001.11433860

Zarevski, P., Marusic, I., Zolotic, S., Bunjevac, T., & Vukosav, Z. (1998). Contribution of Arnett's Inventory of Sensation Seeking and Zuckerman's Sensation Seeking Scale to the differentiation of athletes engaged in high and low risk sports. *Personality and Individual Differences, 25,* 763–768. Retrieved from http://dx.doi.org/10.1016/S0191-8869(98)00119-6

Zuckerman, M. (2007). *Sensation seeking and risky behavior.* Washington, DC: American Psychological Association. Retrieved from http://dx.doi.org/10.1037/11555-000

Critical Thinking

1. Think about skydiving. Does that sound appealing to you? Do you think that would give you an adrenaline surge, or do you think it would be peaceful and calm? Now, think about your first skydive and your 200th skydive. What differences, if any, do you think you would feel between 1 and 200? Explain.
2. What is phenomenology? Explain this concept, as completely as you can, in your own words.

Internet References

Adrenalize Zen: What "Normal People" Can Learn from Extreme Sports

https://theconversation.com/adrenaline-zen-what-normal-people-can-learn-from-extreme-sports-72944

Jumping to Your Death? Motivations of Extreme Sports

https://www.sciencedaily.com/releases/2017/05/170509093619.htm

The Psychology of Extreme Sports: Addicts, Not Loonies

http://www.popularsocialscience.com/2012/11/05/the-psychology-of-extreme-sports-addicts-not-loonies/

The Real Adrenaline Junkies

https://www.psychologytoday.com/us/blog/in-excess/201410/the-real-adrenaline-junkies

Why Do Extreme Athletes Like Dean Potter Risk Their Lives?

http://www.latimes.com/science/sciencenow/la-sci-sn-dean-potter-risk-motivation-20150518-story.html

Brymer, Eric; Schweitzer, Robert D. "Evoking the Ineffable: The Phenomenology of Extreme Sports," *Psychology of Consciousness: Theory, Research, and Practice*, vol. 4, no. 1, 2017, 63–74.

Unit 4

UNIT Learning

Prepared by: R. Eric Landrum, *Boise State University*

Do you remember your first week of college? There were so many new buildings and so many people's names to remember. You needed to remember accurately where all your classes were as well as your professors' names. Just remembering your class schedule was problematic enough. If you lived in a residence hall, you had to remember where your building was, recall the names of individuals living on your floor, and learn how to navigate from your room to other places on campus. Did you ever think you would survive all the quizzes and tests? The material, in terms of difficulty level and amount, was perhaps more than you thought you could manage, especially compared to high school. Or, it may be that it has been many years since you took a test in high school. What a stressful time you experienced when you first came to campus! Much of what created the stress was the strain on your learning and memory systems. Indeed, most students survive just fine—and with memories, learning strategies, and their health intact.

Today, with their sophisticated experimental techniques, psychologists have identified several types of memory processes and have discovered what makes learning more efficient, so that subsequent recall and recognition are more accurate. We also have discovered that humans aren't the only organisms capable of these processes. Nearly all types of animals can learn, even if the organism is as simple as an earthworm or amoeba.

You may be surprised to learn, though, that in addition to researching memory processes and the types of learning you most often experience in school, psychologists have spent a considerable amount of time and effort studying other types of learning, particularly classical conditioning, operant conditioning, and social learning. Classical conditioning is a form of learning that governs much of our involuntary responses to stimuli, such as environmental events and our emotions. Operant conditioning centers on how the consequences of our behavior shape and otherwise influence the frequency with which those behaviors subsequently occur and the circumstances under which they take place. Most of the time, these associations are beneficial to us, but sometimes individuals develop phobias, and operant conditioning can be used to help people "unlearn" the associations that result in irrational fears. Social learning happens when we learn from watching what other people do and how others' actions change the environment—that is, we sometimes learn vicariously from observing others.

Historically, psychologists used nonhuman laboratory animals as well as human participants to study learning processes. Such research has led to many widely accepted principles of learning that appear to be universal across many species. Although nonhuman laboratory research is still a popular area of psychological inquiry, many psychologists today test and extend the application of these principles to humans under a wide array of laboratory and nonlaboratory settings. We explore these principles and their applications in the articles in this unit.

Article

Prepared by: R. Eric Landrum, *Boise State University*

You Have No Idea What Happened

MARIA KONNIKOVA

Learning Outcomes

After reading this article, you will be able to:

- Know the definition of "flashbulb memory."
- Understand the role of the hippocampus in the consolidation of memories.
- Appreciate the connection between memory accuracy and the role that eyewitness testimony plays in the legal system.

R. T. first heard about the *Challenger* explosion as she and her roommate sat watching television in their Emory University dorm room. A news flash came across the screen, shocking them both. R. T., visibly upset, raced upstairs to tell another friend the news. Then she called her parents. Two and a half years after the event, she remembered it as if it were yesterday: the TV, the terrible news, the call home. She could say with absolute certainty that that's precisely how it happened. Except, it turns out, none of what she remembered was accurate.

R. T. was a student in a class taught by Ulric Neisser, a cognitive psychologist who had begun studying memory in the seventies. Early in his career, Neisser became fascinated by the concept of flashbulb memories—the times when a shocking, emotional event seems to leave a particularly vivid imprint on the mind. William James had described such impressions, in 1890, as "so exciting emotionally as almost to leave a *scar* upon the cerebral tissues."

The day following the explosion of the *Challenger*, in January, 1986, Neisser, then a professor of cognitive psychology at Emory, and his assistant, Nicole Harsch, handed out a questionnaire about the event to the hundred and six students in their ten o'clock psychology 101 class, "Personality Development." Where were the students when they heard the news? Whom were they with? What were they doing? The professor and his assistant carefully filed the responses away.

In the fall of 1988, two and a half years later, the questionnaire was given a second time to the same students. It was then that R. T. recalled, with absolute confidence, her dorm-room experience. But when Neisser and Harsch compared the two sets of answers, they found barely any similarities. According to R. T.'s first recounting, she'd been in her religion class when she heard some students begin to talk about an explosion. She didn't know any details of what had happened, "except that it had exploded and the schoolteacher's students had all been watching, which I thought was sad." After class, she went to her room, where she watched the news on TV, by herself, and learned more about the tragedy.

R. T. was far from alone in her misplaced confidence. When the psychologists rated the accuracy of the students' recollections for things like where they were and what they were doing, the average student scored less than three on a scale of seven. A quarter scored zero. But when the students were asked about their confidence levels, with five being the highest, they averaged 4.17. Their memories were vivid, clear—and wrong. There was no relationship at all between confidence and accuracy.

At the time of the *Challenger* explosion, Elizabeth Phelps was a graduate student at Princeton University. After learning about the *Challenger* study, and other work on emotional memories, she decided to focus her career on examining the questions raised by Neisser's findings. Over the past several decades, Phelps has combined Neisser's experiential approach with the neuroscience of emotional memory to explore how such memories work, and why they work the way they do. She has been, for instance, one of the lead collaborators of an ongoing longitudinal study of memories from the attacks of 9/11, where confidence and accuracy judgments have, over the years, been complemented by a neuroscientific study of the subjects' brains as they make their memory determinations. Her hope is to understand how, exactly, emotional memories behave at all stages of the remembering process: how we encode them, how we consolidate and store them, how we retrieve them. When we met recently in her New York University lab to discuss her latest study, she told me that she has concluded that memories of emotional events do indeed differ substantially from regular memories. When it comes to the central details of the event, like that the *Challenger* exploded, they are clearer and more accurate. But when it comes to peripheral details, they are worse. And our confidence in them, while almost always strong, is often misplaced.

Within the brain, memories are formed and consolidated largely due to the help of a small seahorse-like structure called the hippocampus; damage the hippocampus, and you damage the ability to form lasting recollections. The hippocampus is located next to a small almond-shaped structure that is central to the encoding of emotion, the amygdala. Damage that, and basic responses such as fear, arousal, and excitement disappear or become muted.

A key element of emotional-memory formation is the direct line of communication between the amygdala and the visual cortex. That close connection, Phelps has shown, helps the amygdala, in a sense, tell our eyes to pay closer attention at moments of heightened emotion. So we look carefully, we study, and we stare—giving the hippocampus a richer set of inputs to work with. At these moments of arousal, the amygdala may also signal to the hippocampus that it needs to pay special attention to encoding this particular moment. These three parts of the brain work together to insure that we firmly encode memories at times of heightened arousal, which is why emotional memories are stronger and more precise than other, less striking ones. We don't really remember an uneventful day the way that we remember a fight or a first kiss. In one study, Phelps tested this notion in her lab, showing people a series of images, some provoking negative emotions, and some neutral. An hour later, she and her colleagues tested their recall for each scene. Memory for the emotional scenes was significantly higher, and the vividness of the recollection was significantly greater.

When we met, Phelps had just published her latest work, an investigation into how we retrieve emotional memories, which involved collaboration with fellow N.Y.U. neuroscientist Lila Davachi and post-doctoral student Joseph Dunsmoor. In the experiment, the results of which appeared in *Nature* in late January, a group of students was shown a series of sixty images that they had to classify as either animals or tools. All of the images—ladders, kangaroos, saws, horses—were simple and unlikely to arouse any emotion. After a short break, the students were shown a different sequence of animals and tools. This time, however, some of the pictures were paired with an electric shock to the wrist: two out of every three times you saw a tool, for instance, you would be shocked. Next, each student saw a third set of animals and tools, this time without any shocks. Finally, each student received a surprise memory test. Some got the test immediately after the third set of images, some, six hours later, and some, a day later.

What Dunsmoor, Phelps, and Davachi found came as a surprise: it wasn't just the memory of the "emotional" images (those paired with shocks) that received a boost. It was also the memory of all similar images—even those that had been presented in the beginning. That is, if you were shocked when you saw animals, your memory of the *earlier* animals was also enhanced. And, more important, the effect only emerged after six or twenty-four hours: the memory needed time to consolidate. "It turns out that emotion retroactively enhances memory," Davachi said. "Your mind selectively reaches back in time for other, similar things." That would mean, for instance, that after the *Challenger* explosion people would have had better memory for all space-related news in the prior weeks.

The finding was surprising, but also understandable. Davachi gave me an example from everyday life. A new guy starts working at your company. A week goes by, and you have a few uninteresting interactions. He seems nice enough, but you're busy and not paying particularly close attention. On Friday, in the elevator, he asks you out. Suddenly, the details of all of your prior encounters resurface and consolidate in your memory. They have retroactively gone from unremarkable to important, and your brain has adjusted accordingly. Or, in a more negative guise, if you're bitten by a dog in a new neighborhood, your memory of all the dogs that you had seen since moving there might improve.

So, if memory for events is strengthened at emotional times, why does everyone forget what they were doing when the *Challenger* exploded? While the memory of the event itself is enhanced, Phelps explains, the vividness of the memory of the central event tends to come at the expense of the details. We experience a sort of tunnel vision, discarding all the details that seem incidental to the central event.

In the same 2011 study in which Phelps showed people either emotionally negative or neutral images, she also included a second element: each scene was presented within a frame, and, from scene to scene, the color of the frames would change. When it came to the emotional images, memory of color ended up being significantly worse than memory of neutral scenes. Absent the pull of a central, important event, the students took in more peripheral details. When aroused, they blocked the minor details out.

The strength of the central memory seems to make us confident of all of the details when we should only be confident of a few. Because the shock or other negative emotion helps us to remember the animal (or the explosion), we think we also remember the color (or the call to our parents). "You just feel you know it better," Phelps says. "And even when we tell them they're mistaken people still don't buy it."

Our misplaced confidence in recalling dramatic events is troubling when we need to rely on a memory for something important—evidence in court, for instance. For now, juries tend to trust the confident witness: she knows what she saw. But that may be changing. Phelps was recently asked to sit on a committee for the National Academy of Sciences to make recommendations about eyewitness testimony in trials. After reviewing the evidence, the committee made several concrete suggestions to changes in current procedures, including "blinded" eyewitness identification (that is, the person showing potential suspects to the witness shouldn't know which suspect the witness is looking at at any given moment, to avoid giving subconscious cues), standardized instructions to witnesses, along with extensive police training in vision and memory research as it relates to eyewitness testimony, videotaped identification, expert testimony early on in trials about the issues surrounding eyewitness reliability, and early and clear jury instruction on any prior identifications (when and how prior suspects were identified, how confident the witness was at first, and the like). If the committee's conclusions are taken up, the way memory is treated may, over time, change from something unshakeable to something much less valuable to a case. "Something that is incredibly adaptive normally may not be adaptive somewhere like the courtroom," Davachi says. "The goal of memory isn't to keep the details. It's to be able to generalize from what you know so that you are more confident in acting on it." You run away from the dog that looks like the one that bit you, rather than standing around questioning how accurate your recall is.

"The implications for trusting our memories, and getting others to trust them, are huge," Phelps says. "The more we learn about emotional memory, the more we realize that we can never say what someone will or won't remember given a particular set of circumstances." The best we can do, she says, is to err on the side of caution: unless we are talking about the most central part of the recollection, assume that our confidence is misplaced. More often than not, it is.

Critical Thinking

1. With flashbulb memories, the accuracy of the memory can be quite low, but the confidence can be high. Can you think of other situations in which a college student might have over-confidence, and what might be the effect of that over-confidence?
2. After an emotional image is presented to a participant in a research session, not only are memories heightened for that image, but that event enhances memories for images presented before the key emotional image. How does that work?
3. Based on the information presented in this article, if you wanted to remember a key fact for a long time, what would be the best way to ensure your memory for that fact? Explain.

Internet References

Do you really remember where you were on 9/11?
http://www.livescience.com/15914-flashbulb-memory-september-11.html

Flashbulb memory in psychology: Definition and examples
http://study.com/academy/lesson/flashbulb-memory-in-psychology-definition-examples.html

The consistency of flashbulb memories
https://www.psychologytoday.com/blog/ulterior-motives/201506/the-consistency-flashbulb-memories

Article

Prepared by: R. Eric Landrum, *Boise State University*

A 'Learning' Attitude Helps Boost Job Search Success

SCOTT SLEEK, ALEXANDRA MICHEL, AND ANNA MIKULAK

Learning Outcomes

After reading this article, you will be able to:

- Appreciate that in some situations, stress can be helpful.
- Understand that how a person perceives the stress can be related to how the stress affects the person.
- Comprehend the benefit effect of learning from failure when continuing to persevere toward an ultimate goal.

For most jobseekers, the job hunt is no picnic—disappointment, rejection, and desperation seem to have become hallmarks of the typical job search. It's common to hear stories of job hunters who have submitted hundreds of applications before getting a single interview.

No one will argue that looking for a new job isn't stressful, but new research finds that the way people manage and channel this stress could have a big impact on their ultimate success.

Psychological scientists Serge da Motta Veiga from Lehigh University and Daniel Turban of the University of Missouri found that people who viewed their job hunt as an opportunity to learn may increase their odds of successfully landing a job.

The researchers spent 3 months tracking a group of 120 college seniors just getting ready to hit the job market for the first time. While on the search for full-time employment, students completed surveys every other week assessing their levels of stress, mood, and job search activities.

While we may tend to think of stress as [a] bad thing, that's not always the case. Given the right circumstances, a moderate amount of stress can actually help motivate people to accomplish their goals. The researchers hypothesized that an attitude focused on learning—known as a learning goal orientation (LGO)—would help jobseekers deal with rejection and stress in ways that actually helped them accomplish their goals.

While the students high in LGO were dealing with the same kind of stress as students low in LGO, they showed big differences in how they responded to stress and rejection. As expected, regardless of whether their job search was stressful and frustrating or going well, students high in LGO tended to maintain a productive job search strategy.

People lower in LGO may see a lack of progress as a sign of personal failure, tempting them to give up trying altogether. In contrast, da Motta Veiga and Turban found that people high in LGO are more likely to react to disappointment by working harder and finding new ways to tackle problems, ultimately helping them maintain the motivation necessary to succeed.

"Because individuals with higher learning goal orientation see ability as something that can be developed, they are likely to respond to adverse events with increased effort following perceived failure," da Motta Veiga and Turban write in the journal *Organizational Behavior and Human Decision Processes.*

If they felt like the job search was going well, students low in LGO tended to slack off and decrease their job search efforts. Those with a high learning focus, on the other hand, maintained or even increased the intensity of their job search when they felt like things were going well.

This study did not track the students' ultimate success in getting hired. However, previous research has demonstrated that the perseverance shown by individuals high in LGO can result in real-world payoffs in the job market.

Another study looking at 245 unemployed adult job seekers led by Gera Noordzij of Erasmus University Rotterdam found that not only did high learning orientation help people land a job, it was also something that could be effectively taught.

One group of unemployed adults received training in developing a learning-goal orientation, while another group received a standard employment training.

Rather than viewing rejection as an insurmountable problem, LGO training helped jobseekers see it as something that they could successfully learn from. This, in turn, led them to better manage stress and resulted in higher rates of reemployment compared to the comparison group.

"Job seekers, who think they can learn from failure and who are more aware of different strategies, were found to be more likely to plan job-search activities, resulting in higher probabilities to find a job," they conclude in the journal *Personnel Psychology.*

References

da Motta Veiga, S. P., & Turban, D. B. (2014). Are affect and perceived stress detrimental or beneficial to job seekers? The role of learning goal orientation in job search self-regulation. *Organizational Behavior and Human Decision Processes,* 125(2), 193–203. doi:10.1016/j.obhdp.2014.09.007

Noordzij, G., Hooft, E. A., Mierlo, H., Dam, A., & Born, M. P. (2013). The Effects of a Learning-Goal Orientation Training on Self-Regulation: A Field Experiment Among Unemployed Job Seekers. *Personnel Psychology,* 66(3), 723–755. doi: 10.1111/peps.12011

Critical Thinking

1. Under what other conditions might stress have a positive outcome? [Note that this is sometimes referred to as eustress.]
2. What are the strategies that job seekers follow when they are classified as having a high learning goal orientation (LGO)? Explain.
3. The authors claim that a learning goal orientation with regards to job searchers could be taught. What types of techniques do you think would be used in that kind of teaching-learning scenario? Why?

Internet References

A job search structured = excellent learning experience

http://www.job-hunt.org/job-search-for-new-grads/job-search-learning-experience.shtml

How to overcome job-search misery

http://money.usnews.com/money/careers/articles/2015/08/24/how-to-overcome-job-search-misery

Six steps to job search success

https://netimpact.org/careers/six-steps-to-job-search-success

Article

Prepared by: R. Eric Landrum, *Boise State University*

The Science of Learning: Five Classic Studies

TOM STAFFORD

Learning Outcomes

After reading this article, you will be able to:

- Explain one definition of a classic research article.
- Appreciate how studies in psychology's past continue to influence what we understand about human behavior today.

A few classic studies help to define the way we think about the science of learning. A classic study isn't classic just because it uncovered a new fact, but because it neatly demonstrates a profound truth about how we learn – often at the same time showing up our unjustified assumptions about how our minds work.

A classic study defines where research will go next – whether to confirm, disprove or qualify the original finding – and helps us to reorganise our learning to be more effective.

I'm a psychologist, so you won't be surprised that my choice of classic studies concern the mental processes rather than the social processes involved in learning. Other people might pick a different five studies, but these are mine.

1. Bartlett's 'War of the Ghosts'

Frederick Bartlett was a Cambridge psychologist who used a native American folk story called War of the Ghosts to show something fundamental about our memories. The story, and the research study he used it in, are related in his 1932 book Remembering.

The War of the Ghosts is a tale of two young men on a hunting expedition that goes wrong, with one of them becoming involved in a raid on another village in the company of some ghosts. The tale has some familiar elements (the men are hunting seals, they go in a canoe, at one point they hide behind a log, that sort of thing), but it also has some aspects which are, frankly, a bit unusual in western culture: ghosts, a mortal wound that doesn't hurt, and one of the men dying after "something black" comes out of his mouth.

Bartlett had people read the story and then he tested their recall over intervals varying between 15 minutes and 10 years later. He found, of course, that the longer the delay before testing, the less accurate people were. But the most important result concerned the nature of people's inaccuracies. Bartlett saw how the memory errors people made tended to focus around the unfamiliar elements. People's recall was better for things they had a good model of (such as the hunting expedition), but bad for things that they didn't have a model for (such as the ghosts or the strange wound one of the men receives). These elements got dropped, or distorted in their memories, so as to fit with reasonable expectations. The canoes became boats, for example, or the mortal wound was immediately recognised as fatal.

Bartlett's studies showed that memory is a constructive process, not something like a video recorder, but a web of associations from which accurate memories – and plausible false memories – are rebuilt as they are needed.

The moral for learning is that you can't just slot new memories in like writing files to a computer disk. You need to integrate them into what you already know, making connections between old and new information if you're going to successfully recall them.

2. Skinner's Rats and Pigeons

BF Skinner is famous as the father of behaviourism, the school of psychology known for training behaviours in pigeons and rats. To this day, the rat cage with a lever and a food pellet tray is called a Skinner box. His great achievement was to show how schedules of reinforcement, such as the delivery of food pellets to hungry rats, could condition behaviour.

Advertisement

One of Skinner's key claims was that with the right practice conditions – meaning that correct behaviour is appropriately rewarded – any task can be learned using simple associations. This means anything that can form simple associations, even a pigeon, can learn many complex tasks.

The team that, in 1995, taught pigeons to discriminate between Picasso and Monet paintings were intellectual descendants of Skinner. Like him, they believed that we underestimate the power of practice and reward in shaping behaviour. After just a few weeks' training, their pigeons could not only tell a Picasso from a Monet – indicated by pecks on a designated button – but could generalise their learning to discriminate cubist from impressionist works in general.

For a behaviourist, the moral is that even complex learning is supported by fundamental principles of association, practice and reward. It also shows that you can train a pigeon to tell a Renoir from a Matisse, but that doesn't mean it knows a lot about art.

3. Dissociable Memory Systems

We say "it's like riding a bike" precisely because this kind of memory seems different from the kinds of things we easily forget, like names. What is now indisputable is that different memories are supported by different anatomical areas of the brain.

Pioneering work led by Larry Squire showed that amnesic patients who had trouble remembering episodes of their lives had no trouble performing a new skill they had learned. Brain imaging has confirmed the basic division of labour between so-called declarative memory, aka explicit memory (facts and events), and procedural memory, aka implicit memory (habits and skills).

The neuroscience allows us to understand the frustrating fact that you have the insight into what you are learning without yet having acquired the skill, or you can have the skill without the insight. In any complex task, you'll need both. Maybe the next hundred years of the neuroscience of memory will tell us how to coordinate them.

4. Inside the Mind of the Chess Masters

Advertisement

Lab studies of learning tend to ask people to learn something new. Another approach is to take existing experts and look at how they do what they do so well.

Adriaan de Groot was a Dutch chess master as well as a psychologist. His studies of how chess experts think began the modern study of expertise. One of his findings was that chess masters have an amazing memory for patterns on the chess board – able to recall the positions of all the pieces after only a brief glance. Follow-up work showed that they only have this ability if the patterns conform to possible positions in a legal game of chess. When pieces are positioned on the board randomly, however, chess grandmasters have as poor memories as anyone else.

The result confirms the idea that knowledge is a web of associations – when you have a large existing store of knowledge it is easy to spot patterns and so remember the positions of all the pieces. This also helps us to recognise what is wrong with the idea of brain training. Our skills and memories aren't like muscles. You don't get better at remembering faces by practicing remembering digits, and even if you train to become a world-class chess master you won't necessarily develop a better memory in other areas of your life.

5. Ericsson's 10,000 Hours of Deliberate Practice

Anders Ericsson is famous for claiming that all world-class performers have in common is that they have all invested at least 10,000 in deliberate practice. Deliberate practice means effortful, structured practice focusing on reducing your failings and errors, constantly pushing yourself to improve.

Deliberate practice isn't much fun, but whether the domain is figure skating or chess, the thing that distinguished the best of the best from the runners-up was the way they had arranged their lives to prioritise practice. As well as underlining the golden rule of learning – you have to practice – Ericsson's idea also has a strong egalitarian air.

Don't worry about innate talent, just find a way to put the hours in.

No study is perfect. Even without flaws, there are caveats to how they should be applied, and distortions in how they have been interpreted, but for better or worse these studies define how psychologists think about learning.

Critical Thinking

1. What is the relationship between reading, delay until testing, and accuracy of memory?
2. How are the memories of experts different from the memories of novices? Be precise.
3. What is the relationship between practice and the development of expertise? Explain fully.

Internet References

10 psychological studies that will change what you think you know about yourself

http://www.huffingtonpost.com/2013/10/18/20-psychological-studies-_n_4098779.html

Cognitive versus stimulus-response theories of learning

https://www.ncbi.nlm.nih.gov/pmc/articles/PMC3065938/

The 25 more influential psychological experiments in history

http://www.onlinepsychologydegree.info/influential-psychological-experiments/

What is classical conditioning and why does it matter?

https://blogs.scientificamerican.com/thoughtful-animal/what-is-classical-conditioning-and-why-does-it-matter/

Article

Prepared by: R. Eric Landrum, *Boise State University*

B.F. Skinner at Harvard

GREGORY A. BRIKER

Learning Outcomes

After reading this article, you will be able to:

- Appreciate the historical significance of B.F. Skinner's significant time spent at Harvard University.
- Understand the fundamental, foundational principle of behaviorism.
- Relate the occurrence of superstitious behavior to some of Skinner's operant conditioning principles.

Long before there were grab and go lunches and weekly pub trivia nights, slot machines, and pianos filled the basement of Memorial Hall. The lucky gamblers and musicians were not students or faculty, but pigeons.

Established in 1948, the Harvard Pigeon Lab was one of the many Psychological Laboratories occupying the space below Sanders Theater. It was led by a newly tenured professor who had spent the last few years trying to create a pigeon-guided missile program for the U.S. military to use during World War II. Burrhus Frederic Skinner, known to the academic world as B.F. Skinner, would continue to experiment on pigeons, but his years at Harvard proved to be as dynamic and eclectic as his contributions to the fields of psychology and education.

Skinner's connection to Harvard began in 1928 when he enrolled in the graduate program in psychology within what was then the Department of Philosophy and Psychology. He split most of his time between Emerson Hall, where the department was located, and his house three blocks from the Yard on Harvard Street.

The path that brought Skinner to psychology was an unusual one. Jerome Kagan, Professor Emeritus of Psychology, recalled a lunch date with Skinner, in which the eminent psychologist noted, "when he was an undergraduate, he decided to be a writer because his main goal was to change the world. He had very high ambitions. He wanted to have an effect on the world and decided that writing was the best way to do it."

Everything changed for Skinner in his second half of college when, according to Kagan, "he read [John] Watson, who is the original behaviorist, and that persuaded him that if you want to change the world, becoming a psychologist was probably more effective."

Graduate school at Harvard for Skinner was an experience almost completely confined to academics. He would later write in his autobiography, "The Shaping of a Behaviorist," that "Harvard University takes little or no interest in the private lives of its graduate students," explaining that all matters of social and residential life were not of concern to the University. He would also reflect on the fact that graduate school pushed him harder than anything before, consuming nearly all of his daytime hours.

"At Harvard I entered upon the first strict regimen of my life," he wrote. "I would rise at six, study until breakfast, go to classes, laboratories, and libraries with no more than fifteen minutes unscheduled during the day, study until exactly nine o'clock at night, and go to bed. I saw no movies or plays, seldom went to concerts. I had scarcely any dates, and read only psychology and physiology."

Skinner soon became interested in behaviorism, a school of psychology more concerned with behaviors themselves than the unseen mental processes behind them. Kagan explained that behaviorism is rooted in the belief that in order to teach some behavior to an organism, "all we have to do is control the rewards, the desirable things that the animal or human wants, and punish the behaviors that we don't want. There's no mind, there are no thoughts, everything is behavior." Steven Pinker, Professor of Psychology, described behaviorism as "not a theory of psychology," but instead, "really a meta-theory or a philosophy of psychology."

While still a graduate student, Skinner invented the operant conditioning chamber, in which animals are taught certain behaviors by rewarding or punishing the animal's actions. Later known as the Skinner Box, the apparatus was instrumental in pursuing the study of operant conditioning, an alternative to the more widely studied classical conditioning à la Pavlov's dog.

Operant conditioning opened the door to a world of new theories and possibilities regarding control and learning. "What Skinner did was say, 'Well, if we really want to control behavior, we've got to control habits that are not innately biological,'" notes Kagan. "If you want to control what people do—control their aggression, control their work habits, control their study habits—that's all operant conditioning."

Skinner's years as a graduate student were spent surrounded by the giants of a field emerging as its own distinct science. He studied under professors like Henry Murray—the developer of a personality psychology called personology—and took classes alongside students like Fred Keller, who would become a renowned champion of scientific education reform. But despite contact with pioneering members of the field, Skinner largely took his own approach.

After passing his preliminary exams, Skinner all but ignored by-the-book psychology. He noted in his autobiography that upon reading through a copy of the *American Journal of Psychology,* he concluded "there must be a better way to find out what was going on in the field."

"I never learned how to read the 'literature' in psychology, and the literature remained largely unread by me," he went on to write. Even in his research ventures, he recalled working "entirely without supervision" and that "some kind of flimsy report" would usually suffice.

Nevertheless, Skinner would later reflect that in his late graduate years, "that [he] was doing exactly as [he] pleased." He received his PhD. in 1931 and remained at Harvard to do research until 1936. After over a decade of teaching at colleges in the Midwest, he came back to Cambridge in 1948 when Harvard offered him a tenured professorship. He became the Edgar Pierce Professor of Psychology in 1958, a position he maintained until his retirement in 1974.

In his faculty position at Harvard, Skinner was able to continue his research into animal behavior as well as expand to other fields, both in and out of psychology. The Pigeon Lab, set up in Skinner's first year as a professor, used birds to study behavioral principles that could be applied to humans. A *Crimson* article from 1949 observed Skinner in his element. "Skinner places his pigeons in a small closed box with a button in one wall," the article reports. "The birds must peck at this button at least once every five minutes to be paid off with food. The eager but ignorant pigeon, however, not knowing he will get the same reward with less exertion, will hammer away rapidly for great lengths of time to get his dinner." Skinner saw the experiment as providing valuable insight to the work habits and monetary incentives of human beings.

Working out of his office at the south end of Memorial Hall's basement, Skinner put forth theories on topics ranging from the superstitious tendencies of rodents to the synthesis of internal emotions and external behaviors—a field of his own that became known as radical behaviorism.

Memorial Hall was a beloved site for experimentation. Skinner and his colleagues had significant freedom in modifying the space because administrators had little concern for the building's underground level. When William James Hall was built as a new home for the Department of Psychology, Pinker said that Skinner and others "had to be dragged kicking and screaming out of the basement of Memorial Hall." Scientists, Pinker notes, "love space that you can modify yourself indefinitely."

Nonetheless, the Department managed to adapt to the move. "The 7th Floor of William James Hall was [Skinner's] empire," said Pinker. "When the elevator doors opened there were two bumper stickers that you could see. One of them said 'Think Behavior,' and the other one said 'God is a VI,' which is a very nerdy in-joke, VI being a variable interval schedule of reinforcement."

By the time Skinner retired, behaviorism began to see a decline in popularity. A shift toward cognitive elements of psychology was already underway. Kagan describes the move toward study of the brain as occurring because of both technical advances that made it easier to do cognitive imaging and the desire of psychologists to examine people's inner emotions.

"Humans think. Humans feel. Humans feel guilty if they have a bigoted thought. Operant conditioning can't explain that," he says.

Skinner also explored non-psychological fields, contributing to linguistics and philosophy through books like "Verbal Behavior" and "Beyond Freedom and Dignity". One of the fields outside of psychology that was influenced by Skinner's work is educational theory. He predicted that technology would play an increasingly greater role in the classroom, theorizing that "audio-visual aids" would come to supplement, and maybe even replace, lectures and textbooks. He developed pedagogical methods based on his conditioning theories.

Skinner's legacy at Harvard and more broadly in his discipline remains ambiguous. Many of his theories have suffered extensive criticism and even been eclipsed by modern methods. His thoughts on education and philosophy were unique but often controversial. In any case, he was arguably one of the most famous psychologists of his time, with an unmatched drive to leave a mark in some way.

"There are two kinds of scientists," says Kagan. "I call one kind hunters. Hunters win prizes. Hunters want a victory, they want to establish a fact that's reliable, unambiguous, replicable . . . They don't particularly care what the problem is." He goes on, "then there are the birdwatchers. I'm a birdwatcher. Birdwatchers fall in love with a particular domain."

This dichotomy represents, according to Kagan, "the difference between a passion about a domain and a passion to make an important discovery about anything."

"Skinner," he concludes, "was a hunter."

Critical Thinking

1. One has to be careful when thinking about the control of behavior, because in the wrong context, controlling others' behavior could be seen as more evil than good. What type of behavioral control was Skinner interested in, and why?
2. Regarding scientists, it was said that there are hunters and there are birdwatchers. Is it possible for a scientist to be both at the same time? Why or why not?
3. In his own reflections, B.F. Skinner wrote about the regimens that he would follow each day that he believed were related to his success. What are your regimens or routines for each day, and do you think those patterns are related to your successes (or failures)? Why or why not?

Internet References

B.F. Skinner: The man who taught pigeons to play ping-pong and rats to pull levers

http://www.smithsonianmag.com/science-nature/bf-skinner-the-man-who-taught-pigeons-to-play-ping-pong-and-rats-to-pull-levers-5363946/

B.F. Skinner Foundation

http://www.bfskinner.org/archives/biographical-information/

Computing in the classroom

http://harvardmagazine.com/2015/03/computing-in-the-classroom

Unit 5

UNIT

Prepared by: R. Eric Landrum, *Boise State University*

Cognitive Processes

As Reggie watches his four-month-old child, he is convinced that his baby possesses some degree of understanding of the world around her. In fact, Reggie is sure he has one of the smartest babies in the neighborhood. Although he is a proud father, he keeps his thoughts to himself so as not to alienate the parents of less capable babies.

George lives in the same neighborhood as Reggie. George doesn't have any children, but he does own two golden retrievers. Despite George's most concerted efforts, the dogs never come to him when he calls them. In fact, they have been known to run in the opposite direction on occasion. Instead of being furious, George accepts his dogs' disobedience because he is sure the dogs are just not all that bright.

Both of these scenarios illustrate important and interesting ideas about cognitive processes. In the first vignette, Reggie ascribes cognitive abilities and high intelligence to his child; in fact, Reggie perhaps ascribes too much cognitive ability to his four-month-old. On the other hand, George assumes that his dogs are not intelligent; more specifically, that the dogs are incapable of premeditated disobedience, and therefore forgives the dogs.

As you read about Reggie and his child and George and his dogs, you used many well-researched cognitive resources. You deciphered the marks on the page that we call letters and words and made sense of them. As you go through this process of comprehension, you are forming thoughts effortlessly and automatically about the meaning of what you are reading. You may think to yourself, "Reggie is really biased about his baby's intellectual abilities" or that "It's not George's dogs who lack intelligence, it is George." As you are processing this information, you are also drawing on your memories of any experiences you may have had with babies or with golden retrievers or both—although before you started reading this scenario, you probably were not thinking about babies or golden retrievers. The story tapped your long-term memory story, and your previous experiences were brought to mind.

What you are experiencing firsthand is cognition, which psychologists like to define as the mental abilities involved in the acquisition, maintenance, and use of knowledge. Cognition is critical to our survival. Of course, people think differently from one another, and psychologists report on interesting differences in cognitive development and in adult cognition.

Psychologists have also studied, and continue to study, nonhuman (animal) cognition and how it helps these creatures adapt to their unique environmental demands. You may be doing many other tasks while reading this unit, such as listening to music in the background, checking your cell phone for text messages, and chatting with your roommate. While it may feel like you are being productive, dividing your attention to complete many tasks at one time may not be as efficient as you think!

Article

Prepared by: R. Eric Landrum, *Boise State University*

Cognitive Shields

Investigating Protections against Dementia

ANDREW MERLUZZI

Learning Outcomes

After reading this article, you will be able to:

- Comprehend the scope of dementia disorders and the impact they will have culturally in the next 15 years.
- Explain the concept of cognitive reserve and how it may be able to help delay the onset of dementia.
- Understand the impact of movement for adults later in life.

Novelist Terry Pratchett once noted that because aging baby boomers will spend more years as senior citizens than any previous generation, they will "run right into the dementia firing range."

Indeed, dementia afflicts an estimated 35.6 million people across the globe, according to the World Health Organization, and that number is projected to double in the next 15 years. Pratchett himself suffers from an atypical form of Alzheimer's disease.

Unfortunately, cures for various types of dementia remain elusive, making rising life expectancies look like a curse as much as a blessing.

But psychological researchers and other scientists are closely investigating some apparent cognitive shields against age-related impairment. In doing so, they have discovered that several protective factors appear to operate even in brains that have all the molecular signs of dementia. A 2006 study from Rush University, for instance, found that about a third of post-mortem brains with telltale features of dementia—protein tangles or miniature strokes—came from people who never exhibited symptoms during life. How is it that the cellular pathologies so seemingly intertwined with Alzheimer's and other forms of dementia don't always produce illness?

According to psychological scientist Barbara B. Bendlin, Alzheimer's investigator at the University of Wisconsin–Madison, certain individuals may build buffers over their lifetimes, a phenomenon called *cognitive reserve.*

"What's interesting is that there are several protective factors against developing dementia, including higher education, and higher physical and possibly mental fitness," Bendlin explains. "Some individuals remain cognitively healthy even in the face of increasing burdens of brain pathology."

If that's true—if cognitive reserve can help protect against the onset of dementia—the next question is obvious: How do we develop more of it?

Energizing the Mind

Over the last couple of decades, researchers have found evidence that various behavioral therapies can strengthen mental buffers and help people maintain memory later in life, often at a fraction of the cost required for large-scale drug development. These therapies—cognitive training, exercise, and a healthy diet, for instance—are the same factors that ward off other chronic diseases, and psychological scientists are investigating them in earnest as a means to offset a dementia epidemic.

To date, most studies examining lifestyle factors and dementia have been retrospective and correlational, with researchers relying on participants to report how frequently they engaged in certain activities and when their symptoms began to emerge. That kind of research is valuable for tracking trends, but only a few studies have actually examined lifestyle factors in an experimental context, directly pitting one set of activities against another to see which produces the greatest cognitive benefits.

One study published in *Psychological Science* did just that, examining how actively engaging the brain can actually boost older adults' recall power.

In this experiment, Past APS Board Member Denise C. Park and colleagues at the University of Texas at Dallas randomly assigned more than 200 older adults (ages 60–90) to engage in a particular type of activity for 15 hours a week over the course of 3 months. Some participants learned skills that required significant cognitive investment, like digital photography or quilting. Other participants were asked to take part in more leisurely activities—say, listening to classical music or completing word puzzles. Park wanted these activities to mirror the types of activities people might engage in anyway, rather than using obscure memory-training tasks.

"I think it's very important to understand the types of everyday tasks or hobbies that maintain or improve cognitive health," she explains. At the end of 3 months, Park and her colleagues tested the participants' overall cognitive abilities.

As it turned out, the participants who engaged in digital photography or quilting showed a significant improvement in memory compared with those who took part in the leisure activities. Importantly, the researchers accounted for participants' overall social contact throughout the 3-month period, which allowed them to conclude that it was the psychological challenge, and not social interaction, that was critical for bolstering participants' cognitive performance.

Another recent study from the University of California, San Francisco, revealed similarly encouraging results. In this experiment, led by psychological scientists Adam Gazzaley and Joaquin A. Anguera, 16 older adults were recruited to play a videogame called "Neuroracer." In the game, participants attempted to drive a car down a virtual road, keeping constant speed and lane position. While doing so, they also had to pay attention to sporadically appearing shapes, pressing a button whenever they observed a green circle. As participants improved, the game became increasingly more challenging, ensuring that it was always difficult enough to be mentally engaging.

For comparison, another 15 participants played an easier version of the game, requiring that they drive *or* pay attention to the shapes, but not both. Fifteen more participants didn't play Neuroracer at all. After 1 month, the researchers brought all the participants back to complete several cognitive tests.

The results indicated that those who played the difficult version of Neuroracer were much better at multitasking *within* the game, and they also scored better on unrelated cognitive tests. This kind of transfer—with improvement on one task leading to a more general boost in cognitive functioning—has been notoriously elusive in studies of so-called "brain games," making the Neuroracer results particularly intriguing. Brain imaging with EEG revealed noticeable differences at the neural level: Participants who played the difficult version of the game showed more coherent activation patterns in cognitive control networks, including the prefrontal cortex.

And the benefits seemed to last: Adults who played the difficult game maintained the cognitive gains 6 months later.

Although these results are promising, it's not clear how these particular cognitive improvements would actually play out in the daily lives of older adults, much less whether they might aid in curbing full-blown dementia; larger, longitudinal experiments will be required to answer these questions. As Park points out, such studies might address a crucial gap between animal and human dementia research.

"The animal literature suggests that without continued engagement in a stimulating activity, gains for engaging in cognitive challenges are quickly lost," she says. Just like booster shots, periodically revisiting the challenging activities may be necessary to buffer against later dementia.

Still, these experiments reveal that it's never too late to challenge the mind, and that even short stints of training can produce tangible benefits.

Moving to Protect the Brain

Continuing to exercise the mind in the later years of life is important, but research suggests that physical exercise is equally critical. According to Art Kramer, APS Fellow and director of the Beckman Institute for Advanced Science and Technology at the University of Illinois at Urbana–Champaign, both the mind and brain thrive when the body is in motion.

Kramer and colleagues have designed numerous randomized experimental studies to identify the types of exercise that are most effective at boosting cognition later in life.

In one study, Kramer randomly assigned 120 older adults to either an aerobic fitness routine—about 40 minutes of brisk walking 3 days a week—or a less intense stretching routine for the same amount of time. Both groups stuck to their respective routines for about a year, and Kramer used MRI to assess any change in the structure and size of participants' brains over time.

In doing so, he and his colleagues hoped to determine whether demonstrated changes in memory map onto specific changes in the brain. That is, is there evidence for "brain reserve" that can be linked to cognitive reserve?

Their findings suggest so. Participants in the stretching group—who didn't undergo aerobic exercise over that year—showed a typical age-related decrease in volume of the hippocampus, a brain region crucially involved in memory. Participants in the aerobic group, on the other hand, exhibited *increases* in hippocampal volume, effectively offsetting 1–2 years' worth of volume loss.

Together, the findings suggest that aerobic fitness produced increased hippocampal volume, which in turn was directly related to improvements on memory tests in the walking (aerobic training) group. Because of these potential neuroprotective effects, Kramer and his coauthors stress the importance of squeezing in an exercise routine at any stage in life and especially as we age.

Other studies support these findings. Stephen Rao, professor at the Schey Center for Cognitive Neuroimaging at the Cleveland Clinic, was interested in whether exercise can grant neuroprotective effects in people who are at genetic risk for Alzheimer's. Alzheimer's is considered a heritable disease, and a variation in one particular gene, apolipoprotein E (APOE), confers an elevated risk. For this investigation, Rao and his colleagues studied about 100 older adults, many of whom carried the APOE gene. The participants explained their normal exercise habits and had their brains scanned twice over a period of 18 months.

By comparing the first and second brain scans, Rao and his colleagues found evidence suggesting that exercise was critically important for the at-risk group: People with the APOE gene who didn't routinely exercise exhibited about a 3 percent decrease in hippocampal volume over time. By contrast, those carrying the gene who did incorporate exercise into their lives—more than 15 minutes of moderate exercise at least 3 days a week—didn't show any decreases in hippocampal volume. People without the risk gene did not show a decrease in hippocampal volume, whether they were sedentary or exercised regularly. This finding suggests that the neuroprotective effects of exercise may be specific to persons at risk for Alzheimer's.

Although the study doesn't point to a specific mechanism linking exercise and brain volume, Rao and colleagues have some hypotheses: for example, staying active might reduce inflammation in the brain and promote neuronal growth in the hippocampus, effectively building up cognitive reserve *and* brain reserve in people at risk for developing Alzheimer's.

The Language Buffer

Although studies have identified the hippocampus as one area of the brain linked with cognitive reserve and brain reserve, other studies suggest an important role for networks involved in executive control. Investigations of bilingual people have shown that the networks we use for language—and the executive control required for learning new languages—are the same networks that seem to deteriorate with dementia.

The first hints that bilingualism might promote cognitive reserve came from epidemiological research. Two investigations led by APS Fellow Ellen Bialystok and APS William James Fellow Fergus I. M. Craik, psychological scientists from the Rotman Research Institute at Baycrest, Canada, indicated that older adults who regularly used at least two languages for most of their lives were, on average, diagnosed with dementia 4 years later than their monolingual counterparts. And that held true even when the researchers accounted for potentially related factors like education, cognitive skills, occupation history, and immigration status.

Bialystok and Craik believe that because using two languages requires the recruitment of many higher order cognitive abilities, bilingualism may delay dementia in the same ways as other cognitive challenges. The ability to learn diverse grammatical rules, suppress one language in favor of another, and quickly switch sentence styles is difficult, and difficult tasks have the potential to strengthen cognitive reserve.

Several dementia-research studies have provided neural evidence in support of the protective effects of bilingualism. In one investigation, Tom Schweizer from the University of Toronto, Canada, used CT scans to measure brain atrophy in 40 older adults with probable Alzheimer's disease, some of whom were bilingual and some of whom were monolingual. Crucially, the researchers ensured that both groups exhibited the same level of dementia symptoms; that way, any differences in the brain could not be accounted for by dementia severity.

Compared to monolingual individuals, patients who spoke two languages exhibited more atrophy in regions most associated with Alzheimer's disease decline.

These findings may seem paradoxical at first blush, but they are actually directly predicted by the cognitive reserve hypothesis.

As Schweizer and colleagues hypothesized, a lifetime of speaking two languages may build stronger shields *against* the effects of brain atrophy—which may explain why bilinguals' symptoms of dementia weren't worse than their monolingual counterparts, despite the greater degree of atrophy. In effect, it's as if the bilingual individuals were cognitively "younger" than one would predict by simply looking at the deterioration in their brains.

In another recent study, Gigi Luk of Harvard University, along with Craik, Bialystok, and Cheryl Grady of the University of Toronto, discovered that bilingual older adults had more robust white matter tracts than did monolingual participants. This suggests that the myelin on axons in these nerve bundles is more intact (less degraded), which would help to maintain efficient transmission of nerve signals. Ultimately, preservation of white matter among bilinguals may help to buffer against age-related changes in the size and structure of critical areas of the brain.

Mark Antoniou, a psychological scientist from the Chinese University of Hong Kong, is especially convinced by these findings and has suggested that language training later in life might be a useful method for reducing rates of dementia.

"The end result of foreign language learning may be that language function is promoted, the integrity of brain structures involved is maintained, and a greater number of potential neural circuits could be available that allow for compensation of age-related cognitive declines," write Antoniou and his colleagues.

Just as with physical exercise and other cognitive training techniques, however, moving from principle to practice is not so straightforward.

"Motivation also plays a larger role in determining language-learning success in older adults," Antoniou suggests. "Therefore, it is crucial to identify the optimal learning method for older learners, namely by ensuring that older learners are motivated, that the material has immediate practical value, and is personally rewarding."

From Cortex to Community

The results of these studies are exciting, but translating the science of cognitive reserve into healthier people is another problem entirely.

Research has shown, for example, that although people may have a vague understanding that they can shield themselves against age-related memory decline, they're fuzzy on the details. Funded by the US Centers for Disease Control, a collaborative research effort among nine universities found that most people recognize the link between exercise and cognitive health, but they're unsure about how much exercise they should be getting and what types of exercise are most effective. That is, they have difficulty translating what they *should* do into actual healthy actions.

Kristen Felten, a social worker and dementia specialist in the Wisconsin Department of Health Services, believes fixing this problem is of paramount importance.

"You can have a good quality of life, you can mitigate the symptoms of the disease, you can affect the trajectory of its progression with lifestyle changes," Felten explains. "Often, people don't realize they can take control."

As the research suggests, it's crucial that early symptoms be taken seriously. Some symptoms simply reflect the quotidian annoyances of an aging brain, but, in other cases, they may be early signs of dementia.

And this issue underlies perhaps the most critical policy measure societies can take: early dementia screening. Studies have shown that detecting signs of cognitive impairment early and targeting intervention programs appropriately can provide significant government savings in the long run. Furthermore, it can reduce the time patients spend in severe stages of the illness, leading to reduced emotional stress for families.

To address these dementia challenges, state and local authorities are beginning to develop strategic plans using the most recent scientific evidence. In her home state of Wisconsin, Felten has worked tirelessly to construct a systematic response to what is most certainly a large-scale problem, including building public awareness campaigns, disseminating evidence-based educational materials, and conducting outreach with rural and minority populations.

Perhaps most importantly, Felten and others are developing "dementia-capable" communities.

"We work with local businesses, grocery stores, pharmacies, banks, and restaurants—anywhere someone with dementia might go as part of their daily life," she says. "It's important that older individuals stay socially active and engaged, and communities need to be ready and willing to have that happen."

These opportunities for community engagement, she adds, may promote cognitive reserve.

Helping people make lifestyle changes that boost cognitive reserve is an important component of addressing the dementia epidemic, but there is no magic bullet. Invariably, there will be people who exercise, stay mentally fit, and keep an eye out for the early symptoms, but still develop dementia. These cases reinforce the notion that the onset of cognitive impairment is governed by a complex mix of biological and environmental risks, and there is much about the ailment that scientists don't yet know. Detaching dementia from aging will be an important part of ensuring that well-being increases alongside human longevity.

References and Further Reading

Anguera, J. A., Boccanfuso, J., Rintoul, J. L., Al-Hashimi, O., Faraji, F., Janowich, J., . . . Gazzaley, A. (2013). Video game training enhances cognitive control in older adults. *Nature, 501,* 97–101. doi: 10.1038/nature12486

Antoniou, M., Gunasekera, G. M., & Wong, P. (2013). Foreign language training as cognitive therapy for age-related cognitive decline: A hypothesis for future research. *Neuroscience & Biobehavioral Reviews, 37,* 2689–2698. doi: 10.1016/j.neubiorev.2013.09.004

Barnett, J. H., Lewis, L., Blackwell, A. D., & Taylor, M. (2014). Early intervention in Alzheimer's disease: A health economic study of the effects of diagnostic timing. *BMC Neurology, 14,* 101. doi: 10.1186/1471-2377-14-101

Bennett, D. A., Schneider, J. A., Arvanitakis, Z., Kelly, J. F., Aggarwal, N. T., Shah, R. C., & Wilson, R. S. (2006). Neuropathology of older persons without cognitive impairment from two community-based studies. *Neurology, 66,* 1837–1844. doi: 10.1212/01.wnl.0000219668.47116.e6

Bialystok, E., Craik, F. I. M., & Freedman, M. (2007). Bilingualism as a protection against the onset of symptoms of dementia. *Neuropsychologia, 45,* 459–464. doi: 10.1016/j.neuropsychologia.2006.10.009

Centers for Disease Control and Prevention. (2009). *What is a healthy brain? New research explores perceptions of cognitive health among diverse older adults.* Retrieved January 6, 2015 from http://www.cdc.gov/aging/pdf/perceptions_of_cog_hlth_factsheet.pdf

Craik, F. I. M., Bialystok, E., & Freedman, M. (2010). Delaying the onset of Alzheimer's disease: Bilingualism as a form of cognitive reserve. *Neurology, 75,* 1726–1729. doi: 10.1212/WNL.0b013e3181fc2a1c

Erickson, K. I., Voss, M. W., Prakash, R. S., Basek, C., Szabo, A., Chaddock, L. . . . Kramer, A. F. (2011). Exercise training increases size of hippocampus and improves memory. *Proceedings of the National Academy of Sciences, USA, 108,* 3017–3022. doi: 10.1073/pnas.1015950108

Luk, G., Bialystok, E., Craik, F. I., & Grady, C. L. (2011). Lifelong bilingualism maintains white matter integrity in older adults. *Journal of Neuroscience, 31,* 16808–16813. doi: 10.1523/JNEUROSCI.4563-11.2011

Park, D. C., Lodi-Smith, J., Drew, L., Haber, S., Hebrank, A., Bischof, G. N., & Aamodt, W. (2013). The impact of sustained engagement on cognitive function in older adults. *Psychological Science, 25,* 103–112. doi: 10.1177/0956797613499592

Schweizer, T. A., Ware, J., Fischer, C., Craik, F. I. M., & Bialystok, E. (2012). Bilingualism as a contributor to cognitive reserve: Evidence from brain atrophy in Alzheimer's disease. *Cortex, 48,* 991–996. doi: 10.1016/j.cortex.2011.04.009

Smith, J. C., Nielson, K. A., Woodard, J. L., Seidenberg, M., Durgerian, S., Hazlett, K. E., . . . Rao, S. M. (2014). Physical activity reduces hippocampal atrophy in elders at genetic risk for Alzheimer's disease. *Frontiers in Aging Neuroscience, 6.* doi: 10.3389/fnagi.2014.00061

Critical Thinking

1. Was cognitive performance improved more by psychological challenge or social interaction; and what is the explanation for the pattern of results that emerged?
2. Translate this sentence so that a five-year-old would understand the concepts: "Without continued engagement in a stimulating activity, gains for engaging in cognitive challenges are quickly lost."
3. It seems that exercise is critical for older adults, especially those at risk for different types of dementia. Using psychological principles, how might you design an exercise program for older adults that encourages consistent aerobic exercise?

Internet References

A life-course study of cognitive reserve in dementia—from childhood to old age

http://www.sciencedirect.com/science/article/pii/S1064748115000822

Cognitive reserve and Alzheimer's disease

http://www.crisisprevention.com/Blog/August-2010/Cognitive-Reserve-and-Alzheimer-s-Disease

Cognitive reserve: The first line of defense against dementia

https://www.agingcare.com/Articles/cognitive-reserve-avoid-dementia-symptoms-150033.htm

Article

Prepared by: R. Eric Landrum, *Boise State University*

Getting a Scientific Message across Means Taking Human Nature into Account

ROSE HENDRICKS

Learning Outcomes

After reading this article, you will be able to:

- Understand the benefits of communicating scientific knowledge to the public.
- Articulate the idea of cognitive dissonance and explain how humans resolve this dissonance through confirmation bias.
- Appreciate how framing and metaphors can substantially change our perceptions of a problem to be solved or a scenario to be considered.

We humans have collectively accumulated a lot of science knowledge. We've developed vaccines that can eradicate some of the most devastating diseases. We've engineered bridges and cities and the Internet. We've created massive metal vehicles that rise tens of thousands of feet and then safely set down on the other side of the globe. And this is just the tip of the iceberg (which, by the way, we've discovered is melting). While this shared knowledge is impressive, it's not distributed evenly. Not even close. There are too many important issues that science has reached a consensus on that the public has not.

Scientists and the media need to communicate more science and communicate it better. Good communication ensures that scientific progress benefits society, bolsters democracy, weakens the potency of fake news and misinformation, and fulfills researchers' responsibility to engage with the public. Such beliefs have motivated training programs, workshops, and a research agenda from the National Academies of Science, Engineering, and Medicine on learning more about science communication. A resounding question remains for science communicators: What can we do better?

A common intuition is that the main goal of science communication is to present facts; once people encounter those facts, they will think and behave accordingly. The National Academies' recent report refers to this as the "deficit model."

But in reality, just knowing facts doesn't necessarily guarantee that one's opinions and behaviors will be consistent with them. For example, many people "know" that recycling is beneficial but still throw plastic bottles in the trash. Or they read an online article by a scientist about the necessity of vaccines, but leave comments expressing outrage that doctors are trying to further a pro-vaccine agenda. Convincing people that scientific evidence has merit and should guide behavior may be the greatest science communication challenge, particularly in our "post-truth" era.

Luckily, we know a lot about human psychology—how people perceive, reason, and learn about the world—and many lessons from psychology can be applied to science communication endeavors.

Consider Human Nature

Regardless of your religious affiliation, imagine that you've always learned that God created human beings just as we are today. Your parents, teachers, and books all told you so. You've also noticed throughout your life that science is pretty useful—you especially love heating up a frozen dinner in the microwave while browsing Snapchat on your iPhone.

One day you read that scientists have evidence for human evolution. You feel uncomfortable: Were your parents, teachers, and books wrong about where people originally came from? Are these scientists wrong? You experience cognitive dissonance—the uneasiness that results from entertaining two conflicting ideas.

Psychologist Leon Festinger first articulated the theory of cognitive dissonance in 1957, noting that it's human nature to be uncomfortable with maintaining two conflicting beliefs at the same time. That discomfort leads us to try to reconcile the competing ideas we come across. Regardless of political leaning, we're hesitant to accept new information that contradicts our existing worldviews.

One way we subconsciously avoid cognitive dissonance is through confirmation bias—a tendency to seek information that confirms what we already believe and discard information that doesn't.

This human tendency was first exposed by psychologist Peter Wason in the 1960s in a simple logic experiment. He found that people tend to seek confirmatory information and avoid information that would potentially disprove their beliefs.

The concept of confirmation bias scales up to larger issues, too. For example, psychologists John Cook and Stephan Lewandowsky asked people about their beliefs concerning global warming and then gave them information stating that 97 percent of scientists agree that human activity causes climate change. The researchers measured whether the information about the scientific consensus influenced people's beliefs about global warming.

Those who initially opposed the idea of human-caused global warming became even less accepting after reading about the scientific consensus on the issue. People who had already believed that human actions cause global warming supported their position even more strongly after learning about the scientific consensus. Presenting these participants with factual information ended up further polarizing their views, strengthening everyone's resolve in their initial positions. It was a case of confirmation bias at work: new information consistent with prior beliefs strengthened those beliefs; new information conflicting with existing beliefs led people to discredit the message as a way to hold on to their original position.

Overcoming Cognitive Biases

How can science communicators share their messages in a way that leads people to change their beliefs and actions about important science issues, given our natural cognitive biases?

The first step is to acknowledge that every audience has preexisting beliefs about the world. Expect those beliefs to color the way they receive your message. Anticipate that people will accept information that is consistent with their prior beliefs and discredit information that is not.

Then, focus on framing. No message can contain all the information available on a topic, so any communication will emphasize some aspects while downplaying others. While it's unhelpful to cherry-pick and present only evidence in your favor—which can backfire anyway—it is helpful to focus on what an audience cares about.

For example, these University of California researchers point out that the idea of climate change causing rising sea levels may not alarm an inland farmer dealing with drought as much as it does someone living on the coast. Referring to the impact our actions today may have for our grandchildren might be more compelling to those who actually have grandchildren than to those who don't. By anticipating what an audience believes and what's important to them, communicators can choose more effective frames for their messages—focusing on the most compelling aspects of the issue for their audience and presenting it in a way the audience can identify with.

In addition to the ideas expressed in a frame, the specific words used matter. Psychologists Amos Tversky and Daniel Kahneman first showed when numerical information is presented in different ways, people think about it differently. Here's an example from their 1981 study:

> Imagine that the U.S. is preparing for the outbreak of an unusual Asian disease, which is expected to kill 600 people. Two alternative programs to combat the disease have been proposed. Assume that the exact scientific estimate of the consequences of the programs are as follows: If Program A is adopted, 200 people will be saved. If Program B is adopted, there is ⅓ probability that 600 people will be saved and ⅔ probability that no people will be saved.

Both programs have an expected value of 200 lives saved. But 72 percent of participants chose Program A. We reason about mathematically equivalent options differently when they're framed differently: our intuitions are often not consistent with probabilities and other math concepts.

Metaphors can also act as linguistic frames. Psychologists Paul Thibodeau and Lera Boroditsky found that people who read that crime is a beast proposed different solutions than those who read that crime is a virus—even if they had no memory of reading the metaphor. The metaphors guided people's reasoning, encouraging them to transfer solutions they'd propose for real beasts (cage them) or viruses (find the source) to dealing with crime (harsher law enforcement or more social programs).

The words we use to package our ideas can drastically influence how people think about those ideas.

What's Next?

We have a lot to learn. Quantitative research on the efficacy of science communication strategies is in its infancy but becoming an increasing priority. As we continue to untangle more about what works and why, it's important for science communicators to be conscious of the biases they and their audiences bring to their exchanges and the frames they select to share their messages.

Critical Thinking

1. Given the importance of clear communication and how those communications can be manipulated, what steps will you take as a consumer of scientific information to be certain that the information you choose to believe is as true and factual as possible? Be specific.
2. Cognitive dissonance is experienced when a highly intelligent person who understands the dangers of cigarette smoking (attitudes and beliefs) chooses to smoke anyway (behavior). According to cognitive dissonance theory, the dissonance needs to be resolved. Explain at least two methods by which this specific dissonance could be resolved.

Internet References

Fake News, Lies, and Propaganda: How to Sort Fact from Fiction
https://guides.lib.umich.edu/c.php?g=637508&p=4484724

This Article Won't Change Your Mind
https://www.theatlantic.com/science/archive/2017/03/this-article-wont-change-your-mind/519093/

Why Fake News Is So Darn Shareable and Facts Are So Hard to Believe
https://medium.com/s/news-is-breaking/trust-in-news-3c9afc15d3a1

Why Our Brains Love Fake News—and How We Can Resist It
https://www.nyu.edu/about/news-publications/news/2018/june/jay-van-bavel-on-fake-news.html

Unit 6

UNIT

Prepared by: R. Eric Landrum, *Boise State University*

Emotion and Motivation

Jasmine's sister was a working mother who always reminded Jasmine about how exciting life on the road was as a sales representative. Jasmine stayed home because she wanted to take care of her children, two-year-old Jessica, four-year-old Kristen, and newborn Jade. One day, Jasmine was having a difficult time with the children. The baby, Jade, had been crying all day from colic. The other two children had been bickering over their toys. Jasmine, realizing that it was already 5:15 p.m. and her husband would be home any minute, frantically started preparing dinner. She wanted to fix a nice dinner so that she and her husband could eat after the children went to bed, then relax together.

This particular evening, however, did not turn out as expected. Jasmine sat waiting for her no-show husband. When he finally walked in the door at 10:15 p.m., Jasmine was furious. His excuse, that his boss had invited the whole office for dinner, didn't help Jasmine feel better. Jasmine reasoned that her husband could have called to say that he wouldn't be home for dinner; he could have taken five minutes to do that. He said he did but the phone was busy. Her face was red with rage. She screamed at her husband. Suddenly, bursting into tears, she ran into the living room. Her husband retreated to the safety of their bedroom. Exhausted and disappointed, Jasmine sat alone and pondered why she was so angry with her husband. Was she just tired? Was she frustrated by dealing with young children all day and simply wanted to be around another adult? Was she secretly worried and jealous that her husband was seeing another woman and he had lied about his whereabouts? Was she combative because her husband's and her sister's lives seemed so much more rewarding than her own? Jasmine was unsure of how she felt and why she exploded in such rage at her husband, whom she loved dearly.

This fictional story is told to demonstrate that we can be moved by strong emotions. On other occasions, when we expect to cry, we find that our eyes are dry. What are these strange feelings we call emotions? What motivates us to become angry at someone we love? How is it sometimes when we need certain motivations (such as completing an assignment before a deadline), the motivation to do the work is absent until right before the deadline? How can we become more efficient (both at home and in the workplace) in understanding how our emotions influence our behavioral choices?

These questions and others have inspired psychologists to study motivation and emotion. Jasmine's story, besides introducing these topics to you, also illustrates why these two topics are usually interrelated in psychology. Some emotions are pleasant, so pleasant that we are motivated to keep experiencing them. Pleasant emotions are exemplified by love, pride, and joy. Other emotions are terribly draining and oppressive; so negative that we hope they will be over as soon as possible. Negative emotions are exemplified by anger, grief, and jealousy. Motivation, emotion, and their relationship to one another are the focus of this unit.

Article

Prepared by: R. Eric Landrum, *Boise State University*

Hand on the Wheel, Mind on the Mobile: An Analysis of Social Factors Contributing to Texting While Driving

STEVEN J. SEILER

Learning Outcomes

After reading this article, you will be able to:

- Define and understand the term "mobile multiplexing."
- Recognize specific, identifiable dangers in texting while driving.

Introduction

Social life in the new millennium has been defined by instant connectivity to others via mobile phones ("mobile"). Despite the many benefits of remote connections, the numerous accidents and fatalities associated with exchanging text messages ("texting") while driving reveal a much darker side of social technologies.[1,2] The Center for Disease Control estimates that 31% of adult drivers text while driving.[3] Despite numerous awareness-raising campaigns, increasingly strict laws, research providing evidence of cognitive challenges and consequences of texting while driving, and increasing distracted driving fatalities, many people in the United States still choose to text while driving.[3–11] The question remains as to what social factors increase the likelihood of texting while driving. Although previous research provides substantial evidence of the cognitive challenges and consequences of texting while driving,[5–8] very little is known about the *social* structure of texting while driving. The purpose of this study is to examine sociologically social factors that compel people to exchange text messages while driving.

Theoretical Framework

Research provides evidence that people engage in multiplexing—communicating through various media—on their mobiles.[12–14] People rarely use mobiles just for making calls or just for texting; rather, they commonly communicate through a variety of media on their mobile. To establish a baseline reference for such multiplexing, it is hypothesized that:

H1: As the frequency to which people talk on their mobiles increases, the likelihood of texting while driving increases.

Such mobile multiplexing is also likely to occur while driving. Previous studies provide evidence that people who talk on the mobile, text, and access the Internet while driving are at greater risk of receiving traffic citations and crashing.[6,10]

However, it is unclear how people multiplex while driving. Based upon a substantial body of research suggesting people multiplex on their mobiles,[12–17] the following hypotheses are proposed:

H2: People who use the Internet on their mobiles are more likely to text while driving than people who do not use the Internet on their mobiles.

H3: People who talk on the mobile while driving are more likely to text while driving than people who do not talk on the mobile while driving.

Many sociologists argue that people are tethered to their mobiles and thus use them anytime and anywhere.[16–22] Since mobiles are also relationship technologies, people assume that close others are always digitally present through the mobile.[21] Therefore, people learn to navigate social life in between physical and digital interactions.[16–18,21,22] In fact, previous research suggests people text in various social environments (e.g., during meetings, movies, religious services, family dinners).[16,19–26] As people learn to manage their mobiles and their lives outside of their mobiles simultaneously, the digital and physical spaces tend to blend together in a manner that leaves very few social spaces (including driving) off limits. Accordingly, it is hypothesized that:

H4: People who text in inappropriate nondriving environments (e.g., during meetings or movies) are more likely to text while driving than people who do not text in inappropriate nondriving environments.

Behaviors—including mobile behaviors—are learned through the process of socialization (i.e., the lifelong process of learning culture). Such socialization occurs primarily within group life, and group dynamics shape people's perceptions of, and behaviors within, the social world.[27–29] Sociologically, people are more likely to text while driving when they regularly see other friends and family members texting while driving or even using the mobile in a dangerous manner while driving without negative consequences (e.g., without getting into an accident or receiving a traffic citation). As such behaviors become normalized within everyday experiences, people are likely to feel texting, albeit potentially risky, is simply a normative feature of driving.[29] Although people internalize general cultural norms such as driving laws, primary group norms can often override other, more general, cultural norms. Accordingly, the following hypotheses are proposed:

H5: People who ride in vehicles with drivers who send/receive text messages are more likely to text while driving than people who do not ride in vehicles with drivers who send/receive text messages.

H6: People who ride in vehicles with drivers who have used a mobile in a way that put themselves or others in danger are more likely to text while driving than people who do not ride in vehicles with drivers who have used a mobile in a way that put themselves or others in danger.

Texting while driving is undoubtedly a deviant behavior,[30] as nearly every U.S. state prohibits texting while driving.[31] People who engage in moderately deviant behavior rarely focus their deviance in a single area. Instead, such deviance spills over into other areas of life.[32,33] Similarly, people who text while driving are also likely to engage in other forms of technological deviance. A rather extreme form of *technological* deviance is sexting, that is, exchanging nude or partially nude photos or videos via text messages. To test this connection between nondriving technological deviance and texting while driving, it is hypothesized that:

H7: People who sext are more likely to text while driving than people who do not sext.

People have various motivations for using their mobiles, generally, and texting, specifically. Some researchers argue that people are addicted to their devices or compulsively use their devices.[34,35] However, the uniquely social component of texting underscores, complicates, or otherwise exacerbates such addictive behaviors. One motivation for using a mobile that is conceptually distinct from addiction is boredom. People might simply desire preoccupation, and, for many, the mobile provides such mental diversion.[16,35] It is possible, then, that people text while driving as a mental diversion during routine commutes. Formally stated:

H8: People who use their mobiles when they are bored are more likely to text while driving than people who do not use their mobiles when they are bored.

Additionally, since mobiles connect people with significant others, and since such devices become embedded in everyday social experiences,[16,21] people choose to text at inopportune times for various social reasons. Some people might simply text to maintain relationships with their friends and family by sending periodic messages to let their significant others know they are thinking about them (e.g., "Just to say hi"). Others might text more often to check in with or check on significant others to let them know they, or to find out if others, are "okay" (e.g., "How's your day?" "Things going okay?"). Moreover, previous research suggests texting is widely used to coordinate schedules.[23,24,36–39] Finally, mobiles allow the work day to bleed into other areas of social life.[21,36–39] This study explores whether these factors increase the likelihood of texting while driving.

Methods

The data for this study came from the 2010 Spring Change Assessment conducted by the Pew Research Center.[40] The survey consisted of phone interviews with a sample of adults aged 18 years and older living in the United States (n = 2,252). However, to counteract biases arising from demographic inconsistencies, unbalanced sample designs, and nonresponse patterns, weights were included in the original data set. Therefore, this study utilized the weighted sample (n = 8,519) in order to present findings that are representative of the U.S. population. The margin of sampling error for the survey was about – 3 percentage points.

A multivariate logistic regression analysis of the weighted data was conducted to examine the impact of the independent variables on the likelihood of texting while driving. Accordingly, the dependent variable was texting while driving, which was measured using the following survey question: "Have you ever sent or read a text message while driving?" (0 = "No"/1 = "Yes"). See Table 1 for descriptive statistics. For the independent variables, first, three types of mobile use were measured—general mobile talk, mobile Internet use, and talking on a mobile while driving. An additive index for mobile talk was created from responses to the following five questions (α = 0.72): "When you call someone on your cell phone, how often are you calling to…" "just say hello and chat"; "report where you are or check on where someone else is"; "coordinate where you are physically meeting someone"; "do things that are related to work"; and "have a long conversation to discuss important personal matters" (0 = "never"; 1 = "less often"; 2 = "a few times a week"; 3 = "at least once a day"; 4 = "several times a day"). A measure for mobile Internet use was developed from the question, "Do you ever use your cell phone to access the Internet?" A measure of talking on the mobile while driving was measured using the question, "Have you ever talked on a cell phone while driving?" (0 = "No"/1 = "Yes").

Table 1 Descriptive Statistics for Unweighted and Weighted Variables

	No N (*valid %*)	*Yes* N (*valid %*)	*Total* N/*100%*
Text while driving			
Unweighted	676 (56.9)	513 (43.1)	1,189
Weighted	2,660 (53.5)	2,315 (27.2)	4,975
Talk on mobile while driving			
Unweighted	510 (26.6)	1,406 (73.4)	1,916
Weighted	1,709 (20.1)	5,238 (61.5)	6,947
Use Internet on cell			
Unweighted	1,332 (69.5)	585 (30.5)	1,917
Weighted	4,299 (61.8)	2,659 (31.2)	6,959
Ride with texting driver			
Unweighted	1,266 (56.4)	980 (43.5)	2,246
Weighted	4,322 (50.8)	4,179 (49.2)	8,501
Ride with driver using mobile in dangerous manner			
Unweighted	1,334 (59.6)	904 (40.4)	2,238
Weighted	4,753 (56.1)	3,725 (43.9)	8,477
Sent sexts			
Unweighted	1,839 (96.2)	73 (3.8)	1,912
Weighted	6,561 (94.5)	383 (5.5)	6,944

		Disagree N (*valid %*)	*Agree* N (*valid %*)	*Total* N/*100%*
Use mobile when bored				
Unweighted		1,323 (69.5)	581 (30.5)	1,904
Weighted		4,202 (60.8)	2,709 (39.2)	6,911
		Male N (*valid %*)	*Female* N (*valid %*)	*Total* N/*100%*
Gender				
Unweighted		979 (43.5)	1,273 (56.5)	2,252
Weighted		4,126 (48.4)	4,393 (51.6)	8,519
		White N (*valid %*)	*Nonwhite* N (*valid %*)	*Total* N/*100%*
Race				
Unweighted		1,783 (81.2)	413 (18.8)	2,196
Weighted		6,505 (76.4)	1,733 (21.0)	8,238
Ordinal variables:	Never N (valid %)	Once per week or less N (valid %)	Daily N (valid %)	Daily N (valid %)
Use text, inapp. env.				
Unweighted	461 (38.9)	492 (41.5)	233 (19.6)	1,186
Weighted	1,712 (20.1)	2,110 (42.5)	1,143 (23.0)	4,964
Use text to: Just say hi				
Unweighted	214 (18.0)	450 (37.8)	525 (44.2)	1,189
Weighted	777 (15.6)	1,750 (35.2)	2,449 (28.7)	4,975
Check in/on others				
Unweighted	281 (23.7)	495 (22.0)	412 (34.7)	1,188
Weighted	1,061 (21.4)	1,965 (39.6)	1,942 (39.1)	4,968
Coordinate w/ others				
Unweighted	331 (27.9)	586 (49.4)	269 (22.7)	1,186
Weighted	1,205 (24.3)	2,446 (49.3)	1,315 (26.5)	4,965
Use text for work				
Unweighted	543 (49.7)	318 (29.1)	232 (21.2)	1,093
Weighted	2,170 (46.8)	1,403 (30.3)	1,059 (22.9)	4,632
Continuous variables:		M (*SD*)	*Min: Max*	N
Cell talk index				
Unweighted		8.8 (4.7)	0: 20	1,646
Weighted		9.5 (4.6)	0: 20	6,197
Age				
Unweighted		51 (18.4)	18: 79	2,201
Weighted		46 (18.3)	18: 79	8,379

Second, texting in inappropriate nondriving environments was measured using the following question (0 = "never"; 1 = "once a week or less"; 3 = "daily"): "How often do you send or receive text messages to exchange information quietly when you are in a setting where you can't make a voice call, like a meeting or a movie?"

Third, socialization of risky mobile driving behaviors was measured with two survey questions (0 = "No"/1 = "Yes"): "Have you ever been in a car when the driver was sending or reading text messages on their cell phone?" and "Have you ever been in a car when the driver used a cell phone in a way that put themselves or others in danger?"

Fourth, technological deviance focused on sending sexts, which was measured using the question, "Have you ever sent a sexually suggestive nude or nearly nude photo or video of yourself to someone else using your cell phone?" (0 = "No"/1 = "Yes").

Fifth, to measure motivations, using the mobile out of boredom was distinguished from common motivations for texting. A measure for using mobiles when bored was based upon responses to the following statement (0 = "disagree"/ 1 = "agree"): "When I am bored, I use my cell phone to entertain myself." Motivations for texting were measured using the following four questions (0 = "never"/1 = "once a week or less"/3 = "daily"): "How often do you send or receive text messages to." "just say hello and chat"; "report where you are or check on where someone else is"; "coordinate where you are physically meeting someone"; and "do things that are related to work."

Finally, controls were used for gender (0 = "male"/ 1 = "female"), race (0 = "white"/1 = "nonwhite"), and age, which was a continuous variable ranging from 18 to 79 years.

Results

According to the weighted data, consistent with more conservative estimates by other researchers,[2,3,7,11] more than 27% of adults in the United States text while driving, and more than 60% report talking on their mobiles while driving. The multivariate logistic regression analyses (see Table 2) models various text messaging and mobile behaviors to predict the likelihood of texting while driving (χ^2 = 2,155.38; $p < 0.001$). Around 53% of the variance in texting while driving is explained by the independent variables in this analysis (Nagelkerke R^2 = 0.53). Specifically, contrary to H1, as the frequency of talking on a mobile increases, the likelihood of texting while driving decreases (odds = 0.01; $p < 0.01$). Yet, consistent with H2 and H3, people who use the Internet on their mobiles are more likely to text while driving than those who do not use it on their mobiles (odds = 1.24; $p < 0.05$), and people who talk on their mobiles while driving are more likely to text while driving than those who do not talk on their mobiles while driving (odds = 32.00; $p < 0.001$).

Regarding texting in an inappropriate nondriving environment, people who text once per week or less as well as people who text daily in inappropriate nondriving environments were more likely to text while driving than people who never text in such environments (odds = 1.41, $p < 0.001$; odds = 1.55, $p < 0.05$, respectively), which supports H4.

Socialization also impacts the likelihood of texting while driving. Specifically, consistent with H5, people who ride with drivers who text are more likely to text while driving than people who do not ride with texting drivers (odds = 7.08;

Table 2 Logistic Regression Analysis of the Likelihood of Texting While Driving (Weighted N = 8,519)

	B (SE)	*Exp(b)*	*95% CI*
Mobile talk index	– 0.03** (0.06)	0.01	0.95, 0.99
Use Internet on mobile	0.22* (0.09)	1.24	1.03, 1.48
Talk on mobile while driving	3.47*** (0.21)	32.00	21.28, 48.14
Use text in inappropriate environment (never)			
Once per week or less	0.34*** (0.10)	1.41	1.15, 1.72
Daily	0.44*** (0.13)	1.55	1.19, 2.01
Ride with texting driver	1.96*** (0.10)	7.08	5.77, 8.68
Ride with driver using mobile in dangerous manner	0.18*(0.09)	1.19	1.00, 1.43
Sent sexts	0.93***(0.18)	2.53	1.77, 3.62
Use mobile when bored	0.67***(0.10)	1.96	1.62, 2.36
Use text just to say hi (never)			
Once per week or less	0.53*** (0.14)	1.70	1.30, 2.22
Daily	0.76*** (0.14)	2.14	1.63, 2.80
Use text to check in with or on others (never)			
Once per week or less	0.16 (0.13)	1.17	0.91, 1.52
Daily	–0.03 (0.14)	0.97	0.73, 1.29

Use text to coordinate with others (never)			
Once per week or less	−0.28* (0.12)	0.76	0.60, 0.97
Daily	0.40** (0.15)	1.49	1.11, 2.02
Use text for work (never)			
Once per week or less	0.63*** (0.10)	1.89	1.55, 2.30
Daily	0.32** (0.12)	1.38	1.09, 1.74
Female	−0.22** (0.08)	0.80	0.68, 0.95
Nonwhite	−0.66*** (0.10)	0.52	0.43, 0.63
Age	−0.01*** (0.01)	0.99	0.98, 0.99
Constant		−5.23*** (0.31)	
Model χ^2		2,155.38***	
Nagelkerke R^2		0.53	
−2LL		3,809.42	

***$p < 0.001$; **$p < 0.01$; *$p < 0.05$.

$p < 0.001$). Moreover, in line with H6, people who ride with others who use their mobiles in a dangerous manner are more likely to text while driving than people who do not ride with such people (odds = 1.19; $p < 0.05$).

Texting while driving is also connected with other forms of technological deviance. That is, consistent with H7, people who send sexts are more likely to text while driving than people who do not send sexts (odds = 2.53; $p < 0.001$).

Furthermore, various motivations impact the likelihood of texting while driving. People who use their mobiles when they are bored are more likely to text while driving than people who do not use them when bored (odds = 1.96; $p < 0.001$), which supports H8. Regarding the motivations for texting, people who text others daily to simply say "hi" (odds = 2.14; $p < 0.001$), to coordinate activities (odds = 1.49; $p < 0.01$), and for work (odds = 1.38; $p < 0.01$) were more likely to text while driving than people who never text others for these purposes. Importantly, using text messages to check in with or check on others was statistically insignificant.

Finally, men are more likely to text while driving than women (odds = 0.80; $p < 0.01$); white people were more likely to text while driving than nonwhite people (odds = 0.52; $p < 0.001$); and as age increases, the likelihood of texting while driving decreases (odds = 0.99; $p < 0.001$).

Discussion

The findings provide substantial evidence that a variety of complex social factors impact the likelihood of texting while driving. Whereas the frequency of talking on the mobile was inversely related to the likelihood of texting while driving, people who talk on their mobiles *while driving* were more likely to text while driving, which suggests that people, in fact, engage in mobile multiplexing while driving. Furthermore, the positive association between Internet use on the mobile and texting while driving suggests that mobile multiplexing might not be limited to texting and talking. Therefore, although previous research suggests people engage in various distractions while driving,[2,41] future research is necessary to understand the qualitative dimensions of mobile multiplexing. Specifically, researchers should examine the structure, dynamics, and consequences of engaging in various types of mobile multiplexing (e.g., talking, texting, Facebooking, tweeting, searching the Internet) while driving.

The sense of constant connection to others via the mobile was positively associated with texting while driving, which is a particularly critical point for policymakers and technology developers, as it helps explain why people commonly disregard laws prohibiting texting while driving and the numerous educational campaigns about the dangers of texting while driving. Since using a mobile has become normative public behavior, people do not demand explanation for public mobile use. Although texting in many social environments is often considered rude, people have largely accepted such behaviors as a normative condition of daily life. The greatest pressure to avoid, or at least minimize, mobile use comes from the audience within the social environment.[42] In such environments, people develop strategies for minimizing the disruption of their mobile use in various environments, rather than simply turning off their mobile.[42] When driving alone, the driver's audience is primarily limited—at best—to the momentary glances from people in passing vehicle. Driving occurs in a public–private space void of the direct social pressures experienced in other public environments. Therefore, the decision to text while driving is largely influenced by people's primary group norms. Although people are aware of driving norms, the violation of such driving norms, too, has become normative behavior.[6,7]

Texting while driving is a learned behavior reinforced through observing others engaging in such behaviors. Commonsensically, observing people engaging in dangerous driving behaviors would deter people from texting while driving. However, sociologically, riding with others who engage in such behaviors *without consequence* contributes to a culture of multitasking while driving. As such behaviors are routinized into mundane social life, people begin interpreting them as normal and acceptable. Moreover, such learned behavior might emphasize not getting caught texting while driving instead of the inherent dangers of such distracted driving.

However, texting while driving is exacerbated among those who disregard cultural norms. In particular, people who engage in forms of technological deviance, such as sexting, are more likely to text while driving. Minor forms of deviance are often motivated by a lack of acceptance of authority.[32,33] Accordingly, given the absence of immediate accountability while driving, people who tend to engage in technological deviant behavior in other areas of social life are more likely to disregard certain driving rules, and group norms are likely to take precedence over general driving norms.

Finally, the findings provide evidence that texting while driving is associated with various motivations for texting. People who frequently use texts for sending friendly comments (e.g., to say hi) and coordinating activities with significant others and for managing their work lives were more likely to text while driving. Yet, not all daily uses of texts increased the likelihood of texting while driving, as was the case with texting to checking in with, or check on, others.

These findings have important implications for educational campaigns and technology designers. First, campaigns to educate people of the dangers of texting while driving are likely effective in educating people. However, to change behavior, marketing principles of product placement and product saturation through, for example, billboards, online advertisements, television commercials, t-shirts, posters, or *exposés* could meaningfully contribute to people not only internalizing the dangers of texting while driving but also refraining from texting while driving. Such awareness-raising campaigns should emphasize not only the dangers of texting while driving but also the role of indirect peer influence in reinforcing such dangerous behaviors among others. Second, in-vehicle dashboard indicators and sun visor warnings, similar to seatbelt indicators and tags, could provide constant and subtle reminders of the dangers of texting while driving. Third, since the culture of texting while driving is likely to change slowly—if it changes at all—more innovative in-vehicle voice-to-text technologies allowing drivers to use voice prompts to text—and engage in other forms of mobile multiplexing—are necessary. Automobile companies must continue to integrate hands-free technologies for mobile multiplexing into vehicles innovatively and ergonomically.

Although the findings provide a representative snapshot picture of the social factors influencing texting while driving among adults in the United States, the data set has important limitations. In particular, the data only allow for the analysis of the likelihood of texting while driving based largely upon dichotomous variables. Future research should attempt to account for the frequency that people text while driving. Additionally, some of the variables were only tacit measures of our concepts (e.g., sexting as a measure of technological deviance). Future research should focus on more complex and encompassing measures for many of the variables analyzed here.

Texting while driving is undoubtedly a dangerous social phenomenon. This study provides additional evidence that such behaviors are embedded in sociocultural norms in other areas of social life. To increase the effectiveness of awareness campaigns as well as invehicle technologies, additional sociological research is necessary to understand further the social structure and social processes underlying and leading to texting while driving.

Acknowledgments

The data used in this study were obtained from the Pew Research Center (www.pewresearch.org/). The interpretations presented and conclusions reached in this study are those of the authors and do not represent the positions or policies of the Pew Research Center.

Author Disclosure Statement

No competing financial interests exist.

References

1. Wilson FA, Stimpson JP. Trends in fatalities from distracted driving in the United States, 1999 to 2008. American Journal of Public Health 2010; 100:2213–2219.
2. National Highway Traffic Safety Administration. (2013) Distracted driving 2011. Traffic Safety Facts: Research Notes 2013; dot hs 811737.
3. Naumann RB, Dellinger AM. Mobile device use while driving—United States and seven European countries, 2011. Morbidity & Mortality Weekly Report 2013; 62:177–197.
4. Bayer JB, Campbell SW. Texting while driving on automatic: considering the frequency-independent side of habit. Computers in Human Behavior 2012; 28:2083–2090.

5. Caird JK, Johnston KA, Willness CR, et al. A meta-analysis of the effects of texting on driving. Accident Analysis & Prevention 2014; 71:311–318.
6. Cook JL, Jones RM. Texting and accessing the web while driving: traffic citations and crashes among young adult drivers. Traffic Injury Prevention 2011; 12:545–549.
7. Douglas DM, Paullet KL, Pinchot JL. Distracted driving: dying to text you. Issues in Information Systems 2012; 13:275–283.
8. Lee JD. Dynamics of driver distraction: the process of engaging and disengaging. Annals of Advances in Automotive Medicine 2014; 58:24–32.
9. O'Connor SS, Whitehill JM, King KM, et al. Compulsive cell phone use and history of motor vehicle crash. Journal of Adolescent Health 2013; 53:512–519.
10. Olsen EO, Shults RA, Eaton DK. Texting while driving and other risky motor vehicle behaviors among U.S. high school students. Pediatrics 2013; 131:e1708–1715.
11. Owens JM, McLaughlin SB, Sudweeks J. Driver performance while text messaging using handheld and in-vehicle systems. Accident Analysis & Prevention 2011; 43:939–947.
12. Baym N. (2010) *Personal connections in the digital age.* Malden, MA: Polity Press.
13. Mesch G, Talmud I. The quality of online and offline relationships: the role of multiplexity and duration of social relationships. Information Society 2006; 22:137–148.
14. Haythornthwaite C. Exploring multiplexity: social network structures in a computer-supported distance learning class. Information Society 2001; 17:211–226.
15. Boase J, Horrigan J, Wellman B, et al. (2006) *The strength of Internet ties.* Washington DC: Pew Research Center. www.pewinternet.org/files/old-media//Files/Reports/2006/PIP_Internet_ties.pdf.pdf (accessed Jun. 8, 2014).
16. Turkle S. (2008) Always-on/Always-on-you: the tethered self. In Katz J, ed. *The handbook of mobile communications studies.* Cambridge, MA: MIT Press, pp. 121–138.
17. Wei R, Lo V. Staying connected while on the move: cell phone use and social connectedness. New Media & Society 2006; 8:53–72.
18. Katz JE, Aakhus MA. (2002) Introduction: framing the issues. In Katz, JE, Aakhus, MA, eds. *Perpetual contact mobile communication, private talk, public performance.* New York: Cambridge University Press, pp. 1–14.
19. Baron NS. (2008) *Always on: language in an online and mobile world.* New York: Oxford University Press.
20. Agger B. (2013) *Texting toward utopia: kids, writing, and resistance.* Boulder, CO: Paradigm.
21. Gergen K. (2002) The challenge of the absent presence. In Katz JE, Aakhus MA, eds. *Perpetual contact mobile communication, private talk, public performance.* New York: Cambridge University Press, pp. 227–241.
22. Palen L, Salzman M, Youngs E. (2000) Going wireless: behavior and practice of new mobile phone users. In Kellogg W, Whittaker S, eds. *Proceedings of the 2000 ACM Conference on Computer Supported Cooperative Work.* Williamsport, PA: Association for Computing Machinery, pp. 201–110.
23. Green N. On the move: technology, mobility, and the mediation of social time and space. Information Society 2008; 18:281–292.
24. Hanson J. (2007) 24/7: *How cell phones and the Internet change the way we live, work, and play.* Westport, CT: Praeger.
25. Ishii K. Implications of mobility: the uses of personal communication media in everyday life. Journal of Communication 2006; 56:346–365.
26. Kim H, Kim JG, Park HW, et al. Configurations of relationships in different media: FtF, email, instant messenger, mobile phone, and SMS. Journal of Computer-Mediated Communication 2007; 12:1183–1207.
27. Luft J. (1984) *Group processes: an introduction to group dynamics.* 3rd ed. Mountain View, CA: Mayfield.
28. Mills TM. (1984) *The sociology of small groups.* 2nd ed. Upper Saddle River, NJ: Prentice Hall.
29. Shibutani T. Reference groups as perspectives. American Journal of Sociology 1955; 60:562–569.
30. Ricketts ML, Koller C. (2014) Texting and social networks. In Marcum CD, Higgins GE, eds. *Social networking as a criminal enterprise.* Boca Raton, FL: CRC Press, pp. 49–68.
31. Governors Highway Safety Association. (2014) Distracted driving laws. www.ghsa.org/html/stateinfo/laws/cellphone_laws.html (accessed Nov. 21, 2014).
32. Matza D. (2010) *Becoming deviant.* New Brunswick, NJ: Transaction Publishers.
33. Sutherland EH, Cressey DR, Luckenbill D. (1995) The theory of differential association. In: Herman, NJ, Deviance: *A Symbolic Interactionist Approach.* Lanham, MD: General Hall, pp. 64–68.
34. Park WK. (2005) *Mobile phone addiction.* In Ling R, Pedersen PE, eds. Mobile communications: re-negotiation of the social sphere. London: Springer, pp. 253–272.
35. Walsh SP, White KM, Young RM. (2007) Young and connected: psychological influences of mobile phone use amongst Australian youth. In Goggin G, Hjorth L, eds. *Proceedings of an International Conference on Social and Cultural Aspects of Mobile Phones, Convergent Media and Wireless Technologies.* Sydney: University of Sydney, pp. 125–134.
36. Ling R. (2004) *The mobile connection: the cell phone's impact on society.* San Francisco, CA: Morgan Kaufmann.
37. Ling R, Pedersen PE. (2005) *Mobile communications: renegotiation of the social sphere.* London: Springer.
38. Gergen K. (2000) *The saturated self: dilemmas of identity in contemporary life.* New York: Basic Books.

39. Horstmanshof L, Power MR. Mobile phone, SMS, and relationships. Australian Journal of Communication 2005; 32:33–52.

40. Pew Research Center. (2010) Spring Change Assessment Survey 2010 [Data file and code book]. Washington DC. www.pewinternet.org/datasets/ (accessed May 14, 2012).

41. Olson RL, Hanowski RJ, Hickman JS, et al. (2009) *Driver distraction in commercial vehicle operations*. Washington, DC: U.S. Department of Transportation.

42. Plant S. (2001) *On the mobile: the effects of mobile telephones on social and individual life*. Chicago: Motorola. www.motorola.com/mot/doc/0/234_MotDoc.pdf (accessed Jan. 3, 2008).

Critical Thinking

1. If 31% of adult drivers are texting while driving, what does this imply for public safety? Explain.
2. What is the influence of social norms in regard to texting and driving?

Internet References

Safer roads: 23 awesome groups working to end texting and driving
https://independentmotors.net/texting-and-driving/

Texting and driving: Here's why the problem won't go away soon
http://www.huffingtonpost.com/william-morrow/texting-and-driving-heres_b_11654634.html

Texting and driving isn't a millennial problem, it's an engineering problem
https://www.wired.com/2017/02/texting-driving-isnt-millennial-problem-engineering-problem/

The dangers of distracted driving
https://www.fcc.gov/consumers/guides/dangers-texting-while-driving

Article

Prepared by: R. Eric Landrum, *Boise State University*

On the Science of Creepiness

LINDA RODRIGUEZ MCROBBIE

Learning Outcomes

After reading this article, you will be able to:

- Define creepiness.
- Identify the careers that are reported as the most creepy.

It's the spider crawling up the wall next to your bed. Someone knocking at your door late at night. The guy who stands just a bit too close to you on the subway and for a bit too long. "Hello Barbie" with embedded WiFi and Siri-like capabilities. Overgrown graveyards. Clowns.

As with the Supreme Court standard for obscenity, we know creepy when we see it (or perhaps, more accurately, feel it). But what exactly is it? Why do we experience "the creeps"? And is being creeped out useful?

Though the sensation has probably been around since humans began experiencing emotions, it wasn't until the middle of the 19th century that some of us called this touch of the uncanny "the creeps". Charles Dickens, who gave the English language only marginally fewer new words and expressions than Shakespeare, is credited with the first use of the phrase, in his 1849 novel *David Copperfield*, to mean an unpleasant, tingly chill up the spine. In the years after the book, using "creepy" to describe something that causes unease took off – a Google Ngram search shows the instance of the word increasing dramatically since about 1860.

For all its ubiquity, however, the sensation of being "creeped out" has been little studied by psychologists. Frank McAndrew, professor of psychology at Knox College in Illinois, is one of the few. In 2013, he and graduate student Sara Koehnke presented a small and admittedly preliminary paper based on the results of their survey asking more than 1,300 people "what is creepy?" And as it turns out, "creepy" isn't actually all that complicated.

"[Creepy is] about the uncertainty of threat. You're feeling uneasy because you think there might be something to worry about here, but the signals are not clear enough to warrant your doing some sort of desperate, life-saving kind of thing," explains McAndrew.

Being creeped out is different from fear or revulsion, he says; in both of those emotional states, the person experiencing them usually feels no confusion about how to respond. But when you're creeped out, your brain and your body are telling you that something is not quite right and you'd better pay attention because it might hurt you.

This is sometimes manifest in a physical sensation: In 2012, researchers from the University of Groningen in the Netherlands found that when subjects felt creeped out, they felt colder and believed that the temperature in the room had actually dropped. (Dickens might not have used the word in quite the way it soon came to mean, but he did get the chills part right.)

That physical response further heightens your senses, and, continues McAndrew: "You don't know how to act but you're really concerned about getting more information ... It kind of takes your attention and focuses it like a laser on this particular stimulus, whatever it is."

Whatever it is can be things, situations, places and, of course, people. Most creepy research has looked at what makes people seem creepy. For example, the 2012 study successfully creeped people out by exposing them to others who didn't practice normal non-verbal behavior.

In the experiment, subjects interacted with researchers who practiced degrees of subtle mimicry: When the subject scratched her head, the researcher would do something similar, such as touch his nose. Subjects felt creeped out – and colder – when the researcher didn't mimic, indicating a discomfort with people who may not be able to follow social norms and cues.

McAndrew and Koehnke's survey also explored what made creepy people appear creepy, first asking participants to rate the likelihood a person described as creepy exhibited a set of characteristics or behaviors, such as greasy hair, extreme pallor or thinness, or an unwillingness to let a conversation drop. In another section, it asked people to indicate how much they agreed or disagreed with a series of statements about "the nature of creepy people".

Perhaps the biggest predictor of whether someone was considered creepy was unpredictability. "So much of [what is creepy] is about wanting to be able to predict what's going to happen, and that's why creepy people creep us out – because they're unpredictable," explains McAndrews, noting that the 2012 study also seemed to underscore that point. "We find it hard to know what they're going to do next."

Creepiness in people is also related to individuals breaking certain tacit social rules and conventions, even if sometimes that rule breaking is necessary. This becomes more evident when we look at the kinds of jobs a majority of respondents found creepy. However unfairly, taxidermists and funeral directors were among the creepiest professions listed in McAndrew and Koehnke's survey, likely because these people routinely interact with macabre things that most other people would avoid.

"If you're dealing with somebody who's really interested in dead things, that sets off alarm bells. Because if they're different in that way, what other unpleasant ways they might be different?" says McAndrew.

Garbage collectors, who also deal with things that people would rather avoid, were not considered creepy; evidently, the type of thing being avoided needs to be symbolic of or related to a latent threat. But the study respondents did find a fascination with sex to be creepy, so "sex shop owner" was considered a creepy profession.

By far the creepiest profession, according to the survey, was being a clown. Clowns are by nature unpredictable and difficult to fathom – makeup disguises their features and facial cues, and they typically do things outside the social norm, such as give unexpected hugs, with few consequences.

"Creepy" these days is often used to describe things like data surveillance or artificial intelligence (though the creepiness of the Uncanny Valley is best left for other discussions) – anything that has the potential to be used for evil. But creepiness also relies heavily on context: A doll on a child's bed isn't creepy, but a doll who looks eerily like your own child found on your doorstep definitely is.

McAndrew believes that there's an evolutionary advantage to feeling creeped out, one that's in line with the evolutionary psychology theory of "agency detection". The idea is that humans are inclined to construe willful agency behind circumstances, seek out patterns in events and visual stimuli, a phenomenon called pareidolia. This is why we see faces in toast, hear words in static or believe that things "happen for a reason".

Though the theory is most often invoked in explaining the psychological inclination towards religion, McAndrew says it helps make sense of why we get creeped out – because very often, we think that willful agent is malicious.

"We're predisposed to see willful agents that mean us harm in situations that are ambiguous, but this was an adaptive thing to do," he explains. Our ancestors saw a saber-toothed tiger in every shadow and a slithering snake in the motion of the swaying grass because it was better to be safe than sorry.

McAndrew believes that other findings from the survey are consistent with an evolutionary directive behind the creeped-out response: Firstly, that respondents – both men and women—overwhelmingly thought that men were more likely to be creepy than women, and secondly, that women were likely to perceive someone as creepy if that person showed an unwanted sexual interest in them.

From an evolutionary psychology perspective, McAndrew says, this makes sense. Males are perceived as more capable of and responsible for violence than females, while women faced a much wider range of threats, including sexual threats. Acting on even the whisper of such a threat is infinitely preferable to not acting at all and suffering the consequences.

But being afraid of the right things at the right time is only half of the story of creepiness. Just as our brains were being shaped by being constantly on guard against potential threats, they were also being shaped by the practical necessity of getting along in a group.

The quiet creeped-out response is a result of not only being perpetually wary, but also of being wary of overreacting – the same social norms that, when violated, keep that person from reacting in an overtly terrified way. We don't want to seem impolite or suspicious, or jump to the wrong conclusions, so we tread carefully.

There's something appropriate about the fact that the first appearance of the word "creepy" in *The New York Times* was in an 1877 article about a ghost story. Because for all of the evolutionary priming, all of the prey's instincts for self-preservation that seem to have gone into shaping the creeped-out response, there's at least a little part of us that *likes* to be creeped out.

Sort of.

McAndrew points out that truly creepy things and situations are not attractive, not even a little bit: "We don't enjoy real creepy situations, and we will avoid them like the plague. Like if there's a person who creeps you out, you'll cross the street to get away." What we do enjoy is playacting, in the same way we enjoy the vicarious thrills of watching a horror movie.

McAndrew and other psychologists, anthropologists, and even Stephen King, in his 1981 exploration of the genre he dominated, *Danse Macabre*, see horror films as a safe place for us to explore our fears and rehearse what we would do if, say, zombies tore apart our town.

The same thing that keeps us tense and attentive in a truly creepy situation is not unlike what keeps us moving, shrieking and shaking, through a Halloween haunted house. "It's going to trigger a lot of things that scare and startle you, but deep down you know there's no danger," McAndrew says. "You can have all the creepy biological sensations without any real risk." And there's something important (and fun) about that defanged kind of creepy.

Just keep an eye out for the real creeps.

Critical Thinking

1. What is the relationship between uncertainty and feelings of creepiness? Explain.
2. How is being afraid part of the story about the role of creepiness?
3. Based on the data, can someone be creepy and attractive? Explain.

Internet References

A theory of creepiness

https://aeon.co/essays/what-makes-clowns-vampires-and-severed-hands-creepy

Drone footage shows the creepiness of an abandoned West Texas water park

http://www.mysanantonio.com/entertainment/article/Video-Drone-footage-shows-all-the-creepiness-of-11283116.php

The age of creepiness

https://www.newyorker.com/culture/cultural-comment/the-age-of-creepiness

Article

Prepared by: R. Eric Landrum, *Boise State University*

Changing Faces: We Can Look More Trustworthy, but Not More Competent

NEW YORK UNIVERSITY

Learning Outcomes

After reading this article, you will be able to:

- Identify the features of a trustworthy face and a competent face.
- Appreciate the role that a series of experiments can play in helping to understand a complex phenomenon.

We can alter our facial features in ways that make us look more trustworthy, but don't have the same ability to appear more competent, a team of New York University (NYU) psychology researchers has found.

The study, which appears in the *Personality and Social Psychology Bulletin,* points to both the limits and potential we have in visually representing ourselves—from dating and career-networking sites to social media posts.

"Our findings show that facial cues conveying trustworthiness are malleable while facial cues conveying competence and ability are significantly less so," explains Jonathan Freeman, an assistant professor in NYU's Department of Psychology and the study's senior author. "The results suggest you can influence to an extent how trustworthy others perceive you to be in a facial photo, but perceptions of your competence or ability are considerably less able to be changed."

This distinction is due to the fact that judgments of trustworthiness are based on the face's dynamic musculature that can be slightly altered, with a neutral face resembling a happy expression likely to be seen as trustworthy and a neutral face resembling an angry expression likely to be seen as untrustworthy—even when faces aren't overtly smiling or angered. But perceptions of ability are drawn from a face's skeletal structure, which cannot be changed.

The study, whose other authors included Eric Hehman, an NYU post-doctoral researcher, and Jessica Flake, a doctoral candidate at the University of Connecticut, employed four experiments in which female and male subjects examined both photos and computer-generated images of adult males.

In the first, subjects looked at five distinct photos of 10 adult males of different ethnicities. Here, subjects' perceptions of trustworthiness of those pictured varied significantly, with happier-looking faces seen as more trustworthy and angrier-looking faces seen as more untrustworthy. However, the subjects' perceptions of ability, or competence, remained static—judgments were the same no matter which photo of the individual was being judged.

A second experiment replicated the first, but here, subjects evaluated 40 computer-generated faces that slowly evolved from "slightly happy" to "slightly angry," resulting in 20 different neutral instances of each individual face that slightly resembled a happy or angry expression. As with the first experiment, the subjects' perceptions of trustworthiness paralleled the emotion of the faces—the slightly happier the face appeared, the more likely he was seen to be trustworthy and vice versa for faces appearing slightly angrier. However, once again, perceptions of ability remained unchanged.

In the third experiment, the researchers implemented a real-world scenario. Here, subjects were shown an array of computer-generated faces and were asked one of two questions: which face they would choose to be their financial advisor (trustworthiness) and which they thought would be most likely to win a weightlifting competition (ability). Under this condition, the subjects were significantly more likely to choose as their financial advisor the faces resembling more positive, or happy, expressions. By contrast, emotional resemblance made no difference in subjects' selection of successful weightlifters; rather, they were more likely to choose faces with a particular form: those with a comparatively wider facial structure, which prior studies have associated with physical ability and testosterone.

In the fourth experiment, the researchers used a "reverse correlation" technique to uncover how subjects visually represent a trustworthy or competent face and how they visually represent the face of a trusted financial advisor or competent weightlifting champion. This technique allowed the researchers to determine which of all possible facial cues drive these distinct perceptions without specifying any cues in advance.

Here, resemblance to happy and angry expressions conveyed trustworthiness and was more prevalent in the faces of an imagined financial advisor while wider facial structure conveyed ability and was more prevalent in the faces of an imagined weightlifting champion.

These results confirmed the findings of the previous three experiments, further cementing the researchers' conclusion that perceptions of trustworthiness are malleable while those for competence or ability are immutable.

Critical Thinking

1. If an actor wanted to portray trustworthiness, what facial expressions should be used and what facial expressions should be avoided? Why?
2. If you wanted to increase others' perception of your competence, according to the article and the research, what should you do? Why?

Internet References

7 things your face says about you

http://www.businessinsider.com/seven-things-your-face-says-about-you-2014-1

What's in a face?

https://www.psychologytoday.com/articles/201210/whats-in-face

Your facial bone structure has a big influence on how people see you

http://www.scientificamerican.com/article/your-facial-bone-structure-has-a-big-influence-on-how-people-see-you/

Article

Prepared by: R. Eric Landrum, *Boise State University*

Do Cholesterol Drugs Affect Aggression?

Study finds it's possible, but more research is suggested.

Dennis Thompson

Learning Outcomes

After reading this article, you will be able to:

- Articulate how men and women are affected differently by statin drugs.
- Understand the cumulative effects that statins may have on many different aspects of behavior.
- Appreciate interactions, that is, when different levels of different independent variables have differential effects on the outcomes/dependent variables.

Cholesterol-lowering statin drugs might influence a person's aggressive behaviors, increasing or decreasing their irritability and violent tendencies, a new clinical trial suggests.

Men taking statins typically become less aggressive, while women on statins tend to become more aggressive, according to findings published July 1 in the journal *PLOS ONE.*

"Clinicians should be aware of this, and it's not bad for patients to be aware of it," said lead author Dr. Beatrice Golomb, a principal investigator at the University of California, San Diego School of Medicine. "If an individual develops a behavioral change, in my view medication should always be considered as a possibility."

However, the effect appears to be minimal and needs to be verified with follow-up studies, said one outside expert, Robert Geffner, founding president of the Institute on Violence, Abuse & Trauma at Alliant International University in San Diego.

"If I am reading their study right, it looks like they're dealing with really low levels of aggression to begin with," Geffner, a psychology professor at the University, said. "That's interesting, but I'm not sure how meaningful it is."

For the study, researchers randomly assigned more than 1,000 adult men and postmenopausal women to take either a statin medication or a placebo for six months.

The trial was aimed at clarifying a rather muddy picture that has emerged on the role that low blood cholesterol and statins might play in violent behavior, Golomb said.

Prior research has shown that low blood cholesterol levels can increase a person's aggressive behavior, increasing or decreasing the rate of violent death, violent crime, and suicide, she added.

Even though statins reduce blood cholesterol levels, the drugs theoretically should lower aggressive tendencies by reducing testosterone levels and improving the ability of cells to generate energy, Golomb continued. But statins also can alter a person's serotonin levels, causing sleep problems and increasing aggressive behavior, the researchers noted.

The participants' behavioral aggression was measured by tallying any aggressive acts they performed against other people, objects, or themselves in the previous week. Researchers looked for a change in aggression from the start of the study to the end.

They found that statins typically tended to increase aggression in postmenopausal women, with a significant effect on those older than 45. The increase appeared stronger in women who started out with lower levels of aggression, according to the study.

Analysis of the male participants proved trickier. Three men assigned to take statins had very large increases in aggression. When they were included in the review, statins had no effect one way or the other on average aggressive behavior.

But when the three outliers were removed from the group, researchers observed a significant decline in aggressive behavior for male statin users.

Statins' effect on hormone levels appeared to influence behavior, Golomb said. Those who experienced a decrease in testosterone due to statins also experienced a decrease in aggression.

Those who slept worse—possibly due to statins' effect on serotonin levels—experienced an increase in aggression.

The sleep finding helped account for the male outliers, as the two men with the biggest aggression increases both had developed much worse sleep problems, Golomb noted.

Geffner said that it's well-known that "hormones and neurotransmitters are definitely a player" in the way the brain functions.

But he questioned whether excluding the three aggressive male outliers was appropriate in the analysis, since this could be evidence of statins increasing violent behavior.

Geffner also noted that the study started out with 2,400 people, but that nearly 1,400 were left out because they either didn't meet the criteria for the study or declined to participate.

"I just have a lot more questions than answers at this point," he said. "I think there are interesting things to follow up on, but I have many questions."

Source

Beatrice Golomb, M.D., Ph.D., professor of medicine, University of California, San Diego School of Medicine; Robert Geffner, Ph.D., professor of psychology and founding president, Institute on Violence, Abuse & Trauma, Alliant International University, San Diego; July 1, 2015, *PLOS ONE.*

Critical Thinking

1. Explore the idea that there may be a relationship between low blood cholesterol and violent behavior. Why might that be the case? Explain.
2. The researchers in this study looked at changes in aggression from the beginning of the study to the end of the study. What are the advantages of this type of research approach?
3. When a study begins with 2,400 participants but eventually 1,400 participants are excluded, what concerns (if any) should there be about the remaining data? Explain.

Internet References

Cholesterol and your mood

http://www.healthcentral.com/cholesterol/c/59/45680/cholesterol-mood/

Lipitor rage

http://www.slate.com/articles/health_and_science/medical_examiner/2011/11/lipitor_side_effects_statins_and_mental_health_.html

Low cholesterol and suicide

https://www.psychologytoday.com/blog/evolutionary-psychiatry/201103/low-cholesterol-and-suicide

Unit 7

UNIT Development

Prepared by: R. Eric Landrum, *Boise State University*

Two families—the Garcias and the Smiths—are brand new parents. In fact, they are still at the hospital with their newborns. When the babies are not in their mothers' rooms, both sets of parents wander down to the hospital's neonatal nursery where pediatric nurses care for both babies, José Garcia and Kimberly Smith. Kimberly is alert, active, and often cries and squirms when her parents watch her. On the other hand, José is quiet, often asleep, and less attentive to external commotion when his parents view him in the nursery.

Why are these babies so different? Are the differences gender-related? Will these differences disappear as these children develop, or will they be expressed even more prominently? What role will parenting choices play in the development of each child? Will Kimberly excel at sports and José excel at art? Can Kimberly overcome her parents' poverty and succeed in a professional career? Will José become a doctor like his mother or a pharmacist like his father? Will both of these children avoid childhood disease, maltreatment, and the other misfortunes which sometimes occur with children? Developmental psychologists are concerned with all of the Kimberlys and Josés of our world. Developmental psychologists study age-related changes in language, motor and social skills, cognition, and physical health. Developmental psychologists are interested in the common skills shared by all children, as well as the differences among children, and the events that create these differences. And developmental psychologists are not only interested in child development but also in our development over the life span from birth to death.

For just a moment, think back over your developmental path. What kind of person are you? What sorts of skills do you possess? Are you artistic? Are you athletic? Do you enjoy reading? Do you speak more than one language? Are you outgoing or shy? Do you have higher levels of self-control or lower levels of self-control? What about your personal values such as integrity and honor, and how did you acquire these values? Did you have to work hard at becoming the person you are now, or did you just sort of become who you are naturally? Think now about the present and the future. How are you changing as a college student, and is college shaping the way you think and challenging your values and beliefs? Will you ever stop developing or changing or growing or looking at the world in new ways?

In general, developmental psychologists are concerned with the forces that guide and direct development over the course of a lifetime. Some developmental theorists argue that the major forces that shape a child are found in the environment, such as social class, quality of available stimulation, parenting style, and so on. Other theorists insist that genetics and related physiological/biological factors such as hormones are the major forces that underlie human development. A third set of psychologists believe that a combination or interaction of both sets of factors (nature and nurture) are responsible for development. In this unit, we explore what developmental psychologists can tell us about human growth and change over the life span.

Article

Prepared by: R. Eric Landrum, *Boise State University*

A Brief History of Twin Studies

KER THAN

Learning Outcomes

After reading this article, you will be able to:

- Differentiate between the terms identical and fraternal twins.
- Define eugenics.

On Tuesday, NASA astronaut Scott Kelly and Russian cosmonaut Mikhail Kornienko touched down in Kazakhstan after spending a whopping 340 days aboard the International Space Station (ISS).

As part of NASA's "Year in Space" project, Kelly and his Earth-bound identical twin brother, retired astronaut Mark Kelly, provided samples of blood, saliva and urine and underwent a barrage of physical and psychological tests designed to study the effects of long-duration spaceflight on the human body.

Studies of identical and fraternal twins have long been used to untangle the influences of genes and the environment on particular traits. Identical twins share all of their genes, while fraternal twins only share 50 percent. If a trait is more common among identical twins than fraternal twins, it suggests genetic factors are partly responsible.

"Twins studies are the only real way of doing natural experiments in humans," says Tim Spector, a professor of genetic epidemiology at Kings College, London. "By studying twins, you can learn a great deal about what makes us tick, what makes us different, and particularly the roles of nature versus nature that you just can't get any other way."

Spector is director of the TwinsUK Registry, which includes data from 12,000 twins and is used to study the genetic and environmental causes of age-related complex traits and diseases. He estimates that twins research is currently being conducted in more than 100 countries, and that most of those projects draw upon information contained in large databases such as the TwinsUK Registry.

While it may be a while before we see results from the astronaut twins, researchers are hopeful that the opportunity will yield some unique insights into human health. Here are some examples of what we've learned from past twins studies—both famous and infamous:

The Birth of Eugenics

Victorian scientist Francis Galton, a half-cousin of Charles Darwin, was one of the first people to recognize the value of twins for studying the heritability of traits. In an 1875 paper titled "The History of Twins," Galton used twins to estimate the relative effects of nature versus nature (a term that Galton himself coined). But his firm belief that human intelligence is largely a matter of nature led him to a darker path: He became a vocal proponent of eugenics (another term that he coined) and the idea that "a highly gifted race of men" could be produced through selective breeding.

Genes and I.Q.

In 2003, Eric Turkheimer, a psychology professor at the University of Virginia, took a fresh look at the research on the heritability of I.Q., which relied heavily on twin studies. Turkheimer noticed that most of the studies that found I.Q. is largely due to genetics involved twins from middle-class backgrounds, and he wondered what the pattern was among poorer people. When he looked at twins from poor families, he found that the I.Q.s of identical twins varied just as much as the I.Q.s of fraternal twins. In other words, the impact of growing up poor can overwhelm a child's natural intellectual gifts.

Genetic Basis for Everyday Diseases

Working with data and biological samples in the TwinsUK Registry, Spector and his colleagues have shown in more than 600 published papers that many common diseases such as osteoarthritis, cataracts and even back pain have a clear genetic basis to them. "When I started in this field, it was thought that only 'sexy' diseases [such as cancer] were genetic," Spector says. "Our findings changed that perception."

Heritable Eating Disorders

One of the newer twin registries to come online, the Michigan State University Twin Registry (MSUTR) was founded in 2001 to study genetic and environmental influences on a wide range of psychiatric and medical disorders. One of the most surprising findings to come out of the group's research is that many eating disorders such as anorexia have a genetic component to them.

"People thought for the longest time that it was due entirely to culture, the media and social factors," says MSUTR co-director Kelly Klump. "Because of twins studies, we now know that genes account for the same amount of variability in eating disorders as they do in schizophrenia and bipolar disorder. We would have never known that without twins studies."

The Genetics of Obesity

A classic twin study conducted by geneticist Claude Bouchard in 1990 looked at the importance of genes for body-fat storage. Bouchard, now at Louisiana State University, housed a dozen lean young male twins in a dormitory and overfed them by 1,000 calories a day for three months. Although every participant was heavier by the end of the experiment, the amount of weight and fat gained varied considerably, from 9 pounds to 29 pounds. Weight gain within pairs of twins was much more similar than weight gain between different twin pairs, and the twins in each pair tended to gain weight in the same places, whether it be in the abdomen, buttocks or thighs.

Untangling the "Gay Gene"

Numerous twin studies have attempted to elucidate the importance of genes in sexual orientation. In 2008, researchers led by Niklas Langström, a psychiatrist at the Karolinska Institute in Stockholm, drew upon the treasure trove of twin data contained in the Swedish Twin Registry, the largest in the world, to investigate genetic and environmental influences that determine whether or not a person is gay. The scientists found that genetics accounted for only 35 percent of the differences between identical and fraternal gay men and even less—roughly 18 percent—in gay women.

The study, one of the most comprehensive to date, indicates that a complex interplay of genetics and environmental factors work together to shape people's sexual orientations. But like other twins studies on this controversial subject, Langström's study was criticized for possible recruitment bias, since only 12 percent of the males in the Swedish registry were included in the study.

Twins Reared Apart

In 1979, Thomas Bouchard conducted what is perhaps the most fascinating twin study yet. Then director of the Minnesota Center for Twin and Family Research, Bouchard looked at identical and fraternal twins separated in infancy and reared apart. He found that identical twins who had different upbringings often had remarkably similar personalities, interests and attitudes. In one of the most famous examples, Bouchard came across twins who had been separated from birth and reunited at the age of 39.

"The twins," Bouchard later wrote, "were found to have married women named Linda, divorced, and married the second time to women named Betty. One named his son James Allan, the other named his son James Alan, and both named their pet dogs Toy."

But MSUTR's Klump is quick to point out that Bouchard's findings are not proof of genetic determinism. "What they show is that we we enter the world not as random beings or blank slates," Klump says. "As we walk through life, we have a lot of free choice, but some portion of that free choice is probably based on things that we're really good at and things that we like to do. Bouchard's study tells us that there is a dynamic interplay between what we like, what we want and the environments that we choose."

Critical Thinking

1. Based on the research, what is the impact of growing up poor on a person's intellectual development? Be specific.
2. How is heritability related to eating disorders and obesity?

Internet References

A second look at twin studies
http://www.apa.org/monitor/apr04/second.aspx

Double inanity: Twin studies are pretty much useless
http://www.slate.com/articles/life/twins/2011/08/double_inanity.html

Heritability: A handy guide to what it means, what it doesn't mean, and that giant meta-analysis of twin studies
https://scientiasalon.wordpress.com/2015/06/01/heritability-a-handy-guide-to-what-it-means-what-it-doesnt-mean-and-that-giant-meta-analysis-of-twin-studies/

In-depth look at history's largest genetic twin study
https://www.biosciencetechnology.com/article/2015/05/depth-look-historys-largest-genetic-twin-study

Article

Prepared by: R. Eric Landrum, *Boise State University*

How a Newborn Baby Sees You

KJERSTIN GJENGEDAL

Learning Outcomes

After reading this article, you will be able to:

- Comprehend the visual acuity of newborn infants.
- Appreciate the role of motion/movement in babies' early perception of the world.
- Understand the benefit of researchers from different fields being able to collaborate on and solve a problem.

A newborn infant can see its parents' expressions at a distance of 30 centimeters. For the first time researchers have managed to reconstruct infants visual perception of the world.

By combining technology, mathematics and previous knowledge of the visual perception of infants, researchers have finally succeeded in showing to an adult audience how much of its environment a newborn baby can actually see. The results tell us that an infant of 2 to 3 days old can percieve faces, and perhaps also emotional facial expressions, at a distance of 30 centimeters—which corresponds to the distance between a mother and her nursing baby. If the distance is increased to 60 centimeters, the visual image gets too blurred for the baby to perceive faces and expressions.

The study was conducted by researchers at the Institute of Psychology in collaboration with colleagues at the University of Uppsala and Eclipse Optics in Stockholm, Sweden.

Live Pictures

The study plugs a gap in our knowledge about infants' visual world, which was left open for several decades. It may also help explain claims that newborn babies can imitate facial expressions in adults during the first days and weeks of their lives, long before their vision is sufficiently developed to perceive details in their environments. The key word is motion.

"Previously, when researchers have tried to estimate exactly what a newborn baby sees, they have invariably used still photos. But the real world is dynamic. Our idea was to use images in motion," says professor emeritus Svein Magnussen from the Institute of Psychology.

Testing an Old Idea

Early in his career, Magnussen conducted research into the visual perception of humans. One day, about 15 years ago, he found himself discussing with colleagues the problem of testing whether newborn infants are really able to perceive facial expressions in people around them. The researchers agreed that if it were true that babies could see and imitate facial expressions, the reason might be that the faces were moving.

"Back then we had neither the equipment nor the technical competence to test our idea. We dug it out again only a year ago. So, our results are based on an old idea which nobody had tested in the meantime," he says.

What Makes Facial Expressions Intelligible?

In order to carry out the test, the researchers had to combine modern simulation techniques with previous insight into how infants' vision works. We have a great deal of information about young infants' contrast sensitivity and spatial resolution from behavioural studies conducted, for the most part, in the 1980s. At that time, it was discovered that presenting an infant with a figure against a uniformly grey background caused the infant to direct its gaze towards the figure.

"Figures made up of black and white stripes were used. By choosing a certain stripe width and frequency, the field would appear uniformly grey, and the child would not direct its gaze towards it. Changing the width and frequency to make up figures made it possible to determine the exact level of contrast and spatial resolution needed to make the infant direct its gaze towards the figure," Magnussen says.

In other words, the researchers had access to quite accurate information about newborn infants' vision. What was unknown to them, was the practical consequences of this information. Does it, for instance, mean that a newborn baby can see the expression in the face of an adult bending over the baby?

Movement Is Easier to See

It's easier to recognise something that moves, than a blurry still photo. The researchers made video recordings of faces that changed between several emotional expressions, and subsequently filtered out the information which we know is unavailable to newborn infants. Then they let adult participants see the videos. The idea was that if the adults were unable to identify a facial expression, then we can certainly assume that a newborn would also be unable to do so.

The adult participants correctly identified facial expressions in three out of four cases when viewing the video at a distance of 30 centimeters. When the distance was increased to 120 centimeters, the participants' rate of identification were about what one could expect from random responding. This means that the ability to identify facial expressions based on the visual information available to a newborn baby, reaches its limit at a distance of about 30 centimeters.

Filling a Gap in the Foundation Wall

"It's important to remember that we have only investigated what the newborn infant can actually see, not whether they are able to make sense of it," Magnussen points out.

Previous attempts to recreate the newborn baby's visual reality, for instance in students' textbooks, have usually relied on taking a normal photograph and blurring it. Magnussen confesses himself surprised that nobody before them have made use of the detailed information we possess about infants' visual perception. Hence this is the first time that we have a concrete estimate of the visual information available to the newborn baby.

Magnussen and his colleagues are happy to finally have been able to carry out an idea that had been on the back burner for 15 years. But as for developing their results further, they will leave that to others.

"All of us behind this study are really involved in different fields of research now. Our position is: Now a piece of the foundation is in place. If anyone else wants to follow up, that's up to them," says Magnussen.

Reference

Svein Magnussen et al. "Simulating newborn face perception", *Journal of Vision,* doi: 10.1167/14.13.16

Critical Thinking

1. The researchers suggest that newborn infants can see faces and perhaps emotional expressions within two to three days of birth. Why would that be an important skill to possess so early? Explain.
2. Why is movement such a key component to newborn infants' vision? Explain.
3. When a newborn infant "sees" something, does that also mean that they can make sense of what they are seeing? Why or why not?

Internet References

The world according to babies
http://www.parents.com/baby/care/newborn/babies-world/

Your baby's eyes
http://www.bausch.com/vision-and-age/infant-eyes/eye-development#.VgAv-PnF9g0

Your baby's hearing, vision, and other senses: 1 month
http://kidshealth.org/parent/pregnancy_newborn/senses/sense13m.html

Article

Prepared by: R. Eric Landrum, *Boise State University*

One in Five Teens May Be Bullied on Social Media

Review found wide variations in prevalence, but victims were often females who were depressed.

RANDY DOTINGA

Learning Outcomes

After reading this article, you will be able to:

- Understand the difficulty of establishing causation, such as whether depression causes cyberbullying or cyberbullying causes depression.
- Appreciate the challenges in studying the long-term effects of cyberbullying on children.

A new review suggests that estimates of cyberbullying are all over the place, ranging as low as 5 percent and as high as 74 percent.

But some findings are consistent: Bullied kids are more likely to be depressed and to be female, and cyberbullying mostly arises from relationships.

"When children and youth are cyberbullied, they are often reluctant to tell anyone," said review author Michele Hamm, a research associate with the Alberta Research Center for Health Evidence at the University of Alberta in Edmonton, Canada.

"Prevention and management efforts are likely necessary at multiple levels, involving adolescents, parents, teachers, and health care professionals," Hamm said.

Researchers launched the review to get a better understanding of cyberbullying, which they defined as bullying via social media and not in private conversations by text messages or Skype.

"We wanted to find out whether there was evidence that social media could be harmful to kids and if so, be able to inform future prevention strategies," Hamm said.

The researchers looked at 36 studies, mostly from the United States. Of those, 17 reports examined how often cyberbullying occurred. The researchers found that a median of 23 percent of kids reported being bullied via social media. A median is not an average; it's the midpoint in a group of numbers.

The percentage is derived from studies that had a wide variety of definitions of when cyberbullying had to have occurred to count, Hamm said.

In some cases, researchers counted whether kids had ever been bullied; in other cases, bullying only counted if it was repeated, she said.

One expert thought 23 percent was probably an accurate assessment of the prevalence of cyberbullying.

"It would be easy, just from watching the news, to conclude that virtually every child in America is a victim of bullying," said Robert Faris, an associate professor of sociology at the University of California, Davis.

"The prevalence of cyber- and traditional bullying will always vary based on the way they are defined, how the questions are asked and the time period in question," Faris explained. "But regardless of these issues, only a minority of kids can be considered victims. So, the overall estimate is actually in line with other estimates of traditional bullying."

The researchers also found an association between depression and cyberbullying, although it's not clear if one causes the other.

"The associations between cyberbullying and anxiety and self-harm were inconsistent," Hamm added. "Except for one, all of the studies that we found were only looking at relationships at one point in time, so it isn't known whether there is a long-term impact of cyberbullying on kids' mental health."

However, Faris believes cyberbullying by social media poses a special threat to kids and is "probably a lot more damaging to targets" than other forms of bullying. "Harassing messages can be blocked, but public humiliation can't be halted by victims," he said. "And, of course, it involves a much wider audience."

As for helping kids who are bullied, review author Hamm said, "Adolescents are often unaware that anything can be done about cyberbullying, so efforts should be made to increase education regarding how to address it and who to tell, focusing on both recipients and bystanders."

Rachel Annunziato, an assistant professor of clinical psychology at Fordham University in New York City, said, "The best advice we can give parents is to frequently monitor their children's Internet use . . . We are in a position to spot and stop this behavior or help our children if they are recipients of cyberbullying. Another thing we can do is ask about cyberbullying. Our children may not realize that we are aware of this."

Faris agreed that parents must play a role.

"Kids do not tell adults about bullying. Not teachers, not coaches, not parents," he said. "This is largely because they feel adults will not help and can make things worse. So, one crucial lesson is that parents should really monitor what their kids are doing online and on social media, and also ask pressing questions about how things are going at school and with friends."

Source

Michele Hamm, Ph.D., research associate, Alberta Research Center for Health Evidence, department of pediatrics, University of Alberta, Edmonton, Canada; Robert Faris, Ph.D., associate professor, sociology, University of California, Davis; Rachel Annunziato, Ph.D., assistant professor, clinical psychology, Fordham University, New York City; June 22, 2015, *JAMA Pediatrics,* online

Critical Thinking

1. What is the typical response by a bullied child? Describe it, and discuss why you think the response is what it is.
2. In a research study, why is it important to define what "social media" are, and what they are not? Explain.

Internet References

Cyberbullying statistics
http://www.internetsafety101.org/cyberbullyingstatistics.htm

Teen depression and how social media can help or hurt
http://www.cnn.com/2015/08/05/health/teen-depression-social-media/

Teens, kindness and cruelty on social network sites
http://www.pewinternet.org/2011/11/09/teens-kindness-and-cruelty-on-social-network-sites/

Article

Prepared by: R. Eric Landrum, *Boise State University*

How Do Smartphones Affect Childhood Psychology?

AMY WILLIAMS

Learning Outcomes

After reading this article, you will be able to:

- Appreciate the prevalence and widespread use of cellular phones.
- Understand how the use of brain scans can be a research tool to help understand the progress being made in a developing child's brain.
- Comprehend the effect of increased screen time on brain development.

Have you noticed what seems like an epidemic of people who are glued to their smartphone's soft glow?

Unfortunately, you are not alone. Over 1.8 billion people own smartphones and use their devices on a daily basis. Some studies estimate that an average person checks their screen 150 times a day.

This widespread use of technology trickles down to the youngest members of our society. Data from Britain shows almost 70 percent of "11- to 12-year-olds use a mobile phone and this increases to close to 90 percent by the age of 14."

In a recent publication, it was noted that 56 percent of children between the ages of 10 to 13 own a smartphone. While that fact alone may come as a shock, it is estimated that 25 percent of children between the ages of 2 and 5 have a smartphone.

It should come as no surprise that smartphones and tablets have now replaced basketballs and baby dolls on a child's wish list. Elementary school-aged children start asking, or let's say begging, for these forms of technology before they can even tie their shoes.

This raises the question of how mobile technology, typically found in smartphones, affects childhood brain development. This topic has been creating a lot of debate among parents, educators, and researchers. Unfortunately, smartphones are relatively new and a lot of the gathered evidence is unclear or inconsistent.

That means that it is important for parents to consider the potential effects smartphones can have on childhood psychology and development.

A lot of research has been conducted over the years to understand how children learn. There are many theories circulating, but Jean Piaget might be the most respected in the education field. He was one of the first people to study how a child's brain develops.

His cognitive development theory basically explains how learning is a mental process that reorganizes concepts based on biology and experiences. He deduced that children learn the same way—their brains grow and function in similar patterns, moving through four universal stages of development.

Educators have been implementing a variety of techniques and methods into their lessons that build on Piaget's principles. Children need to experience the world around them to accommodate new ideas. Children "construct an understanding of the world around them" and try to understand new ideas based on what they already know and discover.

For children, face-to-face interactions are the primary ways they gain knowledge and learn.

Dr. Jenny Radesky of Boston Medical Center, became concerned when she noticed the lack of interaction between parents and children. She had observed that smartphones and handheld devices were interfering with bonding and parental attention.

Radesky said, "They (children) learn language, they learn about their own emotions, they learn how to regulate them. They learn by watching us how to have a conversation, how to read other people's facial expressions. And if that's not happening, children are missing out on important development milestones."

Screen time takes away from learning and physically exploring the world through play and interactions. It can be noted that doctors and educators are worried how the overexposure to touch-screen technology can impact developing brains.

Radiation from cellphones has long been a primary fear of how smartphones can affect a brain. However, the radiation theory hasn't been proven and many professionals claim cellphones do not expose us to enough radiation to cause harm. That may provide parents a little relief, but it appears that the radio frequencies emitted from a smartphone might actually harm a developing brain.

The temporal and frontal lobes of the brain are still developing in a teen and they are closest to the part of the ear where teens tend to hold their device. In fact, "research has shown that both the temporal and frontal are actively developing during adolescence and are instrumental in aspects of advanced cognitive functioning."

Besides exposing developing brains to radio waves or harmful radiation, researchers are looking into how smartphones and the Internet can hinder or enrich brain function. Dr. Gary Small, head of UCLA's memory and aging research center, performed an experiment that demonstrates how people's brains change in response to Internet use.

He used two groups: those with a lot of computer savvy and those with minimal technology experience. With brain scans, he discovered that the two groups had similar brain functions while reading text from a book. However, the tech group showed "broad brain activity in the left-front part of the brain known as the dorsolateral prefrontal cortex, while the novices showed little, if any, activity in this area."

As a child ages it often feels like they need to practice technology to stay on top of the modern advancements. However, Dr. Small's experiment shows that after a few days of instruction, the novices were soon showing the same brain functions as the computer-savvy group.

Technology and screen time had rewired their brains. It appears that increased screen time neglects the circuits in the brain that control more traditional methods for learning. These are typically used for reading, writing, and concentration.

Smartphones and the Internet also affect communication skills and the emotional development of humans. If a child relies on electronics to communicate, they risk weakening their people skills. Dr. Small suggests that children can become detached from others' feelings.

If a human's mind can be easily molded, imagine the connections and wiring that is happening in a brain still developing.

However, there is no concrete proof that mobile technology is linked to adverse outcomes. Smartphones and technology do offer benefits to our children. Here is a quick rundown of the benefits technology can offer our youth:

- A child is more capable of: handling rapid cybersearches, making quick decisions, developing visual acuity, and multitasking.
- Games help develop peripheral vision.
- Visual motor tasks like tracking objects or visually searching for items is improved.
- Internet users tend to use decision-making and problem-solving brain regions more often.

Many experts and educators feel that interactive media has a place in a child's life. Smartphones and tablets can foster learning concepts, communication, and camaraderie.

Here are a few recommendations to make the most of time spent on a smartphone:

- Children under two should not be using screens or electronic devices.
- Play alongside your children and interact with them face-to-face.
- Make sure smartphones don't interfere with opportunities for play and socializing.
- Limit screen use to one or two hours a day. This includes smartphones, TV, computers, etc.
- It is all right to use a smartphone as an occasional treat.
- Model positive smartphone use.
- Encourage family meals and communication.
- Look for quality apps that promote building vocabulary, mathematical, literacy, and science concepts.
- Keep smartphones out of the bedrooms.

Health officials seem unable to agree on the impact smartphones and similar devices have on developing brains. Studies contradict each other and new benefits to technology are uncovered regularly.

Obviously, parents do need to stay informed. They should be aware of the possible side effects a smartphone can harbor. All of this inconclusive evidence can lead a parent to question when they should allow their children access to smartphones or technology. However, one thing all the experts seem to agree on is that moderation is key.

References

Babycentre. Is screen time good or bad for babies and children? BabyCentre. Retrieved from http://www.babycentre.co.uk/a25006035/is-screen-time-good-or-bad-for-babies-and-children#ixzz3MIEeZN84

Ballve, M. (2013). How Much Time Do We Really Spend On Our Smartphones Every Day? *Business Insider.* Retrieved from http://www.businessinsider.com.au/how-much-time-do-we-spend-on-smartphones-2013-6

Chapman, G.D., & Pellicane, A. (2014). Growing Up Social: Raising Relational Kids in a Screen-Driven World. Retrieved from http://www.amazon.com/Growing-Up-Social-Relational-Screen-Driven-ebook/dp/B00J48B03K

Glatter, R. M.D. (2014). Can Smartphones Adversely Affect Cognitive Development In Teens? *Forbes.* Retrieved from http://www.forbes.com/sites/robertglatter/2014/05/19/can-smartphones-adversely-affect-cognitive-development-in-teens/

Howley, D.P. (2013). Children and Smartphones: What's the Right Age? Laptop Part of Tom's Guide. Retrieved from http://blog.laptopmag.com/kids-smartphones-right-age

McLeod, S. (2009). Jean Piaget. Simply Psychology. Retrieved from http://www.simplypsychology.org/piaget.html

Neighmond, P. (2014). For The Children's Sake, Put Down That Smartphone. *NPR.* Retrieved from http://www.npr.org/blogs/health/2014/04/21/304196338/for-the-childrens-sake-put-down-that-smartphone

Williams, A. (2014). 7 Steps to Ease Your Tween into a Smartphone. *TeenSafe.* Retrieved from http://www.teensafe.com/blog/smartphones/7-steps-ease-tween-smartphone/

Critical Thinking

1. The author reported the estimate that the average person checks their cellphone screen 150 times a day. What type of impact, overall, do you think this behavior has on other behaviors? Explain.
2. The lack of interaction between parents and developing children is a concern to some researchers. What strategies might be used to reverse this trend? Be specific.
3. Based on the recommendations offered in the article, which of those recommendations are the most important to implement immediately, and why?

Internet References

Babies don't need smartphones

http://www.usatoday.com/story/opinion/2015/05/08/technology-babies-speech-development-toddler-column/70940608/

Pacifying toddlers with tablets, smartphones may hurt development, scientists speculate

http://www.thestar.com/life/2015/02/06/pacifying-toddlers-with-tablets-smartphones-may-hurt-development-scientists-speculate.html

Researchers: Using an iPad or smartphone can harm a toddler's learning and social skills

http://www.washingtonpost.com/news/morning-mix/wp/2015/02/02/using-an-ipad-or-smartphone-can-harm-a-toddlers-brain-researchers-says/

Article

Prepared by: R. Eric Landrum, *Boise State University*

The Influence of Health-care Policies on Children's Health and Development

JAMES M. PERRIN, THOMAS F. BOAT, AND KELLY J. KELLEHER

Learning Outcomes

After reading this article, you will be able to:

- Articulate the relationship between poverty and child health and development.
- Explain the relationship between health insurance coverage for children and children's health.

How do current health care policies influence child health and development in America? The US has recently achieved the highest rates of child health insurance coverage in history, in part due to state Medicaid expansions and the continued growth of the state Children's Health Insurance Program (CHIP). Other health care policies—many in the public health arena—influence child health, ranging from infection control programs and policies to public nutrition programs to prevention of injurious exposures to child abuse and neglect reporting to (generally ineffective) gun violence prevention programs. For the most part, these policies provide for basic, not optimal, health protections and access to health care.

Over the past several decades, many of the scourges of child health—infectious diseases such as diphtheria or meningitis, rickets and severe malnutrition, lead poisoning, and early deaths from cancer—have diminished or even almost disappeared, in part due to effective federal policy on sanitation, food, and health care. The decline of many older diseases has been countered by new epidemics of obesity, asthma, neurodevelopmental disorders, and mental health conditions, but federal health policy has moved slowly to address these new issues. Most of the health problems that affect children and youth today reflect social and community influences rather than infections (although social factors also influence acquisition of infections and their severity). The circumstances into which a child is born have stronger relationships to her/his health and development than do genes or direct health care services, limiting the effectiveness of health care to improve health. At the same time, greater understanding of the importance of early life experiences, early education, and family and community influences on child health and development has highlighted new and changing needs for child health care. Additionally, there is clear recognition that improving child health requires integration across multiple sectors as well as having a long-term or life course perspective. Two examples document these needs for new policy directions well—the effects of poverty on child health and the prominence of behavioral health issues for children.

Poverty affects essentially all aspects of child health and development—higher mortality from serious childhood illnesses, higher rates of accidents and injuries, higher rates of common chronic health conditions and resulting disability, less physical endurance as well as poorer school performance and graduation rates, more risky sexual and substance abuse behaviors, and higher rates of incarceration as adolescents. From a health perspective, decreasing poverty will improve health status and response to medical treatments as much or more than improvements in personal health care services for children. Yet, strategies to diminish poverty among U.S. families are not straightforward and require a multifaceted approach, including work to improve household income, housing, nutrition, jobs, and education among families of young children.

Rates of mental health diagnoses have grown rapidly among U.S. children and youth. Here, too, children face a highly fragmented system at every level of care for behavioral and emotional symptoms. Identification of mental health problems can come from community services (e.g., day care or schools), health services, or family referral. Much mental health diagnosis and treatment, especially for low-income children, takes place in the public school system. Health and related service providers have little incentive currently for early identification and treatment (or referral) of children and families for behavioral health, although recent efforts to (re) integrate behavioral health with the rest of the health care sector have promise. Current federal policy in this area maintains separation of health and behavioral health services in many situations, from precluding researchers from accessing behavioral health claims for study to policies that support separation of psychiatric hospitals and institutions from other services.

How do current policies affect and improve child outcomes—and especially help to promote an effective, well-trained, healthy, and competent young adult population? This report addresses those questions and offers proposals to build stronger, cross-sector programs to enhance the health and development of children in America.

Health Insurance for Children and Families Today

Children and youth obtain health insurance through a combination of public and private sources (Bureau of Labor Statistics & the Census Bureau, 2014). The majority (although diminishing in proportion) of children still receive insurance coverage through a parent's employment benefits. Rates of employer coverage of children's insurance have slowly dropped over the past quarter century (from about 75% in 1980 to about 57% in 2014), in part due to decreasing family coverage for employees (Bureau of Labor Statistics & the Census Bureau, 2014). In years past, employee benefits usually included health insurance for the employee's household; increasingly, employers limit health benefits to the employee alone.

Partly as a result of the decline in employer support for dependents, public health insurance has grown substantially as the payer for children's health care.

Medicaid, the major public insurance program for low-income children, differs from Medicare in several critical ways (Iglehart & Sommers, 2015). Medicare, a national health insurance program for all citizens over age 65, has national payment rates, full funding from the federal government, and common covered services for all beneficiaries, regardless of where they live. Medicaid, like Medicare, is an entitlement program, such that any applicant meeting eligibility requirements must be enrolled. But Medicaid, unlike Medicare, has joint funding from the federal government and the states, and states maintain oversight prerogatives regarding the state's Medicaid program. Insofar as Medicaid, too, is an entitlement program, states are unable to predict their Medicaid expenditures each year. Furthermore, when the economy weakens, state revenues fall but more people meet financial eligibility requirements for Medicaid (and other public programs). Medicaid, as a joint federal-state program, has much variation across states in payment level and services covered. On average, Medicaid payments are about 2/3 the level of Medicare payments for the same service (Rosenbaum, 2014). New York and Massachusetts may cover different mental health services and pay very different rates for those services. States set eligibility requirements, payment rates, and methods of payment (e.g., managed care or direct to provider payment), covered services, and scope of benefits (e.g., hospital days or physical therapy may be covered, but the maximum yearly benefit could be just a few days or a few treatments). The variations across state Medicaid programs are dramatic, with little consistency (Kaiser Commission on Medicaid and the Uninsured, 2013).

Medicaid, initially limited to children on welfare or with severe disabilities, now includes many children with household incomes well above the limits required for public assistance through the Temporary Assistance to Needy Families (TANF) program, in most states up to 2 or 3 times the Federal Poverty Line (FPL). In the mid-1990s, Congress passed the Children's Health Insurance Program (CHIP), which provides additional insurance coverage for children in households with incomes too high for Medicaid but not eligible for employer-based programs (Artiga & Cornachione, 2016). CHIP, unlike Medicaid, is a block grant to the states rather than an entitlement program; when a state runs out of its yearly grant, it can refuse to enroll new, eligible children. Finally, implementation of the Affordable Care Act (ACA) has helped insure some additional children, both because they may be directly eligible but also because increasing coverage for adults has led parents to seek different ways to insure their children (Artiga & Cornachione, 2016). Generally, insured parents are more likely to try to find insurance for their children than are uninsured parents, and the process of enrollment for the ACA has helped parents determine whether their children are eligible for Medicaid or other programs.

While more children than ever before are covered, insurance coverage does not guarantee access. First, large numbers of dentists and pediatricians in the US do not accept Medicaid for children in their practices because of low payment rates. Second, parents with both private and public insurance have increasing out-of-pocket costs for a variety of health care expenses from new, high cost treatments to routine visits. Finally, many children with specialty care needs lack needed services because of long wait lists for appointments at regional pediatric specialty centers where the supply of pediatric specialists remains low.

These insurance expansions—most in the public sector—have led to over 94% of children in the US now having some form of health care insurance coverage. Poor children continue to lag behind middle income children, but the gap has markedly narrowed (Bureau of Labor Statistics & the Census Bureau, 2014). This growth in public insurance for children represents substantial growth in public investment. Given the major squeeze on discretionary funding in federal and many state budgets, however, this growth has come at the expense of new funding for other public services in education or social and community services (Rosenbaum & Blum, 2015; Steuerle, 2014).

What Does Insurance Cover?

U.S. health insurance has long focused on paying for services provided—in general, the more work done (i.e., more visits, procedures, treatments), the greater the payments (i.e., fees for services provided). Providers (physicians, nurses, hospitals, health centers) must meet certain requirements for licensure and accreditation but they then receive payment for an array of services mainly focused on disorder assessment and treatment. Public and private payers will pay for a variety of services, increasingly including some preventive care and health promotion, although the original intention of insurance was catastrophic-risk protection against unexpected high (health care) expenses. Preventive services (e.g., immunizations, screening) still account for only a small percentage of total health expenditures for children.

The incentives in traditional insurance arrangements thus are to increase the number of visits or procedures for which insurance will pay. Yet, the relationship between these services and outcomes that might be valued for children and adolescents may be limited.

Assessment of quality of care in traditional arrangements has often focused on assuring performance of certain services, especially monitoring activities (e.g., routine height and weight, assessment for obesity) and some preventive services (e.g., immunizations and certain screenings, such as hearing and vision or lead levels) rather than improvements in outcomes or effectiveness.

Some evidence does indicate that having health insurance improves child health, although clearly other factors—family, social, and community characteristics—have much more influence on a child's health and well-being than does health insurance. In general, most of the evidence is that health care improves access to and use of preventive services, especially routine checkups (Edmunds & Coye, 1998). Children with health insurance appear to have better dental health as well (Leininger & Levy, 2015). But, as an example, although the US has high immunization rates, that achievement in large part reflects requirements for adequate vaccination at school entry rather than the success of health insurance. For very young children, more evidence supports the value of non-reimbursed services like home visiting and nutrition programs (e.g., WIC) than reimbursed routine prenatal care (Rossin-Slater, 2015). Addressing the family and community issues that have the main impact on children's long-term well-being will require major changes in the application of incentives in health insurance—moving from a focus on medical care coverage to strategies to make health care more effective in building healthy communities (Robert Wood Johnson Foundation, 2014).

A sizable number of children experience (individually) relatively rare and complex conditions such as juvenile arthritis, hemophilia, leukemia, brain tumors, sickle cell disease, and chromosomal disorders. Although each condition may be individually rare, adding all approximately 7,000 rare diseases (most of which manifest in childhood) together leads to a large number of children (3.5 million) with conditions that typically require much expertise and cost in their diagnosis, management, assessment for complications, and monitoring over time. This group of children may get a good deal of care from community health providers, although most of them also will need access to care and support from pediatric subspecialists—medical and surgical (Perrin, Anderson, & Van Cleave, 2014). Pediatric subspecialists, unlike many subspecialties in adult medicine, are relatively few in number and typically centralized in specialized children's hospitals and academic programs, often at some distance from where their patients with rarer chronic conditions may live.

Medicaid, as a joint federal-state program, generally serves children within a state's borders. A child who may need to travel to a neighboring or more distant state for specialized care may find that the insurance coverage does not travel with her and may face difficulty in accessing needed care. Most children's hospitals provide specialized care to children in neighboring states as well as in their home communities. While these specialized programs may contract with Medicaid agencies in neighboring states, these contracts may pay less than the in-state rate for care and can be an obstacle to needed specialized treatment. Moves to develop regionalized systems of care, with regionalized Medicaid funding, may help to improve access (Children's Hospital Association, 2015).

Support For Children Living In Poverty and Those with Disabilities

A number of other programs provide some support for children and families, especially in low-income households. The full range of these programs—from nutrition to housing to juvenile justice—is beyond the scope of this report, although all can influence child health. We will focus on two programs with direct effects on poverty amelioration and links to health care eligibility: the Temporary Assistance to Needy Families

(TANF) program and the Supplemental Security Income (SSI) program.

Both programs provide cash assistance to low-income families but with different purposes. TANF, like Medicaid, is a joint federal-state program, with states having much flexibility in determining eligibility and payment rates. In 2012, TANF income eligibility rates varied across the nation, with a national average of about 50% of the FPL—or less than $13,000 for a family of four. Thus, households must generally be extremely poor to gain TANF eligibility (Falk, 2013). State payment rates vary similarly, from a high in New York of $753 per month for a family of three to a low of $170 in Mississippi. TANF rules, outlined in the Personal Responsibility and Work Opportunity Reconciliation Act of 1996, also place limits on the number of years recipients may receive benefits. Furthermore, that welfare reform act ended any increase in funds, such that the total state and federal expenditures for TANF have remained the same for the last two decades, indicating a loss of about 32% in real dollars from inflation. About a third of households receiving TANF have children with disabilities in them, limiting parents' work opportunities and often requiring much parent caretaking over years. TANF acts as a critical safety net for the few families with young children who are eligible for benefits in lifting them out of abject poverty. Although a vital source of income for the relatively small number of households who are eligible, TANF fills a relatively small gap in services and support needed by families raising children with chronic health conditions and other threats to their health and development. Poverty is linked to numerous opportunities for stressful adverse experiences, and persistent adversity can be toxic and contribute to poor behavioral and physical health across the lifespan. Policy that addresses poverty, with understanding of the short- and long-term costs and benefits for individuals and society, should be a national priority.

The Supplemental Security Income (SSI) program provides cash assistance to low-income people with severe disabilities, including children. In general, the level of disability must be quite high—that is, most children with chronic health conditions will not meet the high standard of severity that SSI uses (Boat & Wu, 2015).

Approximately 1.3 million U.S. children and youth currently receive SSI benefits, and the associated income (up to about $8,000 per year) keeps a moderate number of households with children with disabilities above the FPL. SSI is mainly a federally-funded program, although many states supplement the monthly federal benefit. States, through their Disability Determination Services, determine financial and clinical eligibility for applicants, working under federal rules and supervision. Raising a child with a severe disability usually increases family expenses (many needed services and supplies are not covered by private or public health insurance), along with decreasing household income, as often one or both parents must limit or quit the workplace to care for a child with a major disability. Thus, these SSI funds help to replace this income and allow families to meet some of their additional costs. Moreover, SSI eligibility almost always confers eligibility for Medicaid enrollment and services.

Both of these programs, like Medicaid, experience major variations across states. For Medicaid and TANF, states have much flexibility in determining eligibility and benefits. A recent report also documented wide variations in rates of applications, assessments, and determinations of eligibility for SSI across the states, although the reasons for these variations are not clear (and likely do not reflect major variations in rates of severe disability across the states) (Boat & Wu, 2015). Policy that promotes equity in supports and services that improve health outcomes should have a beneficial impact on the health of the U.S. population.

Recent Trends In Health Care Payment

The high rates of inflation in health care expenditures have led to much interest in finding new ways to diminish the growth of health care costs. The Affordable Care Act, especially as implemented through the Center for Medicaid and Medicare Services (CMS), has supported experimentation with new ways to incentivize preventive care for high-risk older populations—groups with high rates of hospital and emergency department care. Based mainly in Medicare and not Medicaid, these strategies have begun to apply new notions of prevention and keeping populations healthy (or healthier). Payment approaches have included sharing financial risk with providers—if providers can cut costs for populations, for example, by decreasing hospital use, the provider may share in the savings accrued. Providers have responded by implementing health care teams, dedicated case management, new health status monitoring technologies (including extensive use of mHealth), home care, and others. Payers, with Medicare leading the way, have experimented with new ways to pay for health care, including incentives to meet newer quality standards, sharing savings through implementing new programs, and fully capitated arrangements, where providers get a fixed dollar amount for providing a full range of services to a defined population over some time period (Burwell, 2015). These strategies have worked relatively well for specific populations that have traditionally used large amounts of health care services, achieving lower expenses in a relatively short period of time (18–36 months; Powers & Chaguturu, 2016). Applying a similar short-term savings approach works less well for children who generate only a small fraction of total U.S. health care costs, and where the opportunities for major health care cost savings in a short period of time are much more limited. Improvement of child health, however, represents an appealing long-term strategy for reducing adult health care costs.

What Are the Needs of Children and Families That Health Care Policies Can Address?

Several characteristics distinguish children from older populations. They have substantially more racial and ethnic diversity than any other group, and their development influences what diseases they experience, how those conditions manifest at different ages, and how children respond to treatment (Forrest, Simpson, & Clancy, 1997; Perrin & Dewitt, 2011). Children depend very much on adults—initially, parents and family and later, teachers and others—for their health care and developmental needs. Although in general, children are healthier than other populations, they too experience much chronic illness, at increasing rates over the past decades. And finally, they have much higher rates of poverty than any other age group, and poverty has pervasive influences on health and wellness and on growth, development, and educational achievement.

The past few decades have seen much change in the health conditions that children face. Many serious infectious diseases have disappeared with effective immunization programs (e.g., measles, diphtheria, tetanus, meningitis). Tuberculosis affects far fewer children than in decades past; many conditions that would have led to early death now have treatments that have greatly improved life expectancy for those who experience them (e.g., leukemia, complex congenital heart disease, cystic fibrosis). Main causes of death today among children and adolescents are accidents and suicides rather than malnutrition and epidemics (Rosenbaum & Blum, 2015).

These strong improvements in child health have been accompanied by major growth in four groups of common health conditions among children: obesity, asthma, mental health conditions (e.g., depression, anxiety, attention deficit hyperactivity disorder), and neurodevelopmental conditions (e.g., autism spectrum disorders, adverse consequences of prematurity). Diagnoses of these conditions, not typically fatal, have experienced huge growth over the past half century. Parents in 1960 reported less than 2% of children as having a chronic health condition severe enough to interfere with their lives on a daily basis. That percent has grown by over 400% to a rate today of over 8% (Field & Jette, 2007).

And rates of less severe chronic conditions (usually in the same four categories) have also grown such that some studies indicate that 25-35% of people under age 20 years will have experienced some chronic health condition in their first two decades (Van Cleave, Gortmaker, & Perrin, 2010). Some of this growth does represent improved survival owing to advances in medical and surgical care that have improved the outcomes of young people with conditions such as spina bifida and cystic fibrosis, but the large majority reflects the growth of these four common condition groups. Recent data also note well the growth of disability among young Americans of working age, with increasing numbers having severe obesity, mental health impairments, or developmental disorders that limit their ability to pursue educational opportunities or employment (Field & Jette, 2007).

Mental and behavioral health play an increasing and critical role in any consideration of child health and its impact on long-term health outcomes. For example, most mental health disorders of adults have their roots in childhood or adolescence. For several decades, child mental health was treated—and paid for—as a set of conditions separate from and distinct from the other conditions that children experience. Prevention in mental health gained little attention. Community physicians and pediatric subspecialists had little incentive or support to identify mental health conditions early or to prevent them through effective parent counseling or referral to community agencies. As a result, children with moderate to severe mental health conditions were not identified until they had quite severe symptoms, where earlier identification and intervention could have had major benefit. In more recent years, payers and program leaders, including a number of state Medicaid programs, have begun to address this separation and are working to reintegrate behavioral health into general pediatric care.

The effects of persistent mental health problems on children's functioning are clear, along with greater recognition that mental health conditions also generate or complicate many other health conditions. For adults, the co-occurrence of mental health conditions with chronic diseases such as heart disease or diabetes is associated with much higher costs (Melek et al., 2013). Children with chronic health conditions have higher rates of mental or behavioral health concerns as well. The opportunities within the health sector include addressing mental health concerns on all visits, systematic early identification through screening, building on longer-term trusting relationships to institute treatment, and providing services directly in the health sector (see below for co-location of mental health practitioners in pediatric settings as well as parent training activities carried out in pediatric practices) (American Academy of Pediatrics Task Force on Mental Health, 2010; Institute of Medicine & National Research Council, 2014). Given the substantial role of public schools in mental health care provision, it is also critical to have effective, ongoing collaboration between schools and (other) health providers. Unfortunately, budget constraints in school districts have diminished availability of health care personnel in schools. Similar attention to early childhood health has been even more spotty in preschool and child care settings.

Families seek responses to their needs in a delivery system that is a good deal broader than medical care, incorporating a wide array of community, public health, education, and other services (Perrin et al., 2007). These service systems are highly fragmented, and families' access to and use of services depends on many factors, including financing, physical access, knowledge, and beliefs. In mental and behavioral health, fragmentation is particularly obvious, with some care from mental health clinicians and primary care providers, especially in screening and identification of younger children, but a good deal more in public schools and for many in the juvenile justice system. Current incentives for collaboration across sectors are limited, but the opportunities that could accrue from coordination and collaboration are substantial (Cuellar, 2015).

Asthma, obesity, mental disorders, and neurodevelopmental conditions all reflect an interaction of genetic susceptibility with the influences of social and other environmental phenomena. Their prevention and management require a multidisciplinary and multi-institutional response, not something that the health care sector alone can manage. It will, nonetheless, be critical to find ways to prevent the onset and severity of these conditions, or the nation will face larger numbers of citizens who depend on public institutions and services for their livelihood, and fewer young people resilient and capable to participate effectively in the nation's economy (Field & Jette, 2007).

Over the past decade, increasing evidence has documented the importance of early life experiences for the well-being of young children—influencing their readiness for school and literacy at age 8 and their ability to succeed in adolescence and young adulthood. Particularly difficult circumstances lead to "toxic stress," where very young children face persistent adversity with consequent impact on their neuroanatomy and the functioning of their brain and other body systems. Toxic stress, much more prevalent among poorer children (although not limited to children growing up in poverty), can have permanent effects on the developing child (American Academy of Pediatrics, Committee on Psychosocial Aspects of Child and Family Health, 2012). Family functioning is a strong predictor of child developmental outcomes and health. Child health and development are inextricably intertwined—healthy children grow better, develop more skills, and have better school readiness. Similarly, children whose development has had support from parents and community services are healthier, pursue less risky behaviors, and have lower rates of the common chronic mental health and other health conditions in childhood and adulthood (Campbell et al., 2014). As addressed above, policies that promote better family functioning and support of children can broadly improve children's health and development.

New Models of Health Care

Recognition of the unaddressed and changing needs of children and families in the presence of changing financial incentives has fostered the development of new models of care. Most of these include the concept of medical homes and some elements of interdisciplinary care teams—associating medical professionals with other professionals who can expand the work and attention of the health care program (Patient-Centered Primary Care Collaborative, n.d.). Team functions (not specific team members) tend to fall into four main areas: chronic condition management, behavioral health integration, improving early childhood experiences, and linking households with critical community services. The growth of common chronic conditions has led to greater use of nurses or nurse practitioners to monitor care and progress over time and to help children and families with adherence to medical treatments. Greater recognition of mental health needs among children and the interconnection of behavioral issues with health and illness has led to programs of co-locating or integrating mental health professionals in pediatric practice (Kolko & Perrin, 2014; Williams, Shore, & Foy, 2006). Other programs to support better attention to behavioral health in pediatric care have included primary care physician backup systems in over 30 states, where physicians can easily and expeditiously consult a mental health practitioner by phone to help care for behavioral issues in the practice (Sarvet et al., 2010). Increasing understanding of the critical importance of early childhood has led practices to include home visiting and other parent support programs among their services or to collaborate with home visiting programs in the community. A focus on two generation health (child and parents) as essential for child well-being has begun to achieve traction in some pediatric health care settings. Finally, many practices have incorporated staff members who are or become knowledgeable about community culture and resources, learn to refer households to appropriate community services, and follow up to assure that families receive the services they need (Berkowitz et al., 2015). In all of these cases, family members (and children in developmentally appropriate ways) are central members of the team—teams reflect co-production with patients and families.

Financial support for these practice innovations has been limited; private payers rarely reward these innovations in traditional payment schemes because they often focus on nonprofessionals, diverse settings, and linkage of social and educational services with medical care, areas without a history of health care payment. Equally challenging, Medicaid (the largest payer for child medical care) has been much less active in child health care reform than with adults. To date, the development of federal policy around value-based purchasing has largely been driven by Medicare policy including the encouragement of both accountable care organizations and bundled payment initiatives. Primary care clinicians participating in the transformation to team-based care and related initiatives complain that they do so at their own financial risk (Chesluk & Holmboe, 2010).

Nevertheless, many clinicians and a few health systems have learned the value of these changes and have worked to obtain external funding or to reorganize the financing of the practice to support the changes. In a number of states, Medicaid programs have supported innovations, developing some incentives for practices similar to those in Medicare (i.e., care coordination, behavioral health integration, and chronic care management) (Centers for Medicare & Medicaid Services, n.d.; Hervey, Summers, & Inama, 2015). The largest of these are the statewide accountable care organizations (ACOs) undertaken by a handful of states to enroll all Medicaid managed care children and adults into provider networks that take both clinical and financial risk for the patients. Anecdotal experience to date suggests that cost growth in these ACOs has been lower than overall Medicaid cost growth in the respective states (Lloyd, Houston, & McGinnis, 2015). CMS has fostered both the start and expansion of some of these and related experiments in care transformation.

With innovation grants and systems improvement awards from CMS, states have experimented with a variety of programs, some focused on specific chronic conditions (obesity, asthma), others on behavioral health integration in primary care, and still others with bundled payments for episodes of care, an intermediate payment state between fee for service and capitation.

The statewide ACO initiatives have not had specific measurement or quality incentives for care focused on children, but fourteen pediatric health systems around the country have engaged in exclusive pediatric risk contracts while many more have plans to do so (Makni, Rothenburger, & Kelleher, 2015). These efforts have had dedicated pediatric networks and child specific goals for care improvement. Two have published evaluations suggesting modest quality improvements and significant cost savings (Christensen & Payne, 2016; Kelleher et al., 2015).

The use of ACO contracting to transform care is shifting incentives markedly in some places, but a larger effect in practice transformation will likely come from the bundled payment initiatives undertaken by Arkansas (Chernew et al., 2015), Ohio, and other states. The provision of incentives for providers that meet minimum quality standards and save money, with corresponding penalties for high cost providers for specific diagnoses and procedures, results in tight referral networks of low cost providers and careful follow up of high cost patients. Notably, these efforts include partnerships among Medicaid and the largest private insurers so that all providers are affected.

Together, these efforts have started a movement to better use newer measures of quality (Anglin & Hossain, 2015; Blumenthal & McGinnis, 2015). What should indicate value in child health care? What outcomes should health care payers (public and private) use to assess care?

Where do patient and parent experience of care and partnership appear in measures? Would school readiness at age 5, literacy at age 8, and high school graduation serve as good measures? Quality of life, functioning at a high level, and freedom from health symptoms and conditions are potentially important considerations. In behavioral health, increasing evidence indicates the greater importance of improving functioning and academic performance than controlling symptoms (Cuellar, 2015).

Training the Pediatric Workforce

While pediatric training has evolved in response to emerging needs of children over the last several decades, several gaps remain for residency and fellowship training that deserve attention. These include health promotion and prevention in general, parent and family health and functioning assessment and support as it influences child health, and behavioral health, along with skills in epidemiology, behavior change, and clinical management. Although training content is not legislated, several important programs and organizations have responsibility to consider and set expectations for pediatric training that can respond more to the overall health needs of children. These include individual training programs, the Pediatric Residency Review Committee (RRC), and the American Board of Pediatrics (ABP). The latter two influence training outcomes by defining criteria for accreditation of training curriculum and experiences (RRC) and expected competencies for post-training certification (ABP). These regulatory bodies de facto set expectations for pediatric training and its outcomes and thereby set national training policy. The organizations must embrace greater attention to health promotion and prevention, family function, and behavioral health of children, and how to embed these elements of care widely into pediatric practice.

Physicians should also have facility and familiarity with digital monitoring and communications devices, basic epidemiology and population health skills to lead community health efforts, and basic business skills to operate in large corporate enterprises across multiple settings.

A further need for pediatric training is experience in creating and working effectively within interdisciplinary teams. Currently, medical trainees rarely work with trainees and practitioners in other relevant health professions such as nurses and nurse practitioners, psychologists and social workers, and community health workers. The needs of children and families call for planning, integration, and delivery of care that is transdisciplinary, a term that has come to define partners who go beyond working in the same place to those who adopt integrated planning and delivery of comprehensive care. An example arises from the creation of integrated behavioral and traditional medical care, where pediatricians should develop competencies in sharing responsibility for behavioral health outcomes of children.

Integration Across Sectors—Beyond Health Care to the Health of Communities Where Children Live

What are potential solutions to the long-standing disconnect between traditional child health services, the growing population of children with chronic conditions including behavioral health, and the social and community determinants of children's health and development?

One innovative solution to expanding funding for health promotion and disease prevention for children and families is the expansion of social financing broadly and social equity or impact bonds (SIBs) in particular.

This class of investments uses innovative finance tools to engage private capital and oversight in addressing social needs and to create "shared value" (Porter, 2010). SIBs also are known as pay-for-success bonds and are not classical bonds in that they have elements of both bonds and stocks. Private investors enter into fixed period investments with return contingent on savings generated by the public agency for successful improvements. In the original Rockefeller Foundation bond at Petersborough prison in London, investors were returned funds based on the effectiveness of the recidivism prevention programs supervised by social agencies and investors. SIBs have been established to prevent teen pregnancy in Washington, DC, special education among young children in Utah, and asthma exacerbations among children in Fresno, CA, and South Carolina. For specific social problems, they show promise, but across broader social issues, inability to project a clear return on SIB investments will be a barrier to their attractiveness.

Two more general approaches for intervention have been suggested to address the multifactorial nature of health and mental health risk and resilience for children, especially the large number of children living in poverty. First, early childhood support programs that connect center-based child activities with family support can have lasting effects. Two carefully-designed and implemented long-term studies have shown that providing comprehensive child and family support during early childhood can have long-lasting payoffs for children and the community. Both the Abecedarian Project (in rural North Carolina) and the Perry Preschool Project (in more urban Michigan) randomized low-income households, predominantly African-American, to intervention and control groups and have now followed the children for over four decades (Campbell et al., 2014). Among the results have been higher high school and college graduation rates for the intervention groups; as well as later first pregnancies, lower rates of obesity, diabetes and hypertension, higher incomes and job retention, and substantially lower rates of incarceration among males (Campbell et al., 2014). Although both of these programs had health components, they mainly represent coordination of family support and early education with other community services.

The second approach is a more recent and rapidly growing attention to 'place-based' or geographically circumscribed, community development interventions that share common principles for neighborhood and child development. These include locally developed coalitions with community residents as leaders and members, asset-based development with local strengths' assessments, support from anchor institutions such as medical centers or universities, and a comprehensive service package to include at a minimum housing, jobs and education reform linked to health care services. Such initiatives presume that long-term sustainability requires neighborhood commitment and involvement, and the health of children and families will always be vulnerable unless underlying risks like homelessness and unemployment are addressed (Fryer & Katz, 2013; U.S. Department of Health and Human Services, n.d.). National foundations have been leaders in this effort including the Casey Foundation Two Generation Approach, the Robert Wood Johnson Foundation Culture of Health initiatives, and the Kellogg Healthy Communities. The federal Promise Neighborhoods are similar. Independent of these efforts, several neighborhood initiatives are being spearheaded by pediatricians and children's hospitals oftentimes connected with Medicaid financial risk contracts. For example, the Lower Price Hill initiative in Cincinnati, the Southern Orchards initiative in Columbus, and the East Milwaukee initiative in Wisconsin all are linked to organizations with Medicaid capitation contracts. Here, the organizations have recognized that investment in non-traditional programs such as housing may lead to decreased health care costs. While many of these initiatives across the country begin with extended provision of health care services in community settings, Medicaid and other payers are often recognizing the importance of the other components, often with the maxim, "Housing First." In fact, Medicaid waivers like the one in New York now allow Medicaid dollars to be used in focused populations for rent support in recognition of the critical role of housing in maintaining health.

A number of promising programs have focused on the integration of public and private efforts to link multiple services at the community level. Much of this work has focused on early childhood, recognizing that interventions must address both child issues and the needs of parents. These programs recognize that parent health and well-being—and meeting the needs of parents—is critical to improving the health of children. Care must address two generations and not focus only on children. Examples include the major commitment of the business community to improving early childhood education (see http://www.americaspromise.org; http://toosmall.org), public efforts to integrate services so that households find a seamless set of programs to help them meet their needs (Fryer & Katz, 2013; U.S. Department of Health and Human Services, n.d.), and the inclusion of early childhood and community investment in a number of state budgets. Governors recognize that one of the major expenses in state budgets involves maintaining or financing prisons for (mainly) young males—an investment with very little return for the state or community. They also have recognized that prevention of the need for incarceration can be a wiser investment. A recent report from the Robert Wood Johnson Foundation calls for greater investment in children and communities and for making the communities where we work and live and raise children "healthy communities" (Robert Wood Johnson Foundation, 2014). Experiences reflecting this approach also have integrated a variety of services at the community level—including health care—to support health and child growth. The Federal Reserve Banks, which invest large amounts of resources each year in communities, have recognized the importance of community development and coalitions to achieve the kinds of communities that will strengthen the local economy and the lives and preparation of workers. Below, we will consider ways that the health care sector can support and engage with these community efforts and how health care policies could aid that integration.

Federal policy is also influential in the link between the education sector and health care. Health insurance and access to a usual source of care can improve academic outcomes (Institute of Medicine, 2009). Specifically, Medicaid access for children results in better grades, fewer missed days, greater graduation rates, and higher long term earnings (Cohodes, Grossman, Kleiner, & Lovenheim, 2014). When schools aid in insurance enrollment during school registration or other events, they are promoting better performance in school. The Patient Protection and Affordable Care Act (ACA) also recognized the link between health and schools. More than $200M was authorized for expansion of school health clinics, purchase of new equipment for school clinics, and modernization of the same. CMS also modified its 'free care policy' allowing Medicaid reimbursement as first payer for school-based services (U.S. Department of Health and Human Services, 2014). Finally, schools, in partnership with health care agencies, can provide wrap around case management to high risk children who are chronically absent, homeless, or at risk of falling behind (Suter & Bruns, 2009).

New Strategies in Health Care—What's Most Promising

New ventures in health care financing and organization could assist the broader attention to prevention, health promotion, and community integration. Health care payment approaches that pay for value rather than services provided, with value defined as outcomes indicative of child and adolescent wellness and development, should be considered (e.g., readiness for next developmental steps, such as school entry). Such incentives move well beyond fee for service to payment for achieving specified goals or potentially global budgeting (payment for all health services over a specified period of time). These payment arrangements provide incentives for health care providers to account for social and community influences on the health status of their patients and to engage community partners to improve those outcomes. Doing this will require incentives for coordination and new measures to assess outcomes related to functioning and performance. CMS recently announced a new program to support healthy neighborhoods—experimenting with payment to enhance health care connections with the community and recognize the multiple community players that influence health (Centers for Medicare & Medicaid Services, n.d.). The neighborhood for a child includes the multiple service programs, including of course schools, that impact a child (Perrin et al., 2007), and for children with more complex chronic conditions, the subspecialists (often not in the same geographic neighborhood) that the child needs.

New information technologies can enhance these systems of community care. Mobile health (mHealth) developments include the ability to monitor a child with a chronic condition (e.g., asthma) at a distance but in real time; to assess the middle ear status of a child with fever and earache while she stays in school; to communicate with children and families about the value of certain health behaviors (including immunizations, safe sex, adequate sleep, physical activity); and to examine growing premature infants for retinopathy at a distance. While these and additional forms of mHealth development hold great promise, their yield and implementation will be determined more by federal policy than by technical limitations because investment and growth are affected by a myriad of federal issues at the moment.

Oversight of mHealth technologies at the federal level is distributed among several agencies. The Food and Drug Administration issued guidance in 2012 that it would regulate some devices and forms of mHealth as 'medical devices' and modified that guidance in 2013 to include mobile medical apps (U.S. Food and Drug Administration, 2013). For items classified as medical devices, registration, pre-release testing and post-release safety monitoring are all required, considerably raising the costs and stakes for development and sales of mHealth devices. The Federal Trade Commission also plays an important role in assessing whether mHealth advertising claims are met or fair and has the lead federal role in data breaches due to device malfunction or negligence. When data breaches do occur, the Office of Civil Rights within the U.S. Department of Health and Human Services supervises penalties which may amount to $50,000 per individual patient's data loss. Finally, the Federal Communications Commission regulates all mHealth tools that use part of the electromagnetic spectrum or transmit personal data as communications devices (Center for Connected Health Policy, n.d.). They specifically set aside part of the electromagnetic spectrum for transmission of personal medical information in 2012 and monitor the use of public airwaves (Office of the National Coordinator for Health Information Technology, n.d.).

Perhaps most importantly, licensing restrictions and outdated federal telemedicine restrictions discourage innovation and spread of telehealth generally. Telehealth offers many opportunities in health care, including decentralizing subspecialty care to communities through distance evaluation and treatment, providing mental health services in homes and community settings, and providing new skills to community practitioners (Burke & Hall, 2015). Licensing of physical therapists, nurses, and physicians, among others, precludes cross-state interactions requiring clinicians from the originating site to seek multiple state licenses. While interstate compacts are being pursued in some places, short-term solutions are not in sight. Similarly, older legislation prevents Medicare and Veterans Administration patients from receiving telemedicine services in urban areas, at home, in community health centers, and in some other locations. The wide-reaching nature of these exclusions strongly discourages investment in mHealth and telemedicine (American Telemedicine Association, n.d.). A variety of bills have been introduced in Congress aimed at individual pieces of the logjam, but progress has been slow.

Finally, the growing collection of biologic data—phenotypic and genomic—will help guide more targeted therapies and support better health surveillance and prediction of health outcomes. Greater understanding of environmental influences—toxic exposures, social and community interactions—will also improve prediction of critical health outcomes, as well as help target useful interventions to improve health.

As the focus sharpens on understanding child and family health risks and orienting medical care to reduce these risks, identifying individual risks will be increasingly possible and important. Risks are not only socially but biologically determined. Children are born with genetic health risks and resilience, and are both born with and acquire epigenetic health risk and resilience traits. National research funding priorities should acknowledge and promote studies aimed at identifying these risk and resilience factors and using that information along with socioeconomic risk and resilience factors to individualize or be selective in efforts to mitigate health risks in early life. A partnership of biological and socioeconomic research has potential to advance the promotion of child health to levels not achievable by either alone.

References

American Academy of Pediatrics, Committee on Psychosocial Aspects of Child and Family Health. (2012). Early childhood adversity, toxic stress, and the role of the pediatrician: Translating developmental science into lifelong health. *Pediatrics, 129*, e224–e231. doi:10.1542/peds.2011-2662

American Academy of Pediatrics Task Force on Mental Health. (2010). Enhancing pediatric mental health. *Pediatrics, 125*, S69–S195.

American Telemedicine Association. (n.d.). *Telehealth in the U.S.* Washington, DC: Author. Retrieved from http://www.americantelemed.org/docs/default-source/policy/telehealth-in-the-u-s-handout.pdf?sfvrsn=2

Anglin, G., & Hossain, M. (2015). *How are CHIPRA quality demonstration states using quality reports to drive health care improvements for children? National evaluation of the CHIPRA quality demonstration grant program* (Evaluation highlight #11). Washington, DC: Agency for Healthcare Research and Quality.

Artiga, S., & Cornachione, E. (2016). *Trends in Medicaid and CHIP eligibility over time.* Washington, DC: Kaiser Commission on Medicaid and the Uninsured. Retrieved from http://files.kff.org/attachment/report-trends-in-medicaid-and-chip-eligibility-over-time-2016-update

Berkowitz, S. A., Hulberg, A. C., Hong, C., Stowell, B. J., Tirozzi, K. J., Traore, C. Y., & Atlas, S. J. (2015). Addressing basic resource needs to improve primary care quality: A community collaboration programme. *British Medical Journal.* Advance online publication. doi:10.1136/bmjqs-2015-004521

Blumenthal, D., & McGinnis, J. M. (2015). Measuring vital signs: An IOM report on core metrics for health and health care progress. *JAMA, 313*, 1901–1902. doi:10.1001/jama.2015.4862

Boat, T. F., & Wu, J. T. (Eds.). (2015). *Mental disorders and disabilities among low-income children.* Washington, DC: National Academies of Science, Engineering, and Medicine.

Bureau of Labor Statistics & the Census Bureau. (2014). *Current population survey (CPS): Annual social and economic (ASEC) supplement.* Washington, DC: Author. Retrieved from https://www.census.gov/hhes/www/cpstables/032015/health/h01_000.htm

Burke, B. L., & Hall, R. W. (2015). Telemedicine: Pediatric applications. *Pediatrics, 136*, e293–e308. doi:10.1542/peds.2015-1517

Burwell, S. M. (2015). Setting value-based payment goals—HHS efforts to improve U.S. health care. *New England Journal of Medicine, 372*, 897–899. doi:10.1056/NEJMp1500445.

Campbell, F., Conti, G., Heckman, J. J., Moon, S. H., Pinto, R., Pungello, E., & Pan, Y. (2014). Early childhood investments substantially boost adult health. *Science, 343*, 1478–1485. doi:10.1126/science.1248429

Center for Connected Health Policy. (n.d.). *mHealth laws and regulations.* Sacramento, CA: Author. Retrieved from http://cchpca.org/mhealth-laws-and-regulations

Centers for Medicare & Medicaid Services. (n.d.). *Accountable health communities model.* Baltimore, MD: Author. Retrieved from https://innovation.cms.gov/initiatives/ahcm/

Centers for Medicare & Medicaid Services. (n.d.). *Medicaid and CHIP (MAC) learning collaboratives.* Baltimore, MD: Author. Retrieved from https://www.medicaid.gov/state-resource-center/mac-learning-collaboratives/medicaid-and-chip-learning-collab.html

Chernew, M. E., Golden, W. E., Mathis, C. H., Fendrick, A. M., Motley, M. W., & Thompson, J. W. (2015). The Arkansas payment improvement initiative: Early perceptions of multi-payer reform in a fragmented provider landscape. *American Journal of Accountable Care, 3*, 35–38.

Chesluk, B. J., & Holmboe, E. S. (2010). How teams work—or don't—in primary care: A field study on internal medicine practices. *Health Affairs, 29*, 874–879. doi:10.1377/hlthaff.2009.1093

Children's Hospital Association. (2015). *ACE Kids Act of 2015 high-level summary (S. 298 and H.R. 546).* Washington, DC: Author. Retrieved from https://www.childrenshospitals.org/Issues-and-Advocacy/Children-With-Medical-Complexity/Issue-Briefs-and-Reports/2015/ACE-Kids-Act-of-2015-High-Level-Summary

Christensen, E. W., & Payne, N. R. (2016). Effect of attribution length on the use and cost of health care for a pediatric Medicaid accountable care organization. *JAMA Pediatrics, 170*, 148–154. doi:10.1001/jamapediatrics.2015.3446

Cohodes, S., Grossman, D., Kleiner, S. & Lovenheim, M. F. (2014). *The effect of child health insurance access on schooling: Evidence from public insurance expansions* (No. 20178). Cambridge, MA: National Bureau of Economic Research.

Cuellar, A. (2015). Preventing and treating child mental health problems. *Future of Children, 25*, 111–134.

Edmunds, M., & Coye, M. J. (Eds.). (1998). *America's children: Health insurance and access to care.* Washington, DC: National Academies Press.

Falk, G. (2013). *The Temporary Assistance for Needy Families block grant: An introduction* (R40946). Washington, DC: U.S. Congressional Research Service.

Field, M. J., & Jette, A. M. (2007). *The future of disability in America.* Washington, DC: National Academies Press.

Forrest, C. B., Simpson, L., & Clancy, C. (1997). Child health services research: Challenges and opportunities. *JAMA, 277*, 1787–1793. doi:10.1001/jama.1997.03540460051032

Fryer, R. G., & Katz, L. F. (2013). Achieving escape velocity: Neighborhood and school interventions to reduce persistent inequality. *American Economic Review, 103*, 232–237. doi:10.1257/aer.103.3.232

Hervey, D., Summers, L., & Inama, M. (2015). *The rise and future of Medicaid ACOs.* Salt Lake City, NV: Leavitt Partners.

Iglehart, J. K., & Sommers, B. D. (2015). Medicaid at 50—From welfare program to nation's largest health insurer. *New England Journal of Medicine, 372*, 2152–2159. doi:10.1056/NEJMhpr1500791

Institute of Medicine. (2009). *America's uninsured crisis: Consequences for health and health care.* Washington, DC: National Academies Press. Retrieved from https://www.nationalacademies.org/hmd/~/media/Files/Report%20Files/2009/Americas-Uninsured-Crisis-Consequences-for-Health-and-Health-Care/Americas%20Uninsured%20Crisis%202009%20Report%20Brief.pdf

Institute of Medicine & National Research Council. (2014). *Strategies for scaling effective family-focused preventive interventions to promote children's cognitive, affective, and behavioral health (Workshop summary).* Washington, DC: National Academies Press.

Kaiser Commission on Medicaid and the Uninsured. (2013). *Medicaid: A primer 2013.* Washington, DC: Author. Retrieved from https://kaiserfamilyfoundation.files.wordpress.com/2010/06/7334-05.pdf

Kelleher, K. J., Cooper, J., Deans, K., Carr, P., Brilli, R. J., Allen, S., & Gardner, W. (2015). Cost saving and quality of care in a pediatric accountable care organization. *Pediatrics, 135*, e582–589. doi:10.1542/peds.2014-2725

Kolko, D. J., & Perrin, E. (2014). The integration of behavioral health interventions in children's health care: Services, science, and suggestions. *Journal of Clinical Child & Adolescent Psychology, 43*, 216–228. doi:10.1080/15374416.2013.862804

Leininger, L., & Levy, H. (2015). Child health and access to medical care. *Future of Children, 25*, 65-90.Lloyd, J., Houston, R., & McGinnis, T. (2015). *Medicaid accountable care organization programs: State profiles.* Hamilton, NJ: Center for Health Care Strategies. Retrieved from http://www.chcs.org/resource/medicaid-accountable-care-organization-programs-state-profiles/

Makni, N., Rothenburger, A., & Kelleher, K. (2015). Survey of twelve children's hospital-based accountable care organizations. *Journal of Hospital Administration, 4*, 64–73. doi:10.5430/jha.v4n2p64

Melek, S. M., Norris, D. T., & Paulus, J. (2013). *Economic impact of integrated medical-behavioral healthcare.* Denver, CO: Milliman. Retrieved from http://www.psychiatry.org/psychiatrists/practice/professional-interests/integrated-care

Office of the National Coordinator for Health Information Technology. (n.d.). *Overview of federal role in mobile health.* Washington, DC: Author. Retrieved from https://www.healthit.gov/policy-researchers-implementers/overview-federal-role-mobile-health

Patient-Centered Primary Care Collaborative. (n.d.). *Defining the medical home: A patient-centered philosophy that drives primary care excellence.* Washington, DC: Author. Retrieved from https://www.pcpcc.org/about/medical-home

Perrin, J. M., Anderson, L. E., & Van Cleave, J. (2014). The rise in chronic conditions among infants, children, and youth can be met with continued health system innovations. *Health Affairs, 33*, 2099–2105. doi:10.1377/hlthaff.2014.0832

Perrin, J. M., & Dewitt, T. G. (2011). Future of academic general pediatrics: Areas of opportunity. *Academic Pediatrics, 11*, 181–188. doi:10.1016/j.acap.2011.03.008

Perrin, J. M., Romm, D., Bloom, S. R., Homer, C. J., Kuhlthau, K. A., Cooley, C., . . . Newacheck, P. (2007). A family-centered, community-based system of services for children and youth with special health care needs. *Archives of Pediatric and Adolescent Medicine, 161*, 933–936. doi:10.1001/archpedi.161.10.933

Porter, M. E. (2010). What is value in health care? *New England Journal of Medicine, 363*, 2477–2481. doi:10.1056/NEJMp1011024

Powers, B. W., & Chaguturu, S. K. (2016). ACOs and high-cost patients. *New England Journal of Medicine, 374*, 203–205. doi:10.1056/NEJMp1511131

Robert Wood Johnson Foundation Commission to Build a Healthier America. (2014). *Time to act: Investing in the health of our children and communities.* Princeton, NJ: Author. Retrieved from http://www.rwjf.org/en/library/research/2014/01/recommendations-from-the-rwjf-commission-to-build-a-healthier-am.html

Rosenbaum, S. (2014). Medicaid payments and access to care. *New England Journal of Medicine, 371*, 2345–2347. doi:10.1056/NEJMp1412488

Rosenbaum, S., & Blum, R. (2015). How healthy are our children? *Future of Children, 25*, 11–34.

Rossin-Slater, M. (2015). Promoting health in early childhood. *Future of Children, 25*, 35–64.

Sarvet, B., Gold, J., Bostic, J. Q., Masek, B. J., Prince, J. B., Jeffers-Terry, M., . . . Straus, J. H. (2010). Improving access to mental health care for children: The Massachusetts Child Psychiatry Access Project. *Pediatrics, 126*, 1191–2000. doi:10.1542/peds.2009-1340

Steuerle, C. E. (2014). *Dead men ruling: How to restore fiscal freedom and rescue our future.* New York, NY: Century Foundation Press.

Suter, J. C., & Bruns, E. J. (2009). Effectiveness of the wraparound process for children with emotional and behavioral disorders: A meta-analysis. *Clinical Child and Family Psychology Review, 12*, 336–351. doi:10.1007/s10567-009-0059-y

U.S. Department of Health and Human Services. (n.d.). *Invitation: Obama administration announces rural IMPACT demonstration.* Baltimore, MD: Author. Retrieved from http://mchb.hrsa.gov/impactdemonstrationannouncement.html

U.S. Department of Health and Human Services. (2014). *Medicaid payment for services provided without charge (free care).* Baltimore, MD: Author. Retrieved from https://www.medicaid.gov/federal-policy-guidance/downloads/smd-medicaid-payment-for-services-provided-without-charge-free-care.pdf

U.S. Food and Drug Administration. (2013). *Cybersecurity for medical devices and hospital networks: FDA safety communication.* Silver Spring, MD: Author. Retrieved from http://www.fda.gov/medicaldevices/safety/alertsandnotices/ucm356423.htm

Van Cleave, J., Gortmaker, S. L., & Perrin, J. M. (2010). Dynamics of obesity and chronic health conditions among children and youth. *JAMA, 303*, 623–630. doi:10.1001/jama.2010.104

Williams, J., Shore, S. E., & Foy, J. M. (2006). Co-location of mental health professionals in primary care settings: Three North Carolina models. *Clinical Pediatrics, 45*, 537–543. doi:10.1177/0009922806290608

Critical Thinking

1. What is the role of health insurance for children? Where have efforts been successful, and what are the developing challenges here regarding children's health?
2. To what extent can health-care policies solve the challenges of providing adequate health care to all children? Explain.

Internet References

Child care: Early childhood education and care

http://www.child-encyclopedia.com/child-care-early-childhood-education-and-care/according-experts/child-care-and-its-impact-young-1

Child development

https://www.cdc.gov/ncbddd/childdevelopment/facts.html

Maternal, infant, and child health

https://www.healthypeople.gov/2020/topics-objectives/topic/maternal-infant-and-child-health

Unit 8

UNIT

Prepared by: R. Eric Landrum, *Boise State University*

Personality Processes

Sabrina and Sadie are identical twins. When the girls were young, their parents tried very hard to treat them equally. They dressed them the same, fed them same meals, and allowed them to play with the same toys. Each had a kitten from the same litter. Whenever Sabrina received a present, Sadie received one, too, and vice versa. Both girls attended dance school and completed early classes in ballet and tap dance. For elementary school, the twins were both placed in the same class with the same teacher. The teacher also tried to treat them the same. In junior high school, Sadie became a tomboy. She loved to play rough-and-tumble sports with the neighborhood boys. On the other hand, Sabrina remained indoors and practiced the piano. Sabrina was keenly interested in hobbies such as painting, needlepoint, and sewing. Sadie was more interested in reading novels, especially science fiction, and watching action movies on television.

As the twins matured, they decided it would be best to attend different colleges. Sabrina went to a small, quiet college in a rural setting, and Sadie entered a large public university. Sabrina majored in English, with a specialty in poetry; Sadie switched majors several times and finally decided on a psychology major. Why, when these twins were exposed to the same childhood environment, did their interests, personalities, and paths diverge later? What makes people, even identical twins, so unique and so different from one another? The study of individual differences resides the domain of personality psychology.

The psychological study of personality includes two major thrusts. The first has focused on the search for the commonalties of human behavior and personality. Its major question is "How are humans, especially their personalities, affected by specific events or activities?" The second has focused on discovering the bases on which individuals differ in their responses to events, such as the self-control exhibited by Sadie and Sabrina as they went off to college. In its early history, this specialty was called genetic psychology because most people assumed that individual differences resulted from differences in inheritance. By the 1950s, the term genetic psychology had given way to the more current terminology: the psychology of individual differences.

Today, most psychologists accept the principle that both genes and the environment are important determinants of any type of behavior, whether it be watching adventure movies or sitting quietly and reading or caring for the elderly. Modern researchers devote much of their efforts to discovering how the two sources of influence (nature and nurture) interact to produce a unique individual. Thus, the focus of this unit is on personality characteristics and the differences and similarities among individuals, with these fascinating differences ranging from cultural expectations and stereotypes to the development of political attitudes.

Article

Prepared by: R. Eric Landrum, *Boise State University*

Good News about Worrying

JAN HOFFMAN

Learning Outcomes

After reading this article, you will be able to:

- Understand the effectiveness of different coping strategies.
- Define defensive pessimism.

In May, Mathieu Putterman and Anna Evans Putterman graduated from law school at Chapman University. In July, the couple took the California bar examination. Results will be posted on Nov. 20, at 6 p.m. The Puttermans are in the final throes of that four-month wait.

Mr. Putterman, 29, is not breaking a sweat.

"I had good preparation, so I'm expecting to pass," he said. "If I don't, I'll cross that bridge when it comes." His wife? Drenched.

"I would never say 'I think I passed,'" whispered Mrs. Putterman, 25. "What if I say it out loud and they haven't graded my essays yet? Will someone hear?"

Mrs. Putterman and fellow worry warriors, take heart.

A new study in the journal Emotion of how people manage stress while waiting for high-stakes results is a validation of sorts for those who embrace their anxiety. During the waiting period, researchers found, those who tried coping techniques failed miserably at suppressing distress. And when the news arrived, the worriers were more elated than their relaxed peers, if it was good; if bad, the worriers were better prepared.

"One definition of waiting well is not having negative emotions. But not going through that thinking process leaves you less prepared to receive the news. That's the paradox, the counterintuitive part of the findings," said Julie K. Norem, the author of "The Positive Power of Negative Thinking," and a professor of psychology at Wellesley, who was not involved in the study.

Most researchers who study how people cope with uncertainty look at how they absorb difficult news — results of a biopsy, college or job application, bar exam — and then move forward.

But this study focused on an area that has received less scrutiny: the waiting period, during which a person is in limbo, powerless to affect a possibly life-altering outcome.

Kate Sweeny, an associate professor of psychology at the University of California, Riverside, and her researchers surveyed 230 law school graduates frequently during the four months after the California bar exam in July 2013.

Could they wait in ways that mitigated anxiety? And would the way they managed their emotions during the waiting period have an effect on how they handled the pain or joy of the results?

People tried to make time fly and their worries disappear: yoga and exercise, work, binge-watching television, talking with friends, not talking with friends. Drinking.

Mr. Putterman reports that he keeps busy with work and caring for the couple's Maltipoo puppy. Mrs. Putterman: "It drives me crazy when people say 'calm down.' "

Studies have shown that immersive activities, such as video games or even rainy-day household chores like closet decluttering, are more successful distractions than passive ones, like watching TV.

But in this study, almost no activity kept the waiters' anxiety at bay over the long haul. The strategies generally separated into three directions.

Some people sought to suppress fears. "But the more you try not to pay attention," Dr. Sweeny said, "the more aware you become."

Others sought silver linings. "They tried to anticipate something good in a bad outcome," Dr. Sweeny said. "'I will grow as a person if I fail the bar exam.'"

But, she contended: "That's defensive posturing. Why would they take the bar exam if they believed that silver lining?"

Others aimed for a time-tested approach: hoping for the best, bracing for the worst. These people worried constructively, doing what researchers call "defensive pessimism," or "proactive coping." They dive into the worry maelstrom, surfacing with contingency plans.

"Set your expectations low and think through the negative possibilities," Dr. Norem said. "It drives optimists crazy. But it shifts your attention away from feelings of anxiety to what you can do to address the disaster that might happen."

When it came to how people handled the news, "The poor waiters did great," Dr. Sweeny said. If the news was bad, the worriers were ready with productive, reasonable responses. "And if they passed, they were elated."

But woe to those who had remained calm.

"Those who sailed through the waiting period were shattered and paralyzed by the bad news," Dr. Sweeny said. "And if they got good news, they felt underwhelmed. You know, like, 'Big whoops!' "

One takeaway, Dr. Norem said, is that "although anxiety is a negative emotion because it feels bad, it is not a negative emotion in that it's bad to feel it. Why wouldn't you feel anxious, waiting for results?"

The study also points to the importance of elation, the thrill of good news, made even more joyous when freed from soul-binding worry.

After the California bar exam in July 2014, Natalia Bialkowska, 25, a graduate of U.C.L.A.'s law school, worried mightily. That is because during the negligence tort essay, her worst nightmare became reality.

Ms. Bialkowska's laptop, purchased in her native Poland, started behaving like a Polish-language keyboard. Z's, N's, O's, A's popped up with accents.

She panicked, deleting, copying, translating from Polish to English to California legal.

The four-month waiting period was excruciating. "I prayed to God to let the graders be able to read in Polish and English," she said.

At 6 p.m., Nov. 21, 2014, Ms. Bialkowska punched in her registration number as a co-worker peered over her shoulder, clutching a bottle of sake.

Red. She failed.

You typed the wrong ID number, the co-worker shouted.

Green! Congratulations!

The co-worker screamed. Ms. Bialkowska sat silent, stunned. "Be happy!" the co-worker commanded, proffering the bottle. Ms. Bialkowska obeyed.

"I teared up and we laughed and celebrated. I texted everyone and called my mom in Poland," she said. "There had been huge, heavy stress, and waiting forever. So the first feeling was relief." And then, she added, "came the utmost happiness: I am 'Esquire'!"

So good luck, Puttermans et al. Don't be happy. Worry.

Critical Thinking

1. Based on the data, what are the best coping strategies when waiting for a decision which will have high impact?
2. Is anxiety a negative emotion or an appropriate emotion? Explain.

Internet References

Are you a defensive pessimist?
http://academics.wellesley.edu/Psychology/Norem/Quiz/quiz.html

Pessimism and anxiety linked to Parkinson's
http://www.webmd.com/parkinsons-disease/news/20050413/pessimism-anxiety-linked-to-parkinsons#1

The ironic health risks of worrying about your health
https://www.forbes.com/sites/alicegwalton/2016/11/18/the-ironic-health-risks-of-worrying-about-your-health/#17af2ea3703f

The positive power of negative thinking
http://www.huffingtonpost.com/adam-grant/the-positive-power-of-neg_b_4107096.html

The upside of pessimism
https://www.theatlantic.com/health/archive/2014/09/dont-think-positively/379993/

Article

Prepared by: R. Eric Landrum, *Boise State University*

How Are Horoscopes Still a Thing?

LINDA RODRIGUEZ MCROBBIE

Learning Outcomes

After reading this article, you will be able to:

- Understand what a natal star chart is.
- Report the general percentage of Americans who read their horoscopes often.

Astrology is either an ancient and valuable system of understanding the natural world and our place in it with roots in early Mesopotamia, China, Egypt and Greece, or complete rubbish, depending on whom you ask.

But newspaper and magazine horoscopes? The ones advising you to not "fight against changes" today, or to "go with the flow," whatever that means, or to "keep things light and breezy with that new hottie today"? They get even less respect, from both skeptics and true believers. So it's a bit surprising, then, that they remain so popular with everyone in between.

The first real newspaper horoscope column is widely credited to R.H. Naylor, a prominent British astrologer of the first half of the 20th century. Naylor was an assistant to high-society neo-shaman, Cheiro (born William Warner, a decidedly less shamanistic name), who'd read the palms of Mark Twain, Grover Cleveland, and Winston Churchill, and who was routinely tapped to do celebrity star charts. Cheiro, however, wasn't available in August 1930 to do the horoscope for the recently born Princess Margaret, so Britain's *Sunday Express* newspaper asked Naylor.

Like most astrologers of the day, Naylor used what's called a natal star chart. Astrology posits that the natural world and we human beings in it are affected by the movements of the sun, moon and stars through the heavens, and that who we are is shaped by the exact position of these celestial bodies at the time of our birth. A natal star chart, therefore, presents the sky on the date and exact time of birth, from which the astrologer extrapolates character traits and predictions.

On August 24, 1930, three days after the Princess's birth, Naylor's published report predicted that her life would be "eventful," an accurate if not entirely inspired forecast given that she was, after all, a princess (he didn't, it appears, foresee the Princess's later star-crossed romances and lifelong love affair with alcohol and cigarettes). He also noted that "events of tremendous importance to the Royal Family and the nation will come about near her seventh year," a prediction that was somewhat more precise – and seemed to ring true right around the time that her uncle, King Edward VIII, abdicated the throne to her father.

Celebrity natal star charts weren't a particularly novel idea; American and British newspapers routinely trotted astrologers out to find out what the stars had in store for society pagers like Helen Gould and "Baby Astor's Half Brother." Even the venerable *New York Times* wasn't above consulting the stars: In 1908, a headline declared that President Theodore Roosevelt, a Sagittarius, "might have been different with another birthday," according to "expert astrologer" Mme. Humphrey.

But though it wasn't the first of its kind, Naylor's article was a tipping point for the popular consumption of horoscopes. Following the interest the public showed in the Princess Margaret horoscope, the paper decided to run several more forecasts from Naylor. One of his next articles included a prediction that "a British aircraft will be in danger" between October 8 and 15. When British airship R101 crashed outside Paris on October 5, killing 48 of the 54 people on board, the tragedy was taken as eerie evidence of Naylor's predictive skill. Suddenly, a lot more people were paying attention to the star column. The then-editor of the paper offered Naylor a weekly column – on the caveat that he make it a bit less dry and bit more the kind of thing that lots of people would want to read – and "What the Stars Foretell," the first real newspaper horoscope column, was born.

The column offered advice to people whose birthdays fell that the week, but within a few years, Naylor (or a clever editor) determined that he needed to come up with something that could apply to larger volumes of readers. By 1937, he'd hit upon the idea using "star signs," also known as "sun signs," the familiar zodiac signs that we see today. "Sun sign" refers to the period of the year when the sun is passing through one of 12 30-degree celestial zones as visible from earth and named after nearby constellations; for example, if you're born in the period when the sun is passing through the constellation Capricornus (the "horned goat," often represented as a half-fish, half-goat), roughly December 22 to January 19, then that makes your sun sign Capricorn.

"The only phenomenon in astrology allowing you make a wild generalizations about everybody born in this period to that period every year without fail is the sun sign," explained Jonathan Cainer, prominent astrologer who writes one of Britain's most-read horoscope columns for *The Daily Mail.*

"[The column] was embraced by an enthusiastic public with open arms and it spawned a thousand imitations. Before we knew it tabloid astrology was born . . . this vast over-simplification of a noble, ancient art," Cainer says. Cainer pointed out that even as newspaper and magazine horoscope writing became more and more popular – which it did and quickly, on both sides of the Atlantic – the practice was largely disregarded by the "proper" astrological community. The accusation, he says, was bolstered by the fact that historically, a lot of horoscope columns weren't written by actual astrologers, but by writers told to read a book on astrology and get cracking.

Astrologers' consternation notwithstanding, the popularity of newspaper and magazine horoscope has never really died down; they became, along with standards like the crossword, newspaper "furniture," as Cainer put it (and people hate it when the furniture is moved, Cainer says). Cainer also noted that there are few places in newspapers and, to some extent magazines, that address the reader directly: "It's an unusual form of language and form of relationship and as such, it lends itself well to a kind of attachment."

Tiffanie Darke, editor of *The Sunday Times* Style section, which runs astrologer Shelley von Strunckel's column, confirmed that via email, saying, "There is a significant readership who buy the paper particularly for Shelley's column, and there is a very considerable readership who you will see on Sundays in the pub, round the kitchen table, across a table at a cafe, reading out her forecasts to each other."

This fits with what newspapers really are and have virtually always been – not just vehicles for hard news and so-called important stories, but also distributors of entertainment gossip and sports scores, advice on love matters and how to get gravy stains out of clothing, practical information about stock prices and TV schedules, recipes and knitting patterns, comics and humor, even games and puzzles. Whether those features are the spoonful of sugar to help the hard news medicine go down or whether people just pick up the paper for the horoscope makes little difference to the bottom line.

So as to why newspapers run horoscopes, the answer is simple: Readers like them.

But the figures on how many readers actually like horoscopes aren't entirely clear. A National Science Foundation survey from 1999 found that just 12 percent of Americans read their horoscope every day or often, while 32 percent read them occasionally. More recently, the American Federation of Astrologers put the number of Americans who read their horoscope every day as high as 70 million, about 23 percent of the population. Anecdotally, enough people read horoscopes to be angry when they're not in their usual place in the paper – Cainer says that he has a clause in his contract allowing him to take holidays, making him a rarity in the business: "The reading public is gloriously unsympathetic to an astrologer's need for time off."

Other evidence indicates that significant numbers of people do read their horoscopes if not daily, then regularly: When in 2011, astronomers claimed that the Earth's naturally occurring orbital "wobble" could change star signs, many people promptly freaked out. (Astrologers, meanwhile, were far more sanguine – your sign is still your sign, they counseled; some, Cainer included, sighed that the wobble story was just another salvo in the fiercely pitched battle between astronomers and astrologers.)

At the same time, a significant portion of the population believe in the underpinnings of newspapers horoscopes. According to a 2009 Harris poll, 26 percent of Americans believe in astrology; that's more people than believe in witches (23 percent), but less than believe in UFOs (32 percent), Creationism (40 percent) and ghosts (42 percent). Respect for astrology itself may be on the rise: A more recent survey from the National Science Foundation, published in 2014, found that fewer Americans rejected astrology as "not scientific" in 2012 than they did in 2010 – 55 percent as compared to 62 percent. The figure hasn't been that low since 1983.

People who read their horoscopes also pay attention to what they say. In 2009, an iVillage poll – to mark the launch of the women-focused entertainment site's dedicated astrology site, Astrology.com – found that of female horoscope readers, 33 percent check their horoscopes before job interviews; 35 percent before starting a new relationship; and 34 percent before buying a lottery ticket. More recent research, published in the October 2013 issue of the *Journal of Consumer Research*, found that people who read a negative horoscope were more likely to indulge in impulsive or self-indulgent behavior soon after.

So what's going on? Why are people willing to re-order their love lives, buy a lottery ticket, or a take a new job based on the advice of someone who knows nothing more about them than their birthdate?

One reason we can rule out is scientific validity. Of all the empirical tests that have been done on astrology, in all fields, says Dr. Chris French, a professor of psychology at London's Goldsmith College who studies belief in the paranormal, "They are pretty uniformly bad news for astrologers."

There's very little scientific proof that astrology is an accurate predictor of personality traits, future destinies, love lives, or anything else that mass-market astrology claims to know. For example, in a 1985 study published in the journal *Nature*, Dr. Shawn Carlson of University of California, Berkeley's Physics department found that seasoned astrologers were unable to match individual's star chart with the results of a personality test any better than random chance; in a second test, individuals were unable to choose their own star charts, detailing their astrologically divined personality and character traits, any better than chance.

A smaller 1990 study conducted by John McGrew and Richard McFall of Indiana University's Psychology department and designed with a group of astrologers, found that astrologers were no better at matching star charts to the corresponding comprehensive case file of a volunteer than a non-astrologer control subject or random chance, and moreover, didn't even agree with each other. A study out in 2003, conducted by former astrologer Dr. Geoffrey Dean and psychologist Dr. Ivan Kelly, tracked the lives of 2,000 subjects who were all born within minutes of one another over several decades. The theory was that if astrological claims about star position and birthdates were true, then the individuals would have shared similar traits; they did not.

Studies that support the claims of astrology have been largely dismissed by the wider scientific community for a "self-attribution" bias – subjects had a prior knowledge of their sign's supposed characteristics and therefore could not be reliable – or because they could not be replicated. Astrologers are, unsurprisingly, not impressed by scientific efforts to prove or disprove astrology, claiming that scientists are going about it all wrong – astrology is not empirical in the way that, say, physics is: "Experiments are set up by people who don't have any context for this, even if they were attempting to do something constructive," says Shelley von Strunckel, American astrologer and horoscope writer whose column appears in *The Sunday Times*, *London Evening Standard* , Chinese *Vogue*, *Tatler* and other major publications. "It's like, 'I'm going to cook this great French meal, I've got this great cook book in French – but I don't speak French.'"

But despite a preponderance of scientific evidence to suggest that the stars do not influence our lives – and even personally demonstrable evidence such as that financial windfall your horoscope told you to expect on the eighth of the month failed to materialize – people continue to believe. (It's important to note, however, that some astrologers balk at the notion of "belief" in astrology: "It's not something you believe in," says Strunckel. "It's kind of like believing in dinner. The planets are there, the cycles of nature are there, the full moons are there, nature relates to all of that, it's not something to believe in.")

The "why" people continue to read and credence their horoscopes is most often explained by psychologist Bertram Forer's classic 1948 "self-validation" study. Forer gave his students a personality test, followed by a description of their personality that was supposedly based on the results of the test. In reality, there was only ever one description, cobbled together from newspaper horoscopes, and everyone received the same one. Forer then asked them to rate, on a scale of 0 (very poor) to 5 (excellent), the description's accuracy; the average score was 4.26 – pretty remarkable, unless all the students really were exactly the same. Forer's observation was quickly dubbed the Forer effect and has often been replicated in other settings.

Part of what was happening was that the descriptions were positive enough, without being unbelievably positive:

You have a great deal of unused capacity which you have not turned to your advantage. While you have some personality weaknesses, you are generally able to compensate for them.

and, importantly, vague enough to be applicable to a wide audience:

At times you have serious doubts as to whether you have made the right decision or done the right thing. At times you are extroverted, affable, sociable, while at other times you are introverted, wary, reserved.

Even horoscope writers admit that some of their success rests in not saying too much. Says Cainer, "The art of writing a successful horoscope column probably confirms what all too many skeptics and cynics eagerly clutch to their bosoms as charlatanry. Because it's writing ability that makes a horoscope column believable . . . ultimately a successful column will avoid specifics wherever possible. You develop the art of being vague."

The other element of the Forer effect is that the individual readers did most of the work, shaping the descriptions to fit themselves – not for nothing is the Forer effect also called the Barnum effect, after the famous showman's claim that his shows "had something for everyone." French, the Goldsmith psychologist, notes that people who read horoscopes are often invested in making their horoscope right for them. "If you buy into the system and the belief, it's you that's kind of making the reading appear to be more specific than it actually is," he explains. "Most days for most people is a mix of good things and bad things, and depending on how you buy into the system . . . if you're told to expect something good that day, then anything good that happens that day is read as confirmation."

Astrologer Cainer has another, more practical explanation for why people read horoscopes: "It's because they're there." There's very much a "can't hurt" and "might help" perception of horoscopes; at the same time, newspaper horoscopes, he says, also allow casual horoscope readers "a glorious sense of detachment: 'I don't believe in this rubbish but I'll have a look.'" This resonates with what Julian Baggini, a British philosopher and writer for *The Guardian*, says about why people read horoscopes: "No matter how much the evidence is staring someone in the face there's nothing in this, there's that 'Well, you never know.'" (Even if you do know.)

But "you never know" and even the Forer effect doesn't entirely explain the longevity of a form that many critics complain has no business being in a newspaper – so maybe there's something else going on. When French taught a course with a section on astrological beliefs, he'd sometimes ask on exams: "Does astrology work?" "Basically, the good answers would be the ones that took part the word 'work,'" he says. On the one hand, the straightforward answer is that, according to a host of scientific studies, astrology does not work. "But you've then got the other question … 'Does astrology provide any psychological benefit, does it have an psychology function?'" he said. "The answer to that is, sometimes, yes."

Psychologists see people on a scale between those who have what's called an external locus of control, where they feel that they are being acted upon by forces out of their influence, and people with an internal locus of control, who believe that they are the actors. "Not so surprisingly, people who believe in astrology tend to have an external locus of control," says French. That observation tallies with what other psychologists say: Margaret Hamilton, a psychologist at the University of Wisconsin who found that people are more likely to believe favorable horoscopes, noted that people who are believers in astrology also tend to be more anxious or neurotic.

Newspaper horoscopes, she said, offer a bit of comfort, a sort of seeing through the veil on a casual level. French agrees: astrology and newspaper horoscopes can give people "some kind of sense of control and some kind of framework to help them understand what's going on in their lives." It's telling that in times of uncertainty, whether on a global, national or personal level, he notes, astrologers, psychics, and others who claim to be able to offer guidance do a pretty brisk business; that belief in astrology is apparently on the rise in America, according to the NSF survey published in 2014, may have something to do with recent financial uncertainty. Cainer agreed that people take horoscopes more seriously when they're in distress: "If they're going through a time of disruption, they suddenly start to take what's written about their sign much more seriously . . .. If you're worried and somebody tells you not to worry, you take that to heart." (On whether astrologers are taking advantage of people, French is clear: "I am not saying that astrologers are deliberate con artists, I'm pretty sure they're not. They've convinced themselves that this system works.")

Philosophically, there is something about reading horoscopes that *does* imply a placing of oneself. As Hamilton notes, "It allows you to see yourself as part of the world: 'Here's where I fit in, oh, I'm Pisces.'" Looking deeper, Baggini, the philosopher, explains, "Human beings are pattern seekers. We have a very, very strong predisposition to notice regularities in nature and the world, to the extent that we see more than there are. There are good evolutionary reasons for this, in short a false positive is less risky than failure to observe a truth." But, more to the point, "We also tend to think things happen for a reason and we tend to leap upon whatever reasons available to us, even if they're not entirely credible."

Horoscopes walk a fine line, and, for many people, an appealing one. "On the one hand, people do want to feel they have some agency or control over the future, but on the other, it's rather frightening to think they have too much," explained Baggini. "So a rather attractive world view is that there is some sense of unfolding benign purpose in the universe, in which you weren't fundamentally responsible for everything, but were given some kind of control … and astrology gives us a bit of both, a balance."

Astrologers might agree. "I'm a great believer in freewill," says Cainer. "There's a lovely old Latin phrase that astrologers like to quote to each other: Astra *inclinant non necessitant*. The stars suggest, but they don't force… I like to think that astrology is about a way of fighting planetary influences, it's not entirely about accepting them."

But really, at the end of the day, are horoscopes doing more harm than good, or more good than harm? It all depends on whom you ask (and, of course, on the appropriateness of the advice being given). Strunckel and Cainer, obviously, see what they do as helping people, although both acknowledge that, as Strunckel says, "Astrology isn't everybody's cup of tea."

Richard Dawkins, the outspoken humanist and militant atheist, came out strongly against astrology and horoscopes in a 1995 *Independent article* published on New Years' Eve, declaring, "Astrology not only demeans astronomy, shrivelling and cheapening the universe with its pre-Copernican dabblings. It is also an insult to the science of psychology and the richness of human personality." Dawkins also took newspapers to task for even entertaining such "dabblings." More recently, in 2011, British rockstar physicist Brian Cox came under fire from astrologers for calling astrology a "load of rubbish" on his *Wonders of the Solar System* program on BBC. After the

BBC fielded a bunch of complaints, Cox offered a statement, which the broadcaster probably wisely chose not to release: "I apologize to the astrology community for not making myself clear. I should have said that this new age drivel is undermining the very fabric of our civilization."

What Dawkins and Cox may not want to acknowledge is that humans don't tend to make decisions based on a logical, rational understanding of facts (there's a reason why "cognitive dissonance" is a thing) – and horoscope reading might be just as good a system of action as any. "Most people don't base their views and opinions the best empirical evidence," French says. "There are all kinds of reasons for believing what you believe, not least of which is believing stuff because it just kind of feels good."

At their heart, horoscopes are a way to offset the uncertainty of daily life. "If the best prediction you've got is still completely rubbish or baseless, it's better than no prediction at all," says Baggini. "If you have no way of controlling the weather, you'll continue to do incantations and dances, because the alternative is doing nothing. And people hate doing nothing."

Critical Thinking

1. What is your opinion about astrology? Provide a detailed opinion.
2. What is the relationship between sun signs in astrology and horoscopes?
3. Describe the Forer effect, and its relationship to understanding the popularity of horoscopes.

Internet References

Astrology: Is it scientific?
http://undsci.berkeley.edu/article/astrology_checklist

Looking for a sign? Scientifically (in)accurate horoscopes
https://www.scientificamerican.com/article/looking-for-a-sign/

Some people think astrology is a science: Here's why
http://theconversation.com/some-people-think-astrology-is-a-science-heres-why-28642

You've probably been reading the wrong horoscope
http://www.popsci.com/your-zodiac-sign-isnt-what-you-think-it-is

Article

Prepared by: R. Eric Landrum, *Boise State University*

Study of 20,000 Finds an Income Advantage for Those Judged to Be Very Unattractive

ALEX FRADERA

Learning Outcomes

After reading this article, you will be able to:

- Understand that based on previous research, employers tend to pay more salary to employees who are more attractive.
- Observe how researchers speculate to explain and interpret unexpected results from survey research.
- Appreciate some of the basics of survey research, including longitudinal designs and survey response scales.

Do chiseled features garner better pay? Researchers have previously found that income is associated with attractiveness, leading to the idea of both a beauty premium and an ugliness penalty. A common explanation is discrimination: employers seek out beautiful people and reject or ignore those harder on the eye. But in the Journal of Business Psychology, Satoshi Kanazawa and Mary Still have published research aiming to upset this. The biggest takeaway is that being perceived as very unattractive may not incur an income penalty at all.

The researchers drew on a longitudinal study of 20,000 young Americans, interviewed at home at age 16 and then on three more occasions up to the age of 29. Each time the interviewer rated the person's physical attractiveness, from very unattractive to very attractive. While previous research often collapses below-average scores into one category, this research treated them separately, which turns out to be important.

Kanazawa and Still wanted to see whether the participants' gross earnings at 29 were associated with their physical attractiveness at that or any previous age. Overall, there was a positive association between attractiveness and earnings. But there was an anomaly: very unattractive participants kept bucking the trend.

Those participants who were rated very unattractive at age 29 were earning significantly more than people judged more attractive than them, including (though to a lesser extent) the very attractive. For attractiveness measures earlier in life, which allow more persuasive claims of causality, echoes of this pattern were present, as the very unattractive went on to earn significantly more at age 29 than those who were earlier rated unattractive, and they earned in the same region or even slightly more than those who were earlier rated as attractive.

The correlation between extreme unattractiveness and higher pay remained using median earnings and looking separately at men and women. The authors argue this is hard to square with the usual discrimination explanation for why attractiveness (or lack of it) is associated with income. After all, why would employers be less discriminatory toward the worst looking people?

An alternative explanation is that the highly unattractive and attractive each favor different high-value industries. But this wasn't supported by the data—even within a given industry, those rated very unattractive still achieved higher incomes than their more attractive counterparts.

Kanazawa and Still prefer an explanation for the attractiveness–income link that is tied into Kanazawa's focus on evolutionary psychology and his sometimes controversial interest in the biological significance of attractiveness.

Kanazawa reasons that attractive people earn more because facial attractiveness is a marker of better developmental health, which in turn correlates with more intelligence, advantageous personality traits, and being stronger, fitter, and taller—all factors that are associated with higher earnings. In this data set, after accounting for these factors, the attractiveness–income link was no longer statistically significant, supporting Kanazawa's claim that it's these correlates of attractiveness that are driving the higher income for more attractive people, not their beauty per se. This analysis also accounted for some of the earnings benefit for the very unattractive, but not all of it—and why would it, if the assumption is that the unattractive should be less healthy developmentally, on average?

It seems likely to me that we are seeing two factors at work. One relates to the income advantage for increasingly attractive people, maybe the developmental health explanation, maybe something else, and then something separate is at work raising income for the very unattractive group.

As to what gives rise to the income advantage for the very unattractive group, the only speculation I can offer is that in this dataset, the personality trait Openness to Experience—which is usually associated with higher pay—was surprisingly correlated with lower earnings and higher attractiveness, meaning it was the only "bad" trait associated with higher attractiveness.

Could this Openness-attractiveness association be an indicator that some of the very unattractive scored especially low on Openness and were perhaps highly devoted to a specific topic area, pursuing it obsessively to the exclusion of all distractions and eventually entering the forefront of their field? We know that Openness correlates negatively with the passion component of "Grit," so such effects are conceivable.

The very unattractive group was small, as extremes are in any population—just a few hundred participants—so we would want to investigate this again to see if these effects hold. For now, this research challenges assumptions about the potential for those born without conventional looks to find uncommon success.

Critical Thinking

1. The relationship between attractiveness and income is a correlational one. Explain the dangers of taking this relational association too far, meaning, what would be the problem if one assumed there was a causal relationship between these two variables?
2. What are the challenges in measuring facial attractiveness? Do you think all people have the same standards regarding facial attractiveness? Males versus females? Older adults versus younger adults? How might the researchers address some of these methodological concerns?
3. Is there any scenario where someone who is more attractive would actually be worthy of more income? How would that work? Explain why or why not.

Internet References

Beauty and Salary: How Does Employee Attractiveness Affect Lifetime Pay

https://www.payscale.com/career-news/2012/03/beauty-and-salary

Do Women Really Value Income over Looks in a Mate?

https://bigthink.com/dollars-and-sex/do-women-really-value-income-over-looks-in-a-mate

Science Asks: Do Pretty People Really Make More Money?

https://www.forbes.com/sites/daviddisalvo/2017/02/21/science-asks-do-pretty-people-really-make-more-money/#c4a92cf2dbd6

Why Women Do Their Hair and Makeup: Attractiveness and Income

https://workinprogress.oowsection.org/2016/09/27/why-women-do-their-hair-and-makeup-attractiveness-and-income/

Article

Prepared by: R. Eric Landrum, *Boise State University*

How Democracy Can Survive Big Data

COLIN KOOPMAN

Learning Outcomes

After reading this article, you will be able to:

- Realize the number of data points that can be available for every adult in the United States.
- Appreciate the origins of personality research via data collection in the United States with psychology during World War I.
- Understand the challenge of designing ethics into data collection when the ethical considerations occur after the fact.

Only a few years ago, the idea that for-profit companies and foreign agents could use powerful data technologies to disrupt American democracy would have seemed laughable to most, a plotline from a Cold War espionage movie. And the idea that the American system would be compromised enough to allow outside meddling with the most basic of its democratic functions—the election of its leaders—would have seemed even more absurd.

Today, we know that this is not fiction but fact. It is a secret so open that even its perpetrators seem half-hearted about hiding it.

"Data drives all that we do." That is the motto emblazoned on the website of Cambridge Analytica, the consulting firm that was employed by the Trump campaign to influence voters and that is now under scrutiny for its unauthorized harvesting of data from at least 50 million social media users.

The heart of Cambridge Analytica's power is an enormous information warehouse—as many as 5,000 data points on each of more than 230 million Americans, according to recent reporting, a fact the company proudly confirms on its website. Its promise of elections driven by data ultimately implies a vision of government steered not by people but by algorithms, and by an expanding data-mining culture operating without restrictions.

That such threats to democracy are now possible is due in part to the fact that our society lacks an information ethics adequate to its deepening dependence on data. Where politics is driven by data, we need a set of ethics to guide that data. But in our rush to deliver on the promises of Big Data, we have not sought one.

An adequate ethics of data for today would include not only regulatory policy and statutory law governing matters like personal data privacy and implicit bias in algorithms. It would also establish cultural expectations, fortified by extensive education in high schools and colleges, requiring us to think about data technologies as we build them, not after they have already profiled, categorized, and otherwise informationalized millions of people. Students who will later turn their talents to the great challenges of data science would also be trained to consider the ethical design and use of the technologies they will someday unleash.

Clearly, we are not there. High schoolers today may aspire to be the next Mark Zuckerberg, but how many dream of designing ethical data technologies? Who would their role models even be? Executives at Facebook, Twitter, and Amazon are among our celebrities today. But how many data ethics advocates can the typical social media user name?

Our approach to the ethics of data is wholly reactive. Investigations are conducted and apologies are extracted only after damage has been done (and only in some instances). Mr. Zuckerberg seemed to take a positive step on Wednesday, when he vowed to take action to better protect Facebook's user data. "We also made mistakes, there's more to do, and we need to step up and do it," he said in, unsurprisingly, a Facebook post.

This is like lashing a rope around the cracking foundation of a building. What we need is for an ethics of data to be engineered right into the information skyscrapers being built today.

We need data ethics by design. Any good building must comply with a complex array of codes, standards, and detailed studies of patterns of use by its eventual inhabitants. But technical systems are today being built with a minimal concern for compliance and a total disregard for the downstream consequences of decades of identifiable data being collected on the babies being born into the most complicated information ecology that has ever existed.

Mr. Zuckerberg and other Silicon Valley chiefs admitted in the wake of the election that their platforms needed fixing to help mitigate the bad actors who had exploited social media for political gain. It is not Mr. Zuckerberg's fault that our society has given him a free pass (and a net worth of $67 billion) for inventing his platform first and asking only later what its social consequences might be. It is all of our faults. Thus, however successful Mr. Zuckerberg will be in making amends, he will assuredly do almost nothing to prevent the next wunderkind from coming along and building the next killer app that will unleash who knows what before anybody even has a chance to notice.

The challenge of designing ethics into data technologies is formidable. This is in part because it requires overcoming a century-long ethos of data science: develop first, question later. Datafication first, regulation afterward. A glimpse at the history of data science shows as much.

The techniques that Cambridge Analytica uses to produce its psychometric profiles are the cutting edge of data-driven methodologies first devised 100 years ago. The science of personality research was born in 1917. That year, in the midst of America's fevered entry into war, Robert Sessions Woodworth of Columbia University created the Personal Data Sheet, a questionnaire that promised to assess the personalities of Army recruits. The war ended before Woodworth's psychological instrument was ready for deployment, but the Army had envisioned its use according to the precedent set by the intelligence tests it had been administering to new recruits under the direction of Robert Yerkes, a professor of psychology at Harvard at the time. The data these tests could produce would help decide who should go to the fronts, who was fit to lead and who should stay well behind the lines.

The stakes of those wartime decisions were particularly stark, but the aftermath of those psychometric instruments is even more unsettling. As the century progressed, such tests—I.Q. tests, college placement exams, and predictive behavioral assessments—would affect the lives of millions of Americans. Schoolchildren who may have once or twice acted out in such a way as to prompt a psychometric evaluation could find themselves labeled, setting them on an inescapable track through the education system.

Researchers like Woodworth and Yerkes (or their Stanford colleague Lewis Terman, who formalized the first SAT) did not anticipate the deep consequences of their work; they were too busy pursuing the great intellectual challenges of their day, much like Mr. Zuckerberg in his pursuit of the next great social media platform. Or like Cambridge Analytica's Christopher Wylie, the twentysomething data scientist who helped build psychometric profiles of ⅔ of all Americans by leveraging personal information gained through uninformed consent. All of these researchers were, quite understandably, obsessed with the great data science challenges of their generation. Their failure to consider the consequences of their pursuits, however, is not so much their fault as it is our collective failing.

For the past 100 years, we have been chasing visions of data with a singular passion. Many of the best minds of each new generation have devoted themselves to delivering on the inspired data science promises of their day: intelligence testing, building the computer, cracking the genetic code, creating the Internet, and now this. We have in the course of a single century built an entire society, economy, and culture that runs on information. Yet we have hardly begun to engineer data ethics appropriate for our extraordinary information carnival. If we do not do so soon, data will drive democracy, and we may well lose our chance to do anything about it.

Critical Thinking

1. When a data company utilizes information freely available from social media, who is responsible for the ultimate use of that data—Is it the data company, the individual user contributing her/his data, the social media site, or government oversight? Explain your answer.
2. Army recruits during World War I were asked to complete something called a Personal Data Sheet as part of personality research. This began in 1917. What types of survey questions do you think were contained on the PDS, and how do you think those questions compare to the types of data being gathered today. Compare and contrast.

Internet References

Building Digital Trust: The Role of Data Ethics in the Digital Age
https://www.accenture.com/us-en/insight-data-ethics

Ethics for the Digital Age
https://dataethics.eu/en/a-new-ethics-for-the-digital-age/

The Ethics of Data: Care, Respect, and Human Dignity in the Digital Age
https://www.i-scoop.eu/the-ethics-of-data-human-truths-and-dignity-in-the-digital-age/

Unit 9

UNIT

Prepared by: R. Eric Landrum, *Boise State University*

Social Processes

We humans are particularly social creatures, as are many of the other species with whom we share the planet. We tend to assemble in groups, some large and some small. We form friendships with all sorts of people. Many of these relationships develop naturally from shared interests and common goals. Some of these friendships are long-lasting and endure hardship. Other kinds of friendships are shorter-term that are often soon forgotten. We form highly unique relationships in which we fall in love with another person and decide to commit the rest of our lives, or at least a large chunk of it, to be this person's most intimate companion. And then there are families, perhaps the most interesting social unit full of fascinating dynamics that emerge as children are born, grow up, and form families of their own.

The responsibility for understanding the complicated facets of human social behavior falls to social psychologists. These psychologists, like most research-focused behavioral scientists, are trained to apply rigorous experimental methods to discovering, understanding, and explaining how people interact with one another. During the past century, social psychologists studied some of the most pressing and fascinating social behaviors of the day. For example, social psychologists examine and continue to study discrimination, prejudice, conformity, and obedience to authority. In addition to these high-profile issues, social psychologists study the more positive side of human social behavior such as liking and loving, attitude formation and change, attributions, group behavior, and decision-making. There are fascinating examples available of the impact of positive psychology, such as the effort of an entire country to invest in its own national happiness.

In the past few decades, psychologists have become more aware of the impact of culture on human social relationships and have turned their attention to exploring differences among cultures with respect to social development, social perception, social influence, and social change. As the world seems to become smaller and smaller, the demand for social psychologists to provide explanations for both positive and negative social behaviors that are impacted by cultural influences will only become greater. Interesting challenges and opportunities occur when individuals from different backgrounds have the chance to live and work together, and social psychologists can often offer advice and tips about how to learn and develop in these environments.

Thus, as you study social psychology in your introductory psychology course, apply the principles you are learning not just to better understanding your own social behavior but also ask yourself how these principles might (or might not) generalize to the social behavior of individuals from different cultures. Doing so might put you in a better position to understand the whys and wherefores of social behavior that would seem (on the surface) to be so radically different from your own.

Article

Prepared by: R. Eric Landrum, *Boise State University*

The Third Wheel: The Impact of Twitter Use on Relationship Infidelity and Divorce

RUSSELL B. CLAYTON

Learning Outcomes

After reading this article, you will be able to:

- Appreciate the research design utilized to study the impact of Twitter use on relationship status.
- Practice the interpretation of statistical results in order to draw conclusions about psychological ideas.

Introduction

The Introduction of Social Networking Sites (SNSs) such as MySpace, Facebook, and Twitter have provided a relatively new platform for interpersonal communication and, as a result, have substantially enhanced and altered the dynamics of interpersonal relationships.[1–7] Twitter, once deemed merely an "information network,"[8] is now considered one of the most popular SNSs, with more than 554 million active users, competing with Facebook, Google+, and LinkedIn.[9] Although Facebook and MySpace have received a great deal of empirical attention,[3,6] research investigating the effects of Twitter use on interpersonal relationships has been somewhat limited, despite Twitter's increasing popularity. Thus, the current study's aim is to examine the effects of Twitter use on romantic relationships.

Evolution of Twitter as a SNS

Since its creation in 2006, the microblogging site Twitter has accumulated more than 554 million active registered users with 58 million tweets per day.[10] Twitter provides users a communication platform to initiate and develop connections in real time with thousands of people with shared interests.[11] It is also a way to get to know strangers who share the details of their daily lives.[12] As Chen[13] notes, Twitter evolved from an online information network where users responded to a simple question: "What are you doing right now?" to a social network that provides a "new economy of info-sharing and connectivity" between people.[10] Johnson and Yang[14] found that those who have Twitter accounts use the site primarily to give and receive advice, gather and share information, and meet new people.

The primary source for providing and obtaining information on Twitter is by reading or communicating 140-character personal updates, now known as "tweets," to those who opt to "follow" the tweeter. Additional features allow users to retweet, abbreviated as RT, others' tweets and privately direct message, or DM, other users. Twitter users can also have public conversations with others by using "@replies" and can engage in larger conversations by hashtagging ("#") words or phrases. Tweets, RTs, @replies, and hashtags are sent to a public newsfeed viewable by others, unless the user designates his or her tweets as private. Twitter updates can be sent to the newsfeed using mobile phone text messaging from Twitter's mobile phone website, phone applications, and from a user's Twitter home web page.[8,14] Although users can access Twitter across many electronic devices,[8,14] Twitter user interactivity is still somewhat limited compared to other SNSs.

While other SNSs, such as Facebook, allow users to share information about their daily lives on their Facebook newsfeeds, or directly communicate with other users via online chat, Twitter does not provide users the same functionality. Twitter does, however, allow users to post photos, videos, and check-ins that display on the Twitter newsfeed through third-party sites, such as Instagram (photos/videos) and Foursquare (check-ins). Although the method of sharing information varies between Facebook and Twitter, the type of information that can be shared publicly is similar. Therefore, the researcher speculates that the effects of Twitter usage on relationships may parallel those of Facebook. For this reason, the researcher will briefly highlight recent literature pertaining to the effects of SNS use on romantic relationships.

SNSs' effects on romantic relationships

The evolution of SNSs, as well as their increasing popularity, has provided communication and psychology researchers with an avenue to investigate, more than ever, computer-mediated communication. As a result, scholars have compiled a body of research that has systematically investigated the dynamic, complex interactions between SNS use, health, and romantic relationship outcomes.[1,3–7,15–24] While SNSs may be beneficial in helping users keep in touch with others,[16] research has shown that excessive SNS use can be detrimental to romantic relationships.[3] As Tong[17] notes, relationships, both personal and impersonal, are social in nature, and therefore involve one's social networks. Since Twitter and Facebook use "maps on to one's social networks almost isomorphically, SNSs' potential role in the process of relationship maintenance and termination seems quite likely."[17(p1)]

In fact, several studies have found that Facebook-induced jealousy, partner survelliance, posting ambiguous information, compulsive Internet use, and online portrayal of intimate relationships can be damaging to romantic relationships.[18–21] Additionally, Lyndon[22] found that Facebook monitoring leads to negative relationship outcomes, such as online and offline relationship intrusion, which may induce jealousy among romantic partners.[23] Marshall[24] found that remaining friends on SNSs, specifically Facebook, after a breakup delays the healing process. One possible explanation for this delay could be due to romantic partners taking advantage of the information Facebook provides of their ex-partner.[17] This type of information visibility, which occurs not only on Facebook but also on Twitter, may lead to similar relationship outcomes for the latter SNS.

Since Twitter now allows users to interact in a similar way as Facebook (i.e., write posts and upload images, videos, and location check-ins), the researcher theorizes that the effects of Twitter use on interpersonal relationships are comparable to those associated with Facebook. Thus, one additional aim of this study is to examine if Twitter uses parallels that of Facebook with regard to negative relationship outcomes.[3]

The current study

The current study is grounded in the methodological framework of Clayton et al.'s[3] survey study examining the influence of Facebook use on romantic relationships. Clayton et al.'s[4] study of 205 Facebook users found that Facebook-related conflict mediated the relationship between Facebook use and negative relationship outcomes (i.e., cheating, breakup, and divorce). This indirect effect was more pronounced for those in relatively newer relationships of 3 years or less.[3] To understand the influence of Twitter usage on romantic relationships, this study used the same mediating variable, now termed "Twitter-related conflict," as well as the negative relationship outcome items.[3] The researcher conceptualized Twitter-related conflict as whether Twitter use increases relationship complications in intimate romantic relationships. Negative relationship outcomes were conceptualized as whether Twitter use influences the likelihood for emotional cheating, physical cheating, relationship breakup, and divorce. As a result, the researcher predicted that active Twitter use and negative relationship outcomes would be positively related and that Twitter-related conflict would mediate the relationship between active Twitter use and negative relationship outcomes.

Clayton et al.'s[3] study found a moderating effect on the mediational relationship for those who are, or have been, in relationships of 3 years or less. Therefore, the current study hypothesizes that the length of the romantic relationship will moderate the indirect effect on the relationship between active Twitter use and negative relationship outcomes. Based on this examination of the literature, the author hypothesizes the following:

H1: The relationship between active Twitter use and negative relationship outcomes will be positively related.

H2: Twitter-related conflict will mediate the relationship between active Twitter use and negative relationship outcomes.

H3: The indirect effect of active Twitter use on negative relationship outcomes through Twitter-related conflict will be greater for those who are, or have been, in shorter duration relationships.

Method

Participants

An online survey was created on qualtrics.com and distributed to Twitter users via the researcher's Twitter account, as well as *The Huffington Post*'s Twitter account. The survey was tweeted a total of 20 times to followers. The total number of users the survey link was tweeted to, not including possible retweets, exceeded 3.4 million Twitter users. The final number of participants was 581 Twitter users. All participants were 18 years of age or older. The participants' ages ranged from 18 to 67 years ($M = 29$, $SD = 8.9$). Most participants (62%) were Caucasian, 15% Asian, 12% Hispanic, 6% African American, and 5% Native American. The majority of participants (63%) were male. This study was approved by the university's Institutional Review Board.

Materials

Following Clayton's[3] methodology, a 20-question survey was designed using qualtrics.com. The survey included demographic questions, as well as questions about participants' perceived levels of Twitter use. Additionally, participants were asked if they had encountered relationship conflict with their current or former partner as a result of Twitter use. Participants were also asked if Twitter use had led to breakup or divorce, emotional cheating, and physical cheating with a current or former partner.

Relationships

The researcher asked the participants to indicate if their partner or former partner had a Twitter account. Those who indicated that their former partner or spouse did not have a Twitter account were not included in further analyses because some items pertained to participants' perceived levels of their current or former partner's Twitter use ($n = 67$). In order for the researcher to understand to whom the participants' answers were directed, the survey also instructed participants to answer the question, "Are you currently in a romantic relationship?" If the participants answered, "Yes," they were then asked to type how many months or years they had been in the relationship with their current partner. If participants answered "No," the researcher could analyze their data in connection with the participants' former partners. After screening participants' responses for initial criteria, the total number of participants included for analyses was 514. Of the 514 participants, 386 (75%) participants responded that they were in a romantic relationship, while 128 (25%) reported being single.

Active Twitter use

Following Rubin's[25] active audience construct and Chen's[13] Twitter use items, active Twitter use was measured by asking participants to rate the following five statements: "How often do you log in into Twitter?" "How often do you Tweet?" "How often do you @replies?" "How often do you direct message followers?" and "How often do you scroll the Twitter newsfeed?" Data were gathered using a Likert-type scale where A = "never," B = "monthly," C = "weekly," D = "daily," E = "hourly," and F = "more than hourly." The Cronbach's alpha for the scale was 0.90. To create a multiplicative index of Twitter use, participants indicated how many hours per day, and how many days per week, they used Twitter. On average, participants used Twitter for 52 minutes per day ($SD = 66.3$), five days per week ($SD = 2.3$).

Twitter-related conflict

The current study adapted the items in Clayton et al.'s[3] Facebook-related conflict scale (Cronbach's $\alpha = 0.85$) to measure Twitter-related conflict. Such items included, "How often do you have an argument with your significant other as a result of excessive Twitter use?" and "How often do you have an argument with your significant other as a result of viewing friends' Twitter profiles?" The questions were answered using a Likert scale ranging from A = "never" to F = "always." The Cronbach's alpha for the scale was 0.94.

Negative relationship outcomes. The current study used Clayton et al.'s[3] negative relationship outcome questions (Kuder Richardson [KR-20] = 0.70) to measure the criterion variable. Such items included, "Have you emotionally cheated on your significant other with someone you have connected or reconnected with on Twitter?" "Have you physically cheated on your significant other with someone you have connected or reconnected with on Twitter?" and "Has Twitter led to a breakup/divorce?" The researcher condensed the answers into dichotomous yes/no answer choices. Once averaged, the KR-20 measure of reliability was 0.72 (see Table 1).

Results

To test the aforementioned hypotheses, moderation–mediation regression analyses using bootstrapping resampling methods were conducted according to the specifications set out by Andrew Hayes's PROCESS for SPSS using model four for simple mediation and model seven to test for moderation–mediation.[26] As Figure 1 shows, active Twitter use was entered

Table 1 Means, Standard Deviations, Correlations, and Alpha Reliabilities[a] for Variables

	M	*SD*	1	2	3
1. Active Twitter use	3.36	1.0	(0.90)		
2. Twitter-related conflict	2.77	1.4	0.52***	(0.94)	
3. Negative relationship outcomes	1.17	0.30	0.33***	0.53***	(0.72)

[a]On diagonal in parentheses.
*$p < 0.05$; **$p < 0.01$; ***$p < 0.001$.

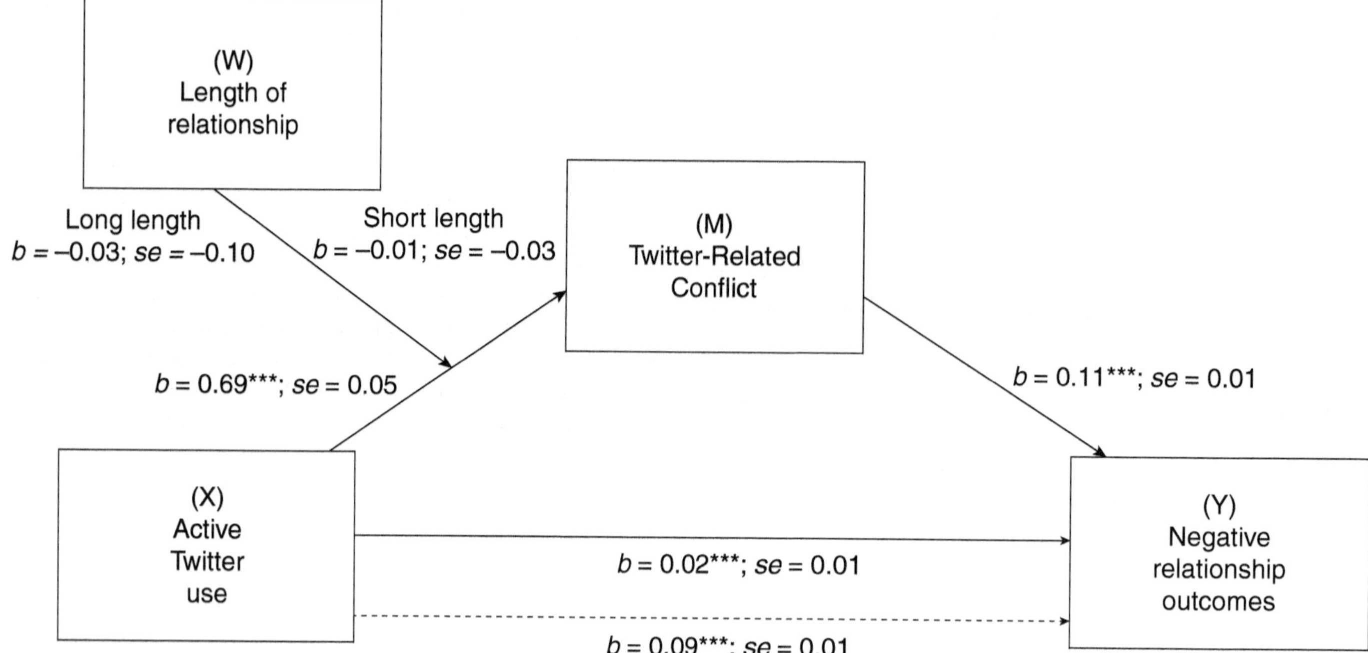

Figure 1 Andrew Hayes's mediation–moderation model 7 conceptual diagram. Path coefficients for simple moderation–mediation model analysis. *Note.* Model four is the same as model seven excluding the moderator variable (W). Dotted line denotes the effect of active Twitter use on negative relationship outcomes when Twitter-related conflict is not included as a mediator. $^{*}p < 0.05$; $^{**}p < 0.01$; $^{***}p < 0.001$.

as the independent variable (X), Twitter-related conflict as the mediator variable (M), length of romantic relationship as the moderator variable (W), and negative relationship outcomes was entered as the criterion variable (Y) in the model.

Mediation

As a test of simple mediation, Twitter-related conflict was entered as the mediator variable (M) in model four of Hayes's PROCESS[26] (see Figure 1). Data analysis using 1,000 bootstrap simulations[26] revealed that the total effect between active Twitter use negative relationship outcomes was positively associated (*effect* = 0.09, *SE* = 0.01, $p < 0.001$ [95% CI 0.07, 0.12]), supporting H1 (see Table 2). Moreover, active Twitter use exerted an indirect effect on negative relationship outcomes through Twitter-related conflict (*effect* = 0.07, *SE* = 0.01, $p < 0.001$ [95% bias-corrected bootstrap CI 0.06, 0.09]), while the direct relationship between active Twitter use and negative relationship outcomes was not significant (*effect* = 0.02, *SE* = 0.01, p = 0.082 [95% CI −0.01, 0.05]), supporting H2 (see Table 2). This indirect effect is statistically different from zero,

Table 2 Total, Direct, and Indirect Effects

	Negative relationship outcomes as criterion				
	Effect	**SE**	**t**	**LLCI**	**ULCI**
Total effect of active Twitter use	0.09	0.01	7.90***	0.07	0.12
Direct effect of active Twitter use	0.02	0.01	1.75	−0.01	0.05
	Effect	**Boot SE**		**BootLLCI**	**BootULCI**
Indirect effect of active Twitter use	0.07***	0.01	—	0.06	0.09

Note. Number of bootstrap samples for bias-corrected bootstrap confidence intervals: 1,000. Level of confidence for all confidence intervals: 95.

$^{*}p < 0.05$; $^{**}p < 0.01$; $^{***}p < 0.001$.

as revealed by a 95% bias-corrected bootstrap confidence interval,[26] and indicates that Twitter-related conflict mediates the relationship between active Twitter use and negative relationship outcomes.

Moderation

As a test of moderation–mediation, negative relationship outcomes was entered as the moderator variable (W) in model seven of Hayes's PROCESS[26] using 1,000 bootstrap simulations[26] (see Figure 1). The sample was divided based upon a median split (median = 18 months). Those participants who reported being in a relationship for 18 months or less were categorized in the shorter length group (n = 194), whereas those who reported being in relationships for more than 18 months were categorized in the longer length group (n = 181). The moderating effect on the indirect relationship between active Twitter use and negative relationship outcomes was not significant for the shorter length group (*effect* = 0.01, SE = 0.02, p = 0.337 [95% CI −0.02, 0.05]) or for the longer length group (*effect* = 0.02, SE = 0.03, p = 0.454 [95% CI −0.03, 0.08]). H3 was not supported.

Discussion

Although a number of variables can contribute to relationship infidelity and separation, the current study hypothesized that SNS use, specifically Twitter use, can contribute to negative relationship outcomes. Therefore, the purpose of this study was to investigate the relationship between active Twitter use and negative romantic relationship outcomes. Moreover, the researcher sought to examine whether the findings of Clayton et al.'s[3] recent study, which concluded that Facebook-related conflict fully mediated the relationship between Facebook use and negative relationship outcomes, were consistent with a different SNS platform—Twitter.

Since Twitter allows users to share similar types of information as Facebook, the researcher argued that Twitter outcomes may parallel those of Facebook regarding SNS use, romantic conflict, and negative relationship outcomes. The researcher theorized that if an individual who is in a romantic relationship is highly active on Twitter (e.g., tweeting, direct messaging others, check-ins, and posting images to the Twitter newsfeed), Twitter use could create conflict within the relationship. If high amounts of Twitter use does, indeed, lead to high amounts of Twitter-related conflict (i.e., arguments pertaining to a partner's Twitter use, etc.) among romantic partners, it is plausible to speculate that such conflict could lead to unfavorable relationship outcomes such as cheating, breakup, or divorce. The results from this study largely support these propositions. In contrast to recent findings,[3] the length of the relationship did not moderate the mediational effect, suggesting that relationship maturity may not influence negative relationship outcomes in terms of Twitter use.

The results of this study partially replicate Clayton et al.'s[3] findings regarding Facebook use and negative relationship outcomes. Based on the findings from both[3] studies, Twitter and Facebook use can have damaging effects on romantic relationships. That is, when SNS use becomes problematic in one's romantic relationship, risk of negative relationship outcomes may follow. In contrast, recent reports have shown that SNS conflict can be reduced when partners share joint accounts.[27] Furthermore, recent SNS applications have been developed to facilitate interpersonal communication between partners by providing a private, secure, and organized environment for two people to share, such as the 2life app[28] for iPhone users. Whether this type of app reduces SNS-related conflict between romantic partners is yet to be determined.

Limitations and implications for further research

The current study has several limitations. The sample included participants who were told before starting the survey that they would be answering questions regarding Twitter use and romantic relationship outcomes, and this may have skewed the data. Additionally, some items were left to participants' interpretation, such as the word "excessive" when answering questions about Twitter-related conflict. Moreover, social desirability is an unavoidable issue when it comes to self-reported data, particularly when the issues under investigation are sensitive, as in the current study. Since the online survey link was distributed by the researcher's Twitter account and *The Huffington Post*'s Twitter account, the current study's sample is limited to only those who use Twitter and who follow the researcher or *The Huffington Post*'s profile on Twitter. This limitation significantly limits the generalizations of the findings. Future research should investigate if engaging in high levels of other SNS usage, such as Instagram and LinkedIn, also predicts negative relationship outcomes. Additional future research should explore other mediators in the current study's model, such as relationship quality and satisfaction.

Conclusion

The results from this study show that active Twitter use leads to greater amounts of Twitter-related conflict among romantic partners, which in turn leads to infidelity, breakup, and divorce. Results from the current study and Clayton et al.'s[3] study demonstrate that Twitter and Facebook use can have damaging effects on romantic relationships.

Author Disclosure Statement

No competing financial interests exist.

References

1. Boyd D, Ellison BN. Social network sites: definition, history, and scholarship. *Journal of Computer-Mediated Communication* 2007; 13.
2. Choi JH. (2008) Living in cyworld: contextualising cy-ties in South Korea. In Bruns A, Jacobs J, eds. *Uses of blogs.* New York: Peter Lang, pp. 173–186.
3. Clayton R, Nagurney A, Smith J. Cheating, breakup, and divorce: is Facebook use to blame? *Cyberpsychology, Behavior, & Social Networking* 2013; 16:717–720.
4. Ellison BN, Steinfield C, Lampe, C. The benefits of Facebook "friends": exploring the relationship between college students' use of online social networks and social capital. *Journal of Computer-Mediated Communication* 2007; 12:article 1.
5. Lampe C, Ellison BN, Steinfield C. Social capital, self-esteem, and use of online social network sites. *Journal of Applied Developmental Psychology* 2008; 29:434–445.
6. Raacke J, Bonds-Raacke J. MySpace and Facebook: applying the uses and gratifications theory to exploring friend-networking sites. *Individual Differences Research Group* 2008; 8:27–33.
7. Fox J, Warber K. Romantic relationship development in the age of Facebook: an exploratory study of emerging adults' perceptions, motives, and behaviors. *Journal of Cyberpsychology, Behavior, & Social Networking* 2013; 16:3–7.
8. About Twitter. https://twitter.com/about (accessed Jun. 20, 2013).
9. 2010 Best social networking site reviews and comparisons. http://social-networking-websites-review.toptenreviews.com (accessed Dec. 28, 2013).
10. Statistics Brain. Twitter statistics. www.statisticbrain.com/twitter-statistics/ (accessed Jun. 20, 2013).
11. Sarno D. On Twitter, mindcasting is the new lifecasting. Los Angeles Times, Mar. 11, 2009. http://latimesblogs.latimes.com/technology/2009/03/on-twitter-mind.html (accessed Jan. 12, 2014).
12. Thompson C. Brave new world of digital intimacy. The New York Times, Sep. 5, 2008. www.nytimes.com/2008/09/07/magazine/07awareness-t.html?_r=1&pagewanted=all (accessed Dec. 29, 2013).
13. Chen G. Tweet this: a uses and gratifications perspective on how active Twitter use gratifies a need to connect with others. *Journal of Computers in Human Behavior* 2011; 27:755–762.
14. Johnson P, Yang S-U. Uses and gratifications of Twitter: an examination of user motives and satisfaction of Twitter use. Paper presented at the Annual Convention of Association for Education in Journalism and Mass Communication in Boston, MA.
15. Clayton R, Osborne R, Miller B, et al. Loneliness, anxiousness, and substance use as predictors of Facebook use. *Computers in Human Behavior* 2013; 29:687–693.
16. Joinson AN. (2008) "Looking at," "looking up" or "keeping up with" people? Motives and uses of Facebook. In: *Proceedings of the 26th Annual SIGCHI Conference on Human Factors in Computing Systems (Florence, Italy, April 5–10, 2008), CHI'08.* New York: ACM Press, pp. 1027–1036.
17. Tong ST. Facebook use during relationship termination: uncertainty reduction and surveillance. *Cyberpsychology, Behavior, & Social Networking* 2013; 16:788–793.
18. Utz S, Beukeboom CJ. The role of social network sites in romantic relationships: effects on jealousy and relationship happiness. *Journal of Computer-Mediated Communication* 2011; 16:511–527.
19. Tokunaga RS. Social networking site or social surveillance site? Understanding the use of interpersonal electronic surveillance in romantic relationships. *Computers in Human Behavior* 2011; 27:705–713.
20. Kerkhof P, Finkenauer C, Muusses, LD. Relational consequences of compulsive internet use: a longitudinal study among newlyweds. *Human Communication Research* 2011; 37:147–173.
21. Papp LM, Danielewicz J, Cayemberg C. "Are we Facebook official?" Implications of dating partners' Facebook use and profiles for intimate relationship satisfaction. *Cyberpsychology, Behavior, & Social Networking* 2012; 15:85–90.
22. Lyndon A, Bonds-Raacke J, Cratty AD. College students' Facebook stalking of ex-partners. *Cyberpsychology, Behavior, & Social Networking* 2011; 14:711–716.
23. Muise A, Christofides E, Desmarais S. More information than you ever wanted: does Facebook bring out the green-eyed monster of jealousy? *Cyberpsychology & Behavior* 2009; 12:441–444.
24. Marshall T. Facebook surveillance of former romantic partners: associations with postbreakup recovery and personal growth. *Cyberpsychology, Behavior, & Social Networking* 2012; 15:521–526.
25. Rubin AM. (2009) Uses and gratifications: an evolving perspective on media effects. In Nabi RL, Oliver MB, eds. *The SAGE handbook of media processes and effect.* Washington, DC: Sage, pp. 147–159.
26. Hayes AF. (2013) *Introduction to mediation, moderation, and conditional process analysis: a regression-based approach.* New York: Guilford Press.
27. Buck S. (2013) When Facebook official isn't enough. Mashable.com. http://mashable.com/2013/08/04/social-media-couples/ (accessed Jan. 10, 2014).
28. 2 For Life Media Inc. (2013) 2Life App description. www.2life.io (accessed Sep. 28, 2013).

Critical Thinking

1. The development of social networking is developing rapidly and changing daily. Why is it important that this article was published in 2014 rather than in 2009? Explain.
2. Some fairly complex results appear in this journal article. What are the takeaway messages that you have after reading the complete article? What reservations might you have about the results and what they mean?

Internet References

Is constant texting good or bad for your relationship?

http://www.psychologytoday.com/blog/meet-catch-and-keep/201403/is-constant-texting-good-or-bad-your-relationship

The effect of technology on relationships

http://www.psychologytoday.com/blog/happiness-in-world/201006/the-effect-technology-relationships

Article

Prepared by: R. Eric Landrum, *Boise State University*

Rethinking One of Psychology's Most Infamous Experiments

CARI ROMM

Learning Outcomes

After reading this article, you will be able to:

- Understand that no real shocks were delivered during the Milgram experiments.
- Appreciate that the patterns of results found by Milgram in the 1960s also hold up today.
- Articulate the importance of the historical context which was in part the motivation for Milgram to carry out his series of experiments.

In the 1960s, Stanley Milgram's electric-shock studies showed that people will obey even the most abhorrent of orders. But recently, researchers have begun to question his conclusions—and offer some of their own.

In 1961, Yale University psychology professor Stanley Milgram placed an advertisement in the *New Haven Register*. "We will pay you $4 for one hour of your time," it read, asking for "500 New Haven men to help us complete a scientific study of memory and learning."

Only part of that was true. Over the next two years, hundreds of people showed up at Milgram's lab for a learning and memory study that quickly turned into something else entirely. Under the watch of the experimenter, the volunteer—dubbed "the teacher"—would read out strings of words to his partner, "the learner," who was hooked up to an electric-shock machine in the other room. Each time the learner made a mistake in repeating the words, the teacher was to deliver a shock of increasing intensity, starting at 15 volts (labeled "slight shock" on the machine) and going all the way up to 450 volts ("Danger: severe shock"). Some people, horrified at what they were being asked to do, stopped the experiment early, defying their supervisor's urging to go on; others continued up to 450 volts, even as the learner pled for mercy, yelled a warning about his heart condition—and then fell alarmingly silent. In the most well-known variation of the experiment, a full 65 percent of people went all the way.

Until they emerged from the lab, the participants didn't know that the shocks weren't real, that the cries of pain were pre-recorded, and that the learner—railroad auditor Jim McDonough—was in on the whole thing, sitting alive and unharmed in the next room. They were also unaware that they had just been used to prove the claim that would soon make Milgram famous: that ordinary people, under the direction of an authority figure, would obey just about any order they were given, even to torture. It's a phenomenon that's been used to explain atrocities from the Holocaust to the Vietnam War's My Lai massacre to the abuse of prisoners at Abu Ghraib. "To a remarkable degree," Peter Baker wrote in *Pacific Standard* in 2013, "Milgram's early research has come to serve as a kind of all-purpose lightning rod for discussions about the human heart of darkness."

Others continued shocking even as the victim pled for mercy, yelled a warning about his heart condition—and then fell alarmingly silent.

In some ways, though, Milgram's study is also—as promised—a study of memory, if not the one he pretended it was.

More than five decades after it was first published in the *Journal of Abnormal and Social Psychology* in 1963, it's earned a place as one of the most famous experiments of the

20th century. Milgram's research has spawned countless spin-off studies among psychologists, sociologists, and historians, even as it's leapt from academia into the realm of pop culture. It's inspired songs by Peter Gabriel (lyrics: "We do what we're told/We do what we're told/Told to do") and Dar Williams ("When I knew it was wrong, I played it just like a game/I pressed the buzzer"); a number of books whose titles make puns out of the word "shocking"; a controversial French documentary disguised as a game show; episodes of *Law and Order* and *Bones;* a made-for-TV movie with William Shatner; a jewelry collection (bizarrely) from the company Enfants Perdus; and most recently, the biopic *The Experimenter,* starring Peter Sarsgaard as the title character—and this list is by no means exhaustive.

But as with human memory, the study—even published, archived, enshrined in psychology textbooks—is malleable. And in the past few years, a new wave of researchers have dedicated themselves to reshaping it, arguing that Milgram's lessons on human obedience are, in fact, misremembered—that his work doesn't prove what he claimed it does.

The problem is, no one can really agree on what it proves instead.

To mark the 50th anniversary of the experiments' publication (or, technically, the 51st), the *Journal of Social Issues* released a themed edition in September 2014 dedicated to all things Milgram. "There is a compelling and timely case for reexamining Milgram's legacy," the editors wrote in the introduction, noting that they were in good company: In 1964, the year after the experiments were published, fewer than 10 published studies referenced Milgram's work; in 2012, that number was more than 60.

It's a trend that surely would have pleased Milgram, who crafted his work with an audience in mind from the beginning. "Milgram was a fantastic dramaturg. His studies are fantastic little pieces of theater. They're beautifully scripted," said Stephen Reicher, a professor of psychology at the University of St. Andrews and a co-editor of the *Journal of Social Issues*' special edition. Capitalizing on the fame his 1963 publication earned him, Milgram went on to publish a book on his experiments in 1974 and a documentary, *Obedience,* with footage from the original experiments.

"His studies are fantastic little pieces of theater. They're beautifully scripted."

But for a man determined to leave a lasting legacy, Milgram also made it remarkably easy for people to pick it apart. The Yale University archives contain boxes upon boxes of papers, videos, and audio recordings, an entire career carefully documented for posterity. Though Milgram's widow Alexandra donated the materials after his death in 1984, they remained largely untouched for years, until Yale's library staff began to digitize all the materials in the early 2000s. Able to easily access troves of material for the first time, the researchers came flocking.

"There's a lot of dirty laundry in those archives," said Arthur Miller, a professor emeritus of psychology at Miami University and another co-editor of the *Journal of Social Issues.* "Critics of Milgram seem to want to—and do—find material in these archives that makes Milgram look bad or unethical or, in some cases, a liar."

One of the most vocal of those critics is Australian author and psychologist Gina Perry, who documented her experience tracking down Milgram's research participants in her 2013 book *Behind the Shock Machine: The Untold Story of the Notorious Milgram Psychology Experiments.* Her project began as an effort to write about the experiments from the perspective of the participants—but when she went back through the archives to confirm some of their stories, she said, she found some glaring issues with Milgram's data. Among her accusations: that the supervisors went off script in their prods to the teachers, that some of the volunteers were aware that the setup was a hoax, and that others weren't debriefed on the whole thing until months later. "My main issue is that methodologically, there have been so many problems with Milgram's research that we have to start reexamining the textbook descriptions of the research," she said.

But many psychologists argue that even with methodological holes and moral lapses, the basic finding of Milgram's work, the rate of obedience, still holds up. Because of the ethical challenge of reproducing the study, the idea survived for decades on a mix of good faith and partial replications—one study had participants administer their shocks in a virtual-reality system, for example—until 2007, when ABC collaborated with Santa Clara University psychologist Jerry Burger to replicate Milgram's experiment for an episode of the TV show *Basic Instincts* titled "The Science of Evil," pegged to Abu Ghraib.

"For years I had heard from my students, 'Well, that was back in the 1960s. People have changed.'"

Burger's way around an ethical breach: In the most well-known experiment, he found, 80 percent of the participants who reached a 150-volt shock continued all the way to the end. "So what I said we could do is take people up to the 150-volt point, see how they reacted, and end the study right there," he said. The rest of the setup was nearly identical to Milgram's lab of the early 1960s (with one notable exception: "Milgram had a gray lab coat and I couldn't find a gray, so I got a light blue.")

At the end of the experiment, Burger was left with an obedience rate around the same as the one Milgram had recorded—proving, he said, not only that Milgram's numbers had been accurate, but that his work was as relevant as ever. "[The results] didn't surprise me," he said, "but for years I had heard from my students and from other people, 'Well, that was back in the 1960s, and somehow now we're more aware of the problems of blind obedience, and people have changed.'"

In recent years, though, much of the attention has focused less on supporting or discrediting Milgram's statistics, and more on rethinking his conclusions. With a paper published earlier this month in the *British Journal of Social Psychology,* Matthew Hollander, a sociology PhD candidate at the University of Wisconsin, is among the most recent to question Milgram's notion of obedience. After analyzing the conversation patterns from audio recordings of 117 study participants, Hollander found that Milgram's original classification of his subjects—either obedient or disobedient—failed to capture the true dynamics of the situation. Rather, he argued, people in both categories tried several different forms of protest—those who successfully ended the experiment early were simply better at resisting than the ones that continued shocking.

"Research subjects may say things like 'I can't do this anymore' or 'I'm not going to do this anymore,'" he said, even those who went all the way to 450 volts. "I understand those practices to be a way of trying to stop the experiment in a relatively aggressive, direct, and explicit way."

It's a far cry from Milgram's idea that the capacity for evil lies dormant in everyone, ready to be awakened with the right set of circumstances. The ability to disobey toxic orders, Hollander said, is a skill that can be taught like any other—all a person needs to learn is what to say and how to say it.

In some ways, the conclusions Milgram drew were as much a product of their time as they were a product of his research. At the time he began his studies, the trial of Adolf Eichmann, one of the major architects of the Holocaust, was already in full swing. In 1963, the same year that Milgram published his studies, writer Hannah Arendt coined the phrase "the banality of evil" to describe Eichmann in her book on the trial, *Eichmann in Jerusalem.*

The ability to disobey toxic orders is a skill that can be learned like any other—all a person needs to learn is what to say.

Milgram, who was born in New York City in 1933 to Jewish immigrant parents, came to view his studies as a validation of Arendt's idea—but the Holocaust had been at the forefront of his mind for years before either of them published their work. "I should have been born into the German-speaking Jewish community of Prague in 1922 and died in a gas chamber some 20 years later," he wrote in a letter to a friend in 1958. "How I came to be born in the Bronx Hospital, I'll never quite understand."

And in the introduction of his 1963 paper, he invoked the Nazis within the first few paragraphs: "Obedience, as a determinant of behavior, is of particular relevance to our time," he wrote. "Gas chambers were built, death camps were guarded; daily quotas of corpses were produced . . . These inhumane policies may have originated in the mind of a single person, but they could only be carried out on a massive scale if a very large number of persons obeyed orders."

Though the term didn't exist at the time, Milgram was a proponent of what today's social psychologists call situationism: the idea that people's behavior is determined largely by what's happening around them. "They're not psychopaths, and they're not hostile, and they're not aggressive or deranged. They're just people, like you and me," Miller said. "If you put us in certain situations, we're more likely to be racist or sexist, or we may lie, or we may cheat. There are studies that show this, thousands and thousands of studies that document the many unsavory aspects of most people."

But continued to its logical extreme, situationism "has an exonerating effect," he said. "In the minds of a lot of people, it tends to excuse the bad behavior . . . it's not the person's fault for doing the bad thing, it's the situation they were put in." Milgram's studies were famous because their implications were also devastating: If the Nazis were just following orders, then he had proved that anyone at all could be a Nazi. If the guards at Abu Ghraib were just following orders, then anyone was capable of torture.

The latter, Reicher said, is part of why interest in Milgram's work has seen a resurgence in recent years. "If you look at acts of human atrocity, they've hardly diminished over time," he said, and news of the abuse at Abu Ghraib was surfacing around the same time that Yale's archival material was digitized, a perfect storm of encouragement for scholars to turn their attention once again to the question of what causes evil.

If the Nazis were just following orders, then he had just proved that anyone at all could be a Nazi.

He and his colleague Alex Haslam, the third co-editor of *The Journal of Social Issues*' Milgram edition and a professor of psychology at the University of Queensland, have come up with a different answer. "The notion that we somehow automatically obey authority, that we are somehow programmed, doesn't account for the variability [in rates of obedience] across conditions," he said; in some iterations of Milgram's study, the rate of compliance was close to 100 percent, while in others it was closer to zero. "We need an account that can explain the variability—when we obey, when we don't."

"We argue that the answer to that question is a matter of identification," he continued. "Do they identify more with the cause of science, and listen to the experimenter as a legitimate representative of science, or do they identify more with the learner as an ordinary person? . . . You're torn between these different voices. Who do you listen to?"

The question, he conceded, applies as much to the study of Milgram today as it does to what went on in his lab. "Trying to get a consensus among academics is like herding cats," Reicher said, but "if there is a consensus, it's that we need a new explanation. I think nearly everybody accepts the fact that Milgram discovered a remarkable phenomenon, but he didn't provide a very compelling explanation of that phenomenon."

What he provided instead was a difficult and deeply uncomfortable set of questions—and his research, flawed as it is, endures not because it clarifies the causes of human atrocities, but because it confuses more than it answers.

Or, as Miller put it: "The whole thing exists in terms of its controversy, how it's excited some and infuriated others. People have tried to knock it down, and it always comes up standing."

Critical Thinking

1. It's unusual for a psychological study to inspire song lyrics. Given this, what do you think the overall impact of the results of the Milgram studies has been on culture? Explain.
2. Milgram classified the participants in his research as obedient or disobedient. What are the potential problems with this approach, and what type of alternative system might have been better employed? Why?
3. What is situationism, and why is this concept particularly important in attempting to understand Milgram's results? Explain.

Internet References

Electric schlock: Did Stanley Milgram's famous obedience experiments prove anything?
http://www.psmag.com/books-and-culture/electric-schlock-65377

Milgram experiment—Obedience to authority
https://explorable.com/stanley-milgram-experiment

Stanley Milgram and the uncertainty of evil
https://www.bostonglobe.com/ideas/2013/09/28/stanley-milgram-and-uncertainty-evil/qUjame9xApiKc6evtgQRqN/story.html

Article

Prepared by: R. Eric Landrum, *Boise State University*

Are People More Disturbed by Dog or Human Suffering?

Influence of victim's species and age

JACK LEVIN, ARNOLD ARLUKE, AND LESLIE IRVINE

Learning Outcomes

After reading this article, you will be able to:

- Appreciate a survey research scenario where undergraduates were asked about their own level of emotional disturbance comparing nonhuman animal or human suffering or abuse.
- Understand the results of the survey research, including the impact of the age of human victim as well as differential responses between males and females.

In the popular perception, media coverage of the abuse of nonhuman animals appears to evoke greater public outrage than reports of comparable mistreatment of human victims. When reports of nonhuman victims reach the media, the attention they receive can seem to overshadow concern for the traumas and tragedies that befall humans. For example, in February 2015, Harrison's Fund, a British charity that supports research for Duchenne muscular dystrophy, ran a fundraising campaign featuring two versions of the same ad. Both contained text that read, "Would you give £5 to save Harrison from a slow, painful death?" One version featured a picture of the real Harrison Smith, an eight-year-old boy diagnosed with Duchenne. The other featured a stock photo of a dog. When the ads ran on MSN's United Kingdom website with links to donate to the charity, the one depicting the dog attracted twice as many clicks as the one with the boy (230, compared with 111; Lambert, 2015).

In addition, in 2014, after a pit bull dog mauled a four-year-old boy in Phoenix, AZ, leaving him with injuries requiring years of reconstructive surgery, a social media campaign rallied a legal team and financial support to save the dog from euthanasia. Within a few weeks, a Facebook page dedicated to Mickey the dog had more than 40,000 "likes," while the page for the support of the boy had barely 500 (Tang & Billeaud, 2014). Critics might point out that Facebook "likes" depend on who shared the story and how, but this only proves the point. Advocates for the dog could quickly leverage social media to reach a wide audience of like-minded supporters.

Despite anecdotal evidence of apparent greater concern for nonhuman than human victims, it would be wrong to assume that animal victims will always elicit a greater degree of emotional distress and sympathy than will human victims of violence. Scholars have noted our society's inconsistent treatment of nonhuman animals and how this ambivalence translates into widespread indifference toward, if not approval of, their harm (Arluke & Sanders, 1996; Herzog, 2010; Plous, 1993). Some people view nonhuman animals as property and treat them like objects; from this perspective, their harm would inspire little if any concern (Vollum et al., 2004).

Even if viewed as more than mere objects, the suffering of nonhuman animals still may not prompt as much concern as humans made to suffer similarly. Of course, views on nonhuman animals vary widely and are rife with contradictions (Arluke & Sanders, 1996). Studies reveal that numerous factors influence people's attitudes (Batt, 2009; Kellert, 1996; Plous, 1993). Anthropomorphized species, including but not limited to those commonly kept as companions, elicit greater concern than do other species. Phylogenetic similarity to humans, perceived intelligence, domestication, and neoteny, or "cuteness," also influence people's views. When it comes to the abuse of nonhuman animals versus children, however, the former lags far behind the latter in terms of the willingness of society to criminalize the violence, intervene to stop it, and provide resources to help the victims.

Social science research has yielded mixed results in studies of empathy felt for nonhuman versus human victims. Much of the inconclusiveness likely stems from differing perspectives on the nature of empathy. Defined as "a vicarious emotional response to another's emotions or states" (Paul, 2000, p. 194), some researchers depict empathy as one continuous capacity directed toward different targets (Eisenberg, 1988; Serpell & Paul, 1994; Signal & Taylor, 2007; Taylor & Signal, 2005). Under this framework, individuals who feel compassion for other people feel similarly toward nonhuman animals and vice versa. Assuming that the same positive correlation holds for a *lack* of compassion, or for cruelty, the idea that a continuous emotion generalizes to different targets has implications for understanding a wide range of antisocial behavior, from animal abuse to violent acts directed at other people (Ascione, 1992).

In contrast, drawing on examples of how empathy for nonhuman animals does *not* generalize to humans, such as the Nazis (Arluke & Sax, 1992) and militant animal liberation activists (Monaghan, 1999), Paul (2000) proposed separate empathy constructs, with one capturing people's response to nonhuman animals and another tapping a similar response involving human targets. Paul's (2000) research found support for the presence of two types of empathy with some shared components, rather than a single, continuous mechanism.

Studies of human–animal interaction have also sought to locate the factors that underlie empathy. Yet, apart from finding gender differences, with females consistently scoring higher than males on attitudes toward nonhuman animals and measures of empathy (Angantyr et al., 2011; Herzog, Betchart, & Pittman, 1991; Matthews & Herzog, 1997; Phillips et al., 2011; Topolski et al., 2013), these studies have been inconclusive. Because many people have close relationships with companion animals, with some claiming to have greater emotional connection to nonhuman animals than to people (Archer, 1997; Bonas, McNicholas, & Collis, 2000), research has examined whether the relationship influences empathy. Here, too, the research offers no definitive conclusions. Although Paul and Serpell (1993) found an association between companion animal ownership in childhood and concern about the welfare of both humans and nonhuman animals, Paul (2000) later found a significant association between current or childhood ownership and empathy directed at animals, but *not* at humans.[1]

Taylor and Signal (2005) found that current companion animal ownership, but not ownership in childhood, correlated with high scores on measures of human–human empathy. Studies by Signal and Taylor (2006) and Meyer, Forkman, and Paul (2014) found that ownership, regardless of life stage, had no effect on concern for nonhuman animals. In a study of children, Daly and Morton (2003) found that having companion animals *did not* result in significantly higher empathy. Daly et al. (2014) found that, while nonhuman animal companionship alone did not make respondents more likely to empathize with animals than humans, level of attachment to the companion animal did significantly mediate respondents' emotional response on behalf of animals. Respondents were generally more "bothered" by the victimization of a human infant than a puppy—with the exception of dedicated companion animal guardians who were more upset by the puppy abuse than any other group.

These and other studies focus on characteristics pertaining to the observers or the person experiencing the empathy. The observer-centered approach seeks the antecedent factors—whether related to personality, demographics, development, psychological skills (e.g., nurturance), or lifestyle choices (e.g., being a vegetarian)—that might influence empathy (see Davis, 2006; Preylo & Arikawa, 2008). Research design may explain the mixed results. By comparing an observer's emotional response to a human versus an animal victim, these studies pit species against each other (e.g., Westbury et al., 2015). Doing so may falsely attribute greater emotional response to a victim's species—animal or human—when the response may be triggered by specific attributes of victims, regardless of their species. In particular, these studies fail to examine the effect of age of victim when comparing human and animal targets. In Angantyr et al. (2011), for example, one set of scenarios compares adult victims (a man, woman, cat, and dog) and another compares young victims (a child, baby, and puppy). In Daly et al.'s (2014) studies, all the scenarios depict the "abuse victims" as young: either as puppies or infants. These studies require respondents to make choices between victims of different species but within the same age category.

A smaller number of studies consider age of the victim as an empathy trigger (Lehmann et al., 2013; Prguda & Neumann, 2014). For example, one study that incorporated age as a potential empathy trigger examined respondents' willingness to help any of the three hypothetical target victims—a 6-year-old child, an adult woman, and a 40-pound dog—portrayed as under attack by an adult man (Laner et al., 2001). Respondents reported willingness to intervene on behalf of any of the victims, but children received the highest mean scores on intention to intervene. Scores for women and dogs, while lower, did not differ significantly. Although the study incorporated age as a potential empathy trigger, it still required respondents to choose between species.

The present study examines the extent to which people's reactions of distress to animal and human suffering stem from the perceived vulnerability of the victim, as characterized by youth. In doing so, we include two potential antecedents to empathy: current need, as depicted by an abuse scenario, and vulnerability, as characterized by the victim's youth. Although the empathic response is considered a response to perceiving another in need, the types of need that elicit empathy (i.e., whether someone is in current need of help or is in a vulnerable position) deserve greater attention (Batson et al., 2005; Lishner et al., 2011). Vulnerability can exist without current need; we can perceive another as defenseless even in the absence of potential harm and doing so would not elicit empathy. Similarly, seeing another in need might not elicit empathy if that other were also seen as capable of resolving the situation without help (Midlarsky & Hannah, 1985).

Research also suggests that the empathic response arises from mechanisms that evolved to promote the care and protection of the young (Dijker, 2010, 2014; Lishner et al., 2008; Lishner et al., 2011). From an evolutionary perspective, a "parental instinct" generalizes to extend care and concern even to nonkin (Lorenz, 1971; McDougal, 1908). Informed by this view and using age as an indicator of vulnerability, we hypothesize that, when reading about a violent act, young rather than adult victims, regardless of species, will elicit greater empathy.

Materials and Methods

Participants

All participants were undergraduate students enrolled in introductory sociology and anthropology classes at a major northeastern university. The approximate enrollment in these classes totaled 380 students; 240 students completed and returned the survey instrument. All participants were in the age range 18–23. One hundred and ninety-six were Caucasian, 16 Black, 19 Asian, and 9 Latino. Some 172 participants were female and 68 were male. Only those students 18 or older were asked to participate. There were no other inclusion/exclusion criteria.

The university's institutional review board reviewed and approved this study.

Procedure

In a regular classroom setting, participants were recruited by asking the students present if they would participate in the study. It was made clear that students' participation was completely voluntary and their acceptance or rejection to participate would not affect their standing at the university or in the class. Before receiving the instrument, verbal informed consent was obtained and participants were given an explanation for completing the instrument. All data were collected during a regular class period. Both oral and written instructions indicated that all answers were to be treated confidentially and that participants could stop at any time, even if they had already started the experiment.

To manipulate the independent variables, consenting participants were randomly given a fictitious newspaper article that described one of the four vignettes (1-year-old infant, 30-year-old adult, a puppy, or 6-year-old adult dog) that detailed an attack perpetrated against the victim. The vignettes differed only by the identification of the victim. All other conditions remained the same. For example, our vignette for the puppy was as follows:

> Please read the following article taken from the *Boston Globe*, October 16th, 2010: *BOSTON—After a noticeable increase of attacks against residents of certain Boston neighborhoods, Police Commissioner Davis has assigned a larger law enforcement presence to crime "hotspots" around the City. Last week, police investigators documented a total of 11 attacks on residents of the South End alone. According to witnesses present, one particularly vicious assault involved a one-year-old puppy that was beaten with a baseball bat by an unknown assailant. Arriving on the scene a few minutes after the attack, a police officer found the victim with one broken leg, multiple lacerations, and unconscious. No arrests have been made in the case.*

Dependent Variable

Participants were then asked to indicate their degree of empathic concern for the victim in the vignette by their responses on an Emotional Response Scale (Batson, 1987). The measure consisted of 16 emotions to which participants responded by indicating how much they felt each toward the victim whose account they read on a series of 7-point rating scales: for example, from 1 (*not at all sympathetic*) to 7 (*extremely sympathetic*). The list included six emotions—*sympathetic, softhearted, warm, compassionate, tender, and moved*—that have been employed in many previous studies to assess feelings of empathic concern (see Batson et al., 2005, 2007).

The ratings on the 16 scales were summarized to yield a total empathic distress score ranging from 7 (*little empathy*) to 112 (*much empathy*). The internal consistency of the overall measure was indicated by Cronbach's $\alpha = .83$. Notwithstanding its lack of explicit validity and reliability data, the Emotional Response Scale has been employed in numerous studies and published in the most selective journals in social psychology, as a measure of empathy and personal distress (see, e.g., Batson, 1991; Batson et al., 1981, 1983, 1986, 1988, 1989, 1995, 1997, 2005, 2007; Fultz et al., 1986; Lishner et al., 2011; Toi & Batson, 1982).

As a check on the effectiveness of the manipulation, participants were asked to recall the age and species of the victim from the vignette they had received. The nine students who gave at least one incorrect response were excluded from the study, leaving a total of 231 participants whose responses were subjected to analysis.

Debriefing

Once participants read one of the fictitious newspaper articles and completed the questionnaire, they were fully debriefed, thanked for their time, and asked to remain in the classroom for their regularly scheduled lecture.

Results

Data were subjected to a 2 (species of victim) × 2 (age of victim) × 2 (gender of participant) analysis of variance in which main effects and interactions were examined. Results indicated that the main effects for age of victim and gender of participant, but not for species of victim, were significant. More specifically, female participants ($M = 74.94$, $SD = 21.58$) were significantly more empathic than their male counterparts ($M = 69.28$, $SD = 20.91$), regardless of species, $F(1,224) = 4.34$, $p = .04$, $d = .28$. This result is consistent with the finding of an earlier study, in which females were found to be more distressed than males regarding victimization generally (Angantyr et al., 2011).

Not surprisingly, participants in the present study were significantly more empathic when the victim was an infant or puppy ($M = 78.22$, $SD = 15.80$) than an adult person or dog ($M = 65.99$, $SD = 20.90$, $F(1,224) = 20.23$, $p = .0001$, $d = .79$). At the same time, the interaction between age and species also yielded significant differences, $F(1,224) = 12.70$, $p = .0001$, $d = .61$, but of an unexpected character. Based on Tukey's multiple comparison test, all of the age categories—infant ($M = 82.76$, $SD = 14.53$), puppy ($M = 75.34$, $SD = 17.06$), and adult dog ($M = 73.15$, $SD = 22.07$)—received significantly greater empathy than did the human adult victim ($M = 62.09$, $SD = 19.72$). Only in comparison with the infant did the adult dog receive significantly less empathy than other victims ($HSD = 8.85$). None of the other interaction effects were significant.

Discussion

Our results indicate that respondents were significantly less distressed when adult humans were victimized, in comparison with human babies, puppies, and adult dogs. Only relative to the infant victim did the adult dog receive lower scores of empathy. These results provide partial support for the assumption that people generally care more about nonhuman animal suffering than human suffering. More specifically, when confronted with hypothetical abuse, individuals report more distress over nonhuman rather than human victimization, unless a human child experiences the suffering.

There are two possible—and related—explanations for these findings, neither of which can be confirmed in the present study. First, the higher scores for the infant over all other victims are consistent with other research highlighting the importance of similarity between respondents and victims. The "perceived similarity" explanation maintains that people feel concern for others whom they perceive as similar to themselves (Batson et al., 2005; Krebs, 1975). Thus, species similarity could account for the preference of the infant over the puppy and dog, as in the study by Daly et al. (2014).

Second, the higher scores for the infant and the puppy suggest the importance of vulnerability, as conveyed by youth, in evoking empathy (Dijker, 2001). Perceived similarity alone did not evoke empathy: it did so only when combined with vulnerability. This is consistent with research suggesting that the empathic response evolved to promote the care and protection of the young (Dijker, 2010, 2014; Lishner et al., 2008; Lishner et al., 2011; Lorenz, 1971). Angantyr et al. (2011) support this explanation. Their study found that participants expressed the same degree of empathy for a baby as for a puppy. However, unlike the research by Angantyr et al., which looked only at main effects of young members of both species (or interactions with gender of participants), we were able to examine the interaction between age and species.

In addition, our results suggest that respondents were similarly concerned for adult dogs as victims. That is, only empathy toward the adult human was significantly lower than empathy expressed toward an infant, a puppy, or an adult dog. It may be that many people appraise dogs as vulnerable, regardless of their age, when compared to adult humans. In other words, dogs, whether young or adult, are seen as possessing many of the same qualities associated with human babies; they are seen as unable to fully protect themselves, compared to adult humans. Additional research could explore this further by asking respondents to rate the perceived vulnerability of the victims.

The vignette in which a human adult appeared did not indicate the victim's gender. In light of the traditional stereotype depicting men as dominant and strong versus women as submissive and weak, it is conceivable that we would have found greater empathy for adult humans if we had specified the female gender of the victim. Future research might vary the gender of the human adult target to determine whether our results apply as well to female as male victims. In addition, examining correlations between the gender of respondents and victims would test the perceived similarity explanation by assessing the degree to which gender, along with species, influences respondents' identification with victims.

Indirect support for our findings comes from studies of how people regard their own companion dogs, some showing that people can consider their dogs, whether full-grown or puppies, as children or babies. For example, Greenebaum's (2004) study of "Yappy Hour" at Fido's Barkery showed that people attending this event on a weekly basis treated their dogs like children and regarded themselves as their dogs' "parents." In fact, Greenebaum's subjects did not view their dogs as animals, but rather as "fur babies," or family members alongside human children. Of course, not everyone will view dogs this way. People who have dominionistic relationships with dogs, for instance, have relatively low regard for their companion animals and value them primarily for protection, compared to people having a humanistic orientation that elevates dogs to the status of surrogate humans (Blouin, 2013).

With regard to the dog and the child being equivalent, this might also stem from respondents' differing perceptions of the vulnerability of the victims. As with a "blaming the victim" situation, respondents might view adults as responsible for and capable of removing themselves from the abusive situation; we expect the adult to walk away, as we would think we would do if in such a situation. With a young child or a dog, respondents might see them as unable to leave a harmful situation.

Of course, making similar attributions to both dogs and human babies also may depend on the specific dog breed. In our study, we did not specify breed in the vignettes. Future research might examine whether the "all dogs are babies" perception is breed-dependent by using vignettes that vary the identity of particular breeds of dogs. Prior research findings have been equivocal about the public's perception of and favorability toward different breeds, with some studies suggesting that people perceive different breeds similarly (Perrine & Wells, 2006), while other studies suggest differences (Budge et al., 1996). There might be less empathy for particular dog breeds stereotyped as highly aggressive, whose owners are also pictured as violent (Twining et al., 2000). Although empathy was not directly studied, the respondents in Wright et al.'s (2007) research found that dogs seen as unfriendly and aggressive were less desirable and adoptable compared with dogs thought to be friendly and not dangerous, suggesting that victimized breeds with the former characteristics might elicit less empathy than the latter.

Whether people have as much empathy for other kinds of victimized companion animals, such as cats or birds, let alone for wildlife, also merits investigation. While many people care about dogs (Plous, 1993), and perhaps other kinds of companion animals, not everyone is likely to have the same degree of empathy for dogs as, say, a squirrel, if the squirrel victim were similarly injured in a vignette. Here, too, as with dog breeds, there is variation in how the public regards various nonhuman species, heavily anthropomorphizing, and perhaps having greater empathy for some species like dolphins or whales while not others, such as snakes (Arluke & Sanders, 1996; Ashley et al., 2007; Herzog & Burghardt, 1988).

Experimental research has the advantage of giving investigators an opportunity to establish cause-and-effect relationships by manipulating their independent variables rather than by merely measuring the effects of variables post hoc. At the same time, experiments including ours tend to have far less external validity than other research methods, typically including for investigation only a few of the many variables that might influence a dependent variable. As a result, it is usually difficult to extrapolate from the respondents in a single experimental study to any larger and more diverse population. We studied college students, most of whom were in their late teens and early twenties and white. Future research might seek to generalize to an older and ethnically more diverse population. Moreover, we excluded a number of variables that might have contributed to differences in empathy such as whether subjects were owners of dogs. Still, the strong internal validity of our experimental approach is a result of the random assignment of respondents to various categories of the independent variables, so that extraneous variables can be assumed to be distributed equally throughout the treatments, and therefore cannot be held accountable for significant differences.

Conclusion

In terms of implications for policy and practice, the results of this study suggest an avenue for cultivating humane attitudes and potentially reducing the likelihood of violence toward human and nonhuman animals. The finding that perceived similarity, coupled with vulnerability, resulted in the highest scores among respondents offers persuasive evidence of the need to shift the scope of existing practices. We suggest that by emphasizing shared vulnerability, rather than focusing on exposure to violence and aggression, innovative programs could reshape the treatment and prevention of animal abuse.

The incorporation of vulnerability has already advanced several other fields. For instance, in the literature on disasters, the "vulnerability paradigm" argues that characteristics of individuals and groups influence their ability to "anticipate, cope with, resist, and recover from the impact" of catastrophic events (Blaikie et al., 1994, p. 94; see also Irvine, 2010; Tierney, 2006). This perspective focuses attention on reducing risks beforehand, and not simply responding after an event.

Current research on medical education underscores the need for physicians and nurses to develop "a sense of what it means to be a vulnerable person, without necessarily focusing on illness" (Holloway & Freshwater, 2007, p. 709; see also Bochner, 2009; Hoffmaster, 2006). The process of incorporating a perspective on vulnerability into specific programs would vary widely, and the details extend beyond the scope of this paper. Nevertheless, because acknowledging vulnerability means acknowledging similarity as embodied beings, similarly subject to harm and pain, it can have a potential impact on a wide range of moral and legal domains related, but not limited to, interactions between humans and nonhuman animals.

Acknowledgment

We would like to thank Abby Huhtala and Kaitlin Nesbitt for their competent assistance in collecting and analyzing data for the study.

Notes

1. We recognize the controversy surrounding "ownership" of non-human animals; we have used the term, as well as "owner," where consistent with the cited literature.

References

Angantyr, M., Jakob, E., & Hansen, E. (2011). A comparison of empathy for humans and empathy for animals. *Anthrozoös, 24*(4), 369–377.

Archer, J. (1997). Why do people love their pets? *Evolution and Human Behavior, 18*(4), 237–259.

Arluke, A., & Sanders, C. (1996). *Regarding animals*. Philadelphia: Temple University Press.

Arluke, A., & Sax, B. (1992). Understanding Nazi animal protection and the Holocaust *Anthrozoös, 5*(1), 6–31.

Ascione, F. R. (1992). Enhancing children's attitudes about the humane treatment of animals: Generalization to human-directed empathy. *Anthrozoös, 5*(3), 176–191.

Ashley, E. P., Kosloski, A., & Petrie, S. A. (2007). Incidence of intentional vehicle—Reptile collisions. *Human Dimensions of Wildlife, 12*(3), 137–143.

Batson, C. D. (1991). *The altruism question: Toward a social psychological answer.* Hillsdale, NJ: Erlbaum.

Batson, C. D., Batson, J. G., Griffitt, C. A., Barrientos, S., Brandt, J., Randall, S. P., & Bayly, M. J. (1989). Negative-state relief and the empathy—altruism hypothesis. *Journal of Personality and Social Psychology, 56*(6), 922–933.

Batson, C. D., Bolen, M. H., Cross, J. A., & Neuringer-Benefiel, H. E. (1986). Where is the altruism in the altruistic personality? *Journal of Personality and Social Psychology, 50*(1), 212–220.

Batson, C. D., Duncan, B. D., Ackerman, P., Buckley, T., & Birch, K. (1981). Is empathic emotion a source of altruistic motivation? *Journal of Personality and Social Psychology, 40*(2), 290–302.

Batson, C. D., Dyck, J. L., Brandt, J. R., Batson, J. G., Powell, A. L., McMaster, M. R., & Griffitt, C. (1988). Five studies testing two new egoistic alternatives to the empathy-altruism hypothesis. *Journal of Personality and Social Psychology, 55*(1), 52–77.

Batson, C. D., Eklund, J., Chermok, V., Hoyt, J., & Biaggio, O. (2007). An additional antecedent of empathic concern: Valuing the welfare of the person in need. *Journal of Personality and Social Psychology, 93*(1), 65–74.

Batson, C. D., Lishner, D. A., Cook, J., & Sawyer, S. (2005). Similarity and nurturance: Two possible sources of empathy for strangers. *Basic and Applied Social Psychology, 27*(1), 15–25.

Batson, C. D., O'Quin, K., Fultz, J., Vanderplas, M., & Isen, A. M. (1983). Influence of self-reported distress and empathy on egoistic versus altruistic motivation to help. *Journal of Personality and Social Psychology, 45*(3), 706–718.

Batson, C. D., Polycarpou, M. P., Harmon-Jones, E., Imhoff, H. J., Mitchener, E. C., Bednar, L. L., Klein, T. R., & Highberger, L. (1997). Empathy and attitudes: Can feeling for a member of a stigmatized group improve feelings toward the group? *Journal of Personality and Social Psychology, 72*(1), 105–118.

Batson, C. D., Turk, C. L., Shaw, L. L., & Klein, T. R. (1995). Information function of empathic emotion: Learning that we value the other's welfare. *Journal of Personality and Social Psychology, 68*(2), 300–313.

Blaikie, P., Cannon, T., Davis, I., & Wisner, B. (1994). *At risk: Natural hazards, people's vulnerability, and disasters.* London: Routledge.

Blouin, D. (2013). Are dogs children, companions, or just animals: Understanding variations in people's orientations toward animals. *Anthrozoös, 26*(2), 279–294.

Bochner, A. P. (2009). Vulnerable medicine. *Journal of Applied Communication Research, 37*(2), 159–166.

Bonas, S., McNicholas, J., & Collis, G. M. (2000). Pets in the network of family relationships: An empirical study. In A. L. Podberscek, E. S. Paul, & J. A. Serpell (Eds.), *Companion animals and us: Exploring the relationships between people and pets* (pp. 209–236). New York: Cambridge University Press.

Budge, C. R., Spicer, J., Jones, B. R., & St. George, R. (1996). The influence of companion animals on owner perception: Gender and species effects. *Anthrozoös, 9*(1), 10–18.

Daly, B., & Morton, L. L. (2003). Children with pets do not show higher empathy: A challenge to current views. *Anthrozoös, 16*(4), 298–314.

Daly, B., Taylor, N., & Signal, T. (2014). Pups and babes: Quantifying sources of difference in emotional and behavioral reactions to accounts of human and animal abuse. *Anthrozoös, 27*(2), 205–217.

Davis, M. H. (2006). Empathy. In J. Stets & J. Turner (Eds.), *Handbook of the sociology of emotions* (pp. 443–466). New York: Springer US.

Dijker, A. J. (2001). The influence of perceived suffering and vulnerability on the experience of pity. *European Journal of Social Psychology, 31*(6), 659–676.

Dijker, A. J. (2010). Perceived vulnerability as a common basis of moral emotions. *British Journal of Social Psychology, 49*(2), 415–423.

Dijker, A. J. (2014). A theory of vulnerability-based morality. *Emotion Review, 6*(2), 175–183.

Eisenberg, N. (1988). Empathy and sympathy: A brief review of the concepts and empirical literature. *Anthrozoös, 2*(1), 15–17.

Eisenberg, N., Fabes, R. A., Bernzweig, J., Karbon, M., Poulin, R., & Hanish, L. (1993). The relations of emotionality and regulation to preschoolers' social skills and sociometric status. *Child Development*, *64*(5), 1418–1438.

Ellingsen, K., Zanella, A. J., Bjerkås, E., & Indrebø, A. (2010). The relationship between empathy, perception of pain and attitudes toward pets among Norwegian dog owners. *Anthrozoös*, *23*(3), 231–243.

Filippi, M., Riccitelli, G., Falini, A., Di Salle, F., & Vuilleumier, P. (2010). The brain functional networks associated to human and animal suffering differ among omnivores, vegetarians and vegans. *PLoS ONE*, *5*(5), e10847. doi:10.1371/journal.pone.0010847

Franklin, R. G., Nelson, A. J., & Barker, M. (2013). Neural responses to perceiving suffering in humans and animals. *Social Neuroscience*, *8*(3), 217-227.

Fultz, J., Batson, C. D., Fortenbach, V. A., Patricia, M. V., & Laurel, L. (1986). Social evaluation and the empathy-altruism hypothesis. *Journal of Personality and Social Psychology*, *50*(4), 761–769.

Gage, M., & Holcomb, R. (1991). Couples' perception of stressfulness of death of the family pet. *Family Relations*, *40*(1), 103–105.

Gerwolls, M., & Labott, S. (1994). Adjustment to the death of a companion animal. *Anthrozoös*, *7*(3), 172–187.

Greenebaum, J. (2004). It's a dog's life: Elevating status from pet to "fur baby" at Yappy Hour. *Society & Animals*, *12*(2), 117–135.

Herzog, H. A. (2007). Gender differences in human–animal interactions: A review. *Anthrozoös*, *20*(1), 7–21.

Herzog, H. A. (2011). *Some we love, some we hate, some we eat.* New York: Harper Perennial.

Herzog, H. A., Betchart, N., & Pittman, R. (1991). Sex role identity and attitudes toward animals. *Anthrozoös*, *4*(3), 184–192.

Herzog, H. A., & Burghardt, G. (1988). Attitudes toward animals: Origins and diversity. *Anthrozoös*, *1*(4), 214–222.

Hoffmaster, B. (2006). What does vulnerability mean? *Hastings Center Report*, *36*(2), 38–45.

Holloway, I., & Freshwater, D. (2007). Vulnerable story telling: Narrative research in nursing. *Journal of Research in Nursing*, *12*(6), 703–711.

Irvine, L. (2010). *Filling the ark: Animal welfare in disasters.* Philadelphia, PA: Temple University Press.

Krebs, D. L. (1975). Empathy and altruism. *Journal of Personality and Social Psychology*, *32*(6), 1134–1146.

Lambert, V. (2015). Why do people donate to dog charities when children are dying? *The Telegraph.* Retrieved from http://www.telegraph.co.uk/lifestyle/11408327/Why-do-people-donate-to-dog-charities-when-children-are-dying.html. Accessed 2/26/15.

Laner, M., Benin, M., & Ventrone, N. (2001). Bystander attitudes toward victims of violence: Who's worth helping? *Deviant Behavior*, *22*(1), 23–42.

Lehmann, V., Huis, E. M., & Vingerhoets, A. J. J. M. (2013). The human and animal baby schema effect: Correlates of individual differences. *Behavioural Processes*, *94*(March), 99–108.

Lishner, D. A., Batson, C. D., & Huss, E. (2011). Tenderness and sympathy: Distinct empathic emotions elicited by different forms of need. *Personality and Social Psychology Bulletin*, *37*(5), 614–625.

Lishner, D. A., Oceja, L. V., Stocks, E. L., & Zaspel, K. (2008). The effect of infant-like characteristics on empathic concern for adults in need. *Motivation and Emotion*, *32*(4), 270–277.

Lorenz, K. (1971). *Studies in animal and human behavior* (Vol. 2). Cambridge: Harvard University Press.

Matthews, S., & Herzog, H. (1997). Personality and attitudes toward the treatment of animals. *Society & Animals*, *5*(2), 57–63.

McDougal, W. (1908). *Introduction to social psychology.* London: Methuen.

Meyer, I., Forkman, B., & Paul, E. S. (2014). Factors affecting the human interpretation of dog behavior. *Anthrozoös*, *27*(1), 127–140.

Midlarsky, E., & Hannah, M. (1985). Competence, reticence, and helping by children and adolescents. *Developmental Psychology*, *21*(3), 534–541.

Monaghan, R. (1999). Terrorism in the name of animal rights. *Terrorism and Political Violence*, *11*(4), 159–169.

Paul, E. S. (1995). Us and them: Scientists' and animal rights campaigners' views of the animal experimentation debate. *Society & Animals*, *3*(4), 1–22.

Paul, E. S. (2000). Empathy with animals and with humans: Are they linked? *Anthrozoös*, *13*(4), 194–202.

Paul, E. S., & Serpell, J. A. (1993). Childhood pet keeping and humane attitudes in young adulthood. *Animal Welfare*, *2*(4), 321–337.

Perrine, R., & Wells, M. (2006). Labradors to Persians: Perceptions of pets in the workplace. *Anthrozoös*, *19*(1), 65–78.

Phillips, C. J. C., Izmirli, S., Aldavood, S. J., Alonso, M., Choe, B., Hanlon, A., . . . Rehn, T. (2011). An international comparison of female and male students' attitudes to the use of animals. *Animals*, *1*(1), 7–26.

Plous, S. (1993). Psychological mechanisms in the human use of animals. *Journal of Social Issues*, *49*(1), 11–52.

Preylo, B. D., & Arikawa, H. (2008). Comparison of vegetarians and non-vegetarians on pet attitude and empathy. *Anthrozoös*, *21*(4), 387–396.

Prguda, E., & Neumann, D. (2014). Inter-human and animal-directed empathy: A test for evolutionary biases in empathic responding. *Behavioural Processes*, *108*(October), 80–86.

Rothgerber, H., & Mican, F. (2014). Childhood pet ownership, attachment to pets, and subsequent meat avoidance: The mediating role of empathy toward animals. *Appetite*, *79*(August), 11–17.

Serpell, J. A., & Paul, E. S. (1994). Pets and the development of positive attitudes to animals. In A. Manning & J. Serpell (Eds.), *Animals and human society: Changing perspectives* (pp. 127–144). London: Routledge.

Signal, T. D., & Taylor, N. (2006). Attitude to animals and empathy: Comparing animal protection and general community samples. *Anthrozoös*, *20*(2), 125–130.

Tang, T., & Billeaud, J. (2014). Petition, advocates help spare 'Mickey,' pit bull who mauled 4-year-old Arizona boy. *Huffington Post.* Retrieved from http://www.huffingtonpost.com/2014/03/26/pit-bull-mauls-arizona-boy_n_5036629.html. Accessed 2/26/15.

Taylor, N., & Signal, T. D. (2005). Empathy and attitudes to animals. *Anthrozoös, 18*(1), 18–27.

Thompson, K., & Gullone, E. (2003). Promotion of empathy and prosocial behaviour in children through humane education. *Australian Psychologist, 38*(3), 175–182.

Thompson, K., & Gullone, E. (2008). Prosocial and antisocial behaviors in adolescents: An investigation into associations with attachment and empathy. *Anthrozoös, 21*(2), 123–137.

Tierney, K. (2006). Foreshadowing Katrina: Recent sociological contributions to vulnerability science. *Contemporary Sociology, 35*(3), 207–212.

Toi, M., & Batson, C. D. (1982). More evidence that empathy is a source of altruistic motivation. *Journal of Personality and Social Psychology, 43*(2), 281–292

Topolski, R., Weaver, J. N., Martin, Z., & McCoy, J. (2013). Choosing between the emotional dog and the rational pal: A moral dilemma with a tail. *Anthrozoös, 26*(2), 253–263.

Twining, H., Arluke, A., & Patronek, G. (2000). Managing the stigma of outlaw breeds: The case of pit bull owners. *Society & Animals, 8*(1), 1–27.

Vollum, S., Buffington-Vollum, J., & Longmire, D. R. (2004). Moral disengagement and attitudes about violence toward animals. *Society & Animals, 12*(3), 209–235.

Westbury, H. R., Neumann, D. L., & Waters, A. M. (2015). Empathy-related ratings to still images of human and nonhuman animal groups in negative contexts graded for phylogenetic similarity. *Anthrozoös, 28*(1), 113–130.

Wright, J., Smith, A., Daniel, K., & Adkins, K. (2007). Dog breed stereotype and exposure to negative behavior: Effects on perceptions of adoptability. *Journal of Applied Animal Welfare Science, 10*(3), 255–265.

Critical Thinking

1. From the Discussion section: "People generally care more about nonhuman animal suffering than human suffering." What do you think about this result? Does it resonate with your own beliefs? Explain.
2. Survey studies are pervasive in psychology and in society. How close do you think they approximate reality? That is, do you think people respond to surveys in such a way that represents how they would actually act in real life? Do people really care more about dog suffering than human suffering, or do they just say that on a survey? Explore this topic a bit and explain your answer.

Internet References

Do Animals Feel Pain in the Same Way as Humans Do?

https://www.independent.co.uk/life-style/health-and-families/features/do-animals-feel-pain-in-the-same-way-as-humans-do-10371800.html

Dogs Feel Empathy for Human Suffering

https://cosmosmagazine.com/biology/dogs-feel-empathy-for-human-suffering

People Care More about Hurt Dogs than Hurt Humans—At Least Sometimes, Study Shows

https://www.miamiherald.com/news/nation-world/national/article182257941.html

Speaking of Research: The Uniqueness of Human Suffering

https://speakingofresearch.com/2015/01/12/the-uniqueness-of-human-suffering-suffering-from-pain/

Unit 10

UNIT

Prepared by: R. Eric Landrum, *Boise State University*

Psychological Disorders

Jay and Harry are two brothers who own a gas station. Harry and Jay have a good working relationship. Harry is the "up-front" man. Taking customer orders, accepting payments, and working with parts distributors, Harry deals directly with the public, delivery personnel, and other people visiting the gas station. Jay works behind the scenes. Although Harry makes the mechanical diagnoses, Jay is the mastermind who does the corrective work. Some of his friends think Jay is a veritable mechanical genius; he can fix anything. Preferring to spend time by himself, Jay has always been a little odd and a bit of a loner. Jay's friends think his emotions have always been inappropriate and more intense than other people, but they pass it off as part of his eccentric talent. On the other hand, Harry is the stalwart of the family. He is the acknowledged leader and decision maker when it comes to family finances.

One day, Jay did not show up for work on time. When he finally did appear, he was dressed in the most garish outfit and was laughing hysterically and talking to himself. At first, Harry suspected that his brother was high. However, Jay's condition persisted and, in fact, worsened. Out of concern, his family took him to their physician, who immediately sent Jay and his family to a psychiatrist. After several visits, the doctor informed the family that Jay suffers from schizophrenia. Jay's maternal uncle had also been schizophrenic. The family somberly left the psychiatrist's office and went to the local pharmacy to fill a prescription for antipsychotic medication.

What caused Jay's drastic change in mental health? Was Jay destined to be schizophrenic because of his family tree? Did competitiveness with his brother and the feeling that he was less revered than Harry cause his descent into mental disorder? (Rest assured the schizophrenia is complicated, and did not occur because of competitiveness). How do psychiatrists and clinical psychologists make accurate diagnoses? Once a diagnosis of mental disorder is made (such as schizophrenia), can the individual ever completely recover? Mental disorders affect millions of people throughout the world. Mental disorders impact every aspect of an individual's life, but work, family, and friendships are especially impacted. Because of their detrimental effect on the individual, mental disorders have been a focal point of psychological research for decades. This important work has revealed the likely origins or causes of mental disorders and has led to breakthroughs in the care and treatment of people with mental disorders. This unit emphasizes the questions that psychologists have attempted to address in their quest to understand the nature of mental illness.

Article Prepared by: R. Eric Landrum, *Boise State University*

Being Neurotic Makes It Harder for You to Remember Things

Emily Mullin

Learning Outcomes

After reading this article, you will be able to:

- Define neuroticism.
- List the five major domains of personality.

If you've ever gone to the grocery store but forgot your shopping list at home, you know just how frustrating it can be trying to remember what to buy. Now, science is revealing why your personality can influence how quickly and accurately you recall items on your list.

Memory has long been a major area of interest to neuroscientists, and previous work has demonstrated that different personality traits affect working memory. But scientists didn't know just what was happening in the brain to link the two.

"Neuroticism is universally implicated in making things difficult for people, whatever they might be doing. These associations have been known, but there was no mechanism to say why one thing influenced the other," says study leader Sophia Frangou at the Icahn School of Medicine at Mount Sinai in New York. The new work by Frangou and her colleagues in the United Kingdom and Switzerland explores the relationship between certain personalities and increased or decreased brain plasticity—the ability of the brain to change the strength of its neural connections based on cognitive demands.

The scientists measured the brain activity of 40 adult participants while they completed a working memory test. To scan the brain, the team used a tried and true neuroimaging technique—functional magnetic resonance imaging (fMRI)—with a relatively new method for interpreting the data called dynamic causal modeling.

"The advantage of dynamic causal modeling is that it moves away from globalness," Frangou explains. "Instead of saying this lobe of the brain is bigger or brighter, it instead looks at what way one region of the brain influences this other brain region during a task." In other words, the technique helps scientists better understand the connections being made in the brain.

The memory test asked study participants to view a sequence of letters on a computer screen and indicate when a current letter matched one from earlier steps in the sequence. Then the investigators evaluated participants' personality traits using a well-known test in psychology called the NEO-PI-R, which measures the five major domains of personality: neuroticism, extraversion, openness to experience, agreeableness and conscientiousness. Two of these personality types were strongly linked to the level of efficiency at which individuals completed the memory task, the team reports this week in *Human Brain Mapping*.

"We found that people who are more neurotic, perhaps because they have the tendency to worry, were less efficient," Frangou says. Meanwhile, subjects who scored higher on the conscientiousness scale, which is defined as having a measure of self-discipline, completed the task more quickly and with a higher accuracy rate.

The dynamic causal modeling helped illuminate why: People who did well on the task showed increased activity in the top part of their brains and made stronger neural connections, while the more neurotic individuals took longer to make the same brain connections.

If you're a worrywart and prone to neurotic behavior, Frangou says you're more likely to take a longer time at the grocery store trying to remember everything on your list. You might miss a few items, too. "But someone who is less prone to distress and is able to focus on the task at hand will be more likely to get everything on the list and do it more quickly," Frangou says.

David Glahn, a professor of psychiatry at the Yale School of Medicine, says the team's study is intriguing because it looks at the association between memory and personality at the microscale. "What they're saying is not only is brain connectivity important to being able to serve working memory function, but it has a direct relationship to long-term, trait-like thinking patterns and behaviors," Glahn says. The study also brings up the possibility of using similar brain connectivity models to learn more about personality disorders.

While the study only included 40 individuals, Glahn notes that the team found such strong links between neuroticism, conscientiousness and working memory that he thinks the results could have wide implications. "I believe this study will allow us to draw conclusions about the broader population, because the individuals in the study were not selected specifically because of their neuroticism scores. They were individuals with normal variations of neuroticism." That said, Glahn would like to see the same methodology applied to people on the more extreme ends of the personality test, such as highly neurotic individuals who have trouble interacting in society.

Frangou and her team are now developing neuroscience-based talk therapies that target neuroticism with the aim of improving cognition. She adds that it is possible for neurotic individuals to improve their memory skills, but the latest study provides additional evidence that these people are more limited than other personality types in their capacity for working memory.

Critical Thinking

1. Regarding memory, what is the relationship between neuroticism and efficiency? Explain.
2. What personality characteristic is aligned with quicker memory performance and higher memory accuracy? Why do you think this is the case?

Internet References

Neuroticism moderates the daily relation between stressors and memory failures

https://www.ncbi.nlm.nih.gov/pmc/articles/PMC4084696/

Retrospective ratings of emotion: The effects of age, daily tiredness, and personality

https://www.ncbi.nlm.nih.gov/pmc/articles/PMC4707248/

The myth of the neurotic creative

https://www.theatlantic.com/science/archive/2016/02/myth-of-the-neurotic-creative/471447/

Trait perspectives on personality

https://courses.lumenlearning.com/boundless-psychology/chapter/trait-perspectives-on-personality/

Article

Prepared by: R. Eric Landrum, *Boise State University*

Overcoming the Shame of a Suicide Attempt

JAMIE BRICKHOUSE

Learning Outcomes

After reading this article, you will be able to:

- Identify the risk factors for suicide.
- Appreciate the roles that stigma and shame play in understanding suicide.

I don't remember much about the first time I tried to kill myself, 21 years ago, because any time the memory popped up I deleted it from my mind like an unflattering photo on Facebook. Despite being open and public about my second attempt, in 2006, which I revealed in a memoir about my alcoholism, I've never told anyone else about that first one – not my partner of 25 years, my therapist of 10 years, family, nor friends – until now.

Here's what I remember about that first time, in 1995. I felt hopeless, that my 27 years of life were done (27!). I'd come home drunk from a glamorous Manhattan book event, which I had organized as the publicist. The wattage of successful artists in literature, fashion and theater was blinding. I felt like a failure, that I would never be more than the hired help, that my own dreams were just thin air. When I came home and poured another drink and remembered the leftover painkillers in my medicine cabinet – prescribed for a sprained ankle earned by a drunken fall – I thought, "Why not?"

My attempt was impulsive, not premeditated. Had it been successful, I'd classify it as suicidal manslaughter. I climbed into the antique wrought iron bed I shared with my partner and passed out. The next morning, I woke up next to him and he was none the wiser. I got up in a daze and went to work feeling like I was moving under water, so heavy was my triple hangover from booze, pills and shame. I kept moving, kept drinking (I was blind then to the cause and effect of booze and depression) and kept silent.

My silence nearly killed me. Eleven years later, I tried again. I had been fantasizing about suicide every day for months. I was more hopeless. I was drunker. That time I did it with sleeping pills I'd been taking to prevent me from drinking as much at night. Booze, pills, suicide attempts: it was all one big happy "Valley of the Dolls" family. That time I took the pills in the morning after my partner left for work, and I didn't wake up on my own. My partner found me in that antique bed when he came home from work. The jig was up, and my winding path to recovery began.

Why bother talking about the first one? Now that I've been sober for almost eight years and my artistic dreams are coming true, the secret made me feel like a house rebuilt on a foundation still riddled with termites. I knew I would have to own the attempt eventually, so when the Centers for Disease Control and Prevention recently released a report that suicides had surged to the highest levels in 30 years, I knew it was time for me to come clean. With two attempts on my score card, I forever remain in a suicide high risk group. According to the Harvard T.H. Chan School of Public Health, a history of suicide attempt is one of the strongest risk factors for suicide, and the American Foundation for Suicide Prevention reports that approximately 40 percent of those who have died by suicide have made a previous suicide attempt at some point in their lives. I don't want the third time to be the charm.

The further away from that first attempt, the deeper the secret grew and the less real it became. *I didn't really do that. I didn't think a few painkillers would kill me. I didn't mean it.* But I *did* do it and I *did* mean it. I'm mortified by that. It was reckless, rash, stupid, selfish, pathetic.

As a recovering alcoholic I know that admitting to my behavior and owning my story is the only way it can no longer own me. I'm not ashamed of being an alcoholic, but I'm still ashamed of trying to kill myself, even though I know I did it under the temporary insanity of alcohol. According to the A.F.S.P., approximately 30 percent of those who die by suicide have blood alcohol levels in the range of intoxication at the time of their deaths.

After my second attempt, I went to rehab and then to sober meetings. The focus quickly shifted from my suicide attempt to my alcoholism, and rightfully so. Once my alcoholism was treated, the depression lifted. It was alcohol that brought on my depression and thoughts of suicide, and ultimately twice gave me the courage to try it. Since I've been sober, I no longer suffer from depression, do not take antidepressants and no longer think about killing myself.

I'm fortunate to live in New York City, where there are almost as many sober meetings as there are bars. These are peer-led meetings of alcoholics helping other alcoholics, free of judgment and condescension. These meetings keep me sober, hence nonsuicidal.

But what about the nonalcoholics and nonaddicts who've attempted suicide? Where are their meetings? I could find only a few peer-led suicide attempt survivor support groups via Google, and none in New York City. When I called the National Suicide Hotline requesting local suicide *attempt* survivor support groups, the operator suggested just one option: a Safe Place Meeting hosted by the Samaritans, a suicide prevention network. But those meetings are for those who have lost loved ones to suicide, and they have no meetings for attempt survivors.

I admitted my second suicide attempt because I was found out, and had to. But shame kept me quiet about my first attempt. I admit it now, and I throw out a call for other closeted suicide attempt survivors to do the same: Own it, and find – or create – a safe group where you can talk about it.

Today I own my story, so that my story doesn't kill me.

Critical Thinking

1. What do you think are the reasons/conditions for the current rate of suicides to be the highest they have been in the past 30 years?
2. What types of support systems need to be put into place for individuals who have attempted suicide? What might those initiatives look like?

Internet References

Shame after a suicide attempt
https://askthepsych.com/atp/2016/01/05/shame-after-a-suicide-attempt/

Suicide and stigma: Moving past silence and shame
http://health.usnews.com/health-news/patient-advice/articles/2015/09/09/suicide-and-stigma-moving-past-silence-and-shame

The stigma of suicide survivorship and related consequences: A systematic review
https://www.ncbi.nlm.nih.gov/pmc/articles/PMC5033475/

Why the stigma of suicide hurts so much
https://www.theguardian.com/commentisfree/2015/dec/16/men-stigma-suicide-michael-mansfield

---

Jamie Brickhouse is the author of Dangerous When Wet: A Memoir of Booze, Sex, and My Mother.

Article Prepared by: R. Eric Landrum, *Boise State University*

China and India Burdened by Untreated Mental Disorders

BENEDICT CAREY

Learning Outcomes

After reading this article, you will be able to:

- Identify the dire state of mental health treatment in China and India.
- Describe the challenges of traditional and alternative health-care providers in working together.

The growing burden of untreated mental disorders in the world's two most populous countries, India and China, cannot be adequately addressed without changes to their health care systems and by training folk healers to become collaborators, a new report has found.

The analysis, published as a part of a series in the journals The Lancet and The Lancet Psychiatry, draws on years of medical surveys in those countries. It represents the latest effort by an international coalition of researchers to put mental health care at the center of the global health agenda; last month, the World Bank and the World Health Organization convened hundreds of public officials, doctors and other specialists in a landmark meeting in Washington to focus attention on global mental health.

The new research, presented in three papers, found that less than 10 percent of people in India and China with a mental disorder received effective treatment, and that the resulting burden of disability from those two countries was higher than in all Western countries combined.

"India and China together represent more than a third of the world's population, and both countries are at a remarkable stage of epidemiologic and demographic transition," said a co-author of one of the papers, Dr. Vikram Patel, a professor of international mental health and co-founder of a community-based mental health center, Sangath, in Goa State in India, in a recorded interview accompanying the articles.

One lesson, experts not involved in the research said, is that investment is still lagging well behind spending on other medical conditions. Both countries spend less than 1 percent of their total medical budget on mental health.

"I think politicians and service planners will find this research valuable," said Dr. Alex Cohen, the course director of the global mental health program at the London School of Hygiene & Tropical Medicine. "But if you don't have the resources to treat more than 2 percent of the people who need it," then the overall burden can seem overwhelming.

In the past decade, both India and China have taken steps to expand access to mental health care. In China, a government program started in 2004 reportedly has trained 10,000 psychiatrists and built hundreds of community mental health centers, in what some consider a historic investment in better psychiatric care. An Indian government program to increase care in communities has effectively reduced hospital costs, in some areas, though implementation has been spotty at best, experts said.

But particularly in rural areas, the majority of people in both countries still have little means or access to psychiatrists or therapists.

"Very few Chinese with common mental illnesses such as depression and anxiety ever seek treatment," Dr. Michael Phillips, of Shanghai Jiao Tong University and Emory University, said in a statement. "And the country as a whole is ill prepared for the coming epidemic of dementia as the population ages rapidly."

One group of practitioners that is very accessible — and one the researchers said policy makers should consider potential allies — include traditional healers, herbalists and spiritual guides. In China, many doctors get some training in traditional healing arts, like herbal treatments, acupuncture and qigong. In India, likewise, many doctors incorporate yoga, and Ayurveda medicine.

A collaboration makes good sense for another reason, the researchers wrote: "In view of the popularity of traditional, complementary and alternative medicine, it is likely that even if sufficient biomedical mental health services were available, people would continue to access other therapeutic systems."

Yet the evidence that medical doctors and folk healers can work together to provide effective mental health care is scarce, experts said. A recent review of the role of traditional healing for mental disorders, led by Dr. Oye Gureje of the University of Ibadan in Nigeria, found that healers "have more readily adopted conventional psychiatric diagnoses such as depression or anxiety" than disorders like schizophrenia or bipolar disorder, which are thought to be spiritual in nature by the healers. And in some developing countries, traditional healers routinely use shackles, isolation and fasting—methods that "might fail to meet widespread understandings of human rights and humane care," the paper concluded.

The growing burden detailed in the new papers was due largely to aging and population growth. Some diagnoses, like attention deficit disorder in China, declined between 1990 and 2013; others, like dementia and abuse of drugs and alcohol, have risen. For reasons no one understands, suicide rates have fallen sharply in China in that time, and risen steadily in India.

Critical Thinking

1. Given that India and China represent one-third of the world's population, and less than 10% of individuals in these countries with mental illness receive mental health treatment, what does that mean for the future. Explain in detail.
2. Considering the situations in both India and China, what plausible explanations might explain why suicide rates have decreased sharply in China but increased steadily in India?

Internet References

10 global health issues to follow in 2016
http://www.humanosphere.org/global-health/2016/01/guest-post-10-global-health-issues-to-follow-in-2016/

2014 mental health atlas
http://apps.who.int/iris/bitstream/10665/178879/1/9789241565011_eng.pdf

Barriers to mental health care
http://www.uniteforsight.org/mental-health/module6

Global mental health
https://www.psychiatry.org/psychiatrists/international/global-mental-health

The state of mental health in America
http://www.mentalhealthamerica.net/issues/state-mental-health-america

Article

Prepared by: R. Eric Landrum, *Boise State University*

A Potent Side Effect to the Flint Water Crisis: Mental Health Problems

Abby Goodnough and Scott Atkinson

Learning Outcomes

After reading this article, you will be able to:

- Articulate the safety standards regarding lead in drinking water.
- Appreciate the levels of anxiety experienced when basic human needs are unmet.

Health-care workers are scrambling to help the people here cope with what many fear will be chronic consequences of the city's water contamination crisis: profound stress, worry, depression and guilt.

Uncertainty about their own health and the health of their children, the open-ended nature of the crisis, and raw anger over government's role in both causing the lead contamination and trying to remedy it, are all taking their toll on Flint's residents.

"The first thing I noticed when I got to Flint, quite honestly, was the level of fear and anxiety and distress," said Dr. Nicole Lurie, an assistant secretary at the Department of Health and Human Services who has been coordinating the federal recovery effort here since January. On Wednesday, President Obama will pay his first visit to the city since the lead contamination was revealed.

A team of behavioral health specialists from the United States Public Health Service began addressing the mental health problem in February by providing "psychological first aid" training for people interested in helping others cope with the water emergency.

Genesee Health System, a local mental health agency, also created the Flint Community Resilience Group, whose members are focusing on the long-term psychological consequences of the water crisis and how to address them.

With a $500,000 emergency grant from the state, the group is offering free crisis counseling at churches and the public library, and has held two community meetings on stress management. Social workers and social work students from around the state are helping with the counseling on a volunteer basis.

But the need probably extends far beyond the 400 people who have been helped since the counseling started in February.

Diane Breckenridge, Genesee Health's liaison to local hospitals, said she had seen "people come into the hospitals directly related to breakdowns, nervous breakdowns, if you will."

"Most of it's been depression or suicidal ideation directly linked to what's going on with their children," she added. "They just feel like they can't even let their children take a bath."

Children, too, are traumatized, said Dexter Clarke, a supervisor at Genesee Health, not least because they constantly hear frightening things on television about the lead crisis, including breathless advertisements by personal injury lawyers seeking clients.

"I teach a fifth-grade class of little girls every Wednesday, and they're from Flint," Ms. Breckenridge said, "and I just get all kinds of questions because they're terrified."

A bill in the United States House of Representatives would provide $5 million for mental health needs in Flint as part of a broader aid package, but has not gotten traction. A separate aid package in the Senate appears to have more momentum, but does not include money for mental health.

The state, meanwhile, is planning to send mobile crisis teams into Flint neighborhoods and to provide help to local pediatricians through a child psychiatric teleprogram.

Michigan's earlier decision to expand Medicaid under the Affordable Care Act will help more low-income residents get psychological help, although officials at Genesee Health System worry about not having enough licensed social workers to meet the eventual demand. About 15,000 additional children and pregnant women here will be eligible for Medicaid, possibly starting this month, under a temporary program that government and local officials are rushing to put together.

One challenge is convincing people to seek mental health care. The Rev. Rigel J. Dawson, pastor of the North Central Church of Christ and a member of the Flint Community Resilience Group, said his focus was on persuading religious-minded residents of the majority-black city to pursue psychological help if they need it.

"There's a history, especially in the African-American church, of 'I'm strong enough spiritually to deal with it,'" Mr. Dawson said. "You see the signs of stress and what it's doing to the community, but we're conditioned to put on our church face and act like it's O.K."

Danis Russell, the chief executive of Genesee Health System, said that while the potential for stigma had kept many here from seeking mental health services in the past, the water crisis might make them more willing.

"Now there's an acceptable reason," he said. "People may say: 'This isn't my fault. Somebody did this to us and everybody's getting help, so I should, too.'"

Still, Mr. Russell added, "What the demand will look like going forward, I don't think anyone knows."

Five Flint residents recently shared their accounts of the psychological impact of the crisis:

'If You go to Sleep, it Feels Like It's All Going to go Away.'

Janice Berryman spends solitary days in a home scattered with pink pillows and angel figurines, following every twist of Flint's water crisis on television and trying to keep her anger at bay.

Her tap water was found to have extremely high lead levels as recently as February, she said. Family members have stopped visiting, including a niece in Arkansas whose twin toddlers Ms. Berryman, 71, is aching to meet. Sometimes her loneliness brings her to tears, she said.

For a while she found it helped to attend protests, and she even took a bus to Lansing in January to march outside the Capitol during Gov. Rick Snyder's State of the State address. But with heart disease, diabetes and other ailments, "I just said, 'I've got to back down.'"

She began sleeping a lot — too much, her relatives told her.

"If you go to sleep, it feels like it's all going to go away," she said. "But it don't."

Her doctor has persuaded her to try the crisis counseling at the public library.

"He said, 'I think you need to, Jan, just to get your feelings out,'" she said. "But if I don't feel it's working? Adios. If they try to start pushing pills on me, I'll be gone. I don't need a bunch of pills to drug me up."

Two of Ms. Berryman's siblings died young, experiences that she said had forced her to learn endurance.

"I think that's why I handle this a little better than others," she said. "No matter what your anger level is, God sees you through."

'I Poisoned Other People's Children.'

Bob and Johanna Atwood Brown thought they were doing everything right.

When reports of lead in the water supply surfaced last summer, they installed a filter on their faucet, which removes lead up to 150 parts per billion. They used bottled water for drinking, but relied on their filtered tap water for cooking, coffee or to make their 10-year-old son and his friends Kool-Aid on hot summer days.

But when they had their water tested in January, they learned that it contained lead at 200 parts per billion — more than their filter was designed to handle, and far more than the federal safety threshold of 15 parts per billion.

Ms. Brown said she was haunted by thoughts of her son and his friends drinking the lemonade and Kool-Aid she had made them.

"The guilt is unreal," she said. "I poisoned other people's children."

Mr. Brown said he felt as if he had failed as a father and protector of his family.

"You beat yourself up," he said. "Why didn't we do something earlier? Why didn't we test earlier?"

Their son received a diagnosis of bipolar disorder and attention deficit disorder before the water crisis, and the Browns said they feared that the lead could exacerbate those problems — or produce others.

He "has special needs as it is, so it's hard to tell if there's a behavioral component," Ms. Brown said. "Things are not clear."

She added: "Are we going to get cancer from this? I'm terrified."

As an outlet, Ms. Brown has started a blog and uses Facebook. She was already seeing a therapist, she said, but now the stress and guilt associated with her home's water contamination dominate her sessions.

Mr. Brown said he did not talk about it much, but as the associate director in Flint for Michigan State University's Center for Economic and Community Development, he finds it therapeutic to share his story when he speaks at events and meetings.

"It never leaves you," Mr. Brown said. "At some point you just want to jump up and down and yell and scream, and then you just try to move forward. Because what are you going to say?"

'Did My Kids Deserve This?'

Too often now, Nicole Lewis cannot sleep.

"I'm up until midnight some nights because I can't shut down," she said. "Just thinking about my life in general — like really, did I deserve this? Did my kids deserve this?"

Ms. Lewis, a 29-year-old accountant and single mother of two boys, said she had also been experiencing chest pains. When they come, she lies down and drinks bottled water.

"Yet I've been told that this bottled water could have lead, too," she said, voicing a common concern here.

To help her nerves, she recently installed a home water filtration system, paying $42.50 a month for the service on her main water supply line. She also bought a blender to make her sons smoothies with lead-leaching vegetables, like spinach and kale.

But still her mind races, especially late at night. Her 7-year-old was just found to have attention deficit disorder, she said. Her 2-year-old is already showing athletic promise, but she wonders whether lead exposure will affect his ability to play sports.

She also worries that living in Flint will brand her as damaged goods if she ever tries to find a job elsewhere.

"When they see my résumé will they say, 'Oh wait, she's from Flint — she might be a huge liability for us'?" she said.

She has no time for a therapist, she said, but regularly talks to her mother in Houston.

"I just vent a lot of stuff out to her," she said. "She's a listening ear."

'This Thing Will Never Be Over.'

As if there were not enough putting Maelores Collins on edge, her dog will not stop barking. She suspects Flint's water is to blame.

"I think he's hallucinating," she said as Wally, a Yorkshire terrier, yapped from a cage near the back door. "We need to get him tested."

The barking adds to a sense of disorder that has agitated Ms. Collins, 48, for months. She is tired of the water bottles cluttering her house, and of eating only microwaved food because she fears cooking with even filtered tap water. Small kindnesses, like her sister bringing over potpies from Kentucky Fried Chicken, keep her going.

Ms. Collins blames the water for a problem that deeply troubles her: Her hair has broken off over the past six months.

Her self-prescribed therapy consists of cruising the aisles of Walmart or playing bid whist, a card game, with friends. A few months ago, her doctor also prescribed Xanax, a tranquilizer, which she takes "to get up" in the morning, she said.

"I'm depressed, I'm angry, my anxiety is running high," said Ms. Collins, a former construction worker who has asthma and is on permanent disability.

Worse off, she said, is her 12-year-old grandson, who refuses to drink even bottled water and will eat only off paper plates. The family jumped several hurdles to secure a psychiatric appointment for him in early May.

"He's freaking out — he's like, 'We're all going to die from the water,'" Ms. Collins said. "I said, 'You're young, you ain't going nowhere.' But I can't convince this boy."

Ms. Collins called the situation "crazy."

"Lose your hair, your family tripping about different things, your kids leaving water bottles all over the house," she said.

She laughed sharply. Wally continued his frantic barking, and she cast a withering glance his way.

"This thing," she said, "will never be over."

Critical Thinking

1. It is complicated to understand a behavioral problem, and try to determine its cause, including one potential cause being the drinking water. How would a psychologist design a study to attempt to understand this situation better?
2. Think about how pervasive our daily exposure is to water. If you were concerned about the safety of your own water, list and describe the potential concerns you might have. Example: The desire to eat from paper plates because leaded water was used in the dishwasher.

Internet References

Environmentally-triggered mental illness
https://doctorsprouse.wordpress.com/2013/07/07/environmentally-triggered-mental-illness/

Lead poisoning and health
http://www.who.int/mediacentre/factsheets/fs379/en/

Lead poisoning's harmful impact on physical and mental health
https://www.sovhealth.com/health-and-wellness/lead-poisonings-harmful-impact-on-physical-and-mental-health/

The toxins that threaten our brains
https://www.theatlantic.com/health/archive/2014/03/the-toxins-that-threaten-our-brains/284466/

Article

Prepared by: R. Eric Landrum, *Boise State University*

A Mad World

A diagnosis of mental illness is more common than ever—did psychiatrists create the problem, or just recognise it?

JOSEPH PIERRE

Learning Outcomes

After reading this article, you will be able to:

- Understand how the role of psychiatry has changed in the past century.
- Appreciate the modern techniques that psychiatrists employ to treat a vast array of psychological issues and problems.
- Articulate "caseness" and the role it plays in psychiatrist's abilities to help individuals.

When a psychiatrist meets people at a party and reveals what he or she does for a living, two responses are typical. People either say, 'I'd better be careful what I say around you,' and then clam up, or they say, 'I could talk to you for hours,' and then launch into a litany of complaints and diagnostic questions, usually about one or another family member, in-law, co-worker or other acquaintance. It seems that people are quick to acknowledge the ubiquity of those who might benefit from a psychiatrist's attention, while expressing a deep reluctance ever to seek it out themselves.

That reluctance is understandable. Although most of us crave support, understanding, and human connection, we also worry that if we reveal our true selves, we'll be judged, criticised, or rejected in some way. And even worse—perhaps calling upon antiquated myths—some worry that, if we were to reveal our inner selves to a psychiatrist, we might be labelled crazy, locked up in an asylum, medicated into oblivion or put into a straitjacket. Of course, such fears are the accompaniment of the very idiosyncrasies, foibles, and life struggles that keep us from unattainably perfect mental health.

As a psychiatrist, I see this as the biggest challenge facing psychiatry today. A large part of the population—perhaps even the majority—might benefit from some form of mental health care, but too many fear that modern psychiatry is on a mission to pathologise normal individuals with some dystopian plan fuelled by the greed of the pharmaceutical industry, all in order to put the populace on mind-numbing medications. Debates about psychiatric overdiagnosis have amplified in the wake of last year's release of the newest edition of the *Diagnostic and Statistical Manual of Mental Disorders* (*DSM*-5), the so-called 'bible of psychiatry', with some particularly vocal critics coming from within the profession.

It's true that the scope of psychiatry has greatly expanded over the past century. A hundred years ago, the profession had a near-exclusive focus on the custodial care of severely ill asylum patients. Now, psychiatric practice includes the office-based management of the 'worried well.' The advent of psychotherapy, starting with the arrival of Sigmund Freud's psychoanalysis at the turn of the 20th century, drove the shift. The ability to treat less severe forms of psychopathology—such as anxiety and so-called adjustment disorders related to life stressors—with the talking cure has had profound effects on mental health care in the United States.

Early forms of psychotherapy paved the way for the Mental Hygiene Movement that lasted from about 1910 through the 1950s. This public health model rejected hard boundaries of mental illness in favour of a view that acknowledged the potential for some degree of mental disorder to exist in nearly everyone. Interventions were recommended not just within a psychiatrist's office, but broadly within society at large; schools and other community settings were all involved in providing support and help.

A new abundance of 'neurotic' symptoms stemming from the trauma experienced by veterans of the First and Second World Wars reinforced a view that mental health and illness existed on a continuous spectrum. And by the time *DSM* was first published in 1952, psychiatrists were treating a much wider swath of the population than ever before. From the first *DSM* through to the most recent revision, inclusiveness and clinical usefulness have been guiding principles, with the profession erring on the side of capturing all of the conditions that bring people to psychiatric care in order to facilitate evaluation and treatment.

In the modern era, psychotherapy has steered away from traditional psychoanalysis in favour of more practical, shorter-term therapies: for instance, psychodynamic therapy explores unconscious conflicts and underlying distress on a weekly basis for as little as a few months' duration, and goal-directed cognitive therapy uses behavioural techniques to correct disruptive distortions in thinking. These streamlined psychotherapeutic techniques have widened the potential consumer base for psychiatric intervention; they have also expanded the range of clinicians who can perform therapy to include not only psychiatrists, but primary care doctors, psychologists, social workers and marriage and family therapists.

In a similar fashion, newer medications with fewer side effects are more likely to be offered to people with less clear-cut psychiatric illnesses. Such medications can be prescribed by a family physician or, in some states, a psychologist or nurse practitioner.

Viewed through the lens of the *DSM,* it is easy to see how extending psychiatry's helping hand deeper into the population is often interpreted as evidence that psychiatrists think more and more people are mentally ill. Recent epidemiological studies based upon *DSM* criteria have suggested that half or more of the US population will meet the threshold for mental disorder at some point in their lives. To many, the idea that it might be normal to have a mental illness sounds oxymoronic at best and conspiratorially threatening at worst. Yet the widening scope of psychiatry has been driven by a belief—on the parts of both mental health consumers and clinicians alike—that psychiatry can help with an increasingly large range of issues.

The diagnostic creep of psychiatry becomes more understandable by conceptualising mental illness, like most things in nature, on a continuum. Many forms of psychiatric disorder, such as schizophrenia or severe dementia, are so severe—that is to say, divergent from normality—that whether they represent illness is rarely debated. Other syndromes, such as generalised anxiety disorder, might more closely resemble what seems, to some, like normal worry. And patients might even complain of isolated symptoms such as insomnia or lack of energy that arise in the absence of any fully formed disorder. In this way, a continuous view of mental illness extends into areas that might actually be normal, but still detract from optimal, day-to-day function.

While a continuous view of mental illness probably reflects underlying reality, it inevitably results in grey areas where 'caseness' (whether someone does or does not have a mental disorder) must be decided based on judgment calls made by experienced clinicians. In psychiatry, those calls usually depend on whether a patient's complaints are associated with significant distress or impaired functioning. Unlike medical disorders where morbidity is often determined by physical limitations or the threat of impending death, the distress and disruption of social functioning associated with mental illness can be fairly subjective. Even those on the softer, less severe end of the mental illness spectrum can experience considerable suffering and impairment. For example, someone with mild depression might not be on the verge of suicide, but could really be struggling with work due to anxiety and poor concentration. Many people might experience sub-clinical conditions that fall short of the threshold for a mental disorder, but still might benefit from intervention.

The truth is that while psychiatric diagnosis is helpful in understanding what ails a patient and formulating a treatment plan, psychiatrists don't waste a lot of time fretting over whether a patient can be neatly categorised in *DSM,* or even whether or not that patient truly has a mental disorder at all. A patient comes in with a complaint of suffering, and the clinician tries to relieve that suffering independent of such exacting distinctions. If anything, such details become most important for insurance billing, where clinicians might err on the side of making a diagnosis to obtain reimbursement for a patient who might not otherwise be able to receive care.

Though many object to psychiatry's perceived encroachment into normality, we rarely hear such complaints about the rest of medicine. Few lament that nearly all of us, at some point in our lives, seek care from a physician and take all manner of medications, most without need of a prescription, for one physical ailment or another. If we can accept that it is completely normal to be medically sick, not only with transient conditions such as coughs and colds, but also chronic disorders such as farsightedness, lower back pain, high blood pressure or diabetes, why can't we accept that it might also be normal to be psychiatrically ill at various points in our lives?

The answer seems to be that psychiatric disorders carry a much greater degree of stigma compared with medical conditions. People worry that psychiatrists think everyone is crazy because they make the mistake of equating any form of psychiatric illness with being crazy. But that's like equating a cough with tuberculosis or lung cancer. To be less stigmatising, psychiatry must support a continuous model of mental health instead of maintaining an exclusive focus on the mental disorders that make up the *DSM.* If general medicine can work within a continuous view of physical health and illness, there is no reason why psychiatry can't as well.

Criticism of this view comes from concern over the type of intervention offered at the healthier end of the continuum. If the scope of psychiatry widens, will psychiatric medications be vastly overprescribed, as is already claimed with stimulants such as methylphenidate (Ritalin) for attention deficit hyperactivity disorder (ADHD)? This concern is well worth fretting over, given the uncertain effectiveness of medications for patients who don't quite meet *DSM* criteria. For example, a 2008 study by the Harvard psychologist Irving Kirsch published in *PLOS Medicine* found that, for milder forms of depression, antidepressants are often no better than placebos. Likewise, recent research suggests that children at risk of developing psychosis—but not diagnosable just yet—might benefit more from fish oil or psychotherapy than antipsychotic drugs.

In the end, implementing pharmacotherapy for a given condition requires solid evidence from peer-reviewed research studies. Although by definition the benefit of medications decreases at the healthier end of a mental health continuum (if one isn't as sick, the degree of improvement will be less), we need not reject all pharmacotherapy at the healthier end of the spectrum, provided medications are safe and effective. Of course, medications aren't candy—most have a long list of potential side effects ranging from trivial to life-threatening. There's a reason such medications require a prescription from a physician and why many psychiatrists are sceptical of proposals to grant prescribing privileges to health practitioners with far less medical training.

Pharmacotherapy for healthier individuals *is* likely to increase in the future as safer medications are developed, just as happened after selective serotonin re-uptake inhibitors (SSRIs) supplanted tricyclic antidepressants (TCAs) during the 1990s. In turn, the shift to medicating the healthier end of the continuum paves a path towards not only maximising wellness but enhancing normal functioning through 'cosmetic' intervention. Ultimately, availability of medications that enhance brain function or make us feel better than normal will be driven by consumer demand, not the Machiavellian plans of psychiatrists. The legal use of drugs to alter our moods is already nearly ubiquitous. We take Ritalin, modafinil (Provigil), or just our daily cup of caffeine to help us focus, stay awake, and make that deadline at work; then we reach for our diazepam (Valium), alcohol, or marijuana to unwind at the end of the day. If a kind of anabolic steroid for the brain were created, say a pill that could increase IQ by an average of 10 points with a minimum of side effects, is there any question that the public would clamour for it? Cosmetic psychiatry is a very real prospect for the future, with myriad moral and ethical implications involved.

In the final analysis, psychiatrists don't think that everyone is crazy, nor are we necessarily guilty of pathologising normal existence and foisting medications upon the populace as pawns of the drug companies. Instead, we are just doing what we can to relieve the suffering of those coming for help, rather than turning those people away.

The good news for mental health consumers is that clinicians worth their mettle (and you might have to shop around to find one) don't rely on the *DSM* as a bible in the way that many imagine, checking off symptoms like a computer might and trying to 'shrink' people into the confines of a diagnostic label. A good psychiatrist draws upon clinical experience to gain empathic understanding of each patient's story, and then offers a tailored range of interventions to ease the suffering, whether it represents a disorder or is part of normal life.

Critical Thinking

1. What role do you think the "bible of psychiatry"—the Diagnostic and Statistical Manual of Mental Disorders, 5th Edition—has to play in how both psychiatrists and clinical psychologists are perceived? Explain.
2. If you hold the belief that everyone in society has some sort of mental disorder, how might that belief affect everyday life? Explain.
3. What are some of the challenges for psychiatrists in the treatment of depression? Be specific.

Internet References

Normal or not? New psychiatric manual stirs controversy

http://www.livescience.com/34496-psychiatric-manual-stirs-controversy.html

Symptoms and treatments of mental disorders

http://psychcentral.com/disorders/

The problem with psychiatry, the 'DSM,' and the way we study mental illness

http://www.psmag.com/books-and-culture/real-problem-with-dsm-study-mental-illness-58843

Joseph Pierre is a professor of psychiatry at the University of California, LA, and co-chief of the Schizophrenia Treatment Unit at the West Los Angeles VA Medical Center. He writes the Psych Unseen blog for *Psychology Today.*

Article

Prepared by: R. Eric Landrum, *Boise State University*

It's Not Just You—Politics Is Stressing Out America's Youth

MELISSA DEJONCKHEERE AND TAMMY CHANG

Learning Outcomes

After reading this article, you will be able to:

- Identify that the time leading up to a national election can be a time of significant stress.
- Understand that American youth aged 14–24 reported feeling overwhelmed and exhausted throughout the election season.
- Know that the rate of depression for young people from 2005 to 2014 rose from 8.7 percent to 11.3 percent, with a similar trend for anxiety disorders.

"I can't sleep."—A 16-year-old

"It's been extremely hard to concentrate."—A 22-year-old

"I got behind in school."—A 22-year-old

"I feel like I could get killed any second."—An 18-year-old

"I'm nervous about whether I need to go to school wearing a gas mask."—A 14-year-old

"I'm scared for my safety."—A 15-year-old

The current political climate has been difficult for Americans of all political stripes. People have been so stressed that, just before the 2016 presidential election, the American Psychological Association released a list of coping strategies to help adults deal with election-related stress.

The focus has been on adults, yet teens and college-aged Americans are exposed to the same headlines. Turns out—youth are feeling it, too. In our survey of 80 youth across the nation, published February 13, we found that a majority experienced physical or emotional distress before and after the 2016 presidential election.

A Barrage of News

For some youth, 2016 may have been their first time voting in a presidential election, engaging in political conversations or even following the news.

Twenty-four-hour-a-day news coverage in print, on the radio, online, and on social media ensured that stories related to the election were easily and constantly accessible. One study showed that 54 percent of adults who used social media during the 2016 election were more likely to say the election is a very or somewhat significant source of stress. The news bombarded everyone, but most certainly youth—the most connected of generations.

Stories of harassment and intimidation dominated news coverage after the election. News headlines reported a barrage of painted swastikas and hate speech, minority students being threatened and assaulted, and an increased incidence of hate crimes.

These events across the country created anxiety about safety, discrimination, and inclusivity in schools and on college campuses.

What Youth Are Saying

In this climate, we wanted to talk to youth about what they were experiencing.

Our team collects weekly survey data from people aged 14–24 across the nation via text messages. Immediately before and two weeks and four months after the 2016 presidential election, 80 youth answered open-ended questions about their emotional and physical responses to the election and the new presidential administration.

We learned that the majority of youth were experiencing, and continue to experience, physical or emotional distress in the current political climate. Physical distress—difficulty concentrating, insomnia, and overeating—was frequently coupled with emotional distress, including depression, anxiety, and fear. Youth felt overwhelmed and exhausted throughout the election season.

Respondents reported fear of potential discrimination. They felt unsafe and hopeless about their future opportunities. Two weeks after the election, a 22-year-old Indian-American explained her worries: "I am scared that I won't have as many opportunities and I will have to fear for my life."

In subsequent months, youth were affected by the rise of racially motivated harassment and crimes across the country. A 19-year-old Muslim-American wrote: "It's been very distressing as a hijabi Muslim-American woman . . . I feel like my family has become a target for harassment and even violence."

The issues the youth in our study care about most—health care, LGBTQ rights, women's rights, immigration—have been the targets of political change in the first year of the current administration. News about the election and postelection implications have been hard to escape, leaving many youth feeling just as stressed as before the election. A 16-year-old explained, "The news and social media coverage is almost unavoidable and always a constant nagging presence."

While one would expect those who voted for a losing candidate to feel disappointed, supporters of both major party candidates and supporters of no candidate described physical or emotional responses following the election.

It's not clear whether this level of stress is normal among youth during elections or political shifts. Among adults, studies have found that psychological and physiological changes occur while voting and after an election, particularly when the political conversation is focused on issues that directly impact them.

Youth Distress Matters

These responses should be concerning to those of us who work with and care about youth. During this tumultuous time, many of us continue to be exposed to news every day, everywhere we turn.

What's more, mental health disorders among young people are currently on the rise. Between 2005 and 2014, rates of depression significantly increased for adolescents, from 8.7 percent to 11.3 percent, and rates of depression among young adults reached 9.6 percent. Similar trends have been observed with anxiety disorders.

There's also much we don't know going forward. Will feelings of hopelessness persist throughout the current administration? How will youth respond to the 2018 midterm elections and 2020 primaries? Will widespread fear, anxiety, and depression affect the future health and well-being of young people?

As one 20-year-old commented, "I've given up and just hope people make it out alive."

Politics is not just politics when it is hurting America's youth. We encourage those who work with young people—such as teachers, clinicians, and parents—to see this as a critical opportunity. Now is the time to model positive coping strategies, embrace thoughtful conversation, encourage voting and volunteer work for causes youth care about, and perhaps instill a sense of hope through our own actions and words.

Critical Thinking

1. Regardless of the political party that wins the election, are there factors now that make elections more salient in our society compared with elections 20 years ago? What factors exist today that possibly contribute to the added stress and anxiety that young adults are experiencing?
2. Feelings of hopelessness have been studied in psychology previously; it's called learned helplessness. How might the principles of learned helplessness be applied to this situation described in the article to give young adults specific strategies to cope with the feelings of fear, discrimination, anxiety, and discrimination?

Internet References

Survey: Months after the Election, Young People Still Feeling Stress and Anxiety

https://labblog.uofmhealth.org/lab-report/survey-months-after-election-young-people-still-feeling-stress-and-anxiety

Teen Depression and Anxiety: Why the Kids Are Not Alright

http://time.com/magazine/us/4547305/november-7th-2016-vol-188-no-19-u-s/

Why Are More American Teenagers than Ever Suffering from Severe Anxiety?

https://www.nytimes.com/2017/10/11/magazine/why-are-more-american-teenagers-than-ever-suffering-from-severe-anxiety.html

Why Millennials Are the Most Anxious Generation in History

https://www.vogue.com.au/beauty/wellbeing/why-millennials-are-the-most-anxious-generation-in-history/news-story/755e7b197bdb20c42b1c11d7f48525cd

Unit 11

UNIT
Psychological Treatments

Prepared by: R. Eric Landrum, *Boise State University*

Have you ever wondered what would happen if we took perfectly normal individuals and institutionalized them in such a dark, dismal place? In one well-known and remarkable study, that is exactly what happened.

In 1973, eight individuals, including a pediatrician, a psychiatrist, and some psychologists, presented themselves to psychiatric hospitals. Each claimed that he or she was hearing voices. The voices, they reported, seemed unclear but appeared to be saying "empty" or "thud." Each of these individuals was admitted to a mental hospital, and most were diagnosed as being schizophrenic. After admission to the hospital, the "pseudopatients" or fake patients gave truthful information and thereafter acted like their usual, normal selves.

Their hospital stays lasted anywhere from 7 to 52 days. The nurses, doctors, psychologists, and other staff members treated them as if they were schizophrenic and never saw through their trickery. Some of the real patients in the hospital, however, recognized that the pseudopatients were perfectly normal. After their discharge, almost all of the pseudopatients received the diagnosis of "schizophrenic in remission," meaning that they were still diagnosed as schizophrenic, but they weren't exhibiting any of the symptoms at the time of release.

What does this classic study demonstrate about the diagnosis and treatment of mental illness? Is genuine mental illness readily detectable? If we can't always pinpoint mental disorders, how can we treat them appropriately? What treatments are available, and which treatments work better for various diagnoses? Although the diagnosis of schizophrenia is dramatic and often of interest to those studying psychology, what about the diagnosis and treatment of much more common disorders, such as depression or addiction?

The treatment of mental disorders is certainly challenging. As you probably know, not all individuals diagnosed as having a mental disorder are institutionalized. In fact, only a relatively small percentage of people suffering from one or more psychological disorders are confined to a mental institution. The most common treatments for mental disorders involve psychotherapy or counseling, medication, or some combination. Depending on the individual and the severity of his or her symptoms, the course of treatment may be relatively short (less than a year) or quite long (several years or more).

The array of available treatments is ever increasing and can be downright bewildering, and not just to the patient or client! Psychotherapists, clinical psychologists, and psychiatrists must weave their way through complicated sets of symptoms, identify the best diagnosis, and then suggest a course of treatment that seems to best address the client's problems in the context of complex health-care delivery systems. In order to demystify and simplify your understanding of treatments and interventions for mental disorders, this unit presents some of these concepts.

Article

Prepared by: R. Eric Landrum, *Boise State University*

Fifty Psychological and Psychiatric Terms to Avoid: A List of Inaccurate, Misleading, Misused, Ambiguous, and Logically Confused Words and Phrases

SCOTT O. LILIENFELD, ET AL.

Learning Outcomes

After reading this article, you will be able to:

- Access a curated list of commonly misunderstood psychological and psychiatric terms.
- Identify frequently misused and ambiguous terms.

"If names be not correct, language is not in accordance with the truth of things."
(Confucius, *The Analects*)

Scientific thinking necessitates clarity, including clarity in writing (Pinker, 2014). In turn, clarity hinges on accuracy in the use of specialized terminology. Clarity is especially critical in such disciplines as psychology and psychiatry, where most phenomena, such as emotions, personality traits, and mental disorders, are "open concepts." Open concepts are characterized by fuzzy boundaries, an indefinitely extendable indicator list, and an unclear inner essence (Pap, 1958; Meehl, 1986).

Many writers, including students, may take the inherent murkiness of many psychological and psychiatric constructs as an implicit license for looseness in language. After all, if the core concepts within a field are themselves ambiguous, the reasoning goes, precision in language may not be essential. In fact, the opposite is true; the inherent openness of many psychological concepts renders it all the more imperative that we insist on rigor in our writing and thinking to avoid misunderstandings (Guze, 1970). Researchers, teachers, and students in psychology and allied fields should therefore be as explicit as possible about what are they are saying and are not saying, as terms in these disciplines readily lend themselves to confusion and misinterpretation.

For at least two reasons, issues of terminology bear crucial implications for the education of forthcoming generations of students in psychology, psychiatry, and related domains. First, many instructors may inadvertently disseminate misinformation or foster unclear thinking by using specialized terms in inaccurate, vague, or idiosyncratic ways. Six decades ago, two prominent psychiatrists bemoaned the tendency of writers to use "jargon to blur implausible concepts and to convey the impression that something real is being disclosed" (Cleckley and Thigpen, 1955, p. 335). We hope that our article offers a friendly, albeit greatly belated, corrective in this regard. Second, if students are allowed, or worse, encouraged, to be imprecise in their language concerning psychological concepts, their thinking about these concepts is likely to follow suit. An insistence on clarity in language forces students to think more deeply and carefully about psychological phenomena, and serves as a potent antidote against intellectual laziness, which can substitute for the meticulous analysis of concepts. The accurate use of terminology is therefore a prerequisite to clear thinking within psychology and related disciplines.

Psychology has long struggled with problems of terminology (Stanovich, 2012). For example, numerous scholars have warned of the *jingle* and *jangle* fallacies, the former being the error of referring to different constructs by the same name and the latter the error of referring to the same construct by different names (Kelley, 1927; Block, 1995; Markon, 2009). As an example of the jingle fallacy, many authors use the term "anxiety" to refer interchangeably to trait anxiety and trait fear. Nevertheless, research consistently shows that fear and anxiety are etiologically separable dispositions and that measures of these constructs are only modestly correlated (Sylvers et al., 2011). As an example of the jangle fallacy, dozens of studies in the 1960s focused on the correlates of the ostensibly distinct personality dimension of repression-sensitization (e.g., Byrne, 1964). Nevertheless, research eventually demonstrated that this dimension was essentially identical to trait anxiety (Watson and Clark, 1984). In the field of social psychology, Hagger (2014) similarly referred to the "deja variable" problem, the ahistorical tendency of researchers to concoct new labels for phenomena that have long been described using other terminology (e.g., the use of 15 different terms to describe the false consensus effect; see Miller and Pedersen, 1999).

In this article, we present a provisional list of 50 commonly used terms in psychology, psychiatry, and allied fields that should be avoided, or at most used sparingly and with explicit caveats. For each term, we (a) explain why it is problematic, (b) delineate one or more examples of its misuse, and (c) when pertinent, offer recommendations for preferable terms. These terms span numerous topical areas within psychology and psychiatry, including neuroscience, genetics, statistics, and clinical, social, cognitive, and forensic psychology. Still, in proposing these 50 terms, we make no pretense at comprehensiveness. We are certain that many readers will have candidates for their own "least favorite" psychological and psychiatric terms, and we encourage them to contact us with their nominees. In addition, we do not include commonly confused terms (e.g., "asocial" with "antisocial," "external validity" with "ecological validity," "negative reinforcement" with "punishment," "mass murderer" with 'serial killer'), as we intend to present a list of these term pairs in a forthcoming publication. We also do not address problematic terms that are restricted primarily to popular ("pop") psychology, such as "codependency," "dysfunctional," "toxic," "inner child," and "boundaries," as our principal focus is on questionable terminology in the academic literature. Nevertheless, we touch on a handful of pop psychology terms (e.g., closure, splitting) that have migrated into at least some academic domains.

Our "eyeball cluster analysis" of these 50 terms has led us to group them into five overarching and partly overlapping categories for expository purposes: inaccurate or misleading terms, frequently misused terms, ambiguous terms, oxymorons, and pleonasms. Terms in all five categories, we contend, have frequently sown the seeds of confusion in psychology, psychiatry, and related fields, and in so doing have potentially impeded (a) their scientific progress and (b) clear thinking among students.

First, some psychological terms are *inaccurate* or *misleading*. For example, the term "hard-wired" as applied to human traits implies that genes rigidly prescribe complex psychological behaviors (e.g., physical aggression) and traits (e.g., extraversion), which is almost never the case. Second, some psychological terms are not incorrect *per se*, but are *frequently misused*. For example, although "splitting" carries a specific meaning as a defensive reaction in psychodynamic theory, it is commonly misused to refer to the propensity of people with borderline personality disorder (BPD) and related conditions to pit staff members against each other. Third, some psychological terms are *ambiguous*, because they can mean several things. For example, the term "medical model" can refer to any one (or more) of at least seven conceptual models of mental illness and its treatment. Fourth, some psychological terms are *oxymorons*. An oxymoron is a term, such as open secret, precise estimate, or final draft, which consists of two conjoined terms that are contradictory. For example, the term "stepwise hierarchical regression" is an oxymoron because stepwise and hierarchical multiple regression are incompatible statistical procedures. Fifth, some psychological terms are *pleonasms*. A pleonasm is a term, such as PIN number, Xerox copy, or advance warning, which consists of two or more conjoined terms that are redundant. For example, the term "latent construct" is a pleonasm because all psychological constructs are hypothetical and therefore unobservable.

Our list of 50 terms, grouped into the five aforementioned categories and presented in alphabetical order within each category, follows.

Inaccurate or Misleading Terms

(1) A gene for. The news media is awash in reports of identifying "genes for" a myriad of phenotypes, including personality traits, mental illnesses, homosexuality, and political attitudes (Sapolsky, 1997). For example, in 2010, *The Telegraph* (2010) trumpeted the headline, "'Liberal gene' discovered by scientists." Nevertheless, because genes code for proteins, there are no "genes for" phenotypes *per se*, including behavioral phenotypes (Falk, 2014). Moreover, genome-wide association studies of major psychiatric disorders, such as schizophrenia and bipolar disorder, suggest that there are probably few or no genes of major effect (Kendler, 2005). In this respect, these disorders are unlike single-gene medical disorders, such as Huntington's disease or cystic fibrosis. The same conclusion probably holds for all personality traits (De Moor et al., 2012).

Not surprisingly, early claims that the monoamine oxidase-A (MAO-A) gene is a "warrior gene" (McDermott et al., 2009) have not withstood scrutiny. This polymorphism appears to be only modestly associated with risk for aggression, and it has been reported to be associated with conditions that are not tied to a markedly heightened risk of aggression, such as major depression, panic disorder, and autism spectrum disorder (Buckholtz and Meyer-Lindenberg, 2013; Ficks and Waldman, 2014). The evidence for a "God gene," which supposedly predisposes people to mystical or spiritual experiences, is arguably even less impressive (Shermer, 2015) and no more compelling than that for a "God spot" in the brain (see "God spot"). Incidentally, the term "gene" should not be confused with the term "allele"; genes are stretches of DNA that code for a given morphological or behavioral characteristic, whereas alleles are differing versions of a specific polymorphism in a gene (Pashley, 1994).

(2) Antidepressant medication. Medications such as tricyclics, selective serotonin reuptake inhibitors, and selective serotonin and norepinephrine reuptake inhibitors, are routinely called "antidepressants." Yet there is little evidence that these medications are more efficacious for treating (or preventing relapse for) mood disorders than for several other conditions, such as anxiety-related disorders (e.g., panic disorder, obsessive—compulsive disorder; Donovan et al., 2010) or bulimia nervosa (Tortorella et al., 2014). Hence, their specificity to depression is doubtful, and their name derives more from historical precedence—the initial evidence for their efficacy stemmed from research on depression (France et al., 2007)—than from scientific evidence. Moreover, some authors argue that these medications are considerably less efficacious than commonly claimed, and are beneficial for only severe, but not mild or moderate, depression, rendering the label of "antidepressant" potentially misleading (Antonuccio and Healy, 2012; but see Kramer, 2011, for an alternative view).

(3) Autism epidemic. Enormous effort has been expended to uncover the sources of the "autism epidemic" (e.g., King, 2011), the supposed massive increase in the incidence and prevalence of autism, now termed autism spectrum disorder, over the past 25 years. The causal factors posited to be implicated in this "epidemic" have included vaccines, television viewing, dietary allergies, antibiotics, and viruses.

Nevertheless, there is meager evidence that this purported epidemic reflects a genuine increase in the rates of autism *per se* as opposed to an increase in autism *diagnoses* stemming from several biases and artifacts, including heightened societal awareness of the features of autism ("detection bias"), growing incentives for school districts to report autism diagnoses, and a lowering of the diagnostic thresholds for autism across successive editions of the Diagnostic and Statistical Manual of Mental Disorders (Gernsbacher et al., 2005; Lilienfeld and Arkowitz, 2007). Indeed, data indicate when the diagnostic criteria for autism were held constant, the rates of this disorder remained essentially constant between 1990 and 2010 (Baxter et al., 2015). If the rates of autism are increasing, the increase would appear to be slight at best, hardly justifying the widespread claim of an "epidemic."

(4) Brain region X lights up. Many authors in the popular and academic literatures use such phrases as "brain area X lit up following manipulation Y" (e.g., Morin, 2011). This phrase is unfortunate for several reasons. First, the bright red and orange colors seen on functional brain imaging scans are superimposed by researchers to reflect regions of higher brain activation. Nevertheless, they may engender a perception of "illumination" in viewers. Second, the activations represented by these colors do not reflect neural activity *per se*; they reflect oxygen uptake by neurons and are at best indirect proxies of brain activity. Even then, this linkage may sometimes be unclear or perhaps absent (Ekstrom, 2010). Third, in almost all cases, the activations observed on brain scans are the products of *subtraction* of one experimental condition from another. Hence, they typically do not reflect the raw levels of neural activation in response to an experimental manipulation. For this reason, referring to a brain region that displays little or no activation in response to an experimental manipulation as a "dead zone" (e.g., Lamont, 2008) is similarly misleading. Fourth, depending on the neurotransmitters released and the brain areas in which they are released, the regions that are "activated" in a brain scan may actually be being inhibited rather than excited (Satel and Lilienfeld, 2013). Hence, from a functional perspective, these areas may be being "lit down" rather than "lit up."

(5) Brainwashing. This term, which originated during the Korean War (Hunter, 1951) but which is still invoked uncritically from time to time in the academic literature (e.g., Ventegodt et al., 2009; Kluft, 2011), implies that powerful individuals wishing to persuade others can capitalize on a unique armamentarium of coercive procedures to change their long-term attitudes. Nevertheless, the attitude-change techniques used by so-called "brainwashers" are no different than standard persuasive methods identified by social psychologists, such as encouraging commitment to goals, manufacturing source credibility, forging an illusion of group consensus, and vivid testimonials (Zimbardo, 1997). Furthermore, there are ample reasons to doubt whether "brainwashing" permanently alters beliefs (Melton, 1999). For example, during the Korean War, only a small minority of the 3500 American political prisoners subjected to intense indoctrination techniques by Chinese captors generated false confessions. Moreover, an even smaller number (probably under 1%) displayed any signs of adherence to Communist ideologies following their return to the US, and even these were individuals who returned to Communist subcultures (Spanos, 1996).

(6) Bystander apathy. The classic work of (e.g., Darley and Latane, 1968; Latane and Rodin, 1969) underscored the counterintuitive point that when it comes to emergencies, there is rarely "safety in numbers." As this and subsequent research demonstrated, the more people present at an emergency, the lower the likelihood of receiving help. In early research, this phenomenon was called "bystander apathy" (Latane and Darley, 1969) a term that endures in many academic articles (e.g., Abbate et al., 2013). Nevertheless, research demonstrates that most bystanders are far from apathetic in emergencies (Glassman and Hadad, 2008). To the contrary, they are typically quite concerned about the victim, but are psychologically "frozen" by well- established psychological processes, such as pluralistic ignorance, diffusion of responsibility, and sheer fears of appearing foolish.

(7) Chemical imbalance. Thanks in part to the success of direct-to-consumer marketing campaigns by drug companies, the notion that major depression and allied disorders are caused by a "chemical imbalance" of neurotransmitters, such as serotonin and norepinephrine, has become a virtual truism in the eyes of the public (France et al., 2007; Deacon and Baird, 2009). This phrase even crops up in some academic sources; for example, one author wrote that one overarching framework for conceptualizing mental illness is a "biophysical model that posits a chemical imbalance" (Wheeler, 2011, p. 151). Nevertheless, the evidence for the chemical imbalance model is at best slim (Lacasse and Leo, 2005; Leo and Lacasse, 2008). One prominent psychiatrist even dubbed it an urban legend (Pies, 2011). There is no known "optimal" level of neurotransmitters in the brain, so it is unclear what would constitute an "imbalance." Nor is there evidence for an optimal ratio among different neurotransmitter levels. Moreover, although serotonin reuptake inhibitors, such as fluoxetine (Prozac) and sertraline (Zoloft), appear to alleviate the symptoms of severe depression, there is evidence that at least one serotonin reuptake *enhancer*, namely tianepine (Stablon), is also efficacious for depression (Akiki, 2014). The fact that two efficacious classes of medications exert opposing effects on serotonin levels raises questions concerning a simplistic chemical imbalance model.

(8) Family genetic studies. The phrase "family genetic studies" is commonly used in psychiatry to refer to designs in which investigators examine the familial aggregation of one or more disorders, such as panic disorder or major depression, within intact (i.e., non-adoptive) families (e.g., Weissman, 1993). Given that the familial aggregation of one or more disorders within intact families could be due to shared environment rather than—or in addition to—shared genes (Smoller and Finn, 2003), the phrase "family genetic study" is misleading. This term implies erroneously that familial clustering of a disorder is necessarily more likely to be genetic than environmental. It may also imply incorrectly (Kendler and Neale, 2009) that studies of intact families permit investigators to disentangle the effects of shared genes from shared environment. Twin or adoption studies are necessary to accomplish this goal.

(9) Genetically determined. Few if any psychological capacities are genetically "determined"; at most, they are genetically influenced. Even schizophrenia, which is among the most heritable of all mental disorders, appears to have a heritability of between 70 and 90% as estimated by twin designs (Mulle, 2012), leaving room for still undetermined environmental influences. Moreover, data strongly suggest that schizophrenia and most other major mental disorders are highly polygenic. In addition, the heritability of most adult personality traits, such as neuroticism and extraversion, appears to be between 30 and 60% (Kandler, 2012). This finding again points to a potent role for environmental influences.

(10) God spot. Seizing on functional imaging findings that religious ideation is associated with activations in specific brain regions, such as circumscribed areas of the temporal lobe, some media and academic sources have referred to the discovery of a "God spot" in the human brain (Connor, 1997). Such language is scientifically dubious given that complex psychological capacities, including religious experiences, are almost surely distributed across several sprawling networks that themselves encompass multiple brain regions. Not surprisingly, studies of people undergoing mystical experiences have reported activation in many brain areas, including the temporal lobe, caudate, inferior parietal lobe, and insula (Beauregard and Paquette, 2006; Jarrett, 2014). As one researcher (Mario Beauregard) observed, "There is no single God spot localized uniquely in the temporal lobe of the human brain" (Biello, 2007, p. 43). The same absence of localizational specificity holds for claims regarding the identification of other purported brain regions, such as an "irony spot" or "humor spot" (Jarrett, 2014).

(11) Gold standard. In the domains of psychological and psychiatric assessment, there are precious few, if any, genuine "gold standards." Essentially all measures, even those with high levels of validity for their intended purposes, are necessarily fallible indicators of their respective constructs (Cronbach and Meehl, 1955; Faraone and Tsuang, 1994). As a consequence, the widespread practice referring to even well-validated measures of personality or psychopathology, such as Hare's (1991/2003) Psychopathy Checklist-Revised, as "gold standards" for their respective constructs (Ermer et al., 2012) is misleading (see Skeem and Cooke, 2010). If authors intend to refer to measures as "extensively validated," they should simply do so.

(12) Hard-wired. The term "hard-wired" has become enormously popular in press accounts and academic writings in reference to human psychological capacities that are presumed by some scholars to be partially innate, such as religion, cognitive biases, prejudice, or aggression. For example, one author team reported that males are more sensitive than females to negative news stories and conjectured that males may be "hard wired for negative news" (Grabe and Kamhawi, 2006, p. 346). Nevertheless, growing data on neural plasticity suggest that, with the possible exception of inborn reflexes, remarkably few psychological capacities in humans are genuinely hard-wired, that is, inflexible in their behavioral expression (Huttenlocher, 2009; Shermer, 2015). Moreover, virtually all psychological capacities, including emotions and language, are modifiable by environmental experiences (Merzenich, 2013).

(13) Hypnotic trance. The notion that hypnosis is characterized by a distinct "trance state" remains one of the enduring myths of popular psychology (Lilienfeld et al., 2009). In a sample of 276 undergraduates, Green (2003; see also Green et al., 2006) found that participants gave high ratings (between 5 and 5.5 on 1–7 scale in two experimental conditions) to the item, "Hypnosis is an altered state of consciousness, quite different from normal waking consciousness" (p. 373). Perhaps not surprisingly, the phrase "hypnotic trance" continues to appear in numerous articles written for the general public (Brody, 2008) as well as in academic sources (Raz, 2011). Nevertheless, the evidence that hypnosis is a distinct "trance" state that differs qualitatively from waking consciousness is scant. There is no consistent evidence for distinctive physiological (e.g., functional brain imaging) markers of hypnosis (Lynn et al., 2007). Nor is there persuasive, or even especially suggestive, evidence that hypnosis is associated with unique behavioral features. For example, suggested responses, including hallucinations, amnesia, and pain reduction, can be achieved in the absence of a "hypnotic induction" and even when participants report being awake and alert (Lynn et al., 2015).

(14) Influence of gender (or social class, education, ethnicity, depression, extraversion, intelligence, etc.) on X. "Influence" and cognate terms, such as effect, are inherently causal in nature. Hence, they should be used extremely judiciously in reference to individual differences, such as personality traits (e.g., extraversion), or group differences (e.g., gender), which cannot be experimentally manipulated. This is not to say that individual or group differences cannot exert a causal influence on behavior (Funder, 1991), only that research designs that examine these differences are virtually always (with the rare exception of "experiments of nature," in which individual differences are altered by unusual events) correlation or quasi-experimental. Hence, researchers should be explicit that when using such phrases as "the influence of gender," they are almost always proposing a hypothesis from the data, not drawing a logically justified conclusion from them. This inferential limitation notwithstanding, the phrase "the influence of gender" alone appears in over 45,000 manuscripts in the *Google Scholar* database (e.g., Bertakis et al., 1995).

(15) Lie detector test. Surely one of the most pernicious misnomers in psychology, the term "lie detector test" is often used synonymously with the storied polygraph test. This test is misnamed: it is an arousal detector, not a lie detector (Saxe et al., 1985). Because it measures non-specific psychophysiological arousal rather than the fear of detection *per se*, it is associated with high false-positive rates, meaning that it frequently misidentifies honest individuals as dishonest (Lykken, 1998). In addition, the polygraph test is susceptible to false-negatives stemming from the use of physical (e.g., biting the tongue) and mental (e.g., performing complex mental arithmetic) countermeasures (Honts et al., 1994). This evidence notwithstanding, the mythical allure of the polygraph test persists. In one survey, 45% of undergraduates agreed that this test is an accurate detector of falsehoods (Taylor and Kowalski, 2010).

(16) Love molecule. Over 6000 websites have dubbed the hormone oxytocin the "love molecule" (e.g., Morse, 2011). Others have named it the "trust molecule" (Dvorsky, 2012), "cuddle hormone" (Griffiths, 2014), or "moral molecule" (Zak, 2013). Nevertheless, data derived from controlled studies imply that all of these appellations are woefully simplistic (Wong, 2012; Jarrett, 2015; Shen, 2015). Most evidence suggests that oxytocin renders individuals more sensitive to social information (Stix, 2014), both positive and negative. For example, although intranasal oxytocin seems to increase within-group trust, it may also increase out- group mistrust (Bethlehem et al., 2014). In addition, among individuals with high levels of trait aggressiveness, oxytocin boosts propensities toward intimate partner violence following provocation (DeWall et al., 2014). Comparable phrases applied to other neural messengers, such as the term "pleasure molecule" as a moniker for dopamine, are equally misleading (see Landau et al., 2008; Kringelbach and Berridge, 2010, for discussions).

(17) Multiple personality disorder. Although the term "multiple personality disorder" was expunged from the American Psychiatric Association's (1994) diagnostic manual over two decades ago and has since been replaced by "dissociative identity disorder" (DID), it persists in many academic sources (e.g., Hayes, 2014). Nevertheless, even ardent proponents of the view that DID is a naturally occurring condition that stems largely from childhood trauma (e.g., Ross, 1994) acknowledge that "multiple personality disorder" is a misnomer (Lilienfeld and Lynn, 2015), because individuals with DID do not genuinely harbor two or more fully developed personalities. Moreover, laboratory studies of the memories of individuals with DID demonstrate that the "alter" personalities or personality states of individuals with DID are not insulated by impenetrable amnestic barriers (Merckelbach et al., 2002).

(18) Neural signature. One group of authors, after observing that compliance with social norms was associated with activations in certain brain regions (lateral orbitofrontal cortex and right dorsolateral cortex), referred to the "neural signature" of social norm compliance (Spitzer et al., 2007, p. 185). Others have referred to neural signatures or "brain signatures" of psychiatric disorders, such as anorexia nervosa (Fladung et al., 2009) and autism spectrum disorder (Pelphrey and McPartland, 2012). Nevertheless, identifying a genuine neural signature would necessitate the discovery of a specific pattern of brain responses that possesses nearly perfect sensitivity and specificity for a given condition or other phenotype. At the present time, neuroscientists are not remotely close to pinpointing such a signature for any psychological disorder or trait (Gillihan and Parens, 2011).

(19) No difference between groups. Many researchers, after reporting a group difference that does not attain conventional levels of statistical significance, will go on to state that "there was no difference between groups." Similarly, many authors will report that a non-significant correlation between two variables means that "there was no association between the variables." But a failure to reject the null hypothesis does not mean that the null hypothesis, strictly speaking, has been confirmed. Indeed, if an investigator finds a correlation of $r = 0.11$ in a sample of 20 participants (which is not statistically significant), the best estimate for the true value of the correlation in the population, presuming that the sample has been randomly ascertained, is 0.11, not 0. Authors are instead advised to write "no significant difference between groups" or "no significant correlation between variables."

(20) Objective personality test. Many authors refer to paper- and-pencil personality instruments that employ a standard (e.g., True–False) item response format, such as the Minnesota Multiphasic Personality Inventory-2 (MMPI-2), as "objective tests" (Proyer and Häusler, 2007), ostensibly to contrast them with more "subjective" measures, such as unstructured interviews or projective techniques (e.g., the Rorschach Inkblot Test). Nevertheless, although the former measures can be scored objectively, that is, with little or no error (but see Allard and Faust, 2000, for evidence of non-trivial error rates in the hand-scoring of the MMPI and other purported "objective" personality tests), they often require considerable subjective judgment on the part of respondents. For example, an item such as "I have many headaches" can be interpreted in numerous ways arising from ambiguity in the meanings of "many" and "headache' (Meehl, 1945). So-called "objective" personality tests are also often subjective with respect to interpretation (Rogers, 2003). For example, even different computerized MMPI-2 interpretive programs display only moderate levels of inter-rater agreement regarding proposed diagnoses (Pant et al., 2014). Not surprisingly, clinicians routinely disagree in their interpretations of profiles on the MMPI-2 and other "objective" tests (Garb, 1998). We therefore recommend that these measures be called "structured" tests (Kaplan and Saccuzzo, 2012), a term that refers only to their response format and that carries no implication that they are interpreted objectively by either examinee or examiner.

(21) Operational definition. The credo that all psychological investigators must develop "operational definitions" of constructs before conducting studies has become something of a truism in many psychology methods textbooks and other research sources (e.g., Burnette, 2007). Operational definitions are strict definitions of concepts in terms of their measurement operations. As a consequence, they are presumed to be exact and exhaustive definitions of these concepts. Perhaps the best known example in psychology is Boring's (1923) definition of intelligence as whatever intelligence tests measure.

Many psychologists appear unaware that the notion of operational definitions was roundly rejected by philosophers of science decades ago (Leahey, 1980; Green, 1992; Gravetter and Forzano, 2012). Operational definitions are unrealistic in virtually all domains of psychology, because constructs are not equivalent to their measurement operations (Meehl, 1986). For example, an "operational definition" of aggression as the amount of hot sauce a participant places in an experimental confederate's drink is not an operational definition at all, because no researcher seriously believes that the amount of hot sauce placed in a drink is a perfect or precise definition of aggression that exhausts all of its potential manifestations. Operational definitions also fell out of favor because they led to logically absurd conclusions. For example, an operational definition of length would imply that length as measured by a wooden ruler cannot be compared with length as measured by a metal ruler, because these rulers are associated with different measurement operations. Hence, the fact that both rulers yield a length for a table of say, 27 inches, could not be taken as converging evidence that the table is in fact 27 inches long (Green, 1992).

Psychological researchers and teachers should therefore almost always steer clear of the term "operational definition." The term "operationalization" is superior, as it avoids the implication of an ironclad definition and is largely free of the problematic logical baggage associated with its sister term.

(22) $p = 0.000$. Even though this statistical expression, used in over 97,000 manuscripts according to *Google Scholar*, makes regular cameo appearances in our computer printouts, we should assiduously avoid inserting it in our *Results* sections. This expression implies erroneously that there is a *zero* probability that the investigators have committed a Type I error, that is, a false rejection of a true null hypothesis (Streiner, 2007). That conclusion is logically absurd, because unless one has examined essentially the entire population, there is always some chance of a Type I error, no matter how meager. Needless to say, the expression "$p < 0.000$" is even worse, as the probability of committing a Type I error cannot be less than zero. Authors whose computer printouts yield significance levels of $p = 0.000$ should instead express these levels out to a large number of decimal places, or at least indicate that the probability level is below a given value, such as $p < 0.01$ or $p < 0.001$.

(23) Psychiatric control group. This phrase and similar phrases (e.g., "normal control group," "psychopathological control group") connote erroneously that (a) groups of ostensibly normal individuals or mixed psychiatric patients who are being compared with (b) groups of individuals with a disorder of interest (e.g., schizophrenia, major depression) are true "control" groups. They are not. They are "comparison groups" and should be referred to accordingly. The phrase "control group" in this context may leave readers with the unwarranted impression that the design of the study is experimental when it is actually quasi- experimental. Just as important, this term may imply that the only difference between the two groups (e.g., a group of patients with anxiety disorder and a group of ostensibly normal individuals) is the presence or absence of the disorder of interest. In fact, these two groups almost surely differ on any number of "nuisance" variables, such as personality traits, co-occurring disorders, and family background, rendering the interpretation of most group differences open to multiple interpretations (Meehl, 1969).

(24) Reliable and valid. If one earned a dollar for every time an author used the sentence "This test is reliable and valid" in a *Method* section, one would be a rich person indeed, as the phrase "reliable and valid" appears in more than 190,000 manuscripts in *Google Scholar*. There are at least three problems with this ubiquitous phrase. First, it implies that a psychological test is either valid or not valid. Much like the testing of scientific theories, the construct validation process is never complete, in essence reflecting a "work in progress." As a consequence, a test cannot be said to be have been conclusively validated or invalidated (Cronbach and Meehl, 1955; Loevinger, 1957; Peter, 1981). Hence, authors should similarly refrain from using the term "validated' with respect to psychological measures. At best, these measures are "empirically supported" or have "accrued substantial evidence for construct validity." The same caveat applies to psychological treatments. When Division 12 (Society of Clinical Psychology) of the American Psychological Association put forth its criteria for, and lists of, psychotherapies found to work in controlled trials for specific mental disorders, it initially termed them "empirically validated therapies" (Chambless et al., 1998). Nevertheless, in recognition of the fact that "validation" implies certainty or finality (Garfield, 1996; Chambless and Hollon, 1998), the committee wisely changed the name to "empirically supported therapies," which is now the term presently in use (Lilienfeld et al., 2013).

Second, the phrase "reliable and valid" implies that reliability and validity are unitary concepts. They are not. There are three major forms of reliability: test–retest, internal consistency, and inter-rater. Contrary to common belief, these forms of reliability often diverge, sometimes markedly (Schmidt and Hunter, 1996). For example, scores derived from the Thematic Apperception Test, a widely used projective technique, frequently display high levels of test–retest reliability but low levels of internal consistency (Entwistle, 1972). There are also multiple forms of validity (e.g., content, criterion-related, incremental), which similarly do not necessarily coincide. For example, a measure may possess high levels of criterion-related validity in multiple samples but little or no incremental validity above and beyond extant information (Garb, 2003).

Third, reliability and validity are conditional on the specific samples examined, and should not be considered inherent properties of a test. Hence, the notion that a test is "reliable and valid" independent of the nature of the sample runs counter to contemporary thinking in psychometrics (American Psychological Association and American Educational Research Association, 2014).

(25) Statistically reliable. This phrase appears in over 62,000 manuscripts according to *Google Scholar*. It is typically invoked when referring to statistical significance, e.g., "Although small in absolute terms, this difference was statistically reliable, $t(157) = 2.86$, $p = 0.005$" (Zurbriggen et al., 2011, p. 453). Nevertheless, despite what many psychologists believe (Tversky and Kahneman, 1971; Krueger, 2001), statistical significance bears at best a modest conceptual and empirical association with a result's "reliability," that is, its replicability or consistency over time (Carver, 1978). Indeed, given the low statistical power of most studies in psychology, a reasonable argument could be advanced that most statistically significant results are unlikely to be reliable. The statistical significance of a result should therefore not be confused with its likelihood of replication (Miller, 2009).

(26) Steep learning curve. Scores of authors use the phrase "steep learning curve" or "sharp learning curve" in reference to a skill that is difficult to master. For example, when referring to the difficulty of learning a complex surgical procedure (endoscopic pituitary surgery), one author team contended that it "requires a steep learning curve" (Koc et al., 2006, p. 299). Nevertheless, from the standpoint of learning theory, these and other authors have it backward, because a steep learning curve, i.e., a curve with a large positive slope, is associated with a skill that is acquired easily and rapidly (Hopper et al., 2007).

(27) The scientific method. Many science textbooks, including those in psychology, present science as a monolithic "method." Most often, they describe this method as a hypothetical-deductive recipe, in which scientists begin with an overarching theory, deduce hypotheses (predictions) from that theory, test these hypotheses, and examine the fit between data and theory. If the data are inconsistent with the theory, the theory is modified or abandoned. It's a nice story, but it rarely works this way (McComas, 1996). Although science sometimes operates by straightforward deduction, serendipity and inductive observations offered in the service of the "context of discovery" also play crucial roles in science. For this reason, the eminent philosopher of science Popper (1983) quipped that, "As a rule, I begin my lectures on Scientific Method by telling my students that the scientific method does not exist.. .".

Contrary to what most scientists themselves appear to believe, science is *not* a method; it is an approach to knowledge (Stanovich, 2012). Specifically, it is an approach that strives to better approximate the state of nature by reducing errors in inferences. Alternatively, one can conceptualize science as a toolbox of finely honed tools designed to minimize mistakes, especially confirmation bias – the ubiquitous propensity to seek out and selectively interpret evidence consistent with our hypotheses and to deny, dismiss, and distort evidence that does not (Tavris and Aronson, 2007; Lilienfeld, 2010). Not surprisingly, the specific research methods used by psychologists bear scant surface resemblance to those used by chemists, astrophysicists, or molecular biologists. Nevertheless, all of these methods share an overarching commitment to reducing errors in inference and thereby arriving at a more accurate understanding of reality.

(28) Truth serum. "Truth serum" is a supposed substance that, when administered intravenously, leads individuals to disclose accurate information that they have withheld. Most so-called truth serums are actually barbiturates, such as sodium amytal or sodium pentothal (Keller, 2005). Even today, some prominent psychiatrists still refer to these substances as truth serums (e.g., Lieberman, 2015), and they are still frequently administered for legal purposes in certain countries, such as India (Pathak and Srivastava, 2011). Nevertheless, there is no evidence that so-called truth serums reveal veridical information regarding past events, such as childhood sexual abuse (Bimmerle, 1993). To the contrary, like other suggestive memory procedures, they are associated with a heightened risk of false memories and false confessions (Macdonald, 1955), probably because they lower the response threshold for reporting all information, accurate and inaccurate alike. Furthermore, individuals can and do readily lie under the influence of truth serum (Piper, 1993).

(29) Underlying biological dysfunction. In this era of the increasing biologization of psychology and psychiatry (Miller, 2010; Satel and Lilienfeld, 2013), authors may be tempted to assume that biological variables, such as parameters of brain functioning, "underlie" psychological phenomena. For example, one set of authors wrote that "cognitive impairments are central to schizophrenia and may mark underlying biological dysfunction" (Bilder et al., 2011, p. 426). Nevertheless, conceptualizing biological functioning as inherently more "fundamental" than (that is, causally prior to) psychological functioning, such as cognitive and emotional functioning, is misleading (Miller, 1996). The relation between biological variables and other variables is virtually always bidirectional. For example, although the magnitude of the P300 event-related potential tends to be diminished among individuals with antisocial personality disorder (ASPD) compared with other individuals (Costa et al., 2000), this finding does not necessarily mean that the P300 deficit precedes, let alone plays a causal role in, ASPD. It is at least equally plausible that the personality dispositions associated with ASPD, such as inattention, low motivation, and poor impulse control, contribute to smaller P300 magnitudes (Lilienfeld, 2014). The same inferential limitation applies to many similar phrases, such as "biological bases of behavior," "brain substrates of mental disorder," and "neural underpinnings of personality" (Miller, 1996).

Frequently Misused Terms

(30) Acting out. Numerous articles use this term as a synonym for any kind of externalizing or antisocial behavior, including delinquency (e.g., Weinberger and Gomes, 1995). In fact, the term "acting out" carries a specific psychoanalytic meaning that refers to the behavioral enactment of unconscious drives that are ostensibly forbidden by the superego (Fenichel, 1945). Hence, this term should not be used interchangeably with disruptive behavior of all kinds and attributable to all causes.

(31) Closure. The term "closure" was introduced by Gestalt psychologists (Koffka, 1922) to refer to the tendency to perceive incomplete figures as wholes. This term has since been misappropriated by popular psychologists (Howard, 2011) and social scientists of various stripes (e.g., Skitka et al., 2004) to describe the purported experience of emotional resolution experienced by victims of trauma following an event of symbolic importance. For example, many advocates of the "closure movement" contend that the execution of a murderer assists the loved ones of victims to put an end to their grieving process. Nevertheless, this use of the term "closure" is hopelessly vague, as it is rarely if ever clear when trauma victims have achieved the desired emotional end-state (Radford, 2003; Weinstein, 2011). Nor is there research support for the proposition that many or most victims experience this end-state after events of symbolic significance, such as executions or funerals (Berns, 2011).

(32) Denial. Denial, a psychodynamic defense mechanism popularized by Freud (1937), is an ostensibly unconscious refusal to acknowledge obvious facts of reality, such as the death of a loved one in an automobile accident (Vaillant, 1977). Nevertheless, thanks largely to the popular psychology industry, this term has been widely misappropriated to refer to the tendency of individuals with a psychological condition, such as alcohol use disorder (formerly called alcoholism), to minimize the extent of their pathology (e.g., Wing, 1995).

(33) Fetish. A fetish, formally referred to as "Fetishistic Disorder" in the current version of the Diagnostic and Statistical Manual of Mental Disorders (DSM-5; American Psychiatric Association, 2013, p. 700), is a psychiatric condition marked by persistent, intense, and psychologically impairing sexual arousal derived from inanimate objects (e.g., shoes) or nongenital body parts (e.g., legs). This term, which is technically a paraphilia, should not be used to refer to generic preferences for specific objects, ideas, or people. One writer, for example, described the national fascination of the Japanese with smartphones as a "feature phone fetish" (Smith, 2015).

(34) Splitting. "Splitting" similarly refers to a psychodynamic defense mechanism, ostensibly ubiquitous in BPD, that forces individuals to see people as all good or all bad rather than in shades of gray, warts and all (Muller, 1992). By engaging in splitting, people with BPD and similar conditions are hypothesized to avoid the anxiety of perceiving those they love as the hopelessly flawed creatures that they are. Nevertheless, this term is consistently misused to refer to the propensity of people with BPD to "pit" staff members on a psychiatric unit (or other caregivers) against one another. This disruptive behavior, sometimes termed "staff splitting" (Linehan, 1989), should not be confused with the formal meaning of splitting.

Ambiguous Terms

(35) Comorbidity. This term, which has become ubiquitous in publications on the relations between two or more mental disorders (appearing in approximately 444,000 citations in *Google Scholar*), refers to the overlap between two diagnoses, such as major depression and generalized anxiety disorder. A similar term, "dual diagnosis," which has acquired considerable currency in the substance abuse literature in particular, refers to the simultaneous presence of a mental disorder, such as schizophrenia, and a substance abuse disorder, such as alcoholism (Dixon, 1999). Some authors have taken the comorbidity concept further, extending it to "trimorbidity" (Cornelius et al., 2001) or "quatromorbidity" (Newman et al., 1998).

Nevertheless, "comorbidity" can mean two quite different things. It can refer to either the (a) covariation (or correlation) between two diagnoses *within a sample or the population* or (b) co-occurrence between two diagnoses *within an individual* (Lilienfeld et al., 1994; Krueger and Markon, 2006). The first meaning refers to the extent to which Condition A and B are statistically associated across individuals; for example, there is substantial covariation between ASPD and BPD (Becker et al., 2014). The second meaning is a conditional probability referring to the proportion of individuals with Condition A who meet diagnostic criteria for Condition B. For example, in the case of the latter meaning, researchers might note that 45% of patients with ASPD also meet diagnostic criteria for BPD. The difference between these two meanings is hardly trivial, because they tend to be differentially influenced by base rates (prevalences). If the base rates of one or more conditions change, the covariation between them will not necessarily be affected but the level of co-occurrence almost always will be (Lilienfeld et al., 1994). Moreover, depending on the base rates of the diagnoses in a sample, two conditions may display little or no covariation but substantial co-occurrence. For example, although ASPD and major depression typically display only modest covariation (Goodwin and Hamilton, 2003), the rates of co-occurrence between ASPD and major depression in an analysis conditioned on major depression (that is, the rates of ASPD among people with major depression) would be extremely high in a prison sample, because most prison inmates meet criteria for ASPD (Flint-Stevens, 1993). Hence, the levels of comorbidity would probably be negligible in the first case but high in the second. If authors elect to use the term "comorbidity," they should therefore be explicit about which meaning (covariation or co-occurrence) they intend.

Some authors (Lilienfeld et al., 1994) have further questioned the routine use of the term comorbidity in psychopathology research given that this term, much like "dual diagnosis," presupposes that the conditions in question are etiologically and pathologically separable entities (but see Rutter, 1994; Spitzer, 1994, for demurrals). For example, although the high level of "comorbidity" between ASPD and BPD may reflect covariation or co-occurrence between two distinct conditions, it may instead reflect the fact that the current diagnostic system is attaching different names to slightly different manifestations of a shared diathesis, thereby falling prey to a jangle fallacy. To take an admittedly extreme example, how likely is it that a participant in a published study who simultaneously met diagnostic criteria for all 10 DSM personality disorders (see Lilienfeld et al., 2013) genuinely possessed 10 distinct disorders at the same time? Critics of the expansive application of the term comorbidity to descriptive psychopathology contend that these diagnostic conundrums are best explained by a flawed diagnostic system that is attaching different names to highly overlapping constructs.

(36) Interaction. As Olweus (1977) observed in the context of the person-situation debate, the term "interaction" has multiple meanings, some of them logically incompatible. For example, the familiar phrase "genes and environment interact for Disorder X" can mean any one of four things: (a) genes and environment are both involved in the causes of Disorder X; (b) the relation between genes and environments are bidirectional, because genes influence the environments to which people are exposed (by means of gene-environment correlations), and environments influence which genes are activated or inactivated (by means of epigenetic processes); (c) the influences of genes and environment are inseparable because of continuous transaction within individuals; or (d) the statistical effects of genes depend on people's environments, and the statistical effects of environments depend on people's genes. Only meaning (d) refers to a statistical interaction in the standard multiple regression or analysis of variance sense.

Two points are worth noting here. First, psychologists routinely confuse meanings (a) and (d). For example, when researchers write that "All reasonable scholars today agree that genes and environment interact to determine complex cognitive outcomes" (Bates et al., 1998, p. 195), some readers may assume that they are referring to the standard statistical meaning of the term "interaction," (McClelland and Judd, 1993), i.e., a multiplicative rather than additive relation between variables, such as that between genetic and environmental influences. Instead, in this case the authors appear to be saying only that both genes and environment play a role in cognitive outcomes, a scenario that does not require a multiplicative relation between genes and environment. Second, meanings (c) and (d) are logically incompatible, because if the effects of genes and environment are not separable, then clearly they cannot be distinguished in statistical designs. The bottom line: when authors use the term "interaction," they should be explicit about which of the four meanings they intend.

(37) Medical model. Although many authors who invoke the term "medical model" presume that it refers to a single conceptualization (e.g., Mann and Himelein, 2008), it does not. Some authors insist that the term is so vague and unhelpful that we are better off without it (Meehl, 1995). Among other things, it has been wielded by various authors to mean (a) the assumption of a categorical rather than dimensional model of psychopathology; (b) an emphasis on underlying "disease" processes rather than on presenting signs and symptoms; (c) an emphasis on the biological etiology of psychopathology; (d) an emphasis on pathology rather than on health; (e) the assumption that mental disorders are better treated by medications and other somatic therapies than by psychotherapy; (f) the assumption that mental disorders are better treated by physicians than by psychologists; or (g) the belief that mentally ill individuals who engage in irresponsible behavior are not fully responsible for such behavior (see Blaney, 1975, 2015, for discussions). Similar semantic and conceptual ambiguities bedevil the term "disease model" when applied to addictions and most other psychological conditions (e.g., Graham, 2013).

(38) Reductionism. There may be no greater insult in psychological circles than to brand a colleague a "reductionist." Indeed, merely accusing a fellow faculty member of "being reductionistic" is often an effective conversation-stopper at cocktail parties. The negative connotation attached to this term neglects the point, overlooked by many authors (e.g., Harris, 2015), that "reductionism" is not one approach. Robinson (1995) delineated multiple forms of reductionism, including (a) nominalistic reduction, i.e., reduction at the level of names ("A brain structure called the amygdala plays a key role in fear processing"); (b) nomological reduction, i.e., reduction at the level of scientific explanation ("The perception of edges is mediated in part by feature detection cells in the visual cortex"); and (c) ontological reduction, i.e., reduction by eliminating immaterial entities ("Neuroscientific data strongly suggest that there is no immaterial soul").

More broadly, we can differentiate between two quite different brands of reductionism: constitutive and eliminative, the latter termed "greedy reductionism" by Dennett (1995). The constitutive reductionist believes merely that everything that is "mental" is ultimately material at some level, and that the "mind" is what the brain and rest of the central nervous system do. Constitutive reductionists (like nomological reductionists; Robinson, 1995), who appear to comprise an overwhelming majority of psychologists and neuroscientists, reject mind-body dualism, the claim that the mind is entirely separable from the brain. In contrast, eliminative reductionists go a large step further (Lilienfeld, 2007). They contend that the "mind" will eventually be *explained away* entirely by lower-level concepts derived from neuroscience, and that mentalist concepts, such as thoughts, motives, and emotions, will ultimately be rendered superfluous by neuroscientific explanations. For eliminative reductionists, the field of psychology will eventually be "gobbled up" by neuroscience. Although we do not attempt to adjudicate the dispute between constitutive and eliminative reductionists here, suffice it to say that "reductionism" does not carry a single meaning in psychology. As a result, psychologists who use "reductionist" as a handy term of opprobrium against their colleagues must be explicit about which form of reductionism they are invoking.

Oxymorons

(39) Hierarchical stepwise regression. Hierarchical and stepwise multiple regression are entirely separate – and incompatible – procedures. Still, they are readily confused, because in hierarchical regression, variables are entered in sequential steps. Specifically, in hierarchical multiple regression the investigator specifies an *a priori* order of entry of the variables, ideally on theoretical grounds. In contrast, in stepwise multiple regression, the investigators allows the computer to select the order of entry of the variables (and the final variables in the equation) on empirical grounds, namely, by choosing each successive predictor based on the highest incremental contribution to variability in the outcome variable (Wampold and Freund, 1987; Petrocelli, 2003). Many authors have wisely warned against the routine use of stepwise regression procedures on the grounds that they typically capitalize heavily on chance fluctuations in datasets and rarely yield replicable results (Thompson, 1989).

(40) Mind-body therapies. The term "mind-body therapy" (e.g., Naliboff et al., 2008) refers to a panoply of treatments, such as relaxation, meditation, Reiki, yoga, and biofeedback, that purportedly harness mental functioning to enhance physical health (Wolsko et al., 2004). This term implies erroneously that the "mind" is materially separate from the "body" and thereby endorses a simplistic version of mind-body dualism. Rather than conceptualizing such interventions as making use of the mind to influence the body, we should conceptualize them as making use of one part of the body to influence another.

(41) Observable symptom. This term, which appears in nearly 700 manuscripts according to *Google Scholar*, conflates signs with symptoms. Signs are observable features of a disorder; symptoms are unobservable features of a disorder that can only be reported by patients (Lilienfeld et al., 2013; Kraft and Keeley, 2015). Symptoms are by definition unobservable.

(42) Personality type. Although typologies have a lengthy history in personality psychology harkening back to the writings of the Roman physician Galen and later, Swiss psychiatrist Carl Jung, the assertion that personality traits fall into distinct categories (e.g., introvert vs. extravert) has received minimal scientific support. Taxometric studies consistently suggest that normal-range personality traits, such as extraversion and impulsivity, are underpinned by dimensions rather than taxa, that is, categories in nature (Haslam et al., 2012). With the possible exception of schizotypal personality disorder (but see Ahmed et al., 2013), the same conclusion holds for personality disorders (Haslam et al., 2012). Hence, if authors elect to use the phrase "personality type," they should qualify it by noting that the evidence for a genuine typology (i.e., a qualitative difference from normality) is in almost all cases negligible within the personality domain.

(43) Prevalence of trait X. Authors in the psychological and psychiatric literatures frequently refer to "the prevalence" or "base rate" of attributes that are dimensionally distributed in the population, such as personality traits and intelligence. For example, one author team referred to the "greater prevalence of extraversion in American students" (p. 1153) compared with Korean students (Song and Kwon, 2012). Nevertheless, such terms as "prevalence," "incidence," "base rate," "false positive," and "false negative" are premised on a taxonic model: they presume that the phenomena in question are inherently categorical, that is, either present or absent in nature. For psychological features that are continuously distributed, such terms should be avoided. In the aforementioned phrase, referring to "higher levels of extraversion in American students" would have been more accurate.

(44) Principal components factor analysis. According to *Google Scholar*, this phrase appears in thousands of articles, including one co-authored by the first author of this manuscript (Reynolds et al., 1988). Nevertheless, this phrase is incoherent, because principal components analysis (which is commonly misspelled as "principle components analysis") and factor analysis are incompatible approaches to data analysis. Principal components analysis is a data reduction technique that relies on the total variance of the variables in a dataset; its principal goal is to create a smaller set of weighted variables (variates) that approximate the variance of the original variables (Weiss, 1970). In contrast, factor analysis relies only on the shared variance of the variables in a dataset, and it is designed to identify underlying *dimensions* that best explain the covariation among these variables (Bryant and Yarnold, 1995). In contrast to principal components analysis, whose primary aim is to simplify a dataset by yielding fewer observed variables, the primary aim of exploratory factor analysis is to identify dimensions that ostensibly account for the covariation among the observed variables.

(45) Scientific proof. The concepts of "proof" and "confirmation" are incompatible with science, which by its very nature is provisional and self-correcting (McComas, 1996). Hence, it is understandable why Popper (1959) preferred the term "corroboration" to "confirmation," as all theories can in principle be overturned by new evidence. Nor is the evidence for scientific theories dichotomous; theories virtually always vary in their degree of corroboration. As a consequence, no theory in science, including psychological science, should be regarded as strictly proven. Proofs should be confined to the pages of mathematics textbooks and journals (Kanazawa, 2008).

Pleonasms

(46) Biological and environmental influences. This phrase implies that biological influences are necessarily genetic, and cannot be environmental. Nevertheless, "environmental influences" encompass everything external to the organism that affects its behavior following its fertilization as a zygote. As a consequence, the environment comprises not only psychosocial influences, but also non-genetic biological influences, such as nutrition, viruses, and exposure to lead and other toxins (e.g., Nisbett et al., 2012). The phrase "biological and environmental influences" is therefore a partial pleonasm.

(47) Empirical data. "Empirical" means based on observation or experience. As a consequence, with the possible exception of information derived from archival sources, all psychological data are empirical (what would "non- empirical" psychological data look like?). Some of the confusion probably stems from the erroneous equation of "empirical" with "experimental" or "quantitative." Data derived from informal observations, such as non-quantified impressions collected during a psychotherapy session, are also empirical. If writers wish to distinguish numerical data from other sources of data, they should simply call them "quantified data."

(48) Latent construct. A "construct" in psychology is a hypothesized attribute of individuals that cannot be directly observed, such as general intelligence, extraversion, or schizophrenia (Cronbach and Meehl, 1955; Messick, 1987). Therefore, all constructs are latent. The same terminological consideration applies to the phrase "hypothetical construct." Authors would be better advised to instead use "construct" or "latent variable."

(49) Mental telepathy. Telepathy, one of the three ostensible types of extrasensory perception (along with clairvoyance and precognition), is the purported ability to read other's minds by means of psychic powers (Hyman, 1995). Hence, all telepathy is necessarily mental. The term "mental telepathy," which appears to be in common currency in the academic literature (e.g., Lüthi, 2013; Sagi-Schwartz et al., 2014), implies erroneously that there are "non-mental" forms of telepathy.

(50) Neurocognition. Many authors have invoked the term "neurocognition" to refer to cognition, especially when conceptualized within a biological framework (e.g., Mesholam-Gately et al., 2009). Nevertheless, because all cognition is necessarily neural at some level of analysis, the simpler term "cognition" will do. In fairness, "neurocognition" is merely one among dozens of terms preceded by the prefix "neuro" that have recently become popular, including neuroeducation, neuroaesthetics, neuropolitics, neuropsychoanalysis, and neurosexology (Satel and Lilienfeld, 2013). In the words of one psychologist, "Unable to persuade others about your viewpoint? Take a Neuro-Prefix – influence grows or your money back" (Laws, 2012).

Concluding Thoughts

We modestly hope that our admittedly selective list of 50 terms to avoid will become recommended, if not required, reading for students, instructors, and researchers in psychology, psychiatry, and similar disciplines. Although jargon has a crucial place in these fields, it must be used with care, as the imprecise use of terminology can engender conceptual confusion. At the very least, we hope that our article encourages further discussion regarding the vital importance of clear writing and clear thinking in science, and underscores the point that clarity in writing and thinking are intimately linked. Clear writing fosters clear thinking, and confused writing fosters confused thinking. In the words of author McCullough (2002), "Writing is thinking. To write well is to think clearly. That's why it's so hard."

References

Abbate, C. S., Ruggieri, S., and Boca, S. (2013). The effect of prosocial priming in the presence of bystanders. *J. Soc. Psychol.* 153, 619–622. doi: 10.1080/00224545.2013.791658

Ahmed, A. O., Green, B. A., Goodrum, N. M., Doane, N. J., Birgenheir, D., and Buckley, P. F. (2013). Does a latent class underlie schizotypal personality disorder? Implications for schizophrenia. *J. Abnorm. Psychol.* 122, 475–491. doi: 10.1037/a0032713

Akiki, T. (2014). The etiology of depression and the therapeutic implications. *Glob. J. Med. Res.* 13. Available at: http://medicalresearchjournal.org/index.php/GJMR/article/viewFile/465/383

Allard, G., and Faust, D. (2000). Errors in scoring objective personality tests. *Assessment* 7, 119–129. doi: 10.1177/107319110000700203

American Psychiatric Association. (1994). *Diagnostic and Statistical Manual of Mental Disorders,* 4th Edn. Washington, DC: American Psychiatric Association.

American Psychiatric Association. (2013). *Diagnostic and Statistical Manual of Mental Disorders*, 5th Edn. Washington, DC: American Psychiatric Association.

American Psychological Association and American Educational Research Association. (2014). *The Standards for Educational and Psychological Testing.* Washington, DC: APA and AERA.

Antonuccio, D., and Healy, D. (2012). Relabeling the medications we call antidepressants. *Scientifica* 2012:965908. doi: 10.6064/2012/965908

Bates, E., Elman, J., Johnson, M., Karmiloff-Smith, A., Parisi, D., and Plunkett, K. (1998). "Innateness and emergentism," in *A Companion to Cognitive Science*, eds W. Bechtel and G. Graham (Oxford: Basil Blackwell), 590–601.

Baxter, A. J., Brugha, T. S., Erskine, H. E., Scheurer, R. W., Vos, T., and Scott, J. G. (2015). The epidemiology and global burden of autism spectrum disorders. *Psychol. Med.* 45, 601–613. doi: 10.1017/S003329171400172X

Beauregard, M., and Paquette, V. (2006). Neural correlates of a mystical experience in Carmelite nuns. *Neurosci. Lett.* 405, 186–190. doi: 10.1016/j.neulet.2006.06.060

Becker, D. F., Grilo, C. M., Edell, W. S., and McGlashan, T. H. (2014). Comorbidity of borderline personality disorder with other personality disorders in hospitalized adolescents and adults. *Am. J. Psychiatry* 157, 2011–2016. doi: 10.1176/appi.ajp.157.12.2011

Berns, N. (2011). *Closure: The Rush to End Grief and What it Costs Us.* Philadelphia, PA: Temple University Press.

Bertakis, K. D., Helms, L. J., Callahan, E. J., Azari, R., and Robbins, J. A. (1995). The influence of gender on physician practice style. *Med. Care* 33, 407–416. doi: 10.1097/00005650-199504000-00007

Bethlehem, R. A., Baron-Cohen, S., van Honk, J., Auyeung, B., and Bos, P. A. (2014). The oxytocin paradox. *Front. Behav. Neurosci.* 8:48. doi: 10.3389/fnbeh.2014.00048

Biello, D. (2007). Searching for God in the brain. *Sci. Am. Mind* 18, 38–45. doi: 10.1038/scientificamericanmind1007-38

Bilder, R. M., Howe, A., Novak, N., Sabb, F. W., and Parker, D. S. (2011). The genetics of cognitive impairment in schizophrenia: a phenomic perspective. *Trends Cogn. Sci.* 15, 428–435. doi: 10.1016/j.tics.2011.07.002

Bimmerle, G. (1993). *Truth Drugs in Interrogation.* Washington, DC: Central Intelligence Agency Library.

Blaney, P. H. (1975). Implications of the medical model and its alternatives. *Am. J. Psychiatry* 132, 911–914. doi: 10.1176/ajp.132.9.911

Blaney, P. H. (2015). "Medical model of mental disorders," in *Encyclopedia of Clinical Psychology,* eds R. L. Cautin and S. O. Lilienfeld (New York: Wiley), 1767–1772.

Block, J. (1995). A contrarian view of the five-factor approach to personality description. *Psychol. Bull.* 117, 187–215. doi: 10.1037/0033-2909.117.2.187

Boring, E. G. (1923). Intelligence as the tests test it. *New Republic* 35, 35–37.

Brody, J. (2008). The possibilities in hypnosis, where the patient has the power. *New York Times*. http://www.nytimes.com/2008/11/04/health/04brody.html? (access November 3, 2008).

Bryant, F. B., and Yarnold, P. R. (1995). "Principal-components analysis and exploratory and confirmatory factor analysis," in *Reading and Understanding Multivariate Statistics*, eds F. B. Bryant, P. R. Yarnold, and L. Grimm (Washington, DC: American Psychological Association), 96–136.

Buckholtz, J. W., and Meyer-Lindenberg, A. (2013). "MAOA and the bioprediction of antisocial behavior: science fact and science fiction," in *Bioprediction Biomarkers, and Bad Behavior: Scientific, Legal, and Ethical Challenges*, eds I. Singh, W. P. Sinnott-Armstrong, and J. Savulescu (Oxford: Oxford University Press), 131.

Burnette, J. L. (2007). "Operationalization," in *Encyclopedia of Social Psychology*, eds R. F. Baumeister and K. D. Vohs (Thousand Oaks, CA: Sage), 636–637. doi: 10.4135/9781412956253.n379

Byrne, D. (1964). Repression-sensitization as a dimension of personality. *Prog. Exp. Personal. Res.* 72, 169–220.

Carver, R. P. (1978). The case against statistical significance testing. *Harv. Educ. Rev.* 48, 378–399. doi: 10.17763/haer.48.3.t490261645281841

Chambless, D. L., Baker, M. J., Baucom, D. H., Beutler, L. E., Calhoun, K. S., Crits-Christoph, P., et al. (1998). Update on empirically validated therapies, II. *Clin. Psychol.* 51, 3–16.

Chambless, D. L., and Hollon, S. D. (1998). Defining empirically supported therapies. *J. Consult. Clin. Psychol.* 66, 7–18. doi: 10.1037/0022-006X.66.1.7

Cleckley, H. M., and Thigpen, C. H. (1955). The dynamics of illusion. *Am. J. Psychiatry* 112, 334–342. doi: 10.1176/ajp.112.5.334

Connor, S. (1997). *"God Spot" is Found in Brain. Los Angeles Times.* Available at: http://members.shaw.ca/tfrisen/Science/God%20Module%20off%20internet.htm (accessed October 29, 1997).

Cornelius, J. R., Salloum, I. M., Lynch, K., Clark, D. B., and Mann, J. J. (2001). Treating the Substance-Abusing Suicidal Patient. *Ann. N. Y. Acad. Sci.* 932, 78–93. doi: 10.1111/j.1749-6632.2001.tb05799.x

Costa, L., Bauer, L., Kuperman, S., Porjesz, B., O'Connor, S., Hesselbrock, V., et al. (2000). Frontal P300 decrements, alcohol dependence, and antisocial personality disorder. *Biol. Psychiatry* 47, 1064–1071. doi: 10.1016/S0006-3223(99)00317-0

Cronbach, L. J., and Meehl, P. E. (1955). Construct validity in psychological tests. *Psychol. Bull.* 52, 281–302. doi: 10.1037/h0040957

Darley, J. M., and Latane, B. (1968). Bystander intervention in emergencies: diffusion of responsibility. *J. Personal. Soc. Psychol.* 8, 377–383. doi: 10.1037/h0025589

Deacon, B. J., and Baird, G. L. (2009). The chemical imbalance explanation of depression: reducing blame at what cost? *J. Soc. Clin. Psychol.* 28, 415–435. doi: 10.1521/jscp.2009.28.4.415

De Moor, M. H., Costa, P. T., Terracciano, A., Krueger, R. F., De Geus, E. J., Toshiko, T., et al. (2012). Meta-analysis of genome-wide association studies for personality. *Mol. Psychiatry* 17, 337–349. doi: 10.1038/mp.2010.128

Dennett, D. C. (1995). Darwin's dangerous idea. *Sciences* 35, 34–40. doi: 10.1002/j.2326-1951.1995.tb03633.x

DeWall, C. N., Gillath, O., Pressman, S. D., Black, L. L., Bartz, J. A., Moskovitz, J., et al. (2014). When the love hormone leads to violence: oxytocin increases intimate partner violence inclinations among high trait aggressive people. *Soc. Psychol. Personal. Sci.* 5, 691–697. doi: 10.1177/19485506135 16876

Dixon, L. (1999). Dual diagnosis of substance abuse in schizophrenia: prevalence and impact on outcomes. *Schizophr. Res.* 35, S93–S100. doi: 10.1016/S0920-9964(98)00161-3

Donovan, M. R., Glue, P., Kolluri, S., and Emir, B. (2010). Comparative efficacy of antidepressants in preventing relapse in anxiety disorders—a meta-analysis. *J. Affect. Disord.* 123, 9–16. doi: 10.1016/j.jad.2009.06.021

Dvorsky, G. (2012). *10 Reasons Why Oxytocin is the Most Amazing Molecule in the World.* Daily 10. Available at: http://io9.com/5925206/10-reasons-why-oxytocin-is-the-most-amazing-molecule-in-the-world (accessed June 21, 2015).

Ekstrom, A. (2010). How and when the fMRI BOLD signal relates to underlying neural activity: the danger in dissociation. *Brain Res. Rev.* 62, 233–244. doi: 10.1016/j.brainresrev.2009.12.004

Entwistle, D. R. (1972). To dispel fantasies about fantasy-based measures of achievement motivation. *Psychol. Bull.* 77, 377–391. doi: 10.1037/h00 20021

Ermer, E., Kahn, R. E., Salovey, P., and Kiehl, K. A. (2012). Emotional intelligence in incarcerated men with psychopathic traits. *J. Pers. Soc. Psychol.* 103, 194–204. doi: 10.1037/a0027328

Falk, R. (2014). The allusion of the gene: misunderstandings of the concepts heredity and gene. *Sci. Educ.* 23, 273–284. doi: 10.1007/s11191-012-9510-4

Faraone, S., and Tsuang, M. (1994). Measuring diagnostic accuracy in the absence of a gold standard. *Am. J. Psychiatry* 151, 650–657. doi: 10.1176/ajp.151.5.650

Fenichel, O. (1945). Neurotic acting out. *Psychoanal. Rev.* 32, 197–206.

Ficks, C. A., and Waldman, I. D. (2014). Candidate genes for aggression and antisocial behavior: a meta-analysis of association studies of the 5HTTLPR and MAOA-uVNTR. *Behav. Genet.* 44, 427–444. doi: 10.1007/s10519-014-9661-y

Fladung, A. K., Grön, G., Grammer, K., Herrnberger, B., Schilly, E., Grasteit, S., et al. (2009). A neural signature of anorexia nervosa in the ventral striatal reward system. *Am. J. Psychiatry* 167, 206–212. doi: 10.1176/appi.ajp.2009.09010071

Flint-Stevens, G. (1993). Applying the diagnosis of antisocial personality to imprisoned offenders: looking for hay in in a haystack. *J. Offender Rehabil.* 19, 1–26. doi: 10.1300/J076v19n01_01

France, C. M., Lysaker, P. H., and Robinson, R. P. (2007). The "chemical imbalance" explanation for depression: origins, lay endorsement, and clinical implications. *Prof. Psychol. Res. Practice* 38, 411–420. doi: 10.1037/0735-7028.38.4.411

Freud, A. (1937). *The Ego and the Mechanisms of Defense,* trans. C. Baines. London: Hogarth Press.

Funder, D. C. (1991). Global traits: a neo-Allportian approach to personality. *Psychol. Sci.* 2, 31–39. doi: 10.1111/j.1467-9280.1991.tb00093.x

Garb, H. N. (1998). *Studying the Clinician: Judgment Research and Psychological Assessment.* Washington, DC: American Psychological Association. doi: 10.1037/10299-000

Garb, H. N. (2003). Incremental validity and the assessment of psychopathology in adults. *Psychol. Assess.* 15, 508–520. doi: 10.1037/1040-3590.15.4.508

Garfield, S. L. (1996). Some problems associated with "validated" forms of psychotherapy. *Clin. Psychol.* 3, 218–229. doi: 10.1111/j.1468-2850.1996. tb00073.x

Gernsbacher, M. A., Dawson, M., and Goldsmith, H. H. (2005). Three reasons not to believe in an autism epidemic. *Curr. Dir. Psychol. Sci.* 14, 55–58. doi: 10.1111/j.0963-7214.2005.00334.x

Gillihan, S. J., and Parens, E. (2011). Should we expect 'neural signatures' for DSM diagnoses? J. Clin. Psychiatry 72, 1383–1389. doi: 10.4088/JCP.10r06332gre

Glassman, W. E., and Hadad, M. (2008). *Approaches to Psychology.* London: Open University Press.

Goodwin, R. D., and Hamilton, S. P. (2003). Lifetime comorbidity of antisocial personality disorder and anxiety disorders among adults in the community. *Psychiatry Res.* 117, 159–166. doi: 10.1016/S0165-1781(02)00320-7

Grabe, M. E., and Kamhawi, R. (2006). Hard wired for negative news? Gender differences in processing broadcast news. *Commun. Res.* 33, 346–369. doi: 10.1177/0093650206291479

Graham, G. (2013). *The Disordered Mind: An Introduction to Philosophy of Mind and Mental Illness.* New York: Routledge.

Gravetter, F. J., and Forzano, L. B. (2012). *Research Methods for the Behavioral Sciences*, 4th Edn. Belmont, CA: Wadsworth.

Green, C. D. (1992). Of immortal mythological beasts: operationism in psychology. *Theory Psychol.* 2, 291–320. doi: 10.1177/09593543920 23003

Green, J. P. (2003). Beliefs about hypnosis: popular beliefs, misconceptions, and the importance of experience. *Int. J. Clin. Exp. Hypn.* 51, 369–381. doi: 10.1076/iceh.51.4.369.16408

Green, J. P., Page, R. A., Rasekhy, R., Johnson, L. K., and Bernhardt, S. E. (2006). Cultural views and attitudes about hypnosis: a survey of college students across four countries. *Int. J. Clin. Exp. Hypn.* 54, 263–280. doi: 10.1080/00207140600689439

Griffiths, S. (2014). *Hugs Can Make You Feel younger: 'Cuddle Hormone' Could Improve Bone Health, and Combat. Muscle Wasting.* Available at: http://www.dailymail.co.uk/sciencetech/article-2654224/Hugs-make-feel-younger-Cuddle-hormone-improve-bone-health-combat-muscle-wasting.html#ixzz3UP2WNT2J

Guze, S. B. (1970). The need for toughmindedness in psychiatric thinking. *South. Med. J.* 63, 662–671. doi: 10.1097/00007611-197006000-00012

Hagger, M. S. (2014). Avoiding the "déjà-variable" phenomenon: social psychology needs more guides to constructs. *Front. Psychol.* 5:52. doi: 10.3389/fpsyg.2014.00052

Hare, R. D. (1991/2003). *Manual for the Hare Psychopathy Checklist-Revised.* Toronto, CA: Multihealth Systems.

Harris, S. (2015). "Our narrow definition of science," in *This Idea Must Die,* ed. J. Brockman (New York: Harper), 136–138.

Haslam, N., Holland, E., and Kuppens, P. (2012). Categories versus dimensions in personality and psychopathology: a quantitative review of taxometric research. *Psychol. Med.* 42, 903–920. doi: 10.1017/S0033291711001966

Hayes, C. (2014). Multiple personality disorder: an introduction for HCAs. *Br. J. Healthcare Assist.* 8, 29–33. doi: 10.12968/bjha.2014.8.1.29

Honts, C. R., Raskin, D. C., and Kircher, J. C. (1994). Mental and physical countermeasures reduce the accuracy of polygraph tests. *J. Appl. Psychol.* 79, 252–259. doi: 10.1037/0021-9010.79.2.252

Hopper, A. N., Jamison, M. H., and Lewis, W. G. (2007). Learning curves in surgical practice. *Postgrad. Med. J.* 83, 777–779. doi: 10.1136/pgmj.2007.057190

Howard, B. S. (2011). *Overcoming Trauma: Find Closure to the Abuse, Tragedies, and Suffering of Life.* St. Louis, MO: Lifetime Media, LLC.

Hunter, E. (1951). *Brain-washing in Red China: The Calculated Destruction of Men's Minds.* New York: Vanguard Press.

Huttenlocher, P. R. (2009). *Neural Plasticity.* Cambridge, MA: Harvard University Press.

Hyman, R. (1995). Evaluation of the program on anomalous mental phenomena. *J. Parapsychol.* 59, 321–352.

Jarrett, C. (2014). *Great Myths of the Brain.* New York: John Wiley & Sons.

Jarrett, C. (2015). *Great Myths of the Brain.* New York: John Wiley & Sons.

Kanazawa, S. (2008). Temperature and evolutionary novelty as forces behind the evolution of general intelligence. *Intelligence* 36, 99–108. doi: 10.1016/j.intell.2007.04.001

Kandler, C. (2012). Nature and nurture in personality development: the case of neuroticism and extraversion. *Curr. Dir. Psychol. Sci.* 21, 290–296. doi: 10.1177/0963721412452557

Kaplan, R., and Saccuzzo, D. (2012). *Psychological Testing: Principles, Applications, and Issues.* Belmont, CA: Cengage Learning.

Keller, L. M. (2005). Is truth serum torture? *Am. Univ. Int. Law Rev.* 20, 521–621.

Kelley, E. L. (1927). *Interpretation of Educational Measurements.* Yonkers, NY: World.

Kendler, K. S. (2005). "A gene for": the nature of gene action in psychiatric disorders. *Am. J. Psychiatry* 162, 1245–1252. doi: 10.1176/appi.ajp.162.7.1243

Kendler, K. S., and Neale, M. C. (2009). "Familiality" or heritability? *Arch. Gen. Psychiatry* 66, 452–453. doi: 10.1001/archgenpsychiatry.2009.14

King, C. R. (2011). A novel embryological theory of autism causation involving endogenous biochemicals capable of initiating cellular gene transcription: a possible link between twelve autism risk factors and the autism 'epidemic'. *Med. Hypotheses* 76, 653–660. doi: 10.1016/j.mehy.2011.01.024

Kluft, R. P. (2011). Ramifications of incest. *Psychiatr. Times* 27, 1–11.

Koc, K., Anik, I., Ozdamar, D., Cabuk, B., Keskin, G., and Ceylan, S. (2006). The learning curve in endoscopic pituitary surgery and our experience. *Neurosurg. Rev.* 29, 298–305. doi: 10.1007/s10143-006-0033-9

Koffka, K. (1922). Perception: an introduction to the Gestalt-theorie. *Psychol. Bull.* 19, 531–585. doi: 10.1037/h0072422

Kraft, N. H., and Keeley, J. W. (2015). "Sign versus symptom," in *Encyclopedia of Clinical Psychology*, eds R. L. Cautin and S. O. Lilienfeld (New York: John Wiley & Sons), 2635–2638.

Kramer, P. D. (2011). In defense of antidepressants. *New York Times.* Available at: http://www.nytimes.com/2011/07/10/opinion/sunday/10antidepressants.html (access July 9, 2011).

Kringelbach, M. L., and Berridge, K. C. (2010). The functional neuroanatomy of pleasure and happiness. *Discov. Med.* 9, 579–587.

Krueger, J. (2001). Null hypothesis significance testing: on the survival of a flawed method. *Am. Psychol.* 56, 16–26. doi: 10.1037/0003-066X.56.1.16

Krueger, R. F., and Markon, K. E. (2006). Reinterpreting comorbidity: a model- based approach to understanding and classifying psychopathology. *Ann. Rev. Clin. Psychol.* 2, 111–133. doi: 10.1146/annurev.clinpsy.2.022305.095213

Lacasse, J. R., and Leo, J. (2005). Serotonin and depression: a disconnect between the advertisements and the scientific literature. *PLoS Med.* 2:e392. doi: 10.1371/journal.pmed.0020392

Lamont, L. (2008). *Commonsense Part of Brain is a "Dead Zone" When Texting. Sydney Morning Herald.* Available at: http://www.smh.com.au/news/specials/science/commonsense-part-of-brain-is-a-dead-zone-when-texting/2008/09/17/1221330929936.html?page

Landau, J., Garrett, J., and Webb, R. (2008). Assisting a concerned person to motivate someone experiencing cybersex into treatment. *J. Marital Fam. Ther.* 34, 498–511. doi: 10.1111/j.1752-0606.2008.00091.x

Latane, B., and Darley, J. (1969). Bystander 'apathy.' *Am. Sci.* 57, 244–268.

Latane, B., and Rodin, J. (1969). A lady in distress: Inhibiting effects of friends and strangers on bystander intervention. *J. Exp. Soc. Psychol.* 5, 189–202. doi: 10.1016/0022-1031(69)90046-8

Laws, K. R. (2012). *Twitter Post.* Available at: http://twitter.com/Keith_Laws/statuses/163218919449962496

Leahey, T. H. (1980). The myth of operationism. *J. Mind Behav.* 1, 127–143.

Leo, J., and Lacasse, J. R. (2008). The media and the chemical imbalance theory of depression. *Society* 45, 35–45. doi: 10.1007/s12115-007-9047-3

Lieberman, J. A. (2015). *Shrinks: The Untold Story of Psychiatry.* New York: Little, Brown, and Company.

Lilienfeld, S. O. (2007). Cognitive neuroscience and depression: legitimate versus illegitimate reductionism and five challenges. *Cogn. Ther. Res.* 31, 263–272. doi: 10.1007/s10608-007-9127-0

Lilienfeld, S. O. (2010). Can psychology become a science? *Personal. Individ. Diff.* 49, 281–288. doi: 10.1016/j.paid.2010.01.024

Lilienfeld, S. O. (2014). The research domain criteria (RDoC): an analysis of methodological and conceptual challenges. *Behav. Res. Ther.* 62, 129–139. doi: 10.1016/j.brat.2014.07.019

Lilienfeld, S. O., and Arkowitz, H. (2007). Is there really an autism epidemic? *Sci. Am.* 17, 58–61. doi: 10.1038/scientificamerican1207-58sp

Lilienfeld, S. O., and Lynn, S. J. (2015). "Dissociative identity disorder: a scientific perspective," in *Science and Pseudoscience in Clinical Psychology*, 2nd Edn, eds S. O. Lilienfeld, S. J. Lynn, and J. M. Lohr (New York: Guilford Press).

Lilienfeld, S. O., Lynn, S. J., Ruscio, J., and Beyerstein, B. L. (2009). *50 Great Myths of Popular Psychology: Shattering Widespread Misconceptions About Human Behavior*. New York: Wiley.

Lilienfeld, S. O., Ritschel, L. A., Lynn, S. J., Cautin, R. L., and Latzman, R. D. (2013). Why many clinical psychologists are resistant to evidence-based practice: root causes and constructive remedies. *Clin. Psychol. Rev.* 33, 883–900. doi: 10.1016/j.cpr.2012.09.008

Lilienfeld, S. O., Waldman, I. D., and Israel, A. C. (1994). A critical examination of the use of the term and concept of comorbidity in psychopathology research. *Clin. Psychol.* 1, 71–83.

Linehan, M. M. (1989). Cognitive and behavior therapy for borderline personality disorder. *Rev. Psychiatry* 8, 84–102.

Loevinger, J. (1957). Objective tests as instruments of psychological theory: monograph supplement 9. *Psychological. Rep.* 3, 635–694. doi: 10.2466/pr0.1957.3.3.635

Lüthi, A. (2013). Sleep spindles where they come from, what they do. *Neuroscientist* 20, 243–256. doi: 10.1177/1073858413500854

Lykken, D. T. (1998). *A Tremor in the Blood: Uses and Abuses of the Lie Detector*. New York: Plenum Press.

Lynn, S. J., Kirsch, I., Knox, J., Fassler, O., and Lilienfeld, S. O. (2007). "Hypnosis and neuroscience: implications for the altered state debate," in *Hypnosis and Conscious States: The Cognitive Neuroscience Perspective,* ed. G. A. Jamieson (Oxford: Oxford University Press), 145–165.

Lynn, S. J., Laurence, J.-R., and Kirsch, I. (2015). Hypnosis, suggestion, and suggestibility: an integrative model. *Am. J. Clin. Hypn.* 57, 314–329. doi: 10.1080/00029157.2014.976783

Macdonald, J. M. (1955). Truth serum. *J. Criminal Law Criminol. Police Sci.* 46, 259–263. doi: 10.2307/1139862

Mann, C. E., and Himelein, M. J. (2008). Putting the person back into psychopathology: an intervention to reduce mental illness stigma in the classroom. *Soc. Psychiatry Psychiatr. Epidemiol.* 43, 545–551. doi: 10.1007/s00127-008-0324-2

Markon, K. E. (2009). Hierarchies in the structure of personality traits. *Soc. Personal. Psychol. Compass* 3, 812–826. doi: 10.1111/j.1751-9004.2009.00213.x

McClelland, G. H., and Judd, C. M. (1993). Statistical difficulties of detecting interactions and moderator effects. *Psychol. Bull.* 114, 376–380. doi: 10.1037/0033-2909.114.2.376

McComas, W. F. (1996). Ten myths of science: reexamining what we think we know about the nature of science. *Sch. Sci. Math.* 96, 10–16. doi: 10.1111/j.1949-8594.1996.tb10205.x

McCullough, D. (2002). *Interview with NEH chairman Bruce Cole. National Endowment for the Humanities*. Available at: http://www.neh.gov/about/awards/jefferson-lecture/david-mccullough-interview (accessed June 23, 2015).

McDermott, R., Tingley, D., Cowden, J., Frazetto, G., and Johnson, D. (2009). The Warrior Gene' (MAOA) predicts behavioral aggression following provocation. *Proc. Natl. Acad. Sci. U.S.A.* 106, 2118–2123. doi: 10.1073/pnas.080837 6106

Meehl, P. E. (1945). The dynamics of "structured" personality tests. *J. Clin. Psychol.* 1, 296–303.

Meehl, P. E. (1969). *Nuisance Variables and the Expost Facto Design*. Report No. PR-69-4. Minneapolis: Department of Psychiatry, University of Minnesota.

Meehl, P. E. (1986). "Diagnostic taxa as open concepts: metatheoretical and statistical questions about reliability and construct validity in the grand strategy of nosological revision," in *Contemporary Directions in Psychopathology*, eds T. Millon and G. L. Klerman (New York: Guilford Press), 215–231.

Meehl, P. E. (1995). Bootstraps taxometrics: solving the classification problem in psychopathology. *Am. Psychol.* 50, 266–275. doi: 10.1037/0003-066X.50.4.266

Melton, G. J. (1999). *Brainwashing and the Cults: The Rise and Fall of a Theory*. Available at: http://www.cesnur.org/testi/melton.htm.

Merckelbach, H., Devilly, G. J., and Rassin, E. (2002). Alters in dissociative identity disorder: metaphors or genuine entities? *Clin. Psychol. Rev.* 22, 481–497. doi: 10.1016/s0272-7358(01)00115-5

Merzenich, M. M. (2013). *Soft-Wired: How the New Science of Brain Plasticity Can Change Your Life*. San Francisco, CA: Parnassus.

Mesholam-Gately, R. I., Giuliano, A. J., Goff, K. P., Faraone, S. V., and Seidman, L. J. (2009). Neurocognition in first-episode schizophrenia: a meta-analytic review. *Neuropsychology* 23, 315–336. doi: 10.1037/a0014708

Messick, S. (1987). Validity. *ETS Res. Rep. Ser.* 2, i208. doi: 10.1002/j.2330- 8516.1987.tb00244.x

Miller, G. A. (1996). How we think about cognition, emotion, and biology in psychopathology. *Psychophysiology* 33, 615–628. doi: 10.1111/j.1469-8986.1996.tb02356.x

Miller, G. A. (2010). Mistreating psychology in the decades of the brain. *Perspect. Psychol. Sci.* 5, 716–743. doi: 10.1177/1745691610388774

Miller, J. (2009). What is the probability of replicating a statistically significant effect? *Psychon. Bull. Rev.* 16, 617–640. doi: 10.3758/PBR.16.4.617

Miller, N., and Pedersen, W. C. (1999). Assessing process distinctiveness. *Psychol. Inq.* 10, 150–155. doi: 10.1207/S15327965PL100210

Morin, C. (2011). Neuromarketing: the new science of consumer behavior. *Society* 48, 131–135. doi: 10.1007/s12115-010-9408-1

Morse, S. (2011). *Tax Compliance and the Love Molecule. Arizona State Law Journal*. Available at: http://arizonastatelawjournal.org/tax-compliance-and-the-love-molecule

Mulle, J. G. (2012). Schizophrenia genetics: progress, at last. *Curr. Opin. Genet. Dev.* 22, 238–244. doi: 10.1016/j.gde.2012.02.011

Muller, R. (1992). Is there a neural basis for borderline splitting? *Compr. Psychiatry* 33, 92–104. doi: 10.1016/0010-440X(92)90004-A

Naliboff, B. D., Frese, M. P., and Rapgay, L. (2008). Mind/body psychological treatments for irritable bowel syndrome. *Evid. Based Complementary Altern. Med.* 5, 41–50. doi: 10.1093/ecam/nem046

Newman, D. L., Moffitt, T. E., Caspi, A., and Silva, P. A. (1998). Comorbid mental disorders: implications for treatment and sample selection. *J. Abnorm. Psychol.* 107, 305–311. doi: 10.1037/0021-843X.107.2.305

Nisbett, R. E., Aronson, J., Blair, C., Dickens, W., Flynn, J., Halpern, D. F., et al., (2012). Intelligence: new findings and theoretical developments. *Am. Psychol.* 67, 130–159. doi: 10.1037/a0026699

Olweus, D. (1977). "A critical analysis of the modern interactionist position," in *Personality at the Crossroads: Current Issues in Interactional Psychology,* eds D. Magnusson and N. S. Endler (New York: Wiley), 221–233.

Pant, H., McCabe, B. J., Deskovitz, M. A., Weed, N. C., and Williams, J. E. (2014). Diagnostic reliability of MMPI-2 computer-based test interpretations. *Psychol. Assess.* 26, 916–924. doi: 10.1037/a0036469

Pap, A. (1958). *Semantics and Necessary Truth.* New Haven, CT: Yale University Press.

Pashley, M. (1994). A-level students: their problems with gene and allele. *J. Biol. Educ.* 28, 120–126. doi: 10.1080/00219266.1994.9655377

Pathak, A., and Srivastava, M. (2011). Narcoanalysis: a critical appraisal. *Indian J. Forensic Med. Toxicol.* 5, 54–57.

Pelphrey, K. A., and McPartland, J. C. (2012). Brain development: neural signature predicts autism's emergence. *Curr. Biol.* 22, R127–R128. doi: 10.1016/j.cub.2012.01.025

Peter, J. P. (1981). Construct validity: a review of basic issues and marketing practices. *J. Mark. Res.* 18, 133–145. doi: 10.2307/3150948

Petrocelli, J. V. (2003). Hierarchical multiple regression in counseling research: common problems and possible remedies. *Meas. Eval. Couns. Dev.* 36, 9–22.

Pies, R. (2011). Psychiatry's new brain-mind and the legend of the chemical imbalance. *Psychiatric Times.* Available at: http://www.psychiatrictimes.com/blog/couchincrisis/content/ (access July 11, 2011).

Pinker, S. (2014). *The Sense of Style: The Thinking Person's Guide to Writing in the 21st Century.* New York: Penguin.

Piper, A. Jr. (1993). Truth serum and recovered memories of sexual abuse: a review of the evidence. *J. Psychiatry Law* 21, 447–471.

Popper, K. R. (1959). *The Logic of Scientific Discovery.* London: Hutchinson.

Popper, K. R. (1983). *Realism and the Aim of Science.* London: Routledge.

Proyer, R. T., and Häusler, J. (2007). Assessing behavior in standardized settings: the role of objective personality tests. *Int. J. Clin. Health Psychol.* 7, 537–546.

Radford, B. (2003). *Media Mythmakers: How Journalists, Activists, and Advertisers Mislead Us.* Amherst, NY: Prometheus Books.

Raz, A. (2011). Does neuroimaging of suggestion elucidate hypnotic trance? *Int. J. Clin. Exp. Hypn.* 59, 363–377. doi: 10.1080/00207144.2011.570682

Reynolds, C. F., Frank, E., Thase, M. E., Houck, P. R., Jennings, J. R., Howell, J. R., et al. (1988). Assessment of sexual function in depressed, impotent, and healthy men: factor analysis of a brief sexual function questionnaire for men. *Psychiatry Res.* 24, 231–250. doi: 10.1016/0165-1781(88)90106-0

Robinson, D. N. (1995). The logic of reductionistic models. *New Ideas Psychol.* 13, 1–8. doi: 10.1016/0732-118X(94)E0032-W

Rogers, R. (2003). Forensic use and abuse of psychological tests: multiscale inventories. *J. Psychiatr. Practice* 9, 316–320. doi: 10.1097/00131746-200307000-00008

Ross, C. A. (1994). *The Osiris Complex: Case Studies in Multiple Personality Disorder.* Toronto, CA: University of Toronto Press.

Rutter, M. (1994). Comorbidity: meanings and mechanisms. *Clin. Psychol.* 1, 100–103. doi: 10.1111/j.1468-2850.1994.tb00012.x

Sagi-Schwartz, A., Van IJzendoorn, M. H., Grossmann, K. E., Joels, T., Grossmann, K., Scharf, M., et al. (2014). Attachment and traumatic stress in female Holocaust child survivors and their daughters. *Am. J. Psychiatry* 160, 1086–1092. doi: 10.1176/appi.ajp.160.6.1086

Sapolsky, R. (1997). A gene for nothing. *Discover* 18, 40–46.

Satel, S., and Lilienfeld, S. O. (2013). *Brainwashed: The Seductive Appeal of Mindless Neuroscience.* New York: Basic Books.

Saxe, L., Dougherty, D., and Cross, T. (1985). The validity of polygraph testing: scientific analysis and public controversy. *Am. Psychol.* 40, 355–366. doi: 10.1037/0003-066X.40.3.355

Schmidt, F. L., and Hunter, J. E. (1996). Measurement error in psychological research: lessons from 26 research scenarios. *Psychol. Methods* 1, 199–223. doi: 10.1037/1082-989X.1.2.199

Shen, H. (2015). Neuroscience: the hard science of oxytocin. *Nature* 522, 410–412. doi: 10.1038/522410a

Shermer, M. (2015). "Hardwired permanent," in *This Idea Must Die,* ed. J. Brockman (New York: Harper), 100–103.

Skeem, J. L., and Cooke, D. J. (2010). Is criminal behavior a central component of psychopathy? Conceptual directions for resolving the debate. *Psychol. Assess.* 22, 433–445. doi: 10.1037/a0008512

Skitka, L. J., Bauman, C. W., and Mullen, E. (2004). Political tolerance and coming to psychological closure following the September 11, 2001, terrorist attacks: an integrative approach. *Personal. Soc. Psychol. Bull.* 30, 743–756. doi: 10.1177/0146167204263968

Smith, M. (2015). *Explaining Japan's Feature Phone Fetish.* Santa Clara, CA: Engadget. Available at: http://www.engadget.com/2015/03/13/japan-loves-feature-phones/

Smoller, J. W., and Finn, C. T. (2003). "Family, twin, and adoption studies of bipolar disorder," in *American Journal of Medical Genetics Part C: Seminars in Medical Genetics,* Vol. 123, eds S. V. Faraone and M. T. Tsuang (New York: Wiley Subscription Services, Inc., A Wiley Company), 48–58.

Song, H., and Kwon, N. (2012). The relationship between personality traits and information competency in Korean and American students. *Soc. Behav. Personal.* 40, 1153–1162. doi: 10.2224/sbp.2012.40.7.1153

Spanos, N. P. (1996). *Multiple Identities and False Memories: A Sociocognitive Perspective*. Washington, DC: American Psychiatric Association. doi: 10.1037/10216-000

Spitzer, M., Fischbacher, U., Herrnberger, B., Grön, G., and Fehr, E. (2007). The neural signature of social norm compliance. *Neuron* 56, 185–196. doi: 10.1016/j.neuron.2007.09.011

Spitzer, R. L. (1994). Psychiatric "co-occurrence"? I'll stick with "comorbidity." *Clin. Psychol.* 1, 88–92.

Stanovich, K. E. (2012). *How to Think Straight About Psychology*. Boston, MA: Pearson Allyn and Bacon.

Stix, G. (2014). *Fact or Fiction? Oxytocin is the "Love Molecule." Scientific American*. Available at: http://www.scientificamerican.com/article/fact-or-fiction-oxytocin-is-the-love-hormone (access September 8, 2014).

Streiner, D. L. (2007). A short cut to rejection: how not to write the results section of a paper. *Can. J. Psychiatry* 52, 385–389.

Sylvers, P., Lilienfeld, S. O., and LaPrairie, J. L. (2011). Differences between trait fear and trait anxiety: Implications for psychopathology. *Clin. Psychol. Rev.* 31, 122–137. doi: 10.1016/j.cpr.2010.08.004

Tavris, C., and Aronson, E. (2007). *Mistakes Were Made (but not by me): Why we Justify Foolish Beliefs, Bad Decisions, and Hurtful Acts*. Boston: Houghton Mifflin Harcourt.

Taylor, A. K., and Kowalski, P. (2010). Naive psychological science: the prevalence, strength, and source of misconceptions. *Psychol. Record* 54, 15–25.

Thompson, B. (1989). Why won't stepwise methods die? *Meas. Eval. Couns. Dev.* 21, 146–148.

Tortorella, A., Fabrazzo, M., Monteleone, A. M., Steardo, L., and Monteleone, P. (2014). The role of drug therapies in the treatment of anorexia and bulimia nervosa: a review of the literature. *J. Psychopathol.* 20, 50–65.

Tversky, A., and Kahneman, D. (1971). Belief in the law of small numbers. *Psychol. Bull.* 76, 105–110. doi: 10.1037/h0031322

Vaillant, G. E. (1977). *Adaptation to Life*. Cambridge, MA: Harvard University Press.

Ventegodt, S., Andersen, N. J., and Merrick, K. (2009). An ethical analysis of contemporary use of coercive persuasion ("brainwashing", "mind control") in psychiatry. *J. Alternat. Med. Res.* 1, 177–188.

Wampold, B. E., and Freund, R. D. (1987). Use of multiple regression in counseling psychology research: a flexible data-analytic strategy. *J. Couns. Psychol.* 34, 372–382. doi: 10.1037/0022-0167.34.4.372

Watson, D., and Clark, L. A. (1984). Negative affectivity: the disposition to experience aversive emotional states. *Psychol. Bull.* 96, 465–490. doi: 10.1037/0033-2909.96.3.465

Weinberger, D. A., and Gomes, M. E. (1995). Changes in daily mood and self-restraint among undercontrolled preadolescents: a time-series analysis of "acting out". *J. Am. Acad. Child Adolesc. Psychiatry* 34, 1473–1482. doi: 10.1097/00004583-199511000-00014

Weinstein, H. M. (2011). Editorial note: the myth of closure, the illusion of reconciliation: final thoughts on five years as co-editor-in-chief. *Int. J. Trans. Justice* 5, 1–10. doi: 10.1093/ijtj/ijr002

Weiss, D. J. (1970). Factor analysis and counseling research. *J. Couns. Psychol.* 17, 477–485. doi: 10.1037/h0029894

Weissman, M. M. (1993). Family genetic studies of panic disorder. *J. Psychiatr. Res.* 27, 69–78. doi: 10.1016/0022-3956(93) 90018-W

Wheeler, K. (2011). A relationship-based model for psychiatric nursing practice. *Perspect. Psychiatr. Care* 47, 151–159. doi: 10.1111/j.1744-6163.2010.00 285.x

Wing, D. M. (1995). Transcending alcoholic denial. *Image* 27, 121–126. doi: 10.1111/j.1547-5069.1995.tb00834.x

Wolsko, P. M., Eisenberg, D. M., Davis, R. B., and Phillips, R. S. (2004). Use of mind–body medical therapies. *J. Gen. Int. Med.* 19, 43–50. doi: 10.1111/j.1525- 1497.2004.21019.x

Wong, E. (2012). *One Molecule for Love, Morality, and Prosperity?* Slate. Available at: http://www.slate.com/articles/health_and_science/medical_examiner/2012/07/oxytocin_is_not_a_love_drug_don_t_give_it_to_kids_with_autism_html (access July 17, 2012).

Zak, P. J. (2013). *The Moral Molecule: The New Science of What Makes us Good or Evil*. New York: Random House.

Zimbardo, P. G. (1997). What messages are behind today's cults? *Am. Psychol. Assoc. Monit.* 28, 14.

Zurbriggen, E. L., Ramsey, L. R., and Jaworski, B. K. (2011). Self- and partner-objectification in romantic relationships: associations with media consumption and relationship satisfaction. *Psychiatry* 132, 911–914. doi: 10.1007/s11199-011- 9933-4

Critical Thinking

1. Differentiate between the jingle and jangle fallacies, and provide a concrete example of each.
2. Out of the 50 possibilities described in the article, select one, and search for examples in the popular press and/or academic literature to see if you can identify additional examples of the improper use of the term.

Internet References

Psychology jargon made simple

https://www.psychologytoday.com/blog/fulfillment-any-age/201202/psychology-jargon-made-simple

General psychology terms

http://people.whitman.edu/~blagovp/resources/psygeneral.html

Psychology glossary

http://www.sparknotes.com/psychology/psych101/glossary/terms.html

Article

Prepared by: R. Eric Landrum, *Boise State University*

Study Finds Virtual Reality Can Help Treat Severe Paranoia

MEDICAL RESEARCH COUNCIL

Learning Outcomes

After reading this article, you will be able to:

- Understand the symptoms of severe paranoia.
- Describe the success rate in using virtual reality in treating individuals with severe paranoia.

Virtual reality can help treat severe paranoia by allowing people to face situations that they fear, an MRC-funded study has found. The virtual reality simulations allowed the patients to learn that the situations they feared were actually safe.

The study, carried out by researchers at Oxford University, is published today in the *British Journal of Psychiatry*. It combines evidence-based psychological treatment techniques with state-of-the-art virtual reality social situations to reduce paranoid fear.

About 1–2% of the population has severe paranoia, typically as a central feature of mental health disorders such as schizophrenia. Patients show extreme mistrust of other people, believing that others are deliberately trying to harm them. The condition can be so debilitating that sufferers may be unable to leave the house.

Coping mechanisms such as avoiding social situations, reducing eye contact or making any social interaction as short as possible worsen the situation, since they reinforce paranoid fears: patients come to believe that they avoided harm because they used these 'defence behaviours'.

The research team, led by Professor Daniel Freeman from Oxford University's Department of Psychiatry, wanted to test whether patients could 're-learn' that a situation was safe, by experiencing situations they feared without using their defence behaviours.

Being in a situation they fear is very difficult for many patients, since it causes intolerable anxiety. To overcome this challenge the team used virtual reality to recreate social situations which patients found fearful.

Thirty patients attending treatment services took part in the study. All the patients went into virtual reality simulations with increasing numbers of computer characters (avatars)—seeing many people at the same time would normally make these patients quite anxious. But participants were told that by staying in the situations, they would relearn that they were safe. A train ride and a lift scene were used.

The patients were randomly given different instructions on how to deal with these situations in virtual reality. One group were encouraged to use their normal defence behaviours: they were told that it would work a bit like getting into cold water, that when you first get in it feels uncomfortable, but after a while you get used to it, as long as you stay in.

The other patients were encouraged drop their defences and try to fully learn that they were safe by approaching the computer characters and looking at them—holding long stares or standing toe-to-toe with avatars.

The patients who fully tested out their fears in virtual reality by lowering their defences showed very substantial reductions in their paranoid delusions. After the virtual reality therapy session, over 50% of these patients no longer had severe paranoia at the end of the testing day.

There were even benefits for those who confronted situations they feared in virtual reality while still using their defences: around 20% of this group no longer having severe paranoia at the end of the testing day.

Patients who fully tested out their fears in virtual reality were later much less distressed even when in a real world situation, such as going to the local shop. Further research is needed to see if the benefits are maintained beyond the testing day.

Professor Freeman, the study lead at Oxford University Department of Psychiatry and clinical psychologist at Oxford Health NHS Foundation Trust, said: "Paranoia all too often leads to isolation, unhappiness, and profound distress.

But the exceptionally positive immediate results for the patients in this study show a new route forward in treatment. In just a thirty minute session, those who used the right psychological techniques showed major reductions in paranoia.

"It's not easy work for patients, since lowering defences takes courage. But as they relearned that being around other people was safe we saw their paranoia begin to melt away. They were then able to go into real social situations and cope far better. This has the potential to be transformative."

Professor David Clark, a member of the study team, said: "There is growing evidence that psychological treatments can have a major beneficial impact on the lives of people suffering from psychosis. Virtual reality assisted treatment has great potential because, as the price of the equipment makes it more accessible, much treatment could be delivered in people's homes."Dr Kathryn Adcock, Head of Neurosciences and Mental Health at the Medical Research Council, which funded the study, said: "Virtual reality is proving extremely effective in the assessment and treatment of mental health problems. This study shows the potential of its application to a major psychiatric problem. There is a lot of work to do be done in testing the approach for treating delusions but this study shows a new way forward."

Critical Thinking

1. If the method to learn how not to be deathly afraid of spiders is to be around spiders, most individuals will continue to be afraid of spiders. Why might virtual reality help a person overcome a severe paranoia or phobia?
2. How important are the instructions given to the participants in this type of research study? Explain.

Internet References

Virtual reality: Expanding use in mental health treatment
https://www.psychiatry.org/news-room/apa-blogs/apa-blog/2017/02/virtual-reality-expanding-use-in-mental-health-treatment

Virtual reality applications in mental health: Challenges and perspectives
https://www.ncbi.nlm.nih.gov/pmc/articles/PMC4361984/

Virtual reality therapy: Treating the global mental health crisis
https://techcrunch.com/2016/01/06/virtual-reality-therapy-treating-the-global-mental-health-crisis/

Why virtual reality could be a mental health gamechanger
https://www.theguardian.com/science/blog/2017/mar/22/why-virtual-reality-could-be-a-mental-health-gamechanger

Article

Prepared by: R. Eric Landrum, *Boise State University*

Could Brain Scans Help Guide Treatment for OCD?

Small study suggests neural activity can point to patients who'll benefit most from psychotherapy.

MARY ELIZABETH DALLAS

Learning Outcomes

After reading this article, you will be able to:

- Understand the component behaviors of obsessive-compulsive disorder (OCD) and how certain beliefs lead to certain actions.
- Appreciate the prevalence of OCD in the United States.
- Comprehend why predicting the success of a treatment is important to an overall approach to improved mental health.

Psychotherapy can help some people avoid the disruptive behaviors linked to obsessive-compulsive disorder (OCD), and a new study suggests that brain scans can help spot those patients for whom the therapy will be most effective.

The treatment is called cognitive behavioral therapy (CBT). It works by placing patients in controlled situations where they are exposed to anxiety-causing stimuli, so that they gradually learn to deal better with these situations.

"Cognitive behavioral therapy is in many cases very effective, at least in the short term," said Dr. Jamie Feusner, an associate professor of psychiatry at University of California, Los Angeles (UCLA), and director of the Semel Institute's Adult OCD Program.

However, the treatment is "costly, time-consuming, difficult for patients and, in many areas, not available," Feusner noted in a UCLA news release. So, "if someone will end up having their symptoms return [after treatment], it would be useful to know before they get treatment," he reasoned.

His team wondered if certain patterns on brain scans might point to those patients who have the most to gain from CBT.

The notion has some merit, said one expert, especially since more reliable treatment is needed for people suffering from OCD.

"OCD is an illness in which patients experience obsessions and then act on them by performing compulsions," explained Dr. Alan Manevitz, a clinical psychiatrist at Lenox Hill Hospital in New York City.

Even though "the patient realizes that these obsessions and compulsions are unwanted, unreasonable, and excessive, he or she cannot stop listening to the thoughts and acting on them," he said.

According to Manevitz, one in every 40 Americans (2.5 percent) has clinical OCD, with symptoms bad enough to interfere with daily living, and another 10 percent have a lower-level form of the illness, where thoughts intrude but do not reach such a disruptive state.

"The past few decades, however, have seen the emergence of many effective treatments, both pharmacological and psychotherapeutic," including CBT, Manevitz said.

But who will gain the most from the psychotherapy? Feusner's team noted that although CBT may be very effective initially, not all patients see long-term benefits, and about 20 percent of patients suffer a relapse of their OCD symptoms.

In the UCLA study, brain scans known as fMRIs were used to study the brains of 17 people with OCD who ranged in age from 21 to 50.

The scans—which measure brain activity in real time—were performed before and after the patients completed intensive CBT.

The patients' symptoms were also monitored for one year.

According to Feusner, people with more efficient brain network "connectivity," as gauged by the brain scans, actually had *worse* long-term outcomes following CBT treatment.

The team also found that the intensity of OCD symptoms prior to treatment, or the patient's initial level of response to the therapy, was not a good predictor of long-term success.

Having a better understanding of which patients will not respond well to specific therapy long-term could help doctors develop a more effective treatment strategy.

The researchers were quick to point out that the study does not suggest that some patients with OCD are "beyond help" when it comes to psychotherapy. Instead, they believe that these patients may simply need longer CBT than the four weeks used in the study, or that they may be helped by medications as well.

"We are now starting to translate knowledge of the brain into useful information that in the future could be used by doctors and patients to make clinical decisions," Feusner said. "Although a brain scan may seem expensive, these scans only took about 15 minutes and thus the cost is not exceptionally high, particularly in comparison to medication or cognitive behavioral therapy treatments, which over time can cost many thousands of dollars."

However, Manevitz did have some reservations about the findings.

"The results are intriguing but this study has a very small sample size: 17 subjects," he said. Plus, those subjects appeared to be especially willing to undertake the rigors of CBT—something not every person with OCD might be amenable to, he said.

All of that "makes it harder to generalize [the findings] to the overall OCD population," Manevitz said. He also believes that while brain network "connectivity" may play a role in the effectiveness of psychotherapy for OCD, that remains only a theory.

The bottom line, according to Manevitz: "It is important to follow up this study with a larger group of participants."

Dr. Emily Stern is assistant professor of psychiatry and neuroscience at the Mount Sinai School of Medicine in New York City. She said that brain scans may have potential "to predict which patients will relapse [and] has the potential to identify those patients who may need further treatment or greater monitoring."

If the findings pan out, "brain network organization may provide a window into patient functioning that cannot be assessed through symptom measures alone," Stern said.

The study was funded by the U.S. National Institute of Mental Health and published recently in the journal *Frontiers in Psychiatry.*

Source

Alan Manevitz, M.D., clinical psychiatrist, Lenox Hill Hospital, New York City; Emily R. Stern, Ph.D. assistant professor, departments of psychiatry and neuroscience, Mount Sinai School of Medicine, New York City; University of California, Los Angeles, news release, June 23, 2015

Critical Thinking

1. Is psychotherapy effective in helping people with obsessive-compulsive disorder? Explain why or why not.
2. When the brains of OCD patients are scanned, what are the results? Explain.

Internet References

Causes of OCD
http://www.anxietycare.org.uk/docs/ocdcauses.asp

Rewiring the brain to treat OCD
http://discovermagazine.com/2013/nov/14-defense-free-will

What does an OCD brain look like?
http://ocd.commons.yale.edu/ocdbrain/

Article

Prepared by: R. Eric Landrum, *Boise State University*

With the Help of Virtual Therapists, People with Eating Disorders Tackle Anxiety in Grocery Stores

JULI FRAGA

Learning Outcomes

After reading this article, you will be able to:

- Appreciate that 1 percent of Americans suffer from anorexia.
- Understand the importance of grocery store therapy to a person with anorexia or binge eating disorder, and how the innovation of having access to a dietitian via video chat.
- Provide an example of exposure therapy, where a person gradually confronts their phobia or anxiety-provoking situation through treatment with a therapist.

Individuals with anorexia, binge eating disorder, and bulimia often feel anxious and overwhelmed when surrounded by food. This anxiety can make grocery shopping and cooking a challenge.

A new form of telemedicine in which people can video chat with a nutritional counselor while at the supermarket aims to help.

According to the National Institute of Mental Health, approximately 1 percent of Americans suffer from anorexia, a sometimes deadly psychiatric illness. Along with anorexia, millions of Americans also struggle with binge eating disorder.

Jamie Lynn Pelletier, 28, of Greensboro, NC, was just 13 when she began counting calories and skipping meals, behavior that eventually led to anorexia, which is characterized by food restriction, extreme weight loss, and distorted body image.

"In junior high, I began to feel unattractive and self-conscious about my body. To lose weight, I started dieting and overexercising," Pelletier said.

Since 2015, Pelletier has completed several residential and outpatient treatment programs in the battle to stop starving herself. Her struggle shows how tough it can be for anorexics to stop seeing food as the enemy.

Recently, Pelletier's dietitian recommended grocery store therapy, which allows her to connect with a dietitian via video chat.

"Going to the grocery store is stressful because seeing foods labeled as low carb and low fat can make me feel like buying the real thing is not okay. With virtual therapy, I FaceTime with my dietitian at the store," said Pelletier, referring to Apple's video chat application. "For privacy, I put in my headphones so I can talk to her discreetly while I'm shopping."

This type of treatment, known as exposure therapy, allows people to face their traumas, phobias, and anxieties by gradually exposing them to the feared stimulus.

"The eating disorder treatment world has adapted exposure therapy to help people face their food fears. Grocery store therapy can be beneficial by allowing individuals to confront their anxieties with the support of a trusted health-care provider," said Kelsey Latimer, a clinical psychologist at the Center for Discovery, a treatment facility for eating disorders in Palm Beach Gardens, Fla.

Earlier, dietitians and counselors would accompany their clients on store outings. Telemedicine allows for virtual help. It can be a game changer for those living in rural areas where access to health-care services may be limited, experts said.

Lois Zsarnay, a therapist and dietitian in Ventura, CA, said telemedicine has expanded the support services she can offer.

"With technology like FaceTime, I can virtually accompany my clients at the grocery store, which allows me to help them at that moment with their food struggles," she said.

Zsarnay first meets with clients in person. They discuss food fears, potential anxiety triggers, and treatment goals. For some, simply stepping inside the store is a huge success; others are ready to take a more significant risk by purchasing a "forbidden" food, such as ice cream, bagels, or potato chips, she said.

When Zsarnay provides virtual grocery store therapy, she begins each session with a breathing exercise to help her clients feel grounded. "At first, we take a few deep breaths together, and then I remind my client about the objectives we reviewed during our planning meeting," she said. Often, clients become triggered when walking down, for example, the cereal aisle. When this fear arises, Zsarnay uses relaxation exercises to help decrease her client's anxiety. If the client becomes too overwhelmed, she reminds them that they can walk back to an area of the store with "safer" foods. Once the anxiety dissipates, she proceeds to guide her client through their shopping list.

Virtual grocery store therapy is relatively new, and there are no studies on its effectiveness. But there is some research on the effectiveness of other forms of virtual therapy to help treat eating disorders.

Athena Robinson, a clinical psychologist and eating disorders researcher at Stanford University, conducted a small study examining the effectiveness of online therapy for eating disorders. The research focused on 34 participants who connected with individual and group therapists and nutritionists through a video conference platform. Robinson and colleagues presented the study's findings at the International Conference on Eating Disorders in April.

"Our initial results show a clinically significant reduction in eating disorder symptoms," Robinson said. She added that future research will examine long-term effectiveness.

For Pelletier, virtual therapy has been a vital part of her healing.

"At the grocery store, I get uneasy reading nutrition labels because I fixate on how many calories are in each food. With grocery store therapy, my dietitian talks me through my fears and reminds me that all foods, even carbohydrates and sweets, are good foods," she said.

Pelletier completed four sessions of grocery store therapy, which her insurance paid for. The treatment helped her realize that no one is judging her food choices or her appearance. Since finishing the treatment, she has been able to shop on her own.

Even though telemedicine can make aspects of eating disorder treatment more accessible, it isn't a replacement for in-person care, experts say. Pelletier continues to meet in person with a psychotherapist and a nutritionist regularly.

"It was validating for my dietitian to acknowledge my worries; it helped me to feel less alone. While recovery is a journey, grocery store therapy gave me additional tools to help guide me through the process," she said.

Critical Thinking

1. Exposure therapy is similar to other therapeutic techniques where the fearful stimulus is gradually introduced to the patient or client under controlled conditions; this technique is called systematic desensitization. What are the underlying behavioral principles of exposure therapy? Explain.
2. What is telemedicine, and what is its specific implementation advantage in this particular therapeutic setting? Be specific.

Internet References

Innovative Support Online for Eating Disorders
https://www.huffingtonpost.com/wendy-adamson/treating-eating-disorders_b_9708312.html

Treatment of Eating Disorders
https://www.sciencedirect.com/topics/neuroscience/treatment-of-eating-disorders

Virtual Reality Therapy: Treating the Global Mental Health Crisis
https://techcrunch.com/2016/01/06/virtual-reality-therapy-treating-the-global-mental-health-crisis/